Selecting Materials for Instruction

Selecting Materials for Instruction

−Three Handbooks for Educators−

Issues and Policies

Media and the Curriculum

Subject Areas and Implementation

Selecting Materials for Instruction

Issues and Policies

Marda Woodbury

Libraries Unlimited, Inc., Littleton, Colorado — 1979

LIBRARIES UNLIMITED, INC.
P.O. Box 263
Littleton, Colorado 80160

Library of Congress Cataloging in Publication Data

Woodbury, Marda.
    Selecting materials for instruction.

    Includes bibliographies and index.
    CONTENTS: [1] Issues and policies.
    1. Audio-visual materials. 2. Teaching--Aids and
devices. I. Title.
LB1043.W664   371.33   79-18400
ISBN 0-87287-197-5 (v.1)

This book is bound with James River (Scott) Graphitek®—C Type II non-
woven material. Graphitek—C meets and exceeds National Association of
State Textbook Administrators' Type II nonwoven material specifications
Class A through E.

PREFACE

"So much has already been written about everything that you cannot find out anything about it."

—James Thurber

■ ■ ■

I began *Selecting Materials for Instruction* with one very full file drawer left over from a Phi Delta Kappa *Fastback, Selecting Instructional Materials*, a research-writing project which in itself took far more time and effort than I had expected.

Reluctant to discard documents and first drafts of two months' research, I decided to whip up the definitive book on selecting instructional materials. I had hoped to simplify and rationalize this multi-faceted topic, using as assets a good knowledge of educational sources, an acquaintance with educational theories, much experience in selecting instructional materials in school situations, and selection principles largely derived from a book selection course taken long ago at Columbia University School of Library Service.

In the intervening months, the research has taken over one entire room of my apartment and threatened to engulf my whole life and my whole apartment. The single volume has grown into three companion texts, and I have had to abandon my smug if naive belief that one book would suffice to simplify and rationalize the complex process of selection.

The result is this series on *Selecting Materials for Instruction*, which comprises *Issues and Policies, Media and the Curriculum* and *Subject Areas and Implementation*. These volumes can, I believe, be used separately by individuals involved at any level in the process of selecting and using instructional materials. *Issues and Policies* is a handbook for the establishing of an effective and efficient selection process. *Media and the Curriculum* approaches the acquisition and evaluation of materials in various print and nonprint media. And *Subject Areas and Implementation* will aid the selector in choosing materials for particular areas of study.

Since educational selection occurs in so many areas for so many purposes at so many levels, it is difficult to see the process as a whole, but these books, so far as I know, are the first to bring together the perspectives, insights, approaches and contributions of that medley or muddle of groups who participate some way, somehow, some time in selecting instructional materials. The groups and individuals who engage in this process include theorists and practitioners; among them educational theorists, curriculum designers and developers, educational evaluators, publishers, producers, distributors, market experts, library educators and librarians, media advocates and practitioners, school board members, administrators, legislators at all levels, citizen groups, advocacy groups, parents and community groups, individual and organized teachers, consultants, and even students, who may sometimes be the victims rather than the beneficiaries of the aggregated procedures. I have actively solicited and gathered information from all sorts of groups and individuals: government agencies, professional associations, publishers, teachers, teacher-librarians, teachers' centers, parents, students, curricular theorists, educational researchers, media specialists, bibliographers, and, of course, librarians. Undoubtedly I have overlooked some organizations and some individuals who should have been consulted.

In organizing this vast amount of data as compactly and practically as I could, I have considered both the ends and the practices of education and the nature of my materials.

For most sections of *Issues and Policies* I have tried to provide background discussions, usable selection criteria and charts, significant references and lists of background readings. I have tried to be comprehensive but selective, not to duplicate the work of others, but to refer to other guides and resources, and to provide background references for individuals who would like to explore particular aspects more thoroughly.

This book includes assorted excerpts, reproductions, and summaries of many other works. In general my criteria for these selections have been authority and utility; to a lesser extent clarity and availability. I have omitted some theoretical works that seemed overly complex or cumbersome, as well as some appealing charts that seemed to lack substance. Some rather lengthy charts and checklists have been included because they come from significant sources or seemed to me to provide or represent significant movements or current thinking. Controversial and stimulating discussions and criteria have also been included to aid in the exchange and development of viewpoint.

While this book covers many—by no means all—issues relating to instructional materials in the United States, ranging from pre-school levels through the secondary level, I have concentrated on the process of selecting materials for classes and individual students, though I have also incorporated many aspects on selection for schools, school systems and states. Unfortunately we have no selection criteria or aggregate of criteria that are simultaneously clear, compact and easy to use, that provide useful information and are universally applicable or acceptable. The users of *Issues and Policies* will have to be selective, themselves. It is not intended as a bible or even a how-to book but as a source of ideas, a stimulating starting place for groups or individuals grappling with the processes or concepts of selection.

My scope excludes selection of "hardware" or equipment, and choosing materials for post-secondary education. Since the book is largely directed to establishing a selection process for materials to be used within our nation and school systems, it would provide relatively little help for selecting appropriate media or programs for underdeveloped countries.

A variety of individuals and agencies have been kind enough to let me reprint their charts, criteria, checklists and the like for low costs or no costs. I greatly appreciate permissions given for these reprints. Such items as are copyrighted should not be reproduced in any way without the written permission of the original issuing agencies (whose addresses are included).

Other forms included in this book were developed at taxpayers' expense, and must remain in the public domain. These forms may be re-used or adapted freely but may not be copyrighted by another.

In the course of preparing *Selecting Materials for Instruction* I have imposed widely on the time, patience and facilities of a variety of individuals—most particularly of colleagues in Bay Area Education Librarians (BAEL) and the Education Division of the Special Libraries Association. The following in particular have gone even beyond their well-honed professional responsibilities in assisting my research.

Special thanks to Lenore Clemens, just retired from the San Mateo County Education Resources Center; Priscilla Watson at Lawrence Hall of Science; Jennifer Futernick and Jean Lee of Far West Laboratory; Joan Thornton from the Education Library at California State University at Hayward; Barbara Nozik and Urania Gluesing of San Francisco State University; and all the patient folks at the reference desk of the Ed-Psych Library at the University of California, Berkeley.

Sue Klein of the National Institute for Education has been extremely helpful in forwarding documents on evaluation. The Multicultural Resources at California State University, Hayward, and its librarians, Margaret Nichols and Peggy O'Neill, have been similarly helpful in providing materials relating to ethnic bias, while the Women's Educational Equity Communications Network has been a substantial source for materials on sex. Bob Muller of Bay Area Media Evaluation Guild (BAMEG), Faith Hektoen of the American Library Association and David Elliot of Educational Products Information Exchange (EPIE) have all simplified the task of research considerably. Wayne Fetter has been generous in sharing his sources. Thanks also to Alice Wittig of Mendocino, California, for taking time from her busy personal and professional life to read and critique this manuscript, and to Joan Rankin, who has an outstanding ability to transcribe scrawls and to correct typographic errors.

"To enrich the quality of life, education must generate curiosity, creativity, competence, and compassion."

—Dr. Albert V. Baez

TABLE OF CONTENTS

PART IV—SOME PARTICIPANT ROLES

PART I
OVERVIEWS

OVERVIEW OF INSTRUCTIONAL MATERIALS

"Instructional materials: any device with instructional content or function that is
used for teaching purposes, including books, textbooks, supplementary reading
materials, and audiovisual and other sensory materials, scripts for radio and television instruction, programs for computer-managed instruction, instruction sheets,
and packaged sets of materials for construction or manipulation."

> —Carter V. Good, *Dictionary of Education*, 3rd ed.,
> 1973

■ ■ ■

Though instructional materials are undoubtedly important in learning (few
teachers since Socrates would want to teach without them) there is surprisingly little
consensus or usable research on their exact role in education. Surveys and studies
indicate that teachers and students currently seem to structure between 80 and 95
percent of their classroom time and 90 percent of their homework around instructional materials. Still, we do not really know to what extent these materials determine the course of instruction or to what extent teachers, librarians and media
specialists choose, use, adapt, are told to use, or fill in time with what happens to
be available.

Though the quality of instruction is obviously affected by the quality of
instructional materials, materials as a variable are rarely studied in any usable way.
Accountability theory tends to hold teachers accountable for the quality of instruction and the quantity of measurable learning, while LVR—Learner Verification and
Revision—places more responsibility on materials. Other studies—of individualization, of the progressive education movement, and a recent Rand study in Los
Angeles—indicate that most children learn more when they are exposed to—and can
choose from—a variety of instructional materials, whether or not these materials are
validated.

Curriculum designers and evaluators, on the other hand, attempt to provide—
and devise tests for—reliable, validated, all-purpose teaching aids, preferably fool-
proof, child-proof, and teacher-proof. To these groups an ideal instructional material is one that succeeds in having all (or at least a high proportion of) students
achieve a certain percentage of particular educational goals or outcomes prescribed
by the curriculum designer. These goals themselves may be derived from common
consent, source-books of instructional objectives, or assessment at some level.
Some seem to be plucked out of air.

Other groups and individuals have different priorities or agendas for instructional materials. For many minority groups, "human values" or freedom from bias—
determined in various ways—are supremely important. Still others would limit educational objectives and materials to those that support "basic" education. Librarians and English teachers tend to support aesthetic standards and literary quality in
instructional materials, while many social studies and math teachers favor materials
organized for teaching concepts. Media enthusiasts emphasize sensory appeal and
camera angles. Administrators want manageable quantities, while publishers, of
necessity, believe in salability.

I will attempt in chapters and sections to provide a fair representation and summary of all these viewpoints on materials, but this book as a whole will emphasize the purpose of selection rather than the intrinsic or desirable or ideal qualities of instructional materials. Clearly, no materials can excel in all these qualities. Clearly, again, all these criteria are valid, some of the time, for some students, in some learning situations. The "complete selector" needs to consider these desiderata and establish priorities among them for particular selections.

Like Carter Good and his co-workers on the *Dictionary of Education*, I take a rather broad view of instructional materials. To me, instructional materials are materials that can be used for instruction, not merely materials designed to be instructive. I would include all materials that can help students acquire skills, gain information, improve cognitive processes or even increase their levels of maturity in physical, emotional or value areas.

Meredith Gall, who teaches a course in the analysis of curriculum materials at the University of Oregon in Eugene, defines curriculum materials as physical objects that contain information intended to bring about learning—including such objects as physical specimens. I would concur largely, although to me the explicit learning intent is less significant than the potential learning content.

I consider many common objects to be excellent instructional materials. The *African Science Program*, for example (developed by Educational Development Center) effectively used such universal substances as sand, clay and water as learning materials. Closer to home, Winston Press from Minnesota put out an excellent *Examining Your Environment* series which explores to the full such commonplace objects as dandelions and snow.

Instructional materials, of course, need not be formally introduced through a teaching guide or a formal curriculum. In spontaneous, effective teaching situations, teachers may bring in their favorite sonnets (sometimes—impressively—from memory) or souvenirs from summer excursions, such as French menus, Japanese boxes or child-made dolls from Guatemala. Students, too, may enrich classroom learning through sharing such items as birds' nests, record collections or original creations. Unfortunately for education there are few acceptable research devices for documenting the value that such contributions may make to learning except for observation and anecdotal records. When I was a high school librarian our library received many comments and queries on certain displays of books, pictures and personal collections (but lacking a research orientation at that time, I never thought to compile or even to count the queries).

Although almost anything—in the right hands, at the right time and in the right situation—can be used for instructional purposes, this book will, of necessity, pay more attention to human-produced materials adaptable to educational purposes. These would include—beyond the categories suggested by the *Dictionary of Education*—toys and games, simulations, tactile devices, art objects, models and printed materials of all kinds. Furthermore, since most instructional materials are communication media of various kinds, this book will deal most extensively with these media—especially with textbooks, library books, and instructional media in various formats. Though these media are selected in rather different ways, they tend to dominate formal education and are highly interrelated in instructional applications.

So far as I know, none of the communication media that are used so extensively for instructional materials was primarily designed for instruction. They are, rather, means of human communication, originally meant to convey knowledge, skills, feelings or attitudes, which have been adapted to educational purposes.

The items we use as instructional materials represent in one sense the communication devices established through human history, all subject to changing times and technology. Pictures (on the walls of caves) go back to pre-history, as do models and various kinds of samplers. The abacus—used for calculation—can also be used to teach number and logic concepts as can the more recent computer. The use of writing or print as a teaching device was greatly amplified by Gutenburg's discovery or reinvention of the printing press—though we still use a lecture system which originated because of the scarcity of books. In the late nineteenth century, the magic lantern and the stereoscope—popular as parlor games—also enriched communication and teaching. While magic lantern projections have largely been replaced by slides, filmstrips and opaque projections, we still use stereoscopic slides for subjects such as anatomy where three-dimensional representation is important. Twentieth century technology extended communication media with audio records and tapes, films, radio, television and computer technology—all of which have trickled down into at least some schools. The proliferation of numbers of media has been accompanied by a proliferation of the sheer numbers of materials.

According to Ken Komoski of Educational Products Information Exchange Institute (EPIE) the number of available textbooks has increased 200 percent in the last 20 years, while the number of 16mm films has increased 600 percent and the number of filmstrips 800 percent. Judging from the indexes of the National Information Center for Educational Media (NICEM), we currently have—at least in theory—more than one-half million instructional media items from which to choose.

One of the paradoxes of the information explosion that encompasses instructional materials is that public budgets for both informational and instructional materials are declining even as the numbers and kinds of materials increase. In schools and other governmental institutions, we are concurrently reducing expenditures for librarians, media specialists, curriculum consultants and other materials experts who have experience or training in selecting, organizing or utilizing these materials.

Because of the various viewpoints, the instructional materials discussed in this book will be classified in several ways: by their instructional purposes, by sensory modes, by formats or by their costs or sources. Some materials—like textbooks, curriculum guides, and basal programs and certain manipulatives—are primarily designed for education. Other human-made materials, both print and nonprint, may have educational values or be adaptable for educational purposes whether or not this was the original intent. For example, commercial toys, trade books and reference books are quite useful in education in different ways. If materials are purchased by the schools and used for educational ends, I am considering them—for the purpose of this book—to be instructional materials. Separate chapters will explore, in greater or lesser detail, characteristics and uses for certain broad genres of materials.

One classification that is very helpful in conceptualizing the whole range of instructional materials is Edgar Dale's Cone of Experience, reprinted here by permission from *Audiovisual Methods in Teaching* (New York, Holt, Rinehart & Winston, 1969), which arranges the means of instruction from direct experience to higher and more abstract levels. Though I do not think this hierarchy is always accurate (are all print materials, for example, always more

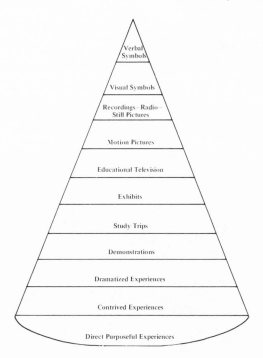

Dale's Cone of Experience

abstract than all visual symbols?), it does provide a good way of ordering the vast array of experiences and materials that can be used for instruction and that are worth considering in selection, somewhat resembling the three-mode model (enactive, iconic and symbolic) discussed in Jerome Bruner's *Toward a Theory of Instruction* (Cambridge, MA, Harvard University, 1966). In using the cone of experience, the basic question is: What kinds of experiences (materials) might help students gain the understanding, skills and attitudes they need? Dale's own rule for selecting materials is: "Go as low on the scale as you need to insure learning, but go as high as you can for the most efficient learning."

While the media/sensory division implicit in Dale's Cone of Experience is one useful parameter for selecting instructional materials, more commonly these are analyzed and selected for their purposes; legality; appropriateness for ages, grades, sequence and developmental levels; their subject content or themes; their research evidence and, sometimes, their quality.

Aside from scope, content, and authenticity, materials for educational uses must be considered in terms of the learning process and the human interactions involved. From the perspective of learning theory, materials might be selected for their differential abilities to perform instructional tasks, such as the "events of instruction" postulated by Robert Gagné in his *The Conditions of Learning* (1965):

- gaining attention
- informing learner of objective(s)
- stimulating recall of prerequisite learning and knowledge
- presenting stimulus
- providing learning guidance
- eliciting performance
- providing feedback
- assessing performance
- enhancing retention and transfer

While some materials—on the surface—seem much better than others for particular "events" (as gaining attention or providing feedback), the events in the learning process can obviously be divided in many ways between materials, teachers and students. Still, materials used in schools should perform at least some of these tasks well.

Another, quite different perspective, paramount in educational selection, stems from the nature of a school as an institution and bureaucracy. Administrative factors in analyzing materials involve such important constraints as:

- special equipment or facilities needed
- teacher qualifications
- time considerations
- price
- storage and processing requirements
- delivery and purchasing deadlines
- useful life expectancy

I will explore such considerations more fully in subsequent chapters.

FOR FURTHER READING

*Items marked with an asterisk include criteria.
+Items marked with a plus include substantial lists of references.

*Allen, W. H. "Media Stimulus and Types of Learning," *Audiovisual Instruction*, v.12, no.1, (Jan. 1967), pp. 27-31.

Bruner, Jerome. *Toward a Theory of Instruction.* Cambridge, MA, Harvard University, 1966.

*Dale, Edgar. *Audiovisual Methods in Teaching.* New York, Holt, Rinehart & Winston, 1969.

+Gagné, Robert M. *The Conditions of Learning.* New York, Holt, Rinehart & Winston, 1965.

+Schramm, Wilbur. *Big Media/Little Media: Tools and Technology for Instruction.* Beverly Hills, CA, Sage Publications, 1977.

OVERVIEW OF SELECTION

"When we mean to build
We first survey the plot, then draw the model."
                                        —William Shakespeare

"The educational system of the United States is unique in its fragmentized,
localized, and independent control. All that curriculum development efforts do is
to place before school boards and other local decision makers new and different
materials that can be adopted or rejected in terms of the needs of the students
and the desires of the community concerned."
                        —William V. Mayer, "Curriculum Development in
                        Crisis," *BSCS Newsletter* 68, September 1977

"The search for universally applicable programs of school improvement that can
be effectively used across the national spectrum has been largely fruitless. Educational environments vary so greatly that we must, instead, search out specific solutions for specific situations."
                        —Louis Rubin, *Curriculum Handbook*, 1977

" . . . education in America is a multi-billion dollar ad hoc enterprise on which
neither its leaders nor its consumers agree."
                        —William V. Mayer, "Curriculum Development in
                        Crisis," *BSCS Newsletter* 68, September 1977

"Most of the substantive content in the traditional subjects now being taught is
obsolete . . . updating is essential."
                        —Louis Rubin, *Curriculum Handbook*, 1977

"We are our choices."
                        —Jean Paul Sartre

■ ■ ■

If instructional materials—both intentional and non-intentional—range widely
in format and quality, the means of selecting these materials also vary considerably.
Major intentional teaching materials such as texts and basal programs are, at least
in theory, selected by carefully composed selection committees following established policies, procedures and criteria. Other intentional instructional materials—
such as activity books, educational games, science equipment or inexpensive manipulatives—are more apt to be purchased by individual teachers, often with their own
money, for their own classes or for individual children in these classes. Media materials and trade publications purchased for school media collections are most often
chosen by library/media specialists who base their selections—to a degree—on
informal needs expressed by teachers, students and administrators. These selectors
tend to locate and select books from reviewing media while they are more apt to
preview expensive items like films and to select inexpensive media items like filmstrips or kits from catalogs. In all these cases, selection is limited—sometimes
sharpened—by the number of dollars available.

All these groups, again, select materials for educational use from established
collections in libraries, textbook rooms, instructional materials centers, teachers'
centers, district resource centers, and state curriculum libraries—with or without

assistance. Selection here is limited by the quality of assistance and by what happens to be available on the shelves at the time of selection.

Selection is a complex decision-making process that involves weighing many factors simultaneously—juggling, at least, need, effectiveness and costs. In selection as in everything else there never seems to be enough time to do the job the way it should be done, and funds are often not available when needed. For some subjects at times there seems to be a bewildering number of choices; at other times, very few materials indeed. The process requires a critical mind, a wide and comparative knowledge of materials and their costs as well as of trends in the teaching and subject areas, and an intimate knowledge of school populations (both teachers and students) and the specific resources currently available to them.

Most approaches to selection are partial and conditioned by the set or perspectives of the would-be problem solvers. Legislators pass laws that may mandate contents, selection procedures or funds. Administrators attempt to cover their bases with policies and administrative procedures. Evaluation experts design complex analyses based on empirical evidence and theories of instructional design. Minorities—of all sorts—devise criteria for fairness, while educators check materials out against basic competencies or standardized lists of objectives. Reviewers may use personal or social criteria for their appraisals of quality, while review journals increasingly supply their own reviewers with institutional guidelines and outlines. Librarians and media people establish standards for quality, quantity and variety in media materials. Teachers' centers develop their own, using their perception of local needs. Interest groups and individual media compile more or less complete lists of materials available in specific fields or media.

Commercial sources, in an effort to supply educators with what they say they need, rely heavily on market research; in some states they are required to verify their materials with learners. These sources—the earliest selectors—also have their own in-house standards and desiderata for physical quality and durability as well as for learning design. In addition, most large educational publishers now have one or more compliance editors reading materials for compliance with state codes and assorted criteria.

Despite or possibly because of all this guidance and assistance, many (perhaps most) instructional materials are purchased with little thought and preparation as funds appear and disappear. In practice, many selectors base their appraisals largely on the reputations of developers, familiarity, or past experiences with particular publishers. As a result, irrespective of quality, relatively few companies supply most of the materials.

There is a widespread passive recognition that guidelines are not the only answer and that evaluation procedures that are time consuming and costly do not necessarily result in better selections, particularly when materials are quite comparable. Though one can use specific criteria or standards to judge, say, the life expectancy of a projector light bulb and choose accordingly, there are no criteria or groups of criteria that make it possible to gauge in advance the exact effectiveness of specific teaching materials for particular classroom settings or school districts.

As a resource librarian in a county office, I was often consulted by conscientious teachers who had been asked by their principals to spend, say, $700 in the next two days—with no guidelines except "for primary" or "for the gifted program." While the greatest selection asset of most of these teachers was their detailed knowledge of their own children and programs, they were being asked, without time or preparation, to pick out materials for unknown children for the following year. But, to develop shopping lists they needed time to articulate their own priorities and philosophies and to become aware of the range of materials that might meet the needs of their programs and students.

In an article in *Educational Technology* (February 1977) Greg Kearsley utilizes a three-dimensional model to illustrate the complexity of the educational process. The structure of his Who-What-How "model of instructional dimensions" is readily adaptable to the illustration of the multiple elements involved in selection. It may be used, for instance, to illustrate the parameters established (in one dimension) by those responsible for selection, (in a second dimension) by the learning processes to be emphasized, the community values to be promoted or the long-range educational objectives to be approached and (in the third dimension) by the information and evaluation materials required for the process of selection itself. The model (shown on page 24) is an application of this three-dimensional construct to the illustration of some of the many factors involved in selection at the local level. Selection at this level involves considering not only the characteristics of the curriculum area to be provided for and the materials available to choose from, but also the restraints placed on selectors by the community as a whole.

TIME FACTORS IN SELECTION

One simple variable in selection is time; materials are selected for use over different periods of time. Those selected for state or district adoption are supposed to be used for perhaps three to five years. At the other end, a teacher may select a few maps for an afternoon's presentation or order a set of free pamphlets for short-range use. Library books may have useful life expectancies of 20 years or one year, depending upon topics. Art, literature, history—the humanities in general—are relatively long lived. Other topics, like science, politics, economics, need constant updating and weeding. Demonstrations, films, study trips or even different texts require somewhat different time allocations for both preparation and classroom use.

In an age of rapid change, audiovisual materials tend to go out of date rather rapidly, even when their condition is satisfactory and their contents or concepts still valid. Most students today tend to snicker at the clothes and mannerisms of even the '50s or the '60s. But generally, materials with artistic integrity tend to survive longer than materials constructed for temporal educational purposes. It could be wise, then, to permabind classroom paperback sets of materials of lasting value, such as Shakespeare's plays, while buying (or borrowing) the cheapest possible versions of ephemeral or topical materials.

Thus, to choose materials for particular schools, one needs to consider the length of the school year, the timing of its holidays, the scheduling and number of hours in a typical school day, the time framework allowed for different subjects, the time span of a classroom period (40 minutes? an hour?), and whether or not mini-courses are given. The choice can also be affected by the time during which students and teachers have access to particular materials. To utilize media centers and library collections, students need some free time during the day before the school bus departs, while teachers need similar convenient blocks of free time to become familiar with and utilize materials in instructional materials centers, teachers' centers or district media collections.

The Dimensions of Selection

COMMUNITY CONSTRAINTS

Available funds

Legal mandates

Political constraints

School environment

Teacher characteristics

Student characteristics

CURRICULUM AREAS

Art

Music

Language Arts

Reading

Social Studies

Science

Health

Existing instructional materials in school or district

Textbooks available (range and rating)

Written media, books, pamphlets, magazines on topic

Community resources (people, places, programs, museums, festivals, etc.)

Teacher center facilities

School library staff and facilities

Professional, college, public libraries

Non-print media (models, films, charts, audio, etc.)

MATERIALS AVAILABLE

As materials are selected to be used for particular time periods (and often kept long beyond their time of optimum use) they are also selected within a time frame of administrative considerations that requires careful planning. When most California school districts responded to Proposition 13 by closing down schools during the summer of 1978, texts and media materials continued to be delivered to— and returned from—many closed schools, a costly and inconvenient process.

Materials, too, need to be considered for their optimal learning time, which might be roughly similar for children of the same age or developmental stage, though differing considerably for individual children.

LEVELS OF DECISION MAKING IN SELECTION

Another obvious variable in selection is that selection takes place and means different things at many levels. Selection occurs at all levels from an international decision-making level (whether to emphasize print materials, radio broadcasts or television programs as educational material in developing nations) on down to the process of helping one child choose materials for a particular assignment. At upper levels, selection necessarily becomes abstract and is largely based on an attempt to evaluate media or materials objectively. Since the nature and circumstances of the users are not known, learner-users (as students in one target group or a particular grade) are assumed to have the same understanding and the same educational requirements, and are expected to use materials in the same ways. At these levels of selection, the teachers who will ultimately use the materials are also considered to start with the same knowledge (which may be supplied) and to use materials in the same ways. (Sometimes variations are built in to handle individuality.) If parents and community are considered at all, they, too, are generalized (as rural, inner-city, college level).

As selection becomes more intimate—when individuals are selecting materials with colleagues they know or for students they know—teachers and children are perceived as having individual needs and strengths. Selection can then be on a more personal, analytic or intuitive level.

Evaluative and market criteria are the bottom line of upper-level selection decisions. At lower levels, materials are chosen on the basis of the particular characteristics of what is known and what is available. In the middle levels (regional and district or sometimes state) approaches vary. Some districts attempt to match abstracted statistical characteristics of the materials to abstracted statistical characteristics of their educational communities.

In international selection—an interesting and important process which is almost completely bypassed in this book—international organizations or world literacy groups set up policies and priorities to select materials and media to meet these priorities. Such groups as Unesco, for example, may work through national governments or international organizations, through volunteers, interested individuals, educational technologists or local organizations. Educational materials in developing countries run the full range from broadcasting facilities (radio and television) to inexpensive text production or to ingenious making-do with local or limited materials.

Selection at our national level is usually expressed in terms of money and policy. Since the 1830s, federal monies available for education have directly or indirectly affected the amount of dollars available for purchasing different kinds of materials. At different times, certain kinds of materials have been heavily subsidized. Schools in the late 1960s in particular were beneficiaries of President Lyndon Johnson's expansive great society funding. Subsequent lowered levels of funding, again, have affected both the kinds and the quantities of materials.

The federal government has spent millions of dollars researching curriculum materials with a substantial amount spent on "development," and a lesser percentage on producing and marketing materials. At the federal level, the selection process is usually expressed in funding or not funding, developing or not developing, a situation which is particularly crucial for handicapped students—particularly for the blind, hard of hearing or multiply-handicapped—because governmental funding priorities largely determine the existence, availability and distribution of materials. Since the national level is, in fact, pervasively determining for selection, decisions made here permeate all other levels of selection. But while the intent is to provide for the public good, the national funding priorities that determine the materials to be funded and distributed are as often based on educational fads and follies as on rational decision-making.

Our national educational priorities are also affected by such external events as Sputnik, the civil rights movement and our recent bicentennial, and by effective pressure groups which may range from professional scientists and educational developers to fundamental religious groups or irate parents. Legislators, too, have a role at the national level in authorizing funds for programs and materials and/or suggesting content. They may in turn be influenced by government bureaucracies, national professional organizations, parents' groups, or interest groups such as radical nutritionists, environmentalists or television producers.

Manufacturers and trade groups who produce and distribute subsidized materials affect our choice and use of materials nationally. Further, most educational products and selection tools are produced for a national market or audience. Therefore, educational producers, many of whom are sincerely concerned with educational quality and relevance, must decide what to publish in light of marketing considerations. As a result of an inertia inherent in education and of their own need for mass sales, publishers produce the best product they can sell rather than the best product they can devise.

In addition, these commercial considerations are further defined by state-level decisions. State legislators, like federal legislators, responding to conscience, the will of the people or effective pressure groups, issue mandates on what should or should not be included in state educational frameworks. These selection policies, often adopted in the past as responses to long-vanished conditions, then define the basic marketing strategies for textbook publishers and other large producers of instructional materials.

Some states influence selection for the better by such niceties as curriculum depository libraries, compilations of reviews, state matrices or materials examination centers. Some states encourage education in selection; others provide statewide approved lists or statewide purchase services. Texas not only selects but also warehouses and distributes text materials.

Selection committees, with varying degrees of power and backup assistance, are delegated to select textbooks and other basal instructional materials at both state and local levels, perhaps in two-thirds to three-fourths of all school districts.

In fact, sometimes the same instructional materials are reviewed at national, state, district, school and classroom levels.

District and county levels seem logical levels for reviewing programs and texts and for preview and/or purchase of expensive items like films. Counties, perhaps more often than states, are apt to provide convenient examination centers or preview services for selectors, local courses in materials production and selections, film collections with catalogs and delivery service, central warehousing, central cataloging, media fairs, and other means to facilitate information exchange about materials and between selectors to enhance the process of selection. But while policies tend to linger on, selection services at both state and local levels are very likely to be eliminated or gutted if or when budgetary cuts are made.

Districts (which can be the same as counties) also offer local inventory, selection and delivery systems. Perhaps two-thirds of them have selection policies, which may or may not be followed in practice. Selection can be easier at this level, which is more attuned to local conditions.

Below the county and district levels, selection decisions—often nebulous—involve choosing—with or without adequate time and information—materials for schools, for grade levels, for individual classes, for media centers and libraries serving teachers and students, and by and for individual students.

In practice, the tone of school-level selection most often is set by the principal, whether or not s/he supports (and fights for) adequate materials, whether or not s/he encourages student or teacher autonomy, whether or not s/he believes in particular programs or levels of achievement, or is good at scrounging funds and materials. (Private schools, which have fewer politics and policies to contend with, are usually confronted with severe money problems.) For library and media materials, a supportive principal and an extraverted librarian are—according to research—the main determinants of use. Teacher activists and teachers' centers, however, also can be extremely important at district, school and classroom levels.

Since the balance of power between state, local and federal influence varies with programs, budgeting, state and local history and personalities, it is extremely hard to generalize on exactly who does what in selection. In my recent pamphlet, *Selecting Instructional Materials* (Phi Delta Kappa Educational Foundation, 1978), I suggested some ideal roles for participants at local and district levels, based in part on actual practices and experience in three California school districts.

SURVEYING THE PROCESS OF SELECTION

Three recent surveys attempting to explore the process of selection provide some help—and also some confusing and contradictory responses. These surveys, which start from different premises, address their questions to different audiences and come up with different appraisals of selection roles.

The Educational Research Service (ERS), "designed to meet the needs of school administrators for objective, reliable and timely research," addressed its questionnaire to district administrators in (what the ERS considered) local selection states in 1976. Questionnaires, mailed to 1,275 selected district administrators in 33 states and the District of Columbia, were returned by about one-third (414) of those queried. Questions considered the existence and nature of selection policies, and the existence, composition, functions and details of service of selection committees, and asked who was responsible for selection.

Of the 414 replies, 75 came from California (a state which has a state adoption program as well as varying degrees of authority for elementary and secondary schools); 36 from Pennsylvania; 29 from Ohio; 28 from Illinois; 24 from New York; and fewer than 20 each from the remaining states including only one response each from six of those states.

While these replies may not be proportionally representative, they provided a great deal of information on the composition and function of the rather elusive selection committee, and showed that about three out of four responding districts had selection policies.

Not surprisingly, about one-half the administrators (51 percent) believed that the local board of education was responsible for selection, followed by the principal (6.2 percent), teachers and principals together (5.9 percent), the district superintendent (4.6 percent), the superintendent and board of education together (2.9 percent) and teachers (only 3.3 percent). While there is no guarantee that all administrators defined "responsibility" the same way, they seemed predominantly to name groups or individuals assigned the *legal* responsibility for selection.

A longitudinal *National Survey and Assessment of Instructional Materials* (NSAIM) carried out from the spring of 1974 to the winter of 1976 by Educational Products Information Exchange (EPIE) queried teachers and principals to identify and evaluate the materials currently used in 90,000 classrooms. This survey was based on the responses of more than 8,000 principals and 12,000 teachers in mathematics, reading, science, and social studies.

EPIE's questionnaire dealt with the quality and nature of the most-used materials (print and nonprint), with the extent of usage, and with teachers' and principals' roles in selection. It uncovered again the fact that many materials are purchased but unused.

The principals and teachers who responded to the NSAIM had quite different perceptions of selection roles. According to principals, print materials are selected by teachers, district-level and building-level committees, department chairpersons, and state-level committees—in that order. Nonprint materials, according to principals, are selected by classroom teachers, librarians and media specialists, department chairpersons, district-level and state-level committees—again, in order of decreasing frequency. Unfortunately no definition was provided for "print" or "nonprint" materials, so that print, conceivably, could encompass library books, pamphlets, worksheets or magazines in addition to textbooks.

Seventy-six percent of surveyed principals said that teachers select "all or many" materials; 5 percent said that teachers select none; and 67 percent said that school staff committees and district-wide committees select "many or some."

The teachers differed: 45 percent of the teachers who responded to EPIE's survey claimed they have no role in selecting materials; 30 percent spend less than one hour per year on the task; while 25 percent spend an average of ten hours selecting materials.

While the ERS and EPIE surveys substantially ignored or by-passed the roles of media personnel and librarians in the selection process, a third survey on the *Marketing, Selection and Acquisition of Materials for School Media Programs* indicated that librarians and media people are actually the prime selectors of both nonprint and print materials. This survey, reported extensively in the Winter and

Spring 1978 issues of the *School Media Quarterly*, was a triple-pronged survey carried out under the aegis of the American Association of School Librarians (AASL) and of the Resources and Technical Services Division (RTSD) of the American Library Association (ALA) with the cooperation of publishers and producers through the Association of American Publishers (AAP). This complex survey used three populations, three survey groups and three task forces, who put their answers together via computer. Its response rate varied somewhat with the groups queried: a 49 percent response from 106 surveys sent to publishers and producers; 44 percent from 516 surveys to school media programs; and only 27 percent from 107 surveys mailed to wholesalers and distributors. While the replies of all those groups correlated well with each other, they differed considerably from those on the other two (ERS and NSAIM) surveys.

The questions here dealt in detail with the processes through which materials are marketed for school media programs and the procedures used to select and acquire these materials. Other broad areas examined were expenditures and budgets (omitted from ERS survey), expectations of growth (or lack of growth) for book and nonprint markets, the impact of ESEA Title IV-B on materials purchases; and other factors that influence the process of selection, such as previewing, producers' catalogs and professional journals. It also asked librarians and media specialists what services they would like to see provided with purchases.

In this survey of media personnel, publishers and producers, media personnel regarded themselves (63 percent of the time) as having the final responsibility for selecting print materials and (64 percent of the time) as having the final responsibility for selecting media materials. Principals were considered to have the final responsibility only two percent of the time, and a reviewing group only one percent of the time. (Very likely the "print" materials in this survey were largely construed to be library books and other nontext materials.)

In this survey, 58 percent of publishers regarded reviewing groups as very important in selecting books, and 54 percent regarded them as important in selecting media. Publishers and producers also rated media personnel very important (57 percent) in selecting books and (62 percent) in selecting media materials.

Media specialists differ considerably from NSAIM principals in their perceptions of who chooses media materials. They believe these are chosen by media specialists (64 percent), acquisition librarians (12 percent), district media coordinators (13 percent), principals (2 percent), teachers (2 percent), reviewing groups (1 percent), and students (less than 1 percent).

According to media personnel (92 percent), teachers participate in the selection process primarily as individuals—usually by requesting materials from the media staff. But they also indicated teachers are involved in selection through requests by subject area teachers (39 percent), through selection committees (17 percent), through exhibits of new materials for faculty preview (42 percent) and through demonstrations of new materials by publishers and distributors (35 percent). These circumscribed selection roles for teachers seem much closer to the roles NSAIM teachers described than the roles that NSAIM principals ascribed to teachers. Principals, however, might have been talking about "some" rather than "typical" teachers.

Another part of the confusion between surveys may be the differing meanings administrators and media personnel attach to the term "responsibility"—the difference between (ultimate) responsibility (theory) and active responsibility (practice).

While there is no easy explanation for the vastly different interpretations of media selection between EPIE's principals and AASL's media personnel, I would tend to credit the AASL survey since it seems a good deal closer to the actual marketing-selection process for media. However, it may be accurate for only those schools—decreasing in number—that have librarians and/or media personnel.

Another study—of principals only—by Donald Orlich and colleagues, attempted to determine how 301 principals in Washington State learned about new programs. Orlich reported that the information sources for science programs are publishers (44 percent), books and journals (27 percent), district experts (42 percent), conferences (21 percent) and colleges (12 percent). One-half of the principals learned about new social studies programs from publishers, 33 percent from books and journals, 43 percent from district experts, 14 percent from conferences, 17 percent from colleagues, and 11 percent from colleges. It is apparent that most principals had more than one source of information.

An earlier (1970) National Education Association study of teachers' roles in selecting instructional materials found teachers "extensively" involved. At that time, 75.4 percent used magazine advertisements for information while 62.9 percent obtained information from educational exhibits and meetings.

Still another study—this one in Northern Ohio, by J. Arch Phillips, Jr. and Richard Hawthorne—considered the roles of many groups in selecting materials. This study, reported in *Educational Leadership* in February 1978, concluded that students are not involved at all, and that parents, individually or collectively, are rarely involved. (If involved at all, they are apt to serve in an advisory capacity.) Teachers tend to be involved in advising and deliberating, not in decision making. Principals and central office personnel are most active in decision-making roles, while superintendents and boards decide or approve curriculum decisions.

Because of the ambiguities and omissions in these questionnaires and surveys, we can only conclude that many groups and individuals are involved in selection and that no one group consistently controls the process. Depending upon what is selected, different groups have varying degrees of input. And finally, none of the groups surveyed had an overview of the total process.

The intent of this book is an overview—compiling, rationalizing and correlating some of the many viewpoints and disciplines that bear somehow on the multi-faceted process of selecting instructional materials. While I feel free to incorporate my own opinions and experiences at appropriate times and places, this book is essentially analytic and descriptive. My purpose is to synthesize and simplify, to present honestly and in proportion the thinking, research and actions of many groups and individuals who play some role in selection.

While I doubt that I can piece together the whole elephant from available fragments, I hope I may outline the beast a little more clearly. I will attempt to cover such aspects as the role of instructional materials in education, the roles of various participants in selection, and some appropriate techniques and criteria for selection.

Since selecting instructional materials is such a multi-faceted process, I have tried to summarize or reprint some criteria that seem significant to me—or that are considered significant by others. I have also devised homemade checklists and question series when these seemed appropriate.

Selection methods generally are discussed under the genre or the area where they seem most relevant (as previewing with films, the selection committee with textbooks, etc.). Similarly, I have attempted to place criteria, checklists and standards within logical, browsable chapters, so that they can be located and consulted as needed. Though I have been lavish in supplying selection aids, I do not consider any of these criteria a substitute for personal judgment.

QUERIES FOR SELECTORS

Some simple questions to consider at the beginning of any selection process are:

- What materials do I want for what purposes? (For which subjects, grade levels, types of students and educational purposes do I need materials?)
- What kinds of materials do we have already? (Are there appropriate materials— and services—in local media centers, public libraries, textbook rooms, museums, curriculum libraries or elsewhere?)
- Who may have prepared appropriate materials? (Commercial publishers, other teachers, local district, community agencies, the state?)
- Who may be aware of relevant materials? (Colleagues, department heads, curriculum specialists, librarians, media specialists, state or county teachers' centers, state or county media offices, the state department of education, publishers' representatives?)
- Is summarizing, descriptive or evaluative literature available? (Source guides, reviews, lists of recommended materials?)
- Can these materials be made available for inspection?
- When will I need these materials?
- For how long will I use these materials?
- Am I capable of evaluating these materials? If not, who can assist me?
- What other limitations do I have? (Costs, purchasing procedures, languages, legal requirements, training time?)

KEY PUBLICATIONS

The brief bibliographies in this chapter include only overviews written from somewhat different perspectives. Many relevant titles are included as Key Publications for further readings in many chapters, especially those on basic learning materials, nonprint media and evaluation.

About Learning Materials, by M. Frances Klein. Washington, DC, Association for
　　Supervision and Curriculum Development, 1978. 45p. $4.50pa.
　　An overview of learning materials from a curriculum perspective, which considers the curriculum reform movement of the 1960s as responsible for the massive production of materials; it includes an intelligent discussion of problems in

developing and evaluating instructional materials, as well as an annotated compilation of 20 guides to materials, and an annotated source bibliography of about 20 criteria. Both of these overlap many items in this book.

It also reprints Richard L. Miller's out-of-print *Selecting New Aids to Teaching* (published by the ASCD in 1971), a concise but thorough outline of the steps that should be taken and criteria that should be followed in selecting instructional units.

Centreville: A Model for Educational Decision Making, by Christopher R. Clarke and Michael L. Fischler. Plymouth, NH, Plymouth State College, 1977. 193p. $7.50pa. (From Plymouth State College, Plymouth, NH 03264.)

This delightfully absurd but all-too-truthful social systems analysis model was intended to provide students with simulated experiences in educational problem solving, using a simulation game based on a mythical composite district. Information is provided on high school student populations (with cumulative folders and class profiles) as well as on state and local systems, feeder elementary schools and other areas to be considered in reaching local educational decisions, one of which involves choosing curriculum.

Improving Materials Selection Procedures: A Basic "How to" Handbook by EPIE. New York, Educational Product Information Exchange Institute, 1973. (EPIE Educational Product "In Depth" Report No. 54). $10.00.

This brief summary of recommendations for rationalizing and systematizing selection procedures covers the roles and requirements of both schools and producers, as well as methods for developing, applying and following through on appropriate criteria, with a criterion checklist.

Instructional Materials: Selection and Purchase, by the National Education Association in cooperation with the Association of American Publishers. Washington, DC, NEA, 1976. 72p. $3.00pa.

This book, a revision of an earlier work by a Joint Committee of the National Education Association and the Association of American Publishers, concentrates on the process of selection, rather than on specific criteria for evaluating materials. It provides a simple but thorough analysis of legal and administrative factors in selection (laws, school boards, administrators) with a systematic indication of the "steps educators should follow to bring the process to a fruitful conclusion." Also recommends an allocation of five percent of average current expenditures on materials.

Politics of Education. 76th Yearbook, by the National Society for the Study of Education. Chicago, NSSE and the University of Chicago, 1977. $12.00.

Provides an overview of some functions of different levels of government in the politics and policies of education; covers local, state and federal roles, including a discussion of the role of the Supreme Court.

Sharper Tools for Better Learning, by the National Association of Secondary School Principals. Reston, VA, NASSP, 1973. 40p. $2.00pa.

This compact little pamphlet addressed to administrators includes a criterion checklist that considers administrative, curricular, pedagogical and evaluation requirements for new materials.

FOR FURTHER READING

*Items marked with an asterisk include criteria.
+Items marked with a plus include further references.

Iannaccone, Laurence. *Three Views of Change in Educational Politics.* Chicago, National Society for the Study of Education, 1977.

*Kearsley, Greg P. "The Who-What-How Model of Instructional Dimensions," *Educational Technology*, v.17, no. 2 (Feb. 1977), pp. 44-45.

+Kunder, Linda R., compiler. *Procedures for Textbook and Instructional Materials Selection.* Arlington, VA, Educational Research Service, 1976.

Lawson, Tom E. *Formative Instructional Product Evaluation.* Englewood Cliffs, NJ, Educational Technology Publications, 1974.

+"Marketing, Selection, and Acquisition of Materials for School Media Programs," *School Media Quarterly*, v.6, no. 2 (Spring 1978), pp. 98-134, and no. 3 (Winter 1978), pp. 171-201.

Moore, J., ed. *Instructional Materials Adoption Data File.* White Plains, NY, Knowledge Industry Publications, 1975.

+National Education Association. *Selection of Instructional Materials and Equipment by Teachers.* Washington, DC, NEA, 1970.

National Survey and Assessment of Instructional Materials (funded by Lilly Endowment). New York, Educational Products Information Exchange Institute, 1977. (EPIE Report 76).

Orlich, Donald C., Thomas P. Ruff, and Henry R. Hansen. "Stalking Curriculum: Where Do Elementary Principals Learn about New Programs?" *Educational Leadership*, v.33, no. 8, (May 1976), pp. 614-21.

Phillips, J. Arch, Jr., and Richard Hawthorne. "Political Dimensions of Curriculum Decision Making," *Educational Leadership*, v.35, no. 5, (Feb. 1978), pp. 362-66.

Philos, Daphne. "Selection and Acquisition of Nonprint Materials," *School Media Quarterly*, v.6, no. 3 (Spring 1978), pp. 179-87.

*+Tyler, Louise L., and M. Frances Klein. *Evaluating and Choosing Curriculum and Instructional Materials.* Glennville, CA, Educational Resource Associates, 1976.

Woodbury, Marda. *Selecting Instructional Materials.* Bloomington, IN, Phi Delta Kappa Educational Foundation, 1978. (Fastback 110).

PART II
PRELIMINARIES

BUDGETING FOR INSTRUCTIONAL MATERIALS

"You cannot teach children to read, and then take away their books."
 —Jimmy Carter

"The number of teaching and learning problems we are asked to deal with seems endless. As a consequence textbooks are taking longer and costing more to produce. Since only seven-tenths of one percent of the money allocated to education is spent for instructional materials, it may well be that the educational community is designing products that, in time, it will not be able to afford."
 —Barbara Thompson Howell (Vice-President, Silver Burdett), Presentation to New Jersey Association of School Administrators, Atlantic City, NJ, May 12, 1977

"We spend an estimated $20 billion annually on cigarettes and cigars—but only half a billion on textbooks for our children. We spend nearly $40 billion on alcohol, $176 billion on 44 major weapons programs, another $40 billion on federal paperwork. And we spend, each day, *five cents* on textbooks for our children— about one-fourth the price of our daily newspaper."
 —Association of American Publishers, *Parents Guide to More Effective Schools*, 1978

■ ■ ■

Our ideal picture of education includes well-trained, competent, dedicated teachers; attractive, well-arranged classroom environments; and children learning from well-selected, up-to-date instructional materials—texts carefully picked for relevance; current films, filmstrips and other media to bring the world into the classroom; and books chosen for individualized learning, independent study, research skills and pleasure reading.

In many of today's classrooms, materials are limited to texts which may be badly out of date, shared by several teachers or students, or so battered and dog-eared as to be almost unusable. My daughter's algebra text may be a typical instance; this book, surplus from another school, was published in 1965. Judging from the scratched and erased signatures inside its back cover, it has passed through the not-so-tender hands of at least 14 children. The title page itself is missing; the cover has been taped and re-taped; at last count, 11 pages were loose and the rest seemed to be hanging in there out of loyalty.

In 1979, while materials are increasing in actual number, in sophistication and diversity, and in number of adaptations, a number of schools have been forced to return to basic frontier teaching tools—blackboards, shared texts, recycled paper and pencil stubs.

Materials budgets and student achievement have shown parallel declines in the 1970s, although the extensive and expensive reports which research the reasons for our declining achievement scores have not, so far as I know, considered the factor of instructional materials. Though we recognize that the quality of instruction is affected by the quality of instructional materials, we have really no accurate measure of the extent to which these affect learning. One informed estimate, by

Roy Barron of the Santa Barbara Unified School District, is that, overall, teacher skills and instructional materials are probably equally responsible for learning—a proportion not reflected in any educational budget.

Our educational budgets in themselves reflect the real rather than an ideal world. Budget setting, of course, should be a rational process. But in the United States in the late 1970s, educational budgets, particularly those of local school jurisdictions, are set in political, emotional and financial contexts dominated by crisis thinking and crisis behavior. Taken together, such factors as inflation, cuts in federal funds, declining enrollments, local taxpayer rebellions and the natural desire of school employees to hold on to their jobs, tend to prevent rational consideration of the roles of instructional materials in the educational process. Spokespersons for materials—mostly librarians and media people—lack clout at this stage of the budget-setting process. Though educators gripe year round at the skimpiness and low quality of available materials, at budget time they act as a pressure group for jobs rather than materials. While individual parents frequently complain of inadequate texts, taxpayer groups tend to agitate for lower school budgets. In these contexts, budgets for materials are cut to the bone. Since materials at best occupy a tiny fraction of the school budgets, these cuts save relatively few dollars though they have a disproportionate effect on learning.

Our outlays for instructional materials have now dwindled to the point where they are only about one percent of our educational budgets—a remarkably low figure. With costs of film and paper rising rapidly, these dollars buy less and less each year. We spend about four times as much per child busing children to and from school as we spend on the materials they use for learning. ("Instructional materials" in this chapter refers only to textbooks, library books, trade books and media materials—and not to such things as laboratory equipment, science supplies, papers and pencils, bats and balls, band instruments or rabbit food, important as these are. Our budgets for these are also exceedingly low.)

To take some concrete examples, our expenditures for textbooks have been declining since 1965. These textbooks, admittedly imperfect, still serve as our major means for assuring continuity in courses where sequential development is important. Certainly most of our achievement tests are correlated with or based on texts. Yet we currently spend only 0.7 percent of our current educational budget for these.

When textbook budgets started declining in the late 1960s, texts were supplanted by other, and sometimes better, instructional materials. In the 1970s we have experienced a decline in the proportion of school budgets spent on all educational media. In a survey of 12,389 teachers and 8,619 principals, EPIE found that instructional materials (again defined as textbooks, library books and media materials) represented less than one percent of their current school budgets. Yet these same 12,389 teachers estimated that they spent 95 percent of their time with these instructional materials; 62.5 percent of their time with print materials; and 32.5 percent with media materials.

The 1977 Survey of Market Data Retrieval's *National Comparison: Local School Costs* (Westport, CT, July 1977) shows a slightly higher budget figure, 1.19 percent, which may be more accurate or possibly more comprehensive but is consistent with the 1.2 percent estimate in the Association of American Publishers' *1976 Industry Statistics*. We seem to spend seven-tenths of one percent on textbooks and about one-quarter of one percent each on other print materials (0.26 percent) and media materials (0.24 percent).

In dollar figures, the average school district spent $16.53 per pupil for all instructional materials out of a total per-pupil cost of $1,614.73 ($1,394.54 for current expenditures). This works out to $8.90 for textbooks (one average or two cheap texts) per student, most of a library book at $4.70 and, at $2.91 for media materials, about one-sixth of a filmstrip. (The dollar budget for instructional materials for the 1975-1976 school year was almost exactly the same—$16.45—but this represented 1.28 percent of the school budget and bought a little more.)

Many districts, of course, spend even less on materials. In its *National Survey and Assessment of Instructional Materials*, EPIE found that a startling 20 percent of their teacher-respondents had no instructional materials other than texts. One teacher, reached by phone, confirmed that she had spent six years trying, without success, to get one globe for her history courses. To an advocate of instructional materials, the cost of one globe spread out over several hundred students would be a very modest investment compared to its educational value.

In California, our most populous state and the state where my three children are being educated, even before Proposition 13, local school districts averaged one-third of one percent of their expenditures on instructional materials—about $4.87 per child. The state supplements of about $12.00 for textbooks were barely enough to cover basic reading and math texts at the elementary level without allowing for extra copies or supplementary materials. Proposition 13 has already affected the amount of materials available at the secondary level.

One fairly typical district that invested heavily in (now aging) media equipment has not bought a new film in nine years. Since the public library in this same community had to discontinue its film program because of Proposition 13 budget constraints, students in this city are limited to those 10-year-old films which are still in good repair and still relevant. This district averages less than $0.80 per student for library books and media materials. In a sizable proportion of schools, no money is spent for books, since book funds and other instructional materials come from inadequate discretionary budgets administered by principals. These budgets, about $11.00 per child at the elementary level, rising to $20.00 per child at the junior high level and $25.00 per high school student, have to cover activities; art, office, and teaching supplies; food for cooking classes; wood for shops and countless miscellaneous items as well. Consequently, about one-fifth of the elementary schools and one-half of the high schools have no district allocation at all for library books. Consistently enough, this particular district, which is worried about the low reading scores of its students, provides no funding for elementary libraries. According to embittered librarians, the school library is "the heart of instruction and the foot of the budget." Typically, school libraries lack current subscriptions and new materials, although some scrounge rather creatively. Recreational reading is down, and library research is seriously limited. Whatever the printed district policy on multicultural enrichment, for instance, you cannot look up new African nations in outdated encyclopedias. You cannot write book reports without books. Certainly, schools located within walking distance of branch libraries can encourage their students to use these branches, but these branch libraries themselves are often struggling with budget and staff cuts and, in some cases, the threat of extinction.

Project funds—such as the Elementary School Aid Act—are intended to supplement district funds, but often substitute for them. Frequently, programs originally funded by school districts are supported for a time with federal project funds. When or if these are cut back, the ultimate level of dollar support may be lower than it was originally. For instance, one junior high library with a student population of about 500 received about $1,600.00 in district funds and $1,200.00 in ESEA Title II funds back in 1968-1969, as well as separate funding for a reference collection. Both district and ESEA II funds gradually shrank through the 1970s to about $400.00 each in 1974-1975. In 1975-1976 the school got $275.00 from district funds and an additional $210.00 for magazine subscriptions, while the project funds were spent on textbooks. In 1976-1977 this library received $800.00 in ESEA funds (Title IVB) and nothing from the district. In 1977-1978 they had a donation of $100.00 from concerned parents but no district funds. Book sales and book donations are now their major supply source.

In other schools, teachers required to develop multicultural or bilingual programs have to rely on PTAs, local public libraries, their own pockets or lucky donations for backup materials. Other schools attempt to teach science without equipment or current information. I was asked more than once by my daughter's junior high school to lend or donate books, posters and science materials for innovative school programs. Though I wish to contribute to the education of my children and other children, I find it hard to go along with a policy that expects parents to supply such instructional items, except through taxes. Many parents and parent groups, however, do take on this responsibility and often contribute toward salaries, shop supplies, art supplies, and special equipment as well. Such support tends to be higher in relatively affluent schools and less in schools that need it the most.

Our declining budget coincides, unhappily, with a real rise in the number and percentage of children under the true poverty line (although the total number of children in our country is declining. According to *America's Children, 1976: A Bicentennial Assessment* (Washington, DC, National Council of Organizations for Children and Youth, 1976), "One of every four American children now lives in poverty," a downward trend that started in 1970. These children, who are particularly dependent upon schools for an enriched environment, are not apt to obtain learning materials or school situations suited to their particular learning styles. They will be especially affected by lowered learning opportunities in bare-budget schools. With short-sighted policies on instructional materials, we can probably expect further declines in our achievement levels as measured by the National Assessment of Educational Progress.

Interestingly, a Rand Corporation comparison of reading programs among 20 minority schools in Los Angeles in 1973-1975 found that teachers' use of a variety of reading materials was the only factor that related strongly and consistently to increased reading achievement (from *Analysis of the School Preferred Reading Program in Selected Los Angeles Minority Schools, R-2007*). When teachers are trained to use these materials, there is an even larger effect on reading achievement. For all other factors studied, such as open classroom, team teaching, word attack and comprehension, there are both effective and ineffective programs, successes and failures.

This is consistent with a great deal of validated research in the progressive school movement which has shown that both elementary students and high school students learn more when they have free choice of a variety of materials.

(More recent reports, on basics as compared to open education, usually do not isolate materials as a factor.)

To determine an ideal (or a minimal) figure or budget percentage for instructional materials, we can use cost analyses, figures supplied by advocates, or past experience. One set of figures is available from the *Guidelines for an Adequate Investment in Instructional Materials* prepared by the Joint Committee of the National Education Association and the American Textbook Publishers Institute in 1967. While this report leaned toward texts, it contained a workchart and a factor analysis whose factors included, among others: need for basic texts, need for variety and flexibility, need for independent study materials, need for materials for differentiated instruction, multiple adoptions, new adoptions for existing programs, new courses and programs, obsolescence, and replacement requirements. The figures in 1966 dollars were $42.00 investment costs and $14.00 replacement costs for each student in grades 1 to 6 (about $71.00 and $24.00, respectively, in 1976 dollars) and $63.00 investment and $21.00 replacement for secondary students (about $107.00 and $36.00 in 1976). The committee's current recommendation is for 5 percent of operational costs per student for all instructional materials except for library books.

School librarians and media experts have long recommended dollar standards and per capita standards which have never been put into effect in the majority of schools—even though they are based on well-thought-out programs and rather thorough analyses of costs. Generally, their percentage figures run from 6 to 10 percent of current school expenditures. In their latest published standard, found in *Media Programs: District and School* (Chicago: American Library Association, 1975), these two groups recommend 10 percent of current expenditures as a consensus figure among school administrators, business managers and media professionals. This figure excludes adoption textbooks (less than 1 percent more) but includes library books, media materials (including replacements and duplicates) and media equipment. They recommend a total collection of 20,000 items for each school of 500 students, which, in this context averages out to 40 items per student. (The American Library Association has a bare bones collection recommendation of 10 items per student; media producers, through the official Association of Media Producers, recommend a more modest 5 percent minimum for all instructional materials.)

The 5 to 6 percent advocated by the NEA, publishers and media producers is based on things as they are; that is, current selection procedures and utilization policies in which media professionals and librarians have a rather marginal role. The 6 to 10 percent figure of media professionals and librarians is based on what can be, rather than what is—and reflects a thoughtful analysis of the costs of a somewhat more individualized and more innovative curriculum.

If we use the past as the basis for guidance, we find that current budget expenditures (not capital outlays) averaged around 3 to 5 percent in the 1960s, though this figure was cited as inadequate many times in the Joint Committee's report and considered low by administrators. In the 1920s, when most schools used only textbooks for instructional materials and some students still bought their own, textbook expenditures averaged out to 2.2 percent of current school expenditures.

To me, the 3 to 5 percent range seems a minimal functional level, with about two-thirds of this for textbooks and library books and one-third for media materials. Below 2.2 percent is criminal; our textbook requirements alone cannot be lower than those of the 1920s. If there is any media program at all, another one-fourth to one-half percent is necessary for media equipment. Realistically, we should add a little to make up for these very lean years. While I am convinced that higher percentages would pay dividends in more exposure and better learning, these require media and clerical staffs which many districts do not have and are not willing to finance.

In the 1960s when I was a school librarian in a fairly well-funded high school, I was responsible, with one overworked all-purpose clerk, for textbooks and media materials as well as for the library in a school of 1,200 students. We were often harassed by housekeeping tasks and the sheer amount of materials we had to select, order, process, catalog, shelve, circulate and inventory. (Since my clerk happened to be a mechanical genius we avoided many repair and maintenance expenses.) Our collection was well selected and very well utilized though textbooks were largely a warehouse operation. All new materials were well-circulated and added to total use. It would have been highly desirable, educationally, to increase our library and media collections and to devote more thought to textbooks, but we would have needed more staff, more space, and above all, more time. (*Media Programs*, referred to earlier, provides good guidelines for these.)

Without these basic ingredients—a trained staff to handle, process, demonstrate, circulate and update materials, to propagandize teachers, to prepare lists and to perform a myriad of other follow-through tasks—instructional materials, no matter how valuable, are apt to be used infrequently if at all. In its survey of instructional materials, EPIE found that thousands of dollars worth of films and filmstrips purchased with federal money were unused. Textbooks, too, were often purchased but unused if no one was responsible for their utilization. Principals, who might be expected to have an overview, generally cannot say what textbooks and materials in social studies, mathematics, science and reading are available to their teachers. They do not know which available texts are being used by their teachers or how they are used on a daily basis. At the district level many districts have no usable central records to help them locate texts that may be surplus or unused in specific locations. Too often, students in one school share texts while extra copies of the same text are stored and forgotten a few miles away in another school.

I have heard my quota of horror stories and have seen well-selected collections sitting in dusty boxes in storage rooms. I have also heard success stories: "My staff and I worked all summer to get out a catalog of our media collection. Circulation went up 500 percent that fall."

Assuming adequate money and staffing, it is still difficult in today's educational circumstances to assign this money to instructional materials and then allocate purchases according to instructional needs and educational priorities. Since funds and authorizations (see chart on page 41) stem from different levels, selections tend to be made at all levels with varying amounts of duplication and coordination. In this hodgepodge, decisions to purchase are often made without consulting the ultimate users or considering the function and value of instructional materials.

Funding Sources (The most usable information on sources of funding is from the principals surveyed by NSAIM.)				
Type of Materials	**Building**	**State**	**Federal**	**Other**	**Unknown**
Print	52.4	32.9	7.8	6.3	0.7
Non-Print	55.2	24.3	11.4	8.4	0.7
All	52.4	26.5	8.8	7.5	5.5

Central urban areas have (slightly) more federal funds for instructional materials; parents and building funds contribute a higher percentage in rural areas.

Media materials and library books, according to the AASL-RTSD survey (discussed in the chapter titled "Overview of Selection") tend to be purchased from local government funds rather than funds from state or federal agencies. These materials, in fact, are quite often dependent upon parent-teacher organizations and/or teacher contributions. In districts with media specialists, 3 percent indicated that they had received all their funding from the PTA, while about 20 percent obtained support from teacher contributions. Quite likely, a higher proportion of other districts did without.

The effect of taxpayers' rebellions—such as that resulting in California's Proposition 13—has been to pass a higher proportion of the burden of school financing on to the state level away from the local levels. In California, so far, Proposition 13 has affected the amount of money for instructional materials (particularly for science materials) at the high school levels. Vocational courses, wood and metal shops, have often had to scrounge for supplies or do without. Media collections and libraries are most affected at elementary grades where there is little or no funding for materials. Often library-media centers are closed down or handed over to volunteers, clerical employees or CETA workers.

While there are no easy solutions for setting budgets for instructional materials, or for budget setting in general, the most appropriate district role seems to be that of setting a firm total for instructional materials, rather than deciding upon individual items. If the state role in financing increases, the state may have to impose a minimum standard or percentage for instructional materials, say 3 to 5 percent, rather than choosing materials. States could also fund media previews and provide exemplary and traveling collections of relevant materials, and/or materials consultants for new programs. And the coordination of funding and planning among different levels would, of course, be vastly improved if they all adopted the same fiscal year and budgeting schedules.

Though some states sometimes attempt to provide some materials funds for mandated programs, there are so many bureaucratic processes involved that often teachers eventually turn out to be responsible for new programs without school materials provisions (such as libraries) or classroom funds for new materials. Thus, funding is quite justifiably perceived as unfair by many teachers.

If state legislators were to require that 3 to 5 percent of instructional budgets be spent on instructional materials, we would improve education immeasurably and without increasing its total cost, since funds could be taken relatively easily from other allocations without significant decline in quality. The federal government, too, when it mandates programs like mainstreaming, should provide funds for needed materials to implement such legislation.

Somehow, before budgets are set for instructional programs, every school and every district needs 1) to assess the quality and currency of its instructional materials available to its students, 2) to correlate this information with intended programs and 3) to estimate in dollars what materials are needed for the coming year. A substantial inflationary figure needs to be built into any budget for materials, since they are subject to a particularly high rate of inflation. Booklets which cost $1.25 each at budget-setting time are apt to cost $2.00 each at the time of purchase. Ideally, the figure set would be an aggregate of the individual budgets submitted. If principals, teachers, administrators and media professionals all participate in the process, the recommended figure will be a consensus figure related to the needs of the district and will probably receive teacher support at budget-setting time. It will not be considered an area which can be cut without affecting the educational program seriously.

At the district level, some relevant questions are:

- What level of support is desirable for instructional materials?
- What is the current level of support in dollars as a percentage of budget?
- Who should set the budget?
- Where can funds be obtained?
- Are there appropriate materials for all programs?
- Who is responsible for long-range planning for instructional materials?
- Who should determine how the budget is spent?
- Are staff and procedures appropriate and adequate for ordering and handling materials?
- What are appropriate budget-setting roles for:
  administrative officers?
  librarian-media staff?
  purchasing agent?
  professional teaching staff?
  existing selection committees?
- Are there mechanisms available to encourage a cooperative figure from this group?
- How should funds be allocated?

Possible Variations for Allocating Funds for Instructional Materials

Method	Advantages	Disadvantages
by broad curricular areas	allows flexibility calls in experts	may slight smaller subject divisions and/or interdisciplinary concerns; not near point of use
by narrower subjects (or particular teachers)	easily monitored; apt to be used	may lack overview, omit interdisciplinary concerns
by forms of materials (textbooks, media, library books)	easy to administer; separates responsibilities; easy for statistics	little relevance to curriculum; no overview; may have concentrations or gaps in one or more collections
by program	adapted to needs	may lack balance
by particular units, individual buildings, etc.	materials are appropriate; more apt to be used	excessive duplication in district
by departments	involves teachers	no overviews; possible duplications
by cost of materials	provides cost comparison across types of media	expensive, but worthwhile items may be slighted
by committee	combines skills of members; fair consensus	time consuming for individuals and process; committee may not be balanced
by grade or levels	provides overview and continuity; may match cost to needs	removed from point of use
by formula based on needs, priorities, and goals	ideal in theory; policies become explicit and articulated rather than fuzzy	lacks flexibility; absolute equity may not be desirable; overlooks quality of available materials, who decides, who weights the formula; overlooks values of subjective and intuitive decisions; may need frequent revision as needs and priorities change

FOR FURTHER READING

*Items marked with an asterisk have criteria for selection.
+Items marked with a plus have extensive lists of references.

*American Association of School Librarians, and the Association for Educational Communications and Technology. *Media Programs, District and Schools.* Chicago, ALA, 1975.
    Includes quantitative and expenditure standards for all types of print and visual materials, services and programs at district and school levels.

Association of American Publishers. *1977 Industry Statistics.* New York, AAP, 1978. (From 1 Park Avenue, New York, NY 10016.)

Association of American Publishers. *Parents Guide to More Effective Schools.* New York, AAP, 1978.

Association of Media Producers. *Survey and Analysis of 1976 Educational Media Sales.* Washington, DC, AMP, 1977. (From 1707 L Street, NW, Suite 515, Washington, DC 20036.)

Barro, S. M., and S. J. Carroll. *Budget Allocation by School Districts: An Analysis of Spending for Teachers and Other Resources.* Santa Monica, CA, Rand Corporation, 1975. (Rand Report R-1797-NIE).

Cronin, Joseph M., and Richard M. Hailer. *Organizing an Urban School System for Diversity.* Lexington, MA, Heath, 1973. (ED 091 494).

Education Commission of the States. *The Fiscal Impacts of Declining Enrollment.* Denver, CO, ECS, 1976.

Education Commission of the States. *School District Expenditures and Tax Controls.* Denver, CO, ECS, 1978.

*Joint Committee of the National Educational Association and the American Textbook Publishers Institute. *Guidelines for an Adequate Investment for Instructional Material.* Washington, DC, National Education Association, 1967.

Knezevich, Stephen J. *Program Budgeting: A Resource Allocation Decision System for Education.* Berkeley, CA, McCutchan, 1973.

Market Data Retrieval. *National Comparisons: Local School Costs.* Westport, CT, Market Data Retrieval, 1977.

Murphy, Gerald. *State Education Agencies and Discretionary Funds.* Lexington, MA, Lexington Books, 1974.

National Council of Organizations for Children and Youth. *America's Children: 1976: A Bicentennial Survey.* Washington, DC, National Council of Organizations for Children and Youth, 1976.

Philos, Daphne. "Selection and Acquisition of Nonprint Media," *School Media Quarterly*, v.6, no. 3 (Spring 1978), pp. 179-87.

Porter, David O., et al. *The Politics of Budgeting Federal Aid: Resource Mobilization in Local School Districts.* Beverly Hills, CA, Sage, 1973. (Sage Professional Papers in Administrative and Policy Studies).

NEEDS ASSESSMENTS

"From each according to his abilities; to each according to his needs."
—Karl Marx, 1875

■ ■ ■

According to educational theory, educational policies and programs should, ideally, start out with a set of educational goals based upon local needs. Since many needs assessments pay relatively little attention to instructional materials per se, I have developed a preliminary instrument for surveying existing instructional materials for quality, scope and relevance to local educational priorities. This particular assessment instrument can be used at school, district or classroom levels. Needs assessments at the national level are considered as surveys. The National Needs Assessment (NNA) for the handicapped is described in the chapter titled "Selection for Special Education."

While the questions and arrangements here are as systematic as I can make them, the answers will, essentially, be more the result of value judgment than of quantitative analysis. (Some quantitative measures are included in the chapter titled "Materials Selection Policies.") The value questions are designed to indicate what kinds of materials exist, whether or not they are meeting their educational purposes, and whether they are appropriate to the community they are supposed to serve. Students, parents, teachers or administrators using the forms here might conceivably come up with different assessments. Since it is important for each of these groups to have a voice on the kinds and numbers of instructional materials, they all need, separately or together, to survey the adequacy of these materials.

More systematic evaluations of adequacy could be performed for specific subject areas and/or specific objectives. Other approaches for analyzing adequacy of materials are surveying long-term trends in materials and/or expenditures, comparison with established standards, or some means of estimating the adequacy of materials in the total role of the school. They can be estimated in terms of excellence, in terms of congruence, or in terms of budgetary expenditures.

The references at the end of this chapter include other forms and approaches for surveying instructional materials needs. Related assessments should include students, faculty, community, goals and facilities. "Evaluating Media Programs" in *Subject Areas and Implementation* covers media program evaluation and has forms and references that could also be helpful in assessing needs.

PRELIMINARY ASSESSMENT OF INSTRUCTIONAL MATERIALS

I CURRICULUM FACTORS

Materials are adequate, quantitatively and qualitatively, to support the overall goals and objectives of the curriculum.

	Poor 1	2	3	4	5	Excellent 6	Not applicable

Specifically, materials are adequate for
  language arts
  mathematics
  social studies
  science
  health
  reading
  other major courses _____
  mini-units _____

Note any subject areas for which instructional materials are
  inaccurate _____
  out of date _____
  not appropriate for current curriculum _____
  not appropriate for student body _____
  not well suited to preferred styles of teaching _____
  poorly chosen _____
  not used _____

What are your plans for improving instructional materials in these areas?

How much money will this require?

Is this budgeted for the near future?

II FORMATS

Materials are systematically acquired in appropriate formats.

Note any formats for which instructional materials are
  nonexistent _____
  out of date or inappropriate re curriculum, style of teaching,
    student body _____

What are your plans for discarding or acquiring instructional materials in these formats?

How much money should this require?

Is this money budgeted?

Audiovisual materials in the following formats are adequate, qualitatively and quantitatively, to support curriculum.

	Poor 1	2	3	4	5	Excellent 6	Not applicable

  realia
  toys
  games
  simulations
  manipulatives
  maps and globes
  filmstrips

(Form continues on next page)

II FORMATS (cont'd)

	Poor 1	2	3	4	5	Excellent 6	Not applicable
films							
audio formats							
trade books							
textbooks							
charts							
pamphlets							
periodicals							
consumable items							

III FACILITIES AND ORGANIZATION

Materials are arranged for convenient use and access

	Poor 1	2	3	4	5	Excellent 6	Not applicable
Location(s) is convenient							
Locations are adequate in size							
Storage is adequate							
Materials are logically arranged and/or indexed							
Materials are accessible at convenient times							
Instructional materials personnel are available as needed							
Supportive equipment is available							
Materials and supportive equipment are well maintained							
Potential users are informed as new materials are acquired							
Facilities are designed to allow a variety of activities to take place							

If improvement is needed, what are your plans to improve the facilities and organization of your instructional materials?

IV TEACHING FACTORS

Appropriate materials for a variety of teaching approaches and methods have been selected, as needed

	Poor 1	2	3	4	5	Excellent 6	Not applicable
individual assignments and homework							
classroom assignments							
computerized approaches							
programmed approaches							
discussion							
debate							
independent study; individualized instruction							
contract learning							
library research							
enrichment on current aspects of topics							
enrichment on history of subject							
discovery							
inquiry							
lecture							
illustrated lectures and demonstration							
simulation							

(Form continues on page 48)

IV TEACHING FACTORS (cont'd)

	Poor 1	2	3	4	5	Excellent 6	Not applicable
drama							
role playing							
team teaching							
tutoring							
learning centers							
problem solving							
multisensory							
outdoor education							
_____							
_____							

What provisions are you making to select materials to meet the strengths and teaching preferences of individual teachers and the educational community?

V STUDENT FACTORS

Materials have been chosen considering the individual needs of students, including such factors as

	Poor 1	2	3	4	5	Excellent 6	Not applicable
ability levels							
learning styles							
learning strengths							
interests							
motivation							
attention span							
current measures of achievement levels							
memorability							
reinforcement							
self direction							
attitude toward school							
previous educational experience							
other learning backgrounds							
aesthetic experiences and attitudes							
feelings and emotions							
family experiences							
disabilities or handicaps							
individual preferences							
inferred intellectual level							
learning modes (preferred media)							

Materials have been chosen considering group needs of students'

	1	2	3	4	5	6	
socio-economic background							
range of achievement							
range of IQ							
community resources							

What means are you using to select materials to meet the individual and group needs of students?

(Form continues on page 49)

VI EVALUATION OF SELECTION PROCESS

What are the official goals of this district?

What kinds of programs and materials seem consistent with these goals?

Are these materials used extensively in the district?

How have funds been invested in the past?

Were these purchases useful?

Are they still being used? How and why?

If used, should they be supplemented or replaced?

If supplemented, how could they best be supplemented?

What materials are being used currently?

How do these meet the needs of the users?

What kinds are needed?

Are they consistent in theory?

How do they work out in practice?

The following Priority Area Needs Assessments (based on a form developed for the National Diffusion Network in *Forms and Formalities*) can be used to assess priority needs for materials as well as for programs.

PRIORITY AREA NEEDS ASSESSMENTS

From the following areas, please indicate the ten (10) which you feel will need the most assistance next year. Rank them one (1) through ten (10), with one being the most critical need for materials. Use the space on the reverse side of this form for questions or other information which will help us become aware of your needs.

All Levels	Elementary	Junior High	Senior High		All Levels	Elementary	Junior High	Senior High	
				Reading					Vocational education
				Math					Physical education
				Career education					Science
				Art-Culture					Cognition
				Learning disabilities					Student attitude–affect
				Handicapped					Decision-making clarification
				Pre-school (parent involvement)					Environmental ed.
				Early childhood					Guidance
				Bilingual-Ethnic education					Library/media materials
				Social studies					Learning Center materials
				Language arts					Individualized programs
				Other curriculum areas— please list					

This Classroom Materials Checklist form was adapted from a similar form in the *Source Book for Evaluation Techniques for Reading* by James Laffey and Carl B. Smith, published by the Measurement and Evaluation Center in Reading Education (MECRE) in Bloomington, IN. It can be adapted again to assess materials for most classes.

CLASSROOM MATERIALS CHECKLIST

1. Is there a well-managed and well-equipped central resource center?   yes ____ no ____

2. Are the classroom libraries frequently changed?   yes ____ no ____

3. Is there a wide variety of interesting reading materials in the subject areas: science? social studies? art? music? physical education?   yes ____ no ____

4. Do these materials relate well to your students' many interests and abilities?   yes ____ no ____

5. Are sufficient trade and paperback books available?   yes ____ no ____

6. Does the teacher have interesting and colorful illustrative ungraded materials to motivate and clarify subject matter understanding?   yes ____ no ____

7. Are games, newspapers and magazines accessible?   yes ____ no ____

8. Are records, filmstrips and other visual materials available?   yes ____ no ____

9. Does the teacher have charts or other means for recording the children's individual progress in cooperative stories, class plans, shared experiences, etc.?   yes ____ no ____

10. Are there enough textbooks?   yes ____ no ____

11. Are workbooks appropriate and well chosen?   yes ____ no ____

12. Are there tables, bookcases or display areas for interest or learning centers?   yes ____ no ____

Classroom surveys or needs assessments of materials can be carried on in various ways; two approaches are included below.

Approach 1
INSTRUCTIONAL MATERIALS CLASSROOM SURVEY

CLASSROOM SURVEY   1   2   3   4   5*

Materials are provided as needed for children in this classroom   _____

Materials are accessible and appropriate for all children   _____

Materials are accessible as needed for the teacher   _____

Materials are *used* by teachers and students   _____

---

*1=No provision. 2=Inadequate provision. 3=Adequate for most classrooms or children. 4=Adequate for all. 5=Superior.

(Form continues on page 51)

Approach 1 (cont'd)

MATERIALS CHECKLIST   1   2   3   4   5

PRINTED MATERIALS (OVERALL EVALUATION)
No. of volumes or books per child (   )
Total number of periodicals (   )
Total number of library books (   )

Media Availability
Models   _____
Globes   _____
Maps   _____
Posters   _____
Specimens   _____
Task cards   _____
Recordings   _____
Films and filmstrips   _____
Supplementary texts   _____
Games   _____
Simulations   _____
Charts   _____
Other _____   _____

RANGE AND VARIATION (OVERALL EVALUATION)
Range in difficulty   _____
Range in interests   _____
Subject range   _____
Choice available per child   _____

ACTIVITIES AND FACILITIES RELATED TO USE (OVERALL RATING)
Visual display   _____
Browsing or selection devices   _____
Flexible use   _____
Learning centers   _____
Records kept of use   _____
Organization for use   _____
Physical facilities   _____

Approach 2 is shown on page 52.

Approach 2
CHECKLIST FOR PHYSICAL FACILITIES
RELATING TO INSTRUCTIONAL MATERIALS

	Un-acceptable	Below standard	Fair	Good	Excellent
	1	2	3	4	5	6
1. adequate file space						
2. adequate, properly-scaled table/ desk space adapted for using all types of materials						
3. display facilities						
4. facilities for preparing instructional materials						
5. flexible table/desk arrangements (variety of shapes for various purposes)						
6. wheeled carts for transporting machines, kits, books, etc.						
7. book and magazine shelving, audiovisual display and storage facilities						
8. provisions for storing and hanging charts, maps, art prints						
9. locked and open storage space						
10. tutoring facilities						
11. conveniently-located electrical outlets in sufficient numbers						
12. convenient means of darkening room						
13. movable room dividers (possibly used also for storage, display, etc.)						
14. well-maintained audiovisual eqmt.						
15. comfortable, movable chairs						
16. accessible reference collection						
17. comfortable reading areas						
18. facilities for small group and conference use						
19. facilities for independent study						

KEY PUBLICATIONS

The publications listed here have forms and/or approaches that can be used or adapted for assessing and/or evaluating the adequacy of instructional materials.

Elementary School Evaluative Criteria: A Guide for School Improvement, by
National Study of School Evaluation. Arlington, VA, National Study of
School Evaluation, 1973. 152p. $6.00. (From National Study of School
Evaluation, 2201 Wilson Blvd., Arlington, VA 22201.)

A thoughtful, structured guide for self-examination and self-assessment of individual elementary schools using the schools' own aims and philosophies and educational commitments. This ten-section guide was developed after three years of field testing. One entire section is on media learning services. Other sections deal with school and community; philosophy, objectives and commitments; designs for learning; school staff and administration; individual faculty data; pupil services; and school plant and facilities.

All sections have questions, implicit or explicit, relating to the roles and extent of instructional materials. For instance, the section on Design for Learning asks:

- Explain the teacher's role in the selection of materials and media, and
- Explain how teachers are involved in determining budget priorities at the building level.

Section B on School and Community has an excellent, compact guide for analyzing the student body as individuals, groups and subgroups.

Evaluative Criteria for Junior High Schools. Washington, DC, National Study of
Secondary School Evaluation, 1963. 329p. price not available.

This guide is a similarly comprehensive guide which considers the kinds, roles and extent of materials for each subject area, with good charts for surveying students and summarizing data.

Forms and Formalities: A Resource Containing Forms Currently Utilized by
Members of the National Diffusion Network, edited by Glenn Clarkson and
Robert Wupinski. San Francisco, Far West Laboratory for Educational
Research and Development, 1978. unpaged. $8.50. Shrink-wrapped and
punched for three-hole notebook.

Originally edited by Clarkson and Wupinski for the Nebraska-Iowa State Facilitator, this resource contains samples of forms for needs assessment, adoption/adaptation agreements, applications, adoption monitoring, awareness evaluation, training workshop evaluation, site visitation evaluation, etc., plus some sample newsletters.

FOR FURTHER READING

The items included here are useful guides or overviews to surveying and assessing districts—adaptable in some ways to needs assessments for instructional materials. The references and bibliographies in the chapter on parents and community groups also can be used in this process. The chapters on individualization and teacher roles in selection also contain references and forms that can be used for assessing how well materials are adapted to students.

*Items marked with an asterisk have other forms or criteria.
+Items marked with a plus have further references.

*+Bradford, Eugene, et al. *Elementary School Evaluation: Administrator's Guide to Accountability.* West Nyack, NJ, Parker, 1972.

+Morgan, James M. *Conducting Local Needs Assessment: A Guide.* Princeton, NJ, ERIC Clearinghouse for Tests, Measurement and Evaluation, 1975. (TM Report 44).
Includes a concise presentation of needs assessment with a 21-item bibliography.

*+National School Public Relations Association. *How to Conduct Low Cost Surveys.* Arlington, VA, NSPRA, 1973.
Provides a rationale and practical guidelines for conducting accurate, economical surveys.

*+White, Bayla F. *Design for a School Rating or Classification System.* Washington, DC, Urban Institute, 1970.
Suggests simple but logical means for identifying and classifying schools, using largely available records, to determine the accomplishment of a school in relationship to schools with similar student populations.

MATERIALS SELECTION POLICIES

"Policy sits above conscience."
                        —William Shakespeare

■ ■ ■

This chapter provides some models and rationales for materials selection policies as well as references to more sources of information on existing and exemplary policies. It also includes a paper that synthesizes and abstracts selection criteria from many printed selection policies. These may prove useful to the relatively small proportion of school districts and state agencies (perhaps one-third) that do not have policies; they may also be useful for larger groups for policy-review purposes.

Particularly since World War II, administrative theorists and organizations for school administrators have encouraged the proliferation of written policies for all contingencies—to guide decisions, to assure consistency and (perhaps most importantly) to protect decision makers. But in practice, selection policies are often for the record (or file) only. One Wisconsin survey indicated that only about 37 percent of teachers are aware of their district's policies. In too many school districts, policies are difficult to locate or to understand; they are rarely reviewed and updated as needed, and are often overlooked or unusable in selection processes. Still other selection situations seem dominated by too many uncoordinated policies.

According to Educational Research Service's survey of 1,275 school districts in 33 local selection states and the District of Columbia, about 72.4 percent of the 414 responding school districts had some sort of written policies for selecting textbooks and/or instructional materials; about one-half (50.7 percent) had policies for supplementary materials. Of the districts that responded, about 61.1 percent included at least some selection criteria in their selection policies, while 36.5 percent had no written criteria.

In theory at least, selectors should be paying attention to assorted mandates that amount to an intricate puzzle of paper policies created by overlapping jurisdictions. In an amusing sketch of this complex process, "Selecting Instructional Materials" (*English Journal*, v.66, January 1977, pp. 9-14), James Sabol compared the process of selection to a play in five acts (with, presumably, a cast of thousands and a muddled plot). His advice for selectors—essentially a third act based on political considerations—was to locate and consult 1) state laws and regulations, 2) printed philosophies and goals from districts, school and state, 3) district policies and procedures, 4) local criteria and process lists and 5) conflict-of-interest codes, and to identify religious, cultural and ethnic considerations.

While any of these overlapping documents might be helpful, they do represent a lot of paperwork and tend to function as constraints and limitations rather than as positive guidance. Or they may be so full of pious generalities and educational jargon that they mean nothing. To be helpful at all, such considerations need to be coordinated and reviewed each year for current applicability. Ideally they should be correlated with current goals of other community institutions—such as libraries, museums and recreation departments—and the philosophy and objectives (or goals) incorporated into materials selection policies should involve clear, simple and distinct goals that express consensus and educational priorities. Finally, since state goals and national goals have quite important effects on funding sources and priorities, these goals need to be at least considered for incorporation into local objectives, for pragmatic reasons.

I hope the policies and rationales below will help to simplify, rather than complicate, the process of selection. The three outlines on the purpose, development and content of an ideal materials selection policy were based on those developed by the California Association of School Librarians in *Instructional Materials: Selection Policies and Procedures* in 1965.

PURPOSE OF A MATERIALS SELECTION POLICY

A materials selection policy should

- Provide a statement of philosophy and objectives for the guidance of those involved in the procedures for selection.
- Define the roles of those who share the responsibility for selection of instructional materials.
- Incorporate legal constraints and other educational realities.
- Set forth criteria for selection and evaluation of materials.
- Correlate selection policies with those of similar community institutions.
- Outline the techniques for the application of the criteria.
- Inform the total educational community on the philosophy and procedures used in evaluating and selecting instructional materials.
- Provide means for evaluating the efficacy of the policy.
- Provide procedures for incorporating suggestions for materials or considering objections relating to particular materials or classes of materials.

DEVELOPMENT OF A MATERIALS SELECTION POLICY

- A materials selection policy should be formulated with input from representatives of all affected groups. These should include:

the school community
{
the teaching staff
the curriculum staff
the library staff
the media staff
the administrative staff
}

the wider community
{
parents
students
other community representatives
libraries and other resource agencies
}

- The materials selection policy should incorporate or append (at logical places) relevant national, state or regional criteria or restraints.
- This selection policy should be reviewed for clarity, legality and enforceability by those groups who will have to work with it.
- The materials selection policy should officially be adopted by a governing board.
- The adopted policy should be communicated and available to all school personnel and to the community.
- The adopted policy should be reviewed frequently (yearly or biannually) and revised as needed.

CONTENT OF A MATERIALS SELECTION POLICY

A materials selection policy should include

- a statement of the agency's philosophy of materials selection
- definitions of materials covered
- an indication of the agency legally responsible for the selection of instructional materials, detailing the delegation of this responsibility to specified agencies and/or individuals
- time frames for selection
- reference to or inclusion of state laws and other relevant documents
- a statement of criteria to be used in the evaluation of materials, including all media, sponsored materials or materials offered as gifts
- a means of correlating selections with those of other agencies
- an outline of the procedures to be used in evaluating and selecting different types of materials, with time-lines and guidelines at each level
- budgetary guidelines for adequacy
- an outline of the procedures to be followed in considering objections to particular materials in the instructional program, with time-lines
- a plan for implementing the use of materials selected
- an outline of the means used to evaluate the utilization of materials and the success of this materials selection policy
- a means of reviewing, discarding and replacing materials that are under-utilized or ineffective

The selection policy of the San Jose Unified School District (reprinted with permission below) serves as a clear model for educational agencies involved in designing or improving their own guidelines or selection policies. San Jose's policy and supplementary forms and Dr. Jenny Armstrong's comprehensive guidelines illustrate effective and efficient application of selection criteria. Sixteen additional well-chosen policy-and-procedure statements (some complete, some excerpted) are included in Educational Research Services' *Procedures for Textbooks and Instructional Materials Selection* (1976).

Good school district selection policies, like the one below, include definitions, purpose and intent, references to state laws, responsibilities, time-lines and guidelines at each level. These policies are excerpted with the permission of the San Jose Unified School District, San Jose, California.

ADMINISTRATIVE POLICIES AND PROCEDURES

3661 Evaluation and Selection of Instructional Materials

A. **Purpose and Intent**

As stated in the Board Policy, the policies and procedures described herein are designed to provide instructional materials of the highest quality available to aid students in realizing the objectives of the district's educational programs.

It is the intent of these policies and procedures to establish the process for the evaluation and selection of instructional materials including textbooks utilizing district personnel and community members.

To be effective, the process must focus on the educational needs of students as identified by the professional staff. The process must also establish the responsibilities of the personnel involved and provide guidelines and direction for carrying out their tasks.

Increased emphasis is placed on the use of the district Learning Continuum and the Board-adopted goals as the basis for selection of instructional materials.

The evaluation and selection of instructional materials involves a large number of personnel whose professional training and experience qualify them for this task. Current State law concerning elementary (K-8) textbook selection requires substantial participation of teachers including those teachers specializing in library-media utilization. The law also encourages schools to involve community members in the selection process.

These policies and procedures provide protection for the rights of students and teachers to maintain access to instructional materials and for the rights of parents and community members to question or challenge materials used in district schools.

To provide a framework for these policies and procedures, the Board of Education of the San Jose Unified School District subscribes in principle to the philosophy for school libraries which has been clearly stated in the *School Library Bill of Rights for School Library-media Center Programs* of the American Association of School Librarians and the *Library Bill of Rights* of the American Library Association. (See Appendix I, II)

B. **Definitions**

1. *District Instructional Materials:*

a. For purposes of this policy, the term "District Instructional Materials" includes materials in two major categories:

(1). *LIBRARY BOOKS*: are books placed in a classroom or school library-media center for use by students and faculty on an individual basis. This term also applies to related written documents such as pamphlets, microfilms, microfiche and periodicals.

(2). *NON-BOOK MEDIA*: refers to instructional materials in other than written formats such as films, filmstrips, records, tapes, study prints, slides, manipulative materials, etc. which are placed in the classroom or school library-media center for use by faculty or by students on an individual basis.

B.   Definitions (cont'd)

       (3).   *STATE INSTRUCTIONAL MATERIALS*: State adopted textbooks and non-book media for grades K-8 purchased by the school to meet curricular needs.

       (4).   *TEXTBOOKS*: – See section on *Textbooks and Supplementary Books - High School* for definition.

C.   Delegation of Responsibility

The responsibility for selection of instructional materials rests with the Board of Education and by Board Policy number 3660 is delegated to the Superintendent and his staff to administer.

1.   *District Responsibility*

The Department of Instruction shall plan, develop, coordinate and administer procedures for the evaluation and selection of instructional materials purchased by individual schools and by the Instructional Materials Division.

2.   *School Responsibility*

    a. Each school shall be responsible for establishing a system for the evaluation and selection of instructional materials which is within the parameters of Board policy and these policies and procedures.

    b. The ultimate responsibility for any and all instructional materials purchased and/or used in the school rests with the school principal.

D.   Guidelines and Procedures

1.   *School Level*

    a. The responsibility for the evaluation of instructional materials often involves many people such as principals, teachers, supervisors, community members, students, and media specialists. The responsibility for coordinating the process of evaluation and selection of instructional materials should be delegated to professionally trained or experienced media personnel, where available.

        Approval of the principal is required prior to the ordering of instructional materials.

        Teachers should be involved in the evaluation process to the fullest extent possible and community members should have opportunity to make recommendations to qualified evaluators.

    b. The materials collection of the school should be acquired according to a plan which will provide breadth and depth of content and represent varied types of materials, points of view and forms of expression. It should provide for a broad range of media formats and meet the requirements of all curriculum areas, accommodating diverse skills and styles of learners at varying maturity and ability levels.

    c. An on-going replacement program for favorite and old books should be established.

    d. A system for acquiring materials for evaluation should be established and qualified evaluators located and trained. Criteria for the evaluation of instructional materials as recommended by the Department of Instruction should be vigorously applied to maintain high standards of quality. (See Appendix III)

(Outline continues on page 60)

D.   Guidelines and Procedures (cont'd)

  e.   Qualified evaluators are certificated district personnel who are familiar with both the subject area involved and with other available district materials which pertain to that subject. In-service training for evaluators shall be available upon request from the Instructional Materials Division.

  f.   The importance of both basic, permanent-value materials and timely, current-value materials on urgent public issues is recognized as essential to the educational process.

  g.   Qualification for selection

   (1).   To qualify for selection, all district instructional materials must have been either (1) recommended by the school library media specialist or library resource teacher; (2) favorably reviewed by at least one of the recognized reviewing agents such as those listed in Appendix IV; or (3) have received at least three favorable evaluations from qualified district evaluators. These evaluations shall be on the Media Evaluation Cards provided by the district and shall be on permanent file in the school. (See Appendix V)

   (2).   Since the value of both student and parent involvement in the evaluation process is recognized, district evaluators are encouraged to utilize these resources in the evaluation of instructional materials.

  h.   Free loan, rental, or gift materials shall be evaluated according to the same criteria and utilize the same evaluation records as materials to be purchased. No materials shall be used which fail to meet the established criteria.

 2.   *District Level*

  a.   Purpose of District Collection

   (1).   The circulating book collection contains books to support four established district programs.

    Supplementary Resource Books—Science, Social Studies, Language Arts, Health & Safety, Math, Career Ed, Guidance, Music, Art, Ethics, Resource books to enrich and reinforce the curriculum.

    Reading and Literature—Supplementary reading books to extend the resources available to teachers in both developmental reading and literature programs.

    Remedial readers—A collection of specialized reading materials of high interest and low reading level to be used for students in need of unique materials to overcome reading deficiencies.

    Literature books—Sets of carefully selected literature books to provide specialized materials to complement the developmental reading programs in district schools.

(Outline continues on page 61)

D.   **Guidelines and Procedures (cont'd)**

b. Evaluation and Selection Procedures

(1).   Each year, the Instructional Materials Division shall prepare a listing of preview priorities which shall guide the procurement of materials for evaluation and their eventual selection for inclusion in the district's central collection.

(a).   The annual priorities listing should reflect needs statements obtained from teachers, department heads, curriculum specialists and other appropriate sources.

(b).   Whenever appropriate, established curriculum groups should be involved in the development and review of the annual priorities listing.

(2).   The Instructional Materials Division shall obtain suitable materials for evaluation and shall send these materials to qualified evaluators together with report forms which are based on the established criteria of evaluation. Before any item may be qualified for selection it must have received three positive evaluations or must have been recommended by one of the recognized reviewing agents listed in Appendix IV for the level involved.

(3).   Evaluators should be selected from a list of volunteer teachers who are familiar with both the subject area involved and the central collection materials which pertain to the subject area.

(4).   Evaluation records shall be maintained by the Instructional Materials Division for all materials currently in the collection. Records of materials evaluated but not accepted shall be kept for a minimum of five years.

(5).   Based upon an analysis of the current collection, established priorities for preview and the projected availability of high quality materials, the Instructional Materials Division shall prepare an annual budget allocation plan, covering all curriculum areas, to be used as a guide in the acquisition of new materials for the current year. This plan shall be made available to curriculum supervisors in the Department of Instruction.

3662 State Adopted Instructional Materials Selection Procedures
Kindergarten through Grade 8

A.   Legal Background

1.   By enacting the George Miller Education Act of 1968, the Legislature recognized the need for districts to develop, within broad state guidelines, educational programs which fit the needs and interests of their pupils, pursuant to the district's stated philosophies, goals and objectives.

Division 8 of the California Education Code as amended during the 1972 legislative session recognizes that because of the common needs and interests of the citizens of this state and the nation, there is a need to establish broad minimum standards and general educational guidelines for the selection of instructional materials for the public schools, but that, because of economic, geographic,

(Outline continues on page 62)

A. **Legal Background (cont'd)**

> physical, political, educational, and social diversity specific choices about instructional materials need to be made at the local level.
>
> It was the intent of the Legislature in adopting these two acts, that district boards be given the authority and responsibility for ordering instructional materials which meet the needs of the pupils in their district and which relate to their adopted courses of study.

2. In accordance with the provisions of California Education Code, Division 8 as amended, 1972, the procedures outlined here are established for the acquisition of State adopted Instructional Materials.

B. **Administrative Policies**

1. The Department of Instruction shall be responsible for implementing procedures for the selection of state adopted instructional materials consistent with Board policy and the intent of the Education Code. These procedures shall include substantial teacher involvement and shall encourage participation of parents and other community members.

2. The San Jose Unified School District subscribes to the philosophy that the selection and use of instructional materials should be determined at the school level. The school principal shall bear the primary responsibility for the evaluation and selection of textbooks and related instructional materials for his school which meet the needs of the pupils and relate to district courses of study adopted pursuant to Division 7 of the Education Code.

3. The Board of Education authorizes the Superintendent to make final decisions concerning the instructional materials orders and to make decisions in respect to the use of district funds to supplement state funds for the purchase of instructional materials.

4. Pursuant to Division 8 of the Education Code, funds authorized by the legislature to the district as part of the annual credit and cash entitlement shall be allocated to each school having students in any grade K-8 on an equitable ADA basis for the purchase of instructional materials.

5. The Board of Education requires that State adopted instructional materials used in district schools comply with the legal and factual requirements established in Education Code, Division 8, Chapter 1, Article 3, Sections 9240 through 9243. State adoption shall constitute said compliance.

C. **Committees**

1. Instructional Materials Advisory Committee

    a. *Membership*—An advisory committee shall be established by the Department of Instruction composed of teachers from any of the K-8 grades, elementary and junior high school site administrators, Department of Instruction personnel and community members. The committee should not exceed 20 in number. Teacher-members shall be a majority of the total appointed committee membership and shall be secured pursuant to existing district policy.

    b. *Term of office*—Committee members shall serve for two years and the initial appointments shall be made so as to provide for staggered terms.

(Outline continues on page 63)

C.   Committees (cont'd)

c. The Director of Educational Services shall recommend members for service to the Associate Superintendent, Instruction who shall review the recommendations and make the necessary appointments.

d. The Director of Educational Services or other Department of Instruction Supervisors shall act as chairman of the Advisory Committee.

e. *Responsibilities*—The Instructional Materials Advisory Committee will have the following responsibilities:

(1). To develop and have approved by the Board of Education a master evaluation and selection calendar for the district.

(2). To develop specific guidelines, procedures and evaluative criteria for use by district level evaluation committees in subject area(s) coming up for local selection.

(3). To secure qualified evaluators to serve on the district evaluation committee(s) and to provide necessary in-service training for them.

(4). To recommend allocation of available released time for evaluation of materials.

(5). To receive evaluation data from district evaluation committees and to prepare final recommendations to the Associate Superintendent, Instruction.

The recommendations shall cover the form, format and contents of the recommended lists of materials and other factors as deemed necessary by the Advisory Committee.

2.   District-Level Evaluation Committees

a. *Membership*—An evaluation committee shall be established by the Advisory Committee for each subject area on the Master Calendar coming up for local selection. These committees shall be composed of qualified volunteer teachers, grades K-8, district administrators and Department of Instruction personnel. Size of the Evaluation Committees shall be determined by the Advisory Committee.

b. *Length of Service*—Membership on the Evaluation Committees shall conclude when final evaluation data is completed and submitted to the Advisory Committee.

c. *Responsibilities*—The district evaluation committees shall evaluate materials in one subject area which have been submitted for state adoption following the evaluative criteria, procedures and guidelines established by the Instructional Materials Advisory Committee.

d. *Released time*—To the extent of the resources available, released time shall be provided for district-level evaluation committee members for the direct evaluation of materials.

(Outline continues on page 64)

C. **Committees (cont'd)**

    3.   School Level Evaluation Committees

        a. *Membership*—The building principal shall establish an evaluation committee for each subject area coming up for selection on the Master Calendar as follows:

            (1).   There should be fairly even representation of primary and upper grade teachers at elementary schools and of 7-8 grade teachers at junior high schools.

            (2).   The library-media resource teacher, Library Media Specialist, or curriculum resource teacher should be a permanent member of the committees.

            (3).   Principals should try to secure interested community members whom they consider qualified to serve on the school level evaluation committee.

        b. *Responsibilities*

            (1).   The school level evaluation committees shall evaluate submitted materials recommended for selection by the district Advisory Committee and other materials which are needed to meet the needs of the students in that school.

            (2).   The school level evaluation committees shall present their recommendations to the school principal who will present them to the entire certificated staff for review, reaction and final recommendation.

            (3).   The principal shall utilize the staff recommendations in preparing the school order. The final decision governing quantities and priorities for ordering rests with the principal.

        c. *Released time*—To the extent of the resources available, released time shall be provided for school-level evaluators. District-level evaluators shall be considered first in determining released time allocations.

3663 High School Textbooks and Supplementary Books—Grades 9-12

A. **Definitions**

    1.   *Textbook*: A textbook is a volume intended for use by pupils and meeting in style, organization, and content, the basic requirements of the course for which it is intended.

    2.   *Supplementary book*: A supplementary book is one which covers part or all of the course affected, that is not intended for use as a textbook but is intended to supply information not found in the textbooks used for the course.

    3.   Reading lists contain books recommended by a department or teacher to direct students to additional optional sources of information concerning the subject.

B. **Responsibility**

    1.   Each high school shall be responsible for establishing a system for the evaluation and selection of textbooks and supplementary books which is within the

(Outline continues on page 65)

B.   **Responsibility (cont'd)**

parameters of Board policy, State Education Code requirements, and these policies and procedures.

2.   The ultimate responsibility for any and all textbooks or supplementary books purchased rests with the school principal.

C.   **Guidelines**

1.   Normally, it is expected that textbooks will be used for five years after adoption. Approval of the Associate Superintendent is required in unusual instances necessitating a shorter period of time.

2.   Supplementary books to be adopted will be presented to the Board of Education as a routine listing on the agenda of each regular meeting.

D.   **Procedures for the Adoption of Textbooks**

1.   The request for textbook adoption may originate with a teacher, a department or division head, and/or district curriculum committee.

2.   Two or more teachers, including those who would use the text, shall read and evaluate the textbook in light of its suitability in the course(s) for which it is being proposed.

3.   Along with a copy of the book, the individual or group proposing the textbook will submit to the department or division chairperson a completed book evaluation form. (See Appendix VI)

4.   The department or division chairperson will consult with the district supervisor to verify that the book is an appropriate text for the goals of the course(s).

5.   The completed form and a copy of the textbook will be submitted to the designated school administrator for his approval who will forward the form and copy to the principal.

6.   The principal will forward a copy of the evaluation form together with the text to the Associate Superintendent, Instruction, who will recommend adoption by the Board of Education.

7.   Upon adoption by the Board of Education, all titles will be added to the list of adopted textbooks.

8.   Though adopted for the grade levels of the majority of the students enrolled in the course, adopted *textbooks* may be used by any secondary school offering the course.

E.   **The Evaluation and Selection of Supplementary Books**

1.   The school principal shall be responsible for carrying out the procedures for evaluating supplementary books. The principal shall follow the pattern given below in adding new titles to his list:

a.   A Committee of teachers under the leadership of the department or division chairperson shall make the basic selection, using the evaluative criteria as listed on the evaluation form.

(Outline continues on page 66)

E.   **The Evaluation and Selection of Supplementary Books (cont'd)**

> b. After approval by the department or division chairperson involved, the recommendation shall be forwarded through the designated school administrator to the principal for approval in his school.
>
> c. The list of supplementary books selected for use in each school, together with completed evaluation forms and sample copies, shall be submitted by the principal to the Associate Superintendent, Instruction who will submit it to the Board of Education for approval.
>
> d. The Associate Superintendent, Instruction shall compile and make available to all principals a list of the approved titles of supplementary books from all secondary schools. Any secondary school may use books from the combined approved list on the grade level(s) for which they were approved.
>
> e. Once a list of approved supplementary books has been established, it shall be continued in effect until amended either through the addition or reduction of titles.

3664 Questioned or challenged materials

A.   Citizens may challenge the usage of books and other forms of instructional materials, using the following procedure:

> 1. The challenger shall register his criticism in writing on the CITIZEN'S REQUEST FOR RECONSIDERATION OF INSTRUCTIONAL MATERIALS. (See Appendix VII) The completed form shall be given to the principal of the school, who will arrange an interview to include himself, the challenger, and the teacher using the material. This group will attempt to resolve the issues. If the citizen's concerns are not resolved at the school level, the principal will write a brief summary of his conference, including the names of people involved and stating the unresolved issues. He will attach this report to the completed Citizen's Request for Reconsideration of Instructional Materials form and forward them through the Associate Superintendent, Instruction and to the Superintendent of Schools for further action. The challenged material shall remain available for use until district action is taken.
>
> 2. The Superintendent shall appoint a committee of certificated personnel of the school district; citizens interested in school matters, including one person without a vested interest in this challenge; and at least one acknowledged expert in the field represented by the materials in question.
>
> > a. The review of questioned material shall be treated objectively, unemotionally, and as an important routine action. Every effort shall be made to meet with the citizen(s) questioning the material and to consider the objections, keeping in mind the best interest of the students, the community, the school and the curriculum.
> >
> > b. The report of the committee shall be completed as rapidly as possible.
> >
> > c. The report of the committee, with its recommendations, shall be final. Administrators, librarians, and teachers shall abide by that action.
> >
> > d. A report of the final action shall be sent to the challenger.
> >
> > e. Formal challenges of instructional materials will be accepted a second time only if, in the opinion of the Superintendent, substantial new evidence is presented to him by the challenger.

3665 Obsolete Textbooks and Instructional Materials

A. Purpose

1.   The purpose of this section is to prescribe standards for the length of time instructional materials must be used in the district and when and under what conditions they shall be declared obsolete.

A further purpose is to provide guidelines and procedures for the sharing among district schools of surplus textbooks and the eventual disposition of both usable and unusable textbooks.

2.   Instructional materials in grades K-8 purchased with state funds shall be considered as the property of the district and not the individual schools for the purpose of sharing or disposition.

B. Elementary School (K-8) Materials

1.   *Basic use requirement*

a. Section 9465 of the Education Code stipulates that after any instructional materials, including any state-adopted textbook, have been placed in use by a district board, they shall be retained in use by the district for a period of not less than 2 years nor more than 6 years after the date of their first use.

b. Each elementary (K-8) school shall maintain records on standardized district forms of the initial use date and anticipated obsolescence date of instructional materials purchased using state funds.

2.   *Determination of Obsolescence*

a. After the minimum use period of two years and up to the 6 year maximum use period, schools shall determine whether instructional materials in their building are obsolete and either usable or unusable for educational purposes.

After the 6 year period, materials will automatically become obsolete and new materials shall be secured to meet the educational needs of the students in each curricular area.

(1).   Schools wishing to exempt materials in use from these requirements may obtain forms from the Department of Instruction for an appeal to the State Board of Education pursuant to Chapter 2, Article 4, Section 9465. (See Appendix VIII)

3.   *Sharing and Disposition Procedures*

a. The Department of Instruction shall request once each year a list from all schools of both the usable obsolete (including surplus) materials and the unusable obsolete materials they have available for sharing or disposition.

b. A consolidated list of usable materials will be prepared and distributed to all district schools and arrangements made for the transfer of materials among them. No charges or obligations will be made for shared materials.

(Outline continues on page 68)

B.   **Elementary School (K-8) Materials (cont'd)**

c. At the conclusion of the sharing process, schools will be urged to donate usable obsolete materials to the children and adults in their attendance area as provided by the law.

(1).   Donated texts must be rubber-stamped "Usable/Obsolete" in the inside back cover.

d. All remaining materials will be collected from the schools and disposed of as prescribed in Chapter 4, Article 2, Section 9820 or Article 3, Section 9840 of the Education Code.

C.   **High School Materials**

1.   *Basic use requirement*

a. Chapter 3, Article 1, Section 9603 of the Education Code requires that after any textbook has been adopted by the district board and placed in use in a high school, it shall be retained in use for a period of not less than 3 years after the date of its first adoption as shown by the official records of the district board.

2.   *Sharing of district textbooks*

a. High schools will participate in the sharing procedures outlined for other district schools.

3.   *Disposition of Textbooks*

a. At the conclusion of the sharing process, high schools may dispose of usable/obsolete textbooks by selling them to students as prescribed in Chapter 3, Article 2, Section 9623 or by selling them on the second-hand market pursuant to Article 3, Section 9640.

b. High schools will be urged to donate remaining usable/obsolete textbooks to students and other adults in their attendance area as provided in Article 2, Section 9820.

(1).   Donated texts must be rubber-stamped "Usable/Obsolete" in the inside back cover.

c. All remaining materials will be collected from the schools and disposed of as prescribed in Chapter 4, Article 2, Section 9820 or Article 3, Section 9840 of the Education Code.

D.   Organizations, agencies, or institutions desiring usable/obsolete instructional materials shall file a written request for notification of materials available with the Department of Instruction, Instructional Materials Division and will be notified at the appropriate time in the disposition process.

CRITERIA FOR EVALUATING INSTRUCTIONAL MATERIALS
(Appendix)

The following criteria are offered as guidelines for use by evaluators. All of the criteria will not apply to each item evaluated.

Does the material relate directly to the district-adopted Learning Continuum?

Is the material the best of its kind available to serve the intended purpose?

Is it authentic, accurate and up-to-date?

Will it stimulate and maintain the user's interest?

Will the user be stimulated to further study or discussion?

Is the content appropriate for the maturity level of students at the level involved?

Is it useful with individuals as well as groups?

Are the format, vocabulary, and concepts appropriate for the intended purpose?

Is it timely or pertinent to library, community or curriculum needs and problems?

Does it fulfill the responsibility of library collections as expressed in the *School Library Bill of Rights*?

Does it complement other printed or audio visual materials in the same subject areas?

Could the subject be better treated by other media?

Are visuals satisfactory and effective?

Is the narrator condescending in mannerisms or style?

Is the production imaginative and creative?

Is it of significant educational, social or artistic value?

Are accompanying guides or notes well written and helpful?

Is the packaging easily manipulated and durable?

Does it avoid both expressed and implied stereotyping of groups of people by sex or ethnicity?

The San Jose Unified School District integrates library association policies and library reviewing media into its instructional materials selection policy.

SCHOOL LIBRARY BILL OF RIGHTS FOR
SCHOOL LIBRARY-MEDIA CENTER PROGRAMS
(Appendix I)

Adopted by The American Association of School Librarians,

"The American Association of School Librarians reaffirms its belief in the Library Bill of Rights of the American Library Association. Media personnel are concerned with generating understanding of American freedoms through the development of informed and responsible citizens. To this end the American Association of School Librarians asserts that the responsibility of the School library media center is:

To provide a comprehensive collection of instructional materials selected in compliance with basic written selection principles, and to provide maximum accessibility to these materials.

To provide materials that will support the curriculum, taking into consideration the individual's needs, and the varied interests, abilities, socio-economic background, and maturity levels of the students served.

To provide materials for teachers and students that will encourage growth in knowledge, and that will develop literary, cultural and aesthetic appreciation, and ethical standards.

To provide materials which reflect the ideas and beliefs of religious, social, political, historical, and ethnic groups and their contribution to the American and

(Continued on page 70)

world heritage and culture, thereby enabling students to develop an intellectual integrity in forming judgments.

To provide a written statement, approved by the local Boards of Education, of the procedures for meeting the challenge of censorship of materials in school library media centers.

To provide qualified professional personnel to serve teachers and students."

LIBRARY BILL OF RIGHTS
(Appendix II)

The Council of the American Library Association reaffirms its belief in the following basic policies which should govern the services of all libraries.

I. As a responsibility of library service, books and other library materials should be chosen for values of interest, information and enlightenment of all people of the community. In no case should library materials be excluded because of the race or nationality or social, political or religious views of the authors.

II. Libraries should provide books and other materials presenting all points of view concerning the problems and issues of our times; no library materials should be prescribed or removed from libraries because of partisan or doctrinal disapproval.

III. Censorship should be challenged by libraries in the maintenance of their responsibility to provide public information and enlightenment.

IV. Libraries should cooperate with all persons and groups concerned with resisting abridgment of free expression and free access to ideas.

V. The rights of an individual to the use of a library should not be denied or abridged because of his age, race, religion, national origins or social or political views.

VI. As an institution of education for democratic living, the library should welcome the use of its meeting rooms for socially useful and cultural activities and discussion of current public questions. Such meeting places should be available on equal terms to all groups in the community regardless of the beliefs and affiliations of their members, provided that the meeting be open to the public.

(Adopted June 18, 1948; amended February 2, 1961, and June 27, 1967, by the ALA Council.)

SUGGESTED REVIEWING AGENTS AND/OR PUBLICATIONS
(Appendix IV)

Pursuant to the Administrative Policies and Procedures governing the evaluation and selection of instructional materials, at least one published favorable review of media materials by any of the recognized reviewing agents such as those listed below shall qualify said materials for purchase by district schools.

Reviewing Agents and/or Publications

RECOMMENDATION BY THE SCHOOL LIBRARY-MEDIA SPECIALIST OR LIBRARY MEDIA RESOURCE TEACHER

BASIC GENERAL LISTS:
ALA Catalog
A Basic Collection for Elementary Grades (ALA)

BASIC GENERAL LISTS (cont'd)
 A Basic Collection for Junior High Schools (ALA)
 A Basic Book Collection for High Schools (ALA)
 Best Books for Children (Bowker)
 Book List for Elementary School Libraries (Calif. Ass'n. of School Librarians)
 Gaver, Mary—Elementary School Library Collection, Phases 1-2-3 (Bro-Dart)
 Hoffman, Hester R.—Reader's Adviser and Bookman's Manual
 Wilson Standard Catalog Series:
  Children's Catalog
  Fiction Catalog
  Junior High School Library Catalog
  Senior High School Library Catalog

CURRENT GENERAL LISTS:
 Book Review Digest

SPECIAL BIBLIOGRAPHIES FOR REFERENCE BOOKS AND PARTICULAR
SUBJECT MATERIALS:
 AAAS Science Book Lists (American Ass'n. for the Advancement of Science)
 English Journal or Elementary English (Nat'l. Council of Teachers of English)
 Winchell, Constance—Guide to Reference Books
 District lists of recommended materials provided by district curriculum
  supervisor

REVIEWING JOURNALS:
 The Booklist (ALA)
 Horn Book
 Library Journal and School Library Journal (Bowker)
 LJ/SLJ Previews (Bowker)
 New York Review of Books
 New York Times Book Review
 Saturday Review

Evaluation cards such as this (reprinted with the permission of the San Jose Unified School District, San Jose, California) are easy to file and compare.

SAN JOSE UNIFIED SCHOOL DISTRICT MEDIA EVALUATION CARD
(Appendix V)

(Front)

```
Type_____ #_____  ·/s,_____Length_____

TITLE/AUTHOR_____  (_____)   Req._____
                                                                         P.O._____
                                                                         Bgt._____
SOURCE _____  (_____)   Terms:
C        /Aq.       Dewey #      r    SUBJECT CODES  P I J S A
Copies   Price                                       ___  ___
                                                        Units
EVALUATOR:  COMPLETE EVERY ITEM OF FOLLOWING IN ORDER FOR REPORT TO BE VALID
                    P        I        J        S        A    (circle range
Suitable for Grades  K  1  2  3    4  5  6    7  8  9   10 11 12  Adult  of grades)

LIST UNDER THESE SUBJECTS: _____
                                   (use terms from subject section of catalog)
Annotation [ ] OK      [ ] Change as indicated on back.

COMMENTS :_____
(note significant features, pro & con and compare with other materials available)


RATING (circle)          EVALUATOR SIGN HERE
1 2   3  4  5
Low ←→ High   S/_____
                                         Location        Date
```

SAN JOSE UNIFIED SCHOOL DISTRICT
INSTRUCTIONAL MATERIALS DIVISION

MEDIA EVALUATION CARD

(Back)

```
RATING        1.  Very poor or completely inappropriate
   AS
EDUCATIONAL   2.  Mediocre quality or not sufficiently useful
 MATERIAL     3.  Passable quality, or only moderately useful
   FOR
   THIS       4.  Good quality, useful
 DISTRICT     5.  Outstanding material, exceptionally useful

(See current instructional materials selection policy)
ANNOTATION




ADDITIONAL COMMENTS
(Student response, correlation with curriculm goals, technical quality)
```

These three special forms, reprinted with the permission of the San Jose Unified School District, are succinct, adequately documented, and adapted to their purposes.

EVALUATION OF A SECONDARY TEXTBOOK RECOMMENDED FOR ADOPTION
(Appendix VI)

Check one:
___Basic Text
___Supplementary

Date Submitted_____

Title_____Author_____

Publisher_____Copyright Date_____

Course(s) and Grade Level(s) for which Textbook is recommended_____

The textbook has been evaluated using the following criteria:

STRUCTURE	Excellent	Good	Fair	Not applicable
1. The organization is educationally suitable.				
2. The bibliography is adequate.				
3. Study aids are appropriate.				
CONTENT				
The materials:				
1. cover essentials in the course (s) of study.				
2. are accurate and in agreement with current research.				
3. deal with U.S. aims, ideals and institutions in an accurate, fair and interesting manner.				
4. depict the contributions of ethnic groups in a manner reflecting current scholarly research.				
5. cover issues fairly and objectively where differences of opinions may exist.				
6. are likely to stimulate further interest and study in the subject and in related fields.				
STYLE				
1. The vocabulary and concepts are appropriate.				
2. The format is attractive and readable.				

DESCRIPTIVE STATEMENT

On the back of this sheet, write the descriptive statement establishing the need for and the appropriateness of this text for the purpose of the course(s).

Read and
evaluated by:_____
                     Teacher

_____
                     Teacher

Recommended
         by:_____
                   Chairperson
         Dept./Division/Dist. Committee

Approved
by:_____
      District Learning Area Supervisor

_____
         Designated Vice-Principal

_____
                  Principal

_____
            Board of Education

(Appendix VII appears on page 74)

CITIZEN'S REQUEST FOR RECONSIDERATION
OF INSTRUCTIONAL MATERIALS
(Appendix VII)

Author_____ Type of materials_____

Title _____

Publisher or Source (if known)_____

Request Initiated By_____

Telephone_____Address_____

City_____Zip Code_____Date_____

Complainant Represents:

_____Himself

_____Name of Organization_____

_____Identify Other Group_____

1. Did you read or view the material completely? Yes____No____If not, what part?
   (Please be specific; if book, cite pages.)_____
   _____

2. To what in the material do you object? (Please be specific)
   _____
   _____
   _____

   In your opinion, what harm to students would result from using this material?__
   _____
   _____

4. In your opinion, for what age group would this material be satisfactory?_____
   _____

5. Is there anything worthwhile about this material?_____What?_____
   _____
   _____

6. In your opinion, what alternate material would convey a fair and objective picture and perspective of this topic?_____
   _____
   _____

7. Other remarks:_____
   _____
   _____
   _____

   If more space is needed, use the back of
   this form or attach additional sheets.

                                        _____
                                                    Signature

TO PURCHASE MATERIALS NOT ADOPTED BY THE
STATE BOARD OF EDUCATION
(Appendix VIII)

Education Code Section 9400 (c)

School District_____Date_____

Subject Area_____

Instructional materials to be purchased: (List author, title, and publisher or
                                          producer)

_____

_____

_____

Grade level (s)_____

Approximate number of copies needed_____

_____

Reason(s)

    1. In an attached statement, explain why the use of materials now in state
adoption would <u>not</u> promote the maximum efficiency of learning for pupils
in your district.

    2. In an attached statement, explain why the materials sought to be approved
will promote the maximum efficiency of learning for pupils in your district.

    3. Check one or more of the following, and in your statement explain in detail:

        ☐ Different type of program from any on list

        ☐ Designed for special group not covered by list

        ☐ Other

    4. If materials requested are characterized by paragraph 4 of the <u>Standards</u> <u>and</u>
<u>Procedures</u>, explain in detail the "overriding extenuating circumstance" you
consider applicable.

    5. Are these instructional materials already in use by district?

        ☐ Yes   ☐ No

Do you desire to address Board Committee?

        ☐ Yes   ☐ No

I hereby certify that the instructional materials specified above will be used as
basic materials, and that in the opinion of the governing board of this district,
these materials comply with the most recent criteria adopted by the State Board of
Education in this subject area.

Curriculum Frameworks and   _____
Instructional Materials   Superintendent
Selection Unit, October 1975

It is also desirable where possible to coordinate local criteria and the objectives announced at other selection levels. This desire has led San Jose to include relevant sections of the California Educational Code in its instructional materials selection policy—an idea which could be expanded to include relevant sections of federal codes as well. The state of Iowa—which does not have a state adoption policy—is working toward the same goal by publishing a model selection policy that contains numerous ethical, educational and legal judgments which the State Department of Public Instruction believes should be considered by local school officials who are developing their own policies and procedures.

Finally, to facilitate this kind of multi-level coordination, the 25 guidelines reprinted below were developed as part of Dr. Jenny R. Armstrong's paper "Minimum Guidelines Used in Consumer Information Analyses" presented at the 1976 annual meeting of the American Educational Research Association. These major guidelines were compiled through a comprehensive review, analysis and summary of existing sets of selection policies or guidelines in current use by federal projects, private agencies and State Departments of Education. They are organized into one comprehensive checklist designed to be used in actual review processes. Data from appropriate categories can be used to develop selection criteria and/or to make selection or adoption decisions.

GUIDELINES FOR THE EVALUATION OF INSTRUCTIONAL MATERIALS

Directions for Use. Each section of the checklist identifies a major instructional materials characteristic to be addressed as a part of the evaluation process. Specific guidelines for evaluation materials relative to these characteristics are provided in each section of the checklist.

These guidelines are value statements about materials. Consequently, you may not agree with all of them. For each guideline provided, decide whether or not you agree with it. If you agree with the stated guideline, put an "X" in the box provided next to the stated position. In this way, you will use only those sets of criteria which you feel are most important to you in evaluating a particular piece of material.

After choosing the guidelines, respond to each of the criterion and/or informational statements provided. Put a ✓ on the blank next to each criterion statement which accurately describes the material you are reviewing. Put NA next to each criterion statement which is NOT APPLICABLE to the particular material you are reviewing. Materials receiving the greatest number of positive checks divided by the total number of applicable criteria should be given the highest rank for selection and/or adoption.

MEDIA

☐ **Guideline 1.** Materials should include complete and accurate identifying information.

This material includes complete and accurate information on the following:

_____Title of Element: [_____] *

_____Title of Program/Series: [_____]

_____Author(s): [_____]

_____Publisher/Producer: [_____]

_____Publisher/Producer address: [_____

_____]

*Record the information given in brackets.

_____Vendor: [_____]

_____Vendor address: [_____

_____]

_____Copyright Date: [_____] _____Production/Publication Date: [_____]

_____Identifying Numbers: ISBN [_____], Catalog Number [_____]

Other Number; Specify: _____ [_____]

_____Media Formats Available; Specify all formats indicated:

[_____Book   _____Slides
_____Film, 8mm   _____Tape, reel to reel
_____Film, 16mm   _____Tape, cassette
_____Filmloop, 8mm   _____Tape, video
_____Filmstrip   _____Transparency
_____Game   _____Other; Specify _____]
_____Realia
_____Record

☐ **Guideline 2.** Materials should include complete and accurate summaries of the content, processes and skills taught.

This material includes complete and accurate information on the:

_____Major content/process areas covered; Specify the content/process areas indicated for coverage:

[_____Affective/Social Development
_____Perceptual-Motor Development
_____Learning Readiness/Conceptual Development
_____Mathematics
_____Science
_____Social Studies
_____Reading
_____Language Arts/English
_____Physical Education
_____Career Education/Vocational Training/Independent Living Skills
_____Fine Arts
_____Other; Specify _____]

_____Specific skills taught; Specify the indicated skills taught:

[_____ _____ _____
_____ _____ _____
_____ _____ _____
_____ _____ _____
_____ _____ _____]

☐ **Guideline 3.** Materials should include summary information on their input/process and response mode requirements.

This material includes information on the following use requirements:

_____Input/process mode requirements; Specify all that are indicated:

[_____Visual   _____Attending   _____Discriminating
_____Auditory   _____Listening   _____Classifying
_____Kinesthetic   _____Manipulating _____Associating
_____Tactual   _____Pressing   _____Identifying/Labeling
_____Olfactory   buttons   _____Abstracting/Generalizing
_____Gustatory   _____Other; Specify: _____Other; Specify:
_____ _____]

(Guideline 3 continues on page 78)

Guideline 3 (cont'd)

_____Response requirements; Specify all that are indicated:

    [_____Pointing, Nodding, Gesturing
    _____Manipulating, Moving Objects
    _____Checking, Marking
    _____Writing
    _____Speaking
    _____Signing
    _____Other; Specify: _____]

☐   **Guideline 4.** Materials should include accurate, summarized, descriptive information on their developmental, instructional, interest, reading, vocabulary and language levels, and the language used (i.e., bilingual-bicultural) and the general interest areas, topics or themes as incorporated in the material.

This material includes accurate, summarized, descriptive information on the following:

_____Instructional Level; Specify the indicated level or range by drawing a line on the scale:

Ages: 0 1 2 3 4 5 6 7 8 9 10 11 12 13 14 15 16 17 18   ADULT

_____Interest Level; Specify indicated level or range:

Ages: 0 1 2 3 4 5 6 7 8 9 10 11 12 13 14 15 16 17 18   ADULT

_____Reading Level; Specify the indicated level or range:

Ages: 0 1 2 3 4 5 6 7 8 9 10 11 12 13 14 15 16 17 18   ADULT

    Pre-Reading   1 2 3 4 5 6 7 8 9 10 11 12
    Readiness   GRADES

_____Language Level; Specify the indicated level or range:

Ages: 0 1 2 3 4 5 6 7 8 9 10 11 12 13 14 15 16 17 18   ADULT

    Pre-School   Primary   Inter-   Junior   High School
    Kindergarten   mediate   High

_____Vocabulary Level; Specify the indicated level or range:

Ages: 0 1 2 3 4 5 6 7 8 9 10 11 12 13 14 15 16 17 18   ADULT

    Pre-School   Primary   Inter-   Secondary
    Kinder-   mediate
    garten

_____Languages; Specify all languages indicated:
    [_____English
    _____Spanish
    _____Other; Specify _____]

Guideline 4 (cont'd)

_____Interest, topical or thematic areas; Specify all areas indicated:

[_____Animals   _____Foreign Affairs
_____Arts & Crafts   _____Hobbies
_____Art: Drawing, Paintings,   _____Industry
       Sculpture   _____Music
_____Aviation   _____Mythology
_____Business   _____Politics
_____Carpentry/Construction   _____Religions
_____Cars   _____Sewing/Design
_____Commerce   _____Sports/Games
_____Cooking   _____Theatre/Drama]

☐   **Guideline 5.** Materials should include clear and complete information on the costs and availability of all items needed to use the material.

This material provides clear and complete information on:

Cost of:	Which is:	For Date:	Availability of:	Immed.	1 Day	1-3 Day	1 Week	2-3 Wk.	1 Mo.	2-3 Mo.	1 Year	1-3 Year	Other	Which is:
_____[	] [	]	_____											Complete Materials Package
_____[	] [	]	_____											Consumables
_____[	] [	]	_____											Replacement Parts
_____[	] [	]	_____											Current Revisions
_____[	] [	]	_____											Projected Revisions
_____[	] [	]	_____											Needed Equipment
_____[	] [	]	_____											Equipment Service
_____[	] [	]	_____											Needed Training

☐   **Guideline 6.** Materials should be designed for ease of use and storage, durability and safety.

A. For this material, all of the parts are:

_____Inventoried and described
_____Easily identified
_____Durable
_____Replaceable
_____Packaged to prevent loss
_____Packaged for ease of location

B. This material and its packaging are:

_____Durable   _____Complete: Contains all of the
_____Easily stored   items needed for use
_____Easily transported   _____Attractive/Appealing
_____Safe

(Guideline 7 appears on page 80)

☐ **Guideline 7.** Information should be provided with the materials on the rationale, purpose, objectives, philosophy, and points of view expressed in the materials and the author's relevant training and expertise should also be described.

For this material, clear and complete statements are provided on the following:

    _____Rationale
    _____Purpose
    _____Objectives
    _____Philosophy
    _____Points of view
    _____Author's relevant training & experience

☐ **Guideline 8.** Materials should provide for a substantial range of individual differences.

This material provides:

    _____Activities, experiences and presentations for children with a wide range of individual learning styles
    _____Different points of entry to the program depending on the child's current skill level
    _____Different options for program use
    _____Activities and experiences which provide for a variety of different presentations–auditory, visual, kinesthetic, tactual, haptic, multi-sensory; and modes for responding–pointing, gesturing, typing, responding through an adaptive device, signing, speaking, and writing
    _____Activities and experiences for a variety of types of social interaction and group participation
    _____Finely detailed and comprehensive skills sequence with a non-graded, non-categorical approach to instruction
    _____A wide range of skills development including the most basic functional skills and the most complex and intricate of skills
    _____A variety of strategies and/or supplementary activities and experiences for: increasing motivation, reteaching difficult concepts, and restructuring the learning environment to accommodate a wider range of individual differences
    _____A variety of optional student learning activities
    _____All levels of instruction: pre-readiness, readiness, and developmental
    _____For the development of social and personal skills for a wide variety of learning styles
    _____Content of interest to students of varied ages, ethnic backgrounds

☐ **Guideline 9.** Materials should provide for learning enhancement and enrichment.

This material:

    _____Provides suggestions for reinforcing learning: questions, simulations, exercises, independent and optional studies and projects.
    _____Provides suggestions for study which promotes an understanding of the material presented.
    _____Has suggested exercises and activities to help the student synthesize, review, and summarize the content.
    _____Provides an introduction, preface, or overview of the content to be presented.
    _____Provides effective summaries, reviews, and bibliographies.
    _____Has graphic aids which are well planned and properly placed to assist in the development of the concepts and the application of ideas
    _____Provides supplementary instructional materials, suggestions for additional activities, recreational and vocational reading, student and class projects.

Guideline 9 (cont'd)

_____Provides opportunities for vocabulary development in the specific subject-matter area.

_____Provides a variety of approaches for meaningfully reinforcing learned concepts.

_____Provides such related and supportive instructional items as: transparencies, tapes, records, ditto masters, worksheets, filmstrips, posters and solution keys.

_____Has options for a multi-media approach for the presentation of concepts.

☐ **Guideline 10.** Materials should provide for the development and enhancement of creative and independent thinking.

This material provides:

_____Activities and experiences which promote exploration, problem-solving and/or discovery

_____For the stimulation of discussion, process, and interaction

_____Activities which provoke thinking, discussing, and discovering insights into occurrences and periods of time

_____Suggestions for study which promotes and stimulates original thinking

_____A presentation of subject-matter which encourages students to think out solutions rather than to memorize specific facts

☐ **Guideline 11.** Materials should include all appropriate reference sources.

This material has the appropriate:

_____Glossaries, indices, tables of contents, appendices

_____Charts, maps, diagrams, graphs

_____Audio-visual resources, illustrations

_____Tests and test keys, problem sets and problem keys

☐ **Guideline 12.** Materials should include provisions for assessment and evaluation.

This material provides:

_____Procedures and/or suggestions for the assessment and evaluation of student progress by the teacher and/or the student

_____Procedures and/or suggestions for the assessment and evaluation of program entry and exit skills

_____Suggestions for teachers and students on how to provide systematic corrective feedback

☐ **Guideline 13.** Materials should provide for the development of independent living skills, vocational and career education.

A. This material provides for the development of:

_____Self-awareness and a positive self-concept

_____Self-care, home and family living skills

_____Community living and general coping skills

_____Occupational and vocational skills

(Guideline 13 continues on page 82)

Guideline 13 (cont'd)

B. This material:

_____Provides up-to-date, realistic, and representative illustrations of real-life careers and occupations

_____Provides reinforcement of the concept of career education in all areas and at all grade levels and as a desirable approach to preparation for living a self-fulfilling life

☐ **Guideline 14.** Materials should meet certain standards of technical quality.

This material has:

_____Clear, legible, visible, visual presentations

_____Clear, discriminable, sound presentations

_____Clear, discriminable, tactile presentations

_____Good sound/visual synchronization

_____Good sound/visual figure-ground contrast

☐ **Guideline 15.** Materials should have up-to-date, accurate, and authoritative content and/or subject-matter.

This material has content and/or subject-matter which is:

_____Accurate

_____Factual

_____Authoritative

_____Realistic, representative of real-life situations

_____Valid

_____Representative of current research, scholarship, and accepted modern practices

☐ **Guideline 16.** Materials should have a comprehensive selection of content which should be logically sequenced and meaningfully organized.

This material has content which is:

_____Meaningfully organized

_____Comprehensive

_____Logically and/or empirically sequenced

_____Representative of the discipline from which it was selected

☐ **Guideline 17.** Materials should treat with fairness and balance human diversity with respect to: sex, race, handicapping conditions, ethnic heritage, age, socio-economic status, attitudes, interests, values, philosophies, religions, political preferences and social customs.

A. This material shows the value of individual differences and examines their development. This material:

_____Explains that all groups have contributed to the growth and development of the United States

_____Presents diversity of race, custom, culture, belief, and sex as a positive influence on our nation's heritage

_____Identifies environmental and historical influences which develop group differences

_____Acknowledges the value of a variety of life-styles

_____Considers people—whatever their ethnic, religious or social class identity, as human beings displaying similar emotions—negative and positive

Guideline 17 (cont'd)

_____Treats customs of different groups with dignity and respect
_____Provides personalized learning experiences
_____Demonstrates consideration for the human worth and dignity of all people
_____Shows positive commitment to equal rights and responsibilities for all citizens
_____Provides opportunities for development of self-expression, self-reliance, initiative and independence
_____Provides experiences for the development of aesthetic and cultural awareness

B. This material shows the diversity of value positions and/or philosophies. This material:

_____Presents a variety of value positions and philosophies
_____Presents and identifies various points of view

C. This material discourages stereotypic views and biases toward diverse human attributes, conditions, attitudes, and/or behaviors. This material:

_____Emphasizes the fact that every group has its achievers, thinkers, writers, artists, scientists, builders, and moral leaders
_____Avoids belittling anyone
_____Shows concerted lack of racial and sexual stereotyping
_____Presents language, situations and cultures in a manner which will not foster stereotyping
_____Avoids references in the form of labels or retorts which tend to demean, stereotype, or be patronizing toward females, males, members of minority groups or handicapped individuals
_____Associates specific emotions—fear, anger, aggression, excitement, or tenderness, equally and randomly among characters regardless of sex, race, national origin, handicapping condition
_____Avoids the depiction of differences in customs or life-styles as undesirable
_____Presents mental activity, creativity, and problem-solving roles, success and failure in these roles, and participation in these roles in fair proportion between whites and minorities, males and females, and handicapped and non-handicapped
_____Depicts whites and minorities in the same range of socio-economic settings
_____Doesn't limit the depiction of diverse ethnic and cultural groups to the root culture but also includes them in the depiction of the mainstream of American life
_____Avoids indicating bias by the use of words which may result in negative value judgments about groups of people
_____Avoids using "man" as the subject of generalized statements that apply to women as well
_____Avoids describing the same behavior differently depending on the sex or other group identification of the persons involved
_____Avoids assigning stereotyped roles
_____Avoids interpreting the statement or act of an individual as representative of the entire group to which he or she belongs
_____Shows unbiased concern for religious, political and intellectual freedom

D. This material represents with fairness and balance the participation of, and the contributions of the many diverse groups in our society. This material:

_____Gives comprehensive, accurate and balanced representation to minority groups, handicapped, and women in all fields of life and culture

(Guideline 17 continues on page 84)

Guideline 17 (cont'd)

_____Provides recognition of minority groups, handicapped, and women, by showing them frequently in positions of leadership

_____Avoids omitting reference to participation by women, handicapped, or minorities in historical events, or to the importance of these events and individuals' participation in the course of history

_____Describes life in urban environments as well as in rural or suburban environments

_____Refers to problems and conditions of all levels and classes of society

_____Shows objective reflection of the multi-ethnic character and cultural diversity of our society

_____Presents accurate accounts of the contributions of various ethnic groups and accurate portrayals of the role of women

_____Accurately portrays the multi-cultural and multi-ethnic diversity of present day society

_____Presents traditional activities engaged in by characters of one sex balanced by the presentation of nontraditional activities for characters of that sex

_____Represents men and women equally in professional or executive roles, or vocations, trades, or other gainful occupations

_____Shows and discusses an equally wide range of aspirations and choices of life-styles for girls as for boys

_____Presents the contributions of women, minorities, and the handicapped to achievement in art, science, or any other field of endeavor

_____Interprets any imbalance or inequality in representation or contribution of minorities, women, or handicapped through the course of history in terms of contemporary standards and circumstances

_____Contains references to, or illustrations of, a fair proportion of diverse ethnic groups, handicapped individuals, and women

E. This material clarifies social values, deals with social action and its consequences, and discusses the undesirable consequences of social bigotry. This material:

_____Identifies and opposes manifestations of racism, sexism, and prejudice toward members of religious and ethnic groups, and those individuals manifesting particular physical, mental or social handicaps

_____Discusses the undesirable consequences of withholding rights, freedom or respect from any individual or group

_____Clarifies social values that reflect unfairly upon persons because of their race, color, creed, national origin, ancestry, sex, occupation, mental, social or physical differences

_____Deals with controversial issues and problems

_____Gives candid treatment, without attempting to rationalize, distort, or ignore unresolved intercultural problems in the United States, including those which involve prejudice and possible discrimination

_____Discusses how controversy and disagreement over public policy are at the heart of the decision-making process

_____Provides opportunities for the student to examine causes and consequences of civil disobedience and of violence on the part of both representatives of authority and those who disagree with them

_____Provides a factual account of the struggles by women, handicapped, and minorities to obtain equal political, educational, legal and human rights and employment

_____Demonstrates consistently the relevancy between knowledge and issues presented and the life-style of the individual

_____Discusses the significance of social reform for all people

_____Illustrates instances of integrated and cooperative groupings and settings to indicate equal status and nonsegregated social relationships as they operate in many places in society

Guideline 17 (cont'd)

F. This material shows an appreciation of and a tolerance for various customs, religious celebrations and rituals, and specific holidays. This material:

_____Shows an appreciation for holidays, festivals, and religious observances of various groups

_____Presents religious content objectively and forthrightly as an integral part of the study of literature, history, and science

_____Avoids holding up to ridicule or portraying as inferior any religious belief or practice

_____Portrays the religious diversity of contemporary American society

_____Presents explanations or descriptions of a religion or practice in a manner which neither encourages nor discourages belief in the matter, nor indoctrinates the student in any particular religious belief, nor otherwise instructs students in religious principles

_____Represents any religious belief presented accurately

G. This material uses and references the work of minorities and women. This material:

_____Utilizes the work of minority and female scholars

_____Provides bibliographies of printed and multi-media materials, including works of minority and female writers and producers

☐ **Guideline 18.** Materials should expose and discredit myths. This material:

_____Exposes and discredits myths which have misrepresented minority groups and women or have served to explain inaccurately aspects of social development in the United States

_____Portrays historical "heroes" on the basis of historical accuracy and/or openly admitted value judgments, rather than on the basis of myths or subtle value judgments

_____Corrects historical interpretations of the past which did not explicitly and thoroughly discuss the extent to which the growth and development of the United States was inconsistent with the values considered by many to be basic to the American political system

_____Presents content which is consistent with the findings of recent and authoritative research concerning minority groups and women in our culture

☐ **Guideline 19.** Materials should encourage the development of an understanding of human and environmental ecology. This material:

_____Includes reports on studies of the environment

_____Accurately presents man's place in ecological systems

_____Portrays the responsibilities of human beings toward a healthy, sanitary environment

_____Encourages a wise use of resources both human and physical

_____Portrays the interdependence of people and their environment

_____Identifies the adverse effects of solutions to environmental problems

_____Suggests appropriate means of protecting the environment

_____Depicts the hazards of the use of tobacco, alcohol, narcotics, and restricted dangerous drugs

_____Avoids glamorizing or encouraging by illustration or discussion the use of tobacco, alcohol, narcotics, or restricted dangerous drugs

(Guideline 20 appears on page 86)

MEDIA X ENVIRONMENT

☐ **Guideline 20.** Materials being selected and/or adopted for use within a particular educational environment should be evaluated relative to the conditions of that environment. This material:

    _____Fulfills a need not currently met by the materials now available for use with the learner

    _____Is reasonable in cost considering the available instructional materials budget

    _____Fits the parameters of the existing physical and/or instructional arrangements

    _____Has a reasonable time requirement for the completion of each lesson considering the amount of time which is available in the daily schedule for instruction in this particular area

    _____Is appropriate for the location of the classroom (e.g., regular self-contained, resource room, institutional setting)

    _____Is relevant to the learner's daily living environment

    _____Is relevant to and compatible with the life space of the community

MEDIA X CURRICULUM

☐ **Guideline 21.** Materials being selected and/or adopted for use within a particular curriculum should have goals and objectives which are defined by that curriculum which are compatible with other allied curricula.

This material has goals and objectives which are:

    _____Included in the curriculum

    _____Addressed by more than one section of the curriculum

    _____Compatible with the curricula of other groups of learners, agencies, and/or instructional levels

    _____Consistent with curriculum goals in general within this content or subject-matter area

    _____Flexible and adaptable to interdisciplinary curriculum programs

☐ **Guideline 22.** Materials being selected and/or adopted for use within a particular curriculum should have the same rationale and philosophical point of reference as that of the curriculum.

This material is compatible with the curriculum with respect to:

    _____Philosophy

    _____Rationale

    _____General value positions represented

    _____Points of view represented

☐ **Guideline 23.** Materials being selected and/or adopted for use within a particular curriculum should have the same scope and sequence as that of the curriculum.

This material provides instruction in the same:

    _____Major content/process areas that are defined in the curriculum

    _____Skills which are included in the curriculum

    _____Sequence as that specified in the curriculum

MEDIA X LEARNER

☐ **Guideline 24.** Materials to be selected and/or adopted for use with particular learners should be evaluated relative to the specific educational requirements and needs of those learners.

This material has:

_____Sensory-motor requirements which are compatible with the learners' needs and preferences

_____Instruction in content/processes/skills which the learners need to learn

_____Instructional levels which are compatible with the functional and/or developmental levels of the learners relative to:

_____Language level

_____Vocabulary level

_____Reading level

_____Conceptual level

_____Knowledge/skill level

_____Interest level

_____Perceptual-motor development level

_____Affective/social development level

_____Instructions and/or directions which are compatible with these learners' level of functioning or development in reading, understanding and carrying out these instructions

_____Response contingencies and feedback systems which are compatible with these learners' requirements for externally managed behavioral control .

_____An appropriate number of instructional steps in the sequence to accommodate the learning needs of these learners

_____An appropriate number of individual lessons on each concept, skill or idea developed to accommodate the learning needs of these learners

_____An appropriate time allotment for exposure to each concept, skill or idea developed to accommodate the learning needs of these learners

_____Enough tasks, activities and experiences for each concept, skill or idea taught to allow for over-learning to take place for these learners

_____Tasks, activities and experiences which begin at a simple enough level to accommodate the entry of these learners into the program

_____Tasks, activities, settings, and experiences which are appropriate to both the functional and interest level of the learners

_____Time allotments which are generous enough to allow these learners to attain mastery of the specified objectives

_____Subject-matter which is meaningfully related to these learners' needs, experiences, interests, and social maturity

_____A format which appeals to these learners and is compatible with their needs and/or preferences in terms of learning style

_____A format which utilizes games, humor, variety of stimuli, suspense, and immediate and corrective feedback to an extent appropriate to the needs and preferences of these learners

_____Vocabulary, sentence and paragraph structure which is appropriate to the needs of these learners

_____A philosophy which reflects a respect for the intellectual, physical, aesthetic-cultural, social and emotional development of these learners

_____Problem-solving experiences which are appropriate to the developmental level of these learners

(Guideline 25 appears on page 88)

MEDIA X TEACHER

☐ **Guideline 25.** Materials to be selected and/or adopted for use by particular teachers should be compatible with the needs, preferences, skills and priorities of these teachers for instructional materials, and consequently, should be evaluated relative to these teachers' characteristics.

This material has:

_____Instructions and directions for the teacher which are compatible with the needs for these instructions and directions by these teachers
_____Implementation requirements which are compatible with these teachers' skills
_____A teacher's edition or manual which is compatible with the needs of these teachers with respect to:

_____the balance between serving as a point of departure for the instruction or providing all of the details for total instructional planning and implementation
_____giving useful introductions to various sections and explanations of arrangements of the material for instruction
_____giving an overview of the material, and providing adequate numbers of suggestions for motivation, follow-up, and extension
_____giving listings of related materials which are integral to the program and which give help and data on the use of the materials
_____providing diagnostic and evaluative strategies to show entry level of students, with prescriptive and reteaching activities to follow such assessment and evaluative strategies for determining mastery
_____the manner in which it is to be used, the ease with which it is used and read
_____the extent to which it provides alternative teaching strategies, ideas for motivation, ideas for follow-up, extension and enrichment, and daily teacher helps
_____its completeness, organization, and format

_____A format which is compatible with these teachers' preference for media format
_____An imbedded teaching style which is compatible with the teachers' preferred styles of interaction (e.g., directive, non-directive, fixed, flexible)
_____Use skill, training and experience requirements which are compatible with those of these teachers
_____Training time and cost requirements which are reasonable and acceptable to these teachers
_____Preparation time requirements which are reasonable and acceptable to these teachers

---

KEY PUBLICATIONS

Procedures for Textbook and Instructional Materials Selection, conducted and reported by Linda H. Kunder. Arlington, VA, Educational Research Service, Inc., 1976. 129p. $10.00pa.

Surveys instructional materials review and selection policies in 33 local adoption states and the District of Columbia, considers the function of the textbooks selection committee and provides samples of state and local instructional materials selection policies and procedures from one state and 16 local agencies. Includes, as well, a substantial bibliography.

FOR FURTHER READING

*Items marked with an asterisk include criteria.
+Items marked with a plus include further references.

American Association of School Administrators, Association for Supervision and Curriculum Development, National Association of Elementary School Principals, and National Association of Secondary School Principals. *Censorship: The Challenge to Freedom in the School: A Joint Publication.* Washington, DC, AASA, ASCD, NAESP, and NASSP, 1975.

California Association of School Librarians. *Instructional Materials: Selection Policies and Procedures.* Daly City, CA, CASL, 1965.

Iowa. Department of Public Instruction. *Selection of Instructional Materials: A Model Policy and Rules.* Des Moines, 1975; reprinted 1977.

Knezevich, Stephen J. *Administration of Public Education.* 3rd ed. New York, Harper & Row, 1975.

*+National Association of Secondary School Principals. *Sharper Tools for Better Learning.* Reston, VA, NASSP, 1973.

Sabol, James W. "Selecting Instructional Materials," *English Journal*, v.66, no.1 (Jan. 1977), pp. 9-14.

Woodworth, Mary L. *Intellectual Freedom, the Young Adult, and Schools: A Wisconsin Perspective.* Communications Program, University of Wisconsin Extension, 1976.

PART III
SELECTION CRITERIA

USING EVALUATION CRITERIA IN
SELECTING INSTRUCTIONAL MATERIALS

This chapter provides reprints, articles, discussion, key works and background readings for some evaluation instruments that have been developed by educational researchers and instructional designers. Generally these approaches were used first for evaluating programs and projects and then extended to materials.

Though I am critical of unthinking misapplications of such instruments to the process of materials selection, they do represent at the very least an attempt to bring rigor and logic into the selection process. Other evaluation materials appear in the discussion of LVR (see page 118) and in a companion volume to this work, *Selecting Materials for Instruction: Media and the Curriculum* (henceforth to be cited as *Media and Curriculum*), which includes other examples such as the Joint Dissemination Review Panel. But while these evaluation approaches are structured and logical, they do entail a certain rigidity as well as a tendency to confuse evaluation with selection—a confusion that can result in poor evaluation and poor selection.

In essence, evaluation—on whatever premises—is a judgment of available materials based on certain specified or implicit criteria. For reviewers, the criterion is generally quality. For instructional researchers and curriculum designers, the basic criteria tend to be adherence to certain constructs of curriculum design and an attempt to measure (rather than intuit or describe) effectiveness, efficiency or accountability. Evaluation models—which seem to stem from applying the precepts of systems management, management by objectives or other managerial approaches to curriculum design—tend to examine materials rigorously on the basis of certain pre-specified criteria in an attempt to predict their effectiveness in all school situations.

Instruments developed by groups like Educational Products Information Exchange Institute (EPIE), the Social Science Education Consortium, and the Far West Laboratory all tend to include an appraisal of objectives, some thought to the organization of materials (often an emphasis on scope and sequence), methods of instruction, means of evaluation (test materials and items related to instructional objectives) and, most importantly, some empirical evidence of evaluation. More recently, the instruments have been broadened in scope to include and subsume other criteria and to provide some means for assessing whether or not materials are appropriate for particular districts or teaching areas.

Instruments used for evaluations range from one page outlines to 127-page categorical analyses with space for typed comments. The longer analyses tend to result in disproportionately long, unwieldy reports which often do not succeed well in conveying unique qualities of particular materials. Despite—or because of—their thoroughness, they may be an unnecessary interface for selectors—obscuring rather than clarifying the materials they attempt to evaluate. A briefer, more cogent descriptive analysis can often be more helpful for selection.

Since selection is a multidimensional process involved with choice, values and need, I strongly suspect that no evaluation instrument—no matter how complex— will ever succeed in bringing together all necessary information in time to be used in selecting instructional materials for particular school situations or audiences. In

many cases—depending upon scarcity, time, quantity, needs and apparent quality—
evaluation may be neither necessary nor possible.

Nonetheless, I have reprinted some laudable attempts by Dr. Susan Klein
and Dr. Jenny Armstrong to arrive at universal minimum consumer standards for
educational products—standards which Louise Tyler advocated in 1971 as analogous
to those adopted for tests. The Evaluation Standards Project is currently developing
such standards.

Whether or not universal evaluation or standards are possible, evaluation is a
time-consuming, cumbersome task. It is probably best performed by producers
and publishers using their own criteria and standards—based on their own
philosophies—to determine whether their own products are meeting their own goals.
Even here, it can be an overly expensive process for small publishers and producers.
If mandated as recommended by LVR, it could cut out some promising materials.

Despite limitations, long, structured evaluations are probably appropriate for
expensive, long-lasting materials that are being considered for funding or for purchase for large numbers of teaching applications. When such evaluations are consulted, individuals engaged in selection should be aware of their potential hazards
and limitations. Some standard difficulties in achieving the "complete" evaluation
for materials are:

- Reports are hard to find and/or hard to use.

- Competing materials may not be evaluated.

- Because of the time required for evaluation, products and packages can become
  obsolete, in part or in whole, before all the information is in.

- For local selection, national data may be misleading or less relevant than educators' understanding of student requirements.

- Criteria used may not be congruent with materials.

- Criteria used may reflect current educational fads or be adapted to please educational funding agencies.

- Actual qualities of materials may be inconsistent with their stated objectives
  or imposed criteria.

- There may be no consensus on criteria.

- Criteria may not be clearly stated.

As educational evaluators and developers get involved in evaluation, they sometimes tend to focus on the quality and reliability of evidence supporting educational products. While this has its value in encouraging better research and evidence,
it does not necessarily result in better selection, since the products with the best
research designs are not necessarily the best products for particular purposes. Conversely, useful materials may lack convincing evidence or may have been evaluated
on inappropriate criteria

The problem of measurability haunts evaluation. Since evaluation usually is
based on measurement, objectives—appropriate or not—may be reorganized to be
readily measurable, whether or not these are meaningful.

As a consequence, evaluation may:

- focus on short-range behavior
- include irrelevant measures
- exclude relevant measures
- overlook potential applications
- use instruments with built-in results
- evaluate research designs rather than materials
- distort objectives to become measurable
- judge programs on arbitrary, imposed goals
- use some (unduly complex) format for all types of materials

Less rigorous evaluations have other defects, which include inappropriate control groups and inconsistent reporting. And for almost all evaluations, there is a built-in "Hawthorne" effect in that the personal testimony of participating teachers almost always yields positive evaluations of the projects involved. If both teachers and students appreciate the extra attention and interest, student scores may be higher. If they feel pushed by the extra tests, their scores may be lower.

In light of these difficulties, if and when comprehensive evaluations are used, whether at national, state or local levels, printed reports on these evaluations— ideally rewritten or recompiled into simple, usable formats—should be fed into data banks and should accompany materials on their journeys to subsequent selectors.

GENERAL EVALUATION CRITERIA

The evaluation models and the key publications introduced in this chapter were chosen because they represent trends in the thinking of evaluators and are, individually and collectively, comprehensive, structured and thorough models for examining instructional materials. To the thoughtful selector, they offer an array of criteria from which to choose or adapt for particular selection situations. They can often be sharpened as selection tools by using extra columns to incorporate C. Lynn Jenks' "Categories for Assessing Compatibility" (reprinted in the chapter titled "Selecting Basic Learning Materials").

The questions listed below were adapted from Louise Tyler's *Recommendations for Curriculum and Instructional Materials* (Los Angeles, Tyl Press, 1971) by the Far West Laboratory for Educational Research and Development as a sort of checklist for evaluators. This instructional design approach considers instructional materials almost solely as part of a total curriculum package, firmly committed to a set of instructional objectives, expressed in terms of measurable behavioral changes and educational outcomes.

- For what audience or type(s) of students are the materials intended? Can you determine the characteristics of those students who participated in the developmental process? Do they match well with your intended users?
- Are the objectives clearly stated? What rationale guided their selection? Is content clearly relevant to these objectives?

- Are the learning activities congruent with the behavior either implicit or explicitly stated in the objectives?

- What evaluation plans and instruments come with the materials? Do they match well with the objectives and the activities? Do they seem appropriate for your students? Were these evaluation materials prepared and used from the beginning?

- What evidence(s) are reported that support any claims for effectiveness and/or efficiency?

- Does the evidence reported relate in an understandable way to the objectives? Also, are unintended outcomes reported and discussed?

- Is evaluative data given for all the different kinds of students for whom the material is recommended?

- Are the specific teacher skills needed in using the materials described? Is there a manual for teachers offering suggestions for implementing the activities?

- Are the administrative and logistical requirements specified? Are these compatible with your teaching style and situation?

These criteria require field tryouts, extensive follow-up information, and systematic evaluation somewhere in development. They may be more appropriate for developers than for selectors.

The model for evaluating instructional materials reprinted below—by permission of the ERIC Clearinghouse—is a variant of the system developed by Maurice J. Eash and used by EPIE. The information on pages 95 to 97 was reproduced from ERIC/TM Report 45: *Evaluation of Instructional Materials* by Maurice J. Eash, Harriet Talmage and Herbert J. Walberg, published by the ERIC Clearinghouse on Tests, Measurement, and Evaluation under contract with the National Institute of Education. The Clearinghouse is located at Educational Testing Service, Princeton, New Jersey.

Constructs of Curriculum Design

I. OBJECTIVES
   A. What is the nature of the general goals of the material stated?
   B. Are specific objectives stated for teacher use?
   C. If neither of the above are stated, list what you believe are the intended objectives of the material.
   D. What are the main emphases in the objectives?
   E. On the scale below, rate the objectives of the materials. Please circle an exact point.

Objectives not useful to a　　1　2　3　4　5　6　　*Objectives give clear direction*
teacher.　　　　　　　　　　　　　　　　　　　　　*for instruction and are useful for a*
　　　　　　　　　　　　　　　　　　　　　　　　　　teacher.

II. ORGANIZATION OF MATERIALS (SCOPE AND SEQUENCE)
   A. What is the scope of content covered in the materials?
   B. How is the scope of the materials organized?
   C. Is there a specified sequence in the material?
   D. What is the basis for the suggested sequence?

(Item II continues on page 96)

II. ORGANIZATION OF MATERIALS (cont'd)

    E.   On the scale below, rate the scope and sequence of the material. Please circle an exact point.

Scope inadequate, sequence 1 2 3 4 5 6   *Scope adequate for grade or*
not logical or incomplete.   *group, sequence tasks carefully*
                                                     interrelated and planned.

III. METHODS OF INSTRUCTION

    A.   What method or methods of instruction are suggested?
    B.   What role is emphasized in the method: teacher, pupil, or both?
    C.   What are the specific features of the method or methods recommended?
    D.   Is the suggested method one that requires the teacher to do extensive prior preparation or participate in specific training?
    E.   On the scale below, rate the methods of instruction. Please circle an exact point.

No methods suggested or   1 2 3 4 5 6   *Very carefully developed*
implied that are helpful to a   *methods. Very useful to both*
teacher.   *teacher and pupil.*

IV. EVALUATION

    A.   What test materials are included for the student's and teacher's use?
    B.   Are the test items adequate for informing a teacher of students' progress toward the instructional objectives set for the materials?
    C.   What do the tests measure?
    D.   Is there information on the tests' reliability and validity?
    E.   Is there any information from the producer on how the materials were tested with students when they were being developed?
    F.   On the scale below, rate the evaluation components of these materials and the evaluation of the materials by the producer as they were developed. Please circle an exact point.

No test materials or sug-   1 2 3 4 5 6   *A wide range of test materials*
gested checks on student   *and evaluation suggestions.*
learning included. No data   *Evaluation data on field test con-*
on the evaluation of mate-   *ducted and materials included.*
rials by the producer.

V. TOTAL RATING OF THE MATERIAL

    A.   Draw up a brief statement on how these materials compare with those currently being used in your curriculum.
    B.   On the scale below, rate overall potential effectiveness of these materials. Please circle an exact point.

Materials contain many weak- 1 2 3 4 5 6   *Very strong in all areas of design.*
nesses in instructional design.   *Strong potential to develop a*
Difficult to use, expensive,   *wide variety of learnings. Of high*
inferior for learning.   *interest to teachers and pupils.*
                                              Very cost effective.

VI. CONSTRUCT RATING PROFILE

    A.   After completing the instrument, fill out the following profile for the evaluated material:

VI.   CONSTRUCT RATING PROFILE (cont'd)

RATING

6

5

4

3

2

1

CONSTRUCT   I   II   III   IV   V

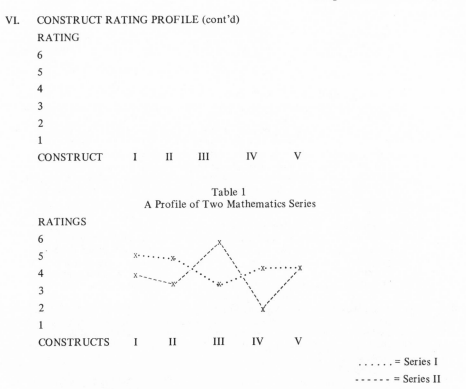

Table 1
A Profile of Two Mathematics Series

RATINGS

6

5

4

3

2

1

CONSTRUCTS   I   II   III   IV   V

. . . . . . = Series I

- - - - - - = Series II

In adapting Each's model into the materials-analysis instrument they call *EPIEform A* the Educational Products Information Exchange Institute has replaced Each's first four categories (objectives, organization, methods of instruction and evaluation) with their own. EPIE's summary of the gist of *EPIEform A* is reprinted below with permission from *EPIEgram*, V.5, No. 6, December 15, 1976.

EPIE'S CONSTRUCTS OF CURRICULUM DESIGN

Can we capsulate *EPIEform A* into an easy-to-use checklist for adoption committees? No. If we knew how to do this, we would not spend two-and-one-half days in training people in the use of this system of analysis. Well, is there any help EPIE can offer? We think so. First, we do offer materials-analysis training sessions, under contract, to up to 30 people per session. Second, we can point out right now a few considerations worth keeping in mind when you examine instructional materials.

*   *intents:* Expressions of the intents—the expected results of any course of action—are the developer's underlying rationale and the learner goals and objectives of instructional materials. Examine the materials to see if the developer has stated them clearly enough so that you, your students, and any interested member of the school community can readily understand them. Only then can you judge whether the intents are a good fit with your own and your school's goals and objectives.

(Summary continues on page 98)

* *contents:* The contents of instructional materials is usually thought of as the range of subject matter or skills covered in the pursuit of goals and objectives. When you examine materials, try to determine if the scope and the sequence seem to reflect and seem likely to realize the intents.

* *methodology:* The many kinds of methodologies all inevitably involve the kinds of teaching and learning activities or "transactions" that are carried on by teachers and learners in order to pursue their goals and objectives through selected contents. When you consider methodology as you examine materials, consider whether or not you, as a teacher, will be comfortable with the prescribed methodologies and whether your students can be reached with the teaching approaches you will be expected to use. Also, and most important, consider whether your students will actually *learn* from the materials rather than simply *cover* the curriculum; so often adoption committees spend much of their time determining whether the materials will cover the curriculum that they seldom attend to the issue of whether the teacher will have time to teach what the materials do cover.

* *means of evaluation:* Evaluation of student performance can take place at a number of points in the instructional process, and through the use of different kinds of standards, and by learners alone as well as by teachers and learners. Check the materials you examine to see if tests and other means of evaluation do indeed reflect what students are supposed to be learning or if they misleadingly reflect what the developers merely claim in their statement of intents.

If you keep in mind these four considerations, you'll be doing a lot. Also, you will be dealing with what we call the four constructs that constitute the instructional design of materials. But don't stop. Consider congruence. Does each construct have internal integrity and do the four constructs together have integrity or congruence? Do they fit? Or as your young students might say, "Does it all hang together?"

There are other considerations that may be critical to you: cost; whether the producer provides inservice workshops, if they are necessary; accuracy of contents; whether the materials are covertly racist; or sexist; how parents might react, if at all, to their children's using these materials; and the like. And two final considerations should be critical variables for everyone. First find out if the materials were developed with the aid of direct feedback from learners or if they have been revised (and, consequently, improved) on the basis of such feedback. Second, if you find materials that seem to fit, try to find time to ask a few of your students to work through portions of the materials. You can learn a lot this way about how "right" the materials are for you.

The Submission Form of the Joint Dissemination Review Panel (reprinted from its *Ideabook*, annotated on page 114) requires rigorous information on costs and effectiveness. These requirements were developed jointly by the U.S. Office of Education and the National Institute of Education for federally-funded projects, but could be used to check the effectiveness and costs in other products.

FORMAT FOR SUBMITTING MATERIALS TO THE JOINT DISSEMINATION REVIEW PANEL

PROGRAM AREA: (e.g., Title III, reading, career education, environmental education, education for the handicapped)

I. INTERVENTION TITLE, LOCATION:
    Specify the title of the intervention and the location for which evidence of effectiveness is being submitted.

II. DEVELOPED BY:
Indicate who developed the intervention originally, even if this happened at a different site than the one for which evidence of effectiveness is being presented.

III. SOURCE AND LEVEL OF FUNDING:
List all funding sources for the intervention at the location for which evidence of effectiveness is presented and, for each source, list the amount of funds (see Figure 1 for an example).

Figure 1
An illustration of a table shell for showing costs

Source and Level of Funding of Intervention		
	INSTALLATION (Non-recurring Costs)	SUBSEQUENT YEARS (Recurring Costs)
Personnel		
Personnel Training		
Facilities		
Equipment & Materials		
Consumables		
Other Costs*–Specify:		
_____		
_____		
_____		
TOTAL		
*E.g., transportation, technical assistance, public relations, etc.		

IV. YEARS OF INTERVENTION DEVELOPMENT:
Indicate the year or years during which the intervention was originally developed or tested.

V. BRIEF DESCRIPTION OF INTERVENTION:
Briefly describe the intervention for which claims of effectiveness are being made. The description should cover at least the following points:

What is the intervention?
What are its objectives?
What claims of effectiveness are being made?
What is the context in which it operates?
Who are the intended users and beneficiaries?
What are the characteristics of the groups on which the intervention was developed and tested?
What are the salient features of the intervention?
What are the costs for adoption and maintenance of the intervention?

VI. EVIDENCE OF EFFECTIVENESS:
Describe the evidence of effectiveness for the intervention. This section should deal with each of the following points, although not necessarily in the same order:

(Outline continues on page 100)

VI.   EVIDENCE OF EFFECTIVENESS (cont'd)

Interpretability of measures: Evidence that the quantitative measures are reliable and valid indicators of the effects claimed.

Credibility of evidence: Who collected and analyzed the data, what assurances are there that the findings are objective?

Evidence of impact: What is the evidence that something happened? What are the effects claimed for the intervention?

Evidence of statistical reliability of the effects: What is the evidence that the effects happened often enough and with sufficient reliability to be likely to happen again under similar circumstances?

Evidence that the effects are educationally meaningful: What is the evidence that the effects are large enough, powerful enough, or important enough to be educationally meaningful, regardless of their statistical significance?

Evidence that the effects are attributable to the intervention: Can alternative explanations such as practice effects, maturation, selection of superior treatment groups, etc., be ruled out?

Evidence of generalizability to the populations for which the product or practice is intended: Evidence that the product or practice has been tested widely enough and under sufficiently diverse circumstances to give assurance that the effects claimed may be similar when the product or practice is used elsewhere for the populations intended.

The following brief but comprehensive evaluation instrument for instructional materials was developed by Wayne R. Fetter, currently Assistant Professor of Education at Ashland College, Ohio. It is copyrighted as of 1978 and reprinted here from pages 55-56 of the October 1978 issue of *Educational Technology*, vol. 18, no. 10, by the kind permission of the author and the publisher. Beyond its function in evaluating instructional materials, it is designed to evaluate the appropriateness of particular materials for particular learning environments. Categories X and XI, evaluation and product revision, call attention to the importance of evaluation and product revision and to the responsibility of producers to supply such information on their products.

EVALUATION OF INSTRUCTIONAL MATERIALS

  I. Product Title or Name: ....
      ....
      Publisher: ....
      Publishing Date: .... Unit Cost: ....

 II. Type of Product: (Check appropriate description)
      A. Textbook ....   D. Topic Booklet ....
      B. Model ....   E. Graph or Chart ....
      C. Filmstrip ....   F. Programmed Materials ....
      G. Other (describe) ....

III. Target Population: (List the appropriate grade and ability levels)
      A. Grade Level: B. Ability Level:
         ....

 IV. Resources Needed: (Indicate cost per unit)
      A. What is the estimated annual replacement cost? ....
      B. What is the estimated annual maintenance cost? ....
      C. If additional support materials need to be purchased, what is needed and what is the estimated unit cost?

  V. Appropriateness:
      A.   Are the stated objectives of the course being met by this product?   Yes ..... No .....
      B.   Are there important long-range goals being met?   Yes ..... No .....
      C.   Can materials be used with other than the stated population?   Yes ..... No .....
      D.   Can materials be used to accomplish other than the stated goals?   Yes ..... No .....

E.	Is the product adaptable to various teachers or situations?	Yes ..... No .....
F.	May individual differences be met by use of the product?	Yes ..... No .....
G.	Are alternative learning opportunities suggested/provided for?	Yes ..... No .....
H.	Are there alternative methods, procedures, etc., for teaching various topics provided for use with the product?	Yes ..... No .....
I.	Does product usage require special training of teachers?	Yes ..... No .....
J.	Is there a definite need for this particular product in teaching the course?	Yes ..... No .....

VI. Content:
- A. Is the content of this instructional material sufficient in quantity to adequately cover the course as provided in the syllabus? — Yes ..... No .....
- B. Is the content of this instructional material sufficient in quality to adequately cover the course as provided in the syllabus? — Yes ..... No .....

VII. Remedial/Enrichment Content:
- A. Does the instructional material provide adequate quantity and quality of additional content to provide for remedial instruction? — Yes ..... No .....
- B. Does the instructional material provide adequate quantity and quality of additional content to provide for enrichment exercises for individuals? — Yes ..... No .....

VIII. Organization: How well does the sequencing of materials in this product match the sequencing of topics in the course syllabus? — Excellent .... Good .... Fair .... Poor ....

IX. Technical or Teacher's Manual:
- A. Is a manual included with the product? — Yes ..... No .....
- B. Does the manual indicate the necessary qualifications of teachers for using the product effectively? — Yes ..... No .....
- C. Does the manual describe the necessary support system needed for effective use of the product? — Yes ..... No .....
- D. Does the manual list field data on the product's effectiveness as an instructional aid? — Yes ..... No .....
- E. Does the manual list field data on typical users of the product? — Yes ..... No .....
- F. Does the manual suggest a typical setting or time frame for product usage? — Yes ..... No .....

X. Evaluation: (of learners)
- A. Are instruments for the evaluation of learners included with the product? — Yes ..... No .....
- B. If *YES*, do the instruments meet the course objectives and the stated objectives of the materials? — Yes ..... No .....
- C. If *NO*, can evaluation instruments be easily developed which will accomplish the evaluation of the learner meeting the course objectives through use of the product? — Yes ..... No .....

XI. Product Revision: Is there evidence that the product has been regularly revised and updated? — Yes ..... No .....

XII. Narrative Comments: Use this space to make any comments concerning any question on the evaluation form. Please refer to *both* the Section number *and* Question letter when making comments.

In "A Pragmatic Note on Program Selection or Will It Work in Your District?" from vol. 7, no. 2 of *Interchange: A Journal of Educational Studies* (published quarterly by the Ontario Institute for Studies in Education) C. Lynn Jenks approaches the complex process of evaluating proposed curriculum innovations. He concludes that adoption decisions must be made on the basis of 1) whether the objectives of a proposed innovation are consistent with those of the adopting school or district, 2) whether the innovation will be acceptable to its intended users and 3) whether those users possess the necessary capabilities to perform as they are expected. In the example reproduced on page 102, Jenks illustrates that by defining the proposed materials from a series of perspectives (content organization, teacher role, student role, etc.) and then determining whether the characteristics each perspective emphasizes would present problems (rated, in effect, on a scale of severity from 0 to 4), evaluators can generate quantitative data on the innovation's feasibility. This item is reproduced with the permission of the author and the publisher and is not to be reproduced without permission.

Current Issues Social Studies Program

A. *Content Scope.* The program is based on an interdisciplinary approach and does not provide for specific instruction in geography, history, economics, etc.

1. Would the involved teachers support an interdisciplinary approach to social studies?[1]

___ Virtually the entire staff would be supportive.

___ One-half or more would be supportive.

_x_ Only a few staff members would presently be supportive.

___ Virtually no support presently exists.

B. *Content Organization.* The program does not have a predetermined sequence of learning steps. Rather, students select topics for study and, together with the teacher, plan projects.

1. What is the attitude of staff toward programs of instruction in which the content of learning is not presequenced?

___ This would be acceptable to everyone.

_x_ Some would object, but this probably would not prevent adoption.

___ There would be fairly serious problems with many teachers.

___ Such programs would definitely not be adopted.

C. *Teacher Role.* With this program, teachers function as coordinators and facilitators. Their role therefore includes group work, planning with and advising individual students, and frequent encounters with community people.

1. Would there be any resistance among involved staff to work in this way?

___ No.

_x_ Yes, some resistance.

___ Many would resist.

___ No one would be agreeable.

2. Is there a sufficient number of staff members who have experience and are capable of performing this kind of role?

___ Yes, most teachers are able to do so.

_x_ Very likely, but some minimal training may be needed.

___ Doubtful; an intensive in-service program would be required for some.

___ No; massive retraining would be necessary.

D. *Student Role.* The student is the primary planner and performer. The student is expected to select topics of interest and design a project indicating learning activities, desired resources, and evidence of project completion.

1. Would staff be willing to permit students to assume this kind of role in the classroom?

___ Yes, most staff would like to give students a stronger voice in instructional decision-making.

_x_ Many staff would be willing.

___ Most would resist.

___ No one would permit such a thing.

2. Would parents be supportive of such a student role?

___ Yes, most parents would be agreeable.

_x_ Yes, some parents would be agreeable.

___ There would be serious problems with most parents.

___ No.

3. Could students work in this manner?

___ Practically all students could.

___ Many students could.

_x_ Perhaps a few students in upper grades could.

___ Most students would not function very well.

E. *Teaching/Learning Method.* A variety of methods are used, including discussion/seminars, discovery/inquiry, research/synthesis.

1. Do involved staff have the motivation to work in this way?

___ Definitely.

_x_ There are a few who could be identified.

___ Not sure, most have fairly stylized classroom techniques of presentation, discussion, and application.

___ Definitely not.

2. Do involved staff have such capabilities?

___ Absolutely.

___ There are sufficient numbers of capable staff to make it work.

_x_ Quite a bit of in-service training would be needed.

___ No; teachers who would be involved have not worked this way.

F. *Student Grouping.* The program is non-graded in terms of content and is also multi-graded in terms of student grade classification. Small groups, when they are formed, are usually heterogeneous and interest-based. Thus a teacher has responsibility for a group composed of both 11th and 12th graders.

1. Are non-graded as well as multi-graded programs acceptable to teachers?

___ There is heavy involvement with such grouping and it would present no problem.

_x_ There is some of this and could probably be more.

___ Organization for this on a small scale might be possible, given enough lead time.

___ Not at present.

G. *Materials.* A teacher manual is available that provides general guidelines for teachers, sample projects, and suggested learning topics. Teachers and students are expected to locate learning resources (books, articles, people) for use with projects.

1. Would there be any objection to adopting an instructional program that provides only a framework, guidelines, examples, and suggested procedures and leaves content selection, sequence, and design of learning activities to the student and teacher?

___ Not at all.

_x_ Maybe some.

___ Quite a few would object.

___ There would be overwhelming objections.

2. Does the staff have the capabilities to work with students in selecting and sequencing content and identifying useful learning resources?

___ Yes.

___ For the most part.

_x_ Not very many do.

___ No.

H. *Physical Setting.* In addition to some time in a classroom, students are expected to spend up to 30% of their time on their own with learning resources outside the classroom, including work with community

people, in libraries, museums, courts, etc.
1. Would this new student freedom be acceptable to staff?
____ Yes.
____ It would bother a few, but not seriously.
_x_ It would present real problems for several.
____ No.

I. *Student Evaluation.* Evaluation is criterion-referenced and often subjective. Since projects vary widely, evaluation is individualized and includes the student in assessing progress. Standardized tests are not recommended.

1. Would this type of evaluation be acceptable to staff?
____ Yes.
_x_ Most would be willing to try this approach.
____ Most would object and would be concerned about objectivity.
____ Reliance is on standardized tests and teacher-made tests for the assessment of student work.

J. *Staff Reorganization.* The program recommends that social studies teachers form planning teams and work together as much as possible.
1. Would the involved staff be willing to work together as a team?
____ Yes.
____ Most would.
_x_ Many could not work this way.
____ There would probably be a rebellion.
2. Do staff members have the necessary skills (leadership, interaction, etc.) to work in teaching teams?
____ Yes, staff are experienced with this.
_x_ Some teachers could, if carefully selected.
____ Most could not without some kind of training.
____ Massive retraining would be required.

Dr. Susan Klein of the NIE is also concerned with the variety of perspectives that should be considered in evaluating instructional materials. The criteria clusters reproduced below were developed by Dr. Klein to simplify this complex process by arranging 22 desiderata into six broad categories.

SUSAN KLEIN'S CRITERIA CLUSTERS

Desirability	Practicality	Intrinsic Quality	Product Development	User Effects	Spinoffs
Need (1)	Adaptability (1)	Sex, race, ethnic age, socio-economic fairness or balance (1)	Learner verification and revision (1)	Cognitive skills, performance, attitude, motivation, learning rate, attendance, impact on others (1)	Model for other work (1)
Appropriate for intended users (2)	Ease of use (2)	Content accuracy and currency (2)	Quality design (2)	Credibility of evidence supporting claimed effects (2)	Contributes to knowledge (2)
Adherence to social, moral and instructional values (3)	Reasonable fiscal and psychic costs (3)	Uniqueness (3)	Expert staff (3)	(3)	(3)
Demand (4)	Availability and acceptability to users (4)	Instructional quality, clear purpose, rationale (4)	(4)	(4)	(4)
(5)	Ability to receive any needed training to use product (5)	Technical quality of physical features of materials (5)	(5)	(5)	(5)
(6)	(6)	Appeal to learners (6)	(6)	(6)	(6)

This *Standard Criteria for the Selection and Evaluation of Instructional Material*, issued by the National Center on Educational Media and Materials for the Handicapped in 1976, is the result of a ten-year project sponsored by the Bureau of Education for the Handicapped from 1966 to 1976 at Ohio State University and elsewhere. These national criteria, originally intended to evaluate instructional materials for groups of handicapped learners, can often be used or adapted for other groups of learners.

This instrument, a microcosm of the selection process, involves needs assessment, screening, review, student requirements, teacher requirements, materials characteristics, and a means of matching materials to learners.

SELECTION AND EVALUATION CRITERIA OF NCEMMH

National Level

I. IDENTIFICATION OF NEEDS

The outcome of stage I will be: identification of the availability and adequacy of sources of need information prior to any selection of suitable instructional materials.

A. Sources

___ 1. The National Needs Assessment sponsored by the Bureau of Education for the Handicapped

___ 2. Consumers who are currently working with handicapped children

___ 3. Analysis of curriculums and instructional priorities at Learner Level

___ 4. Analysis of learner characteristics

___ 5. Availability of appropriate materials for curricular areas

___ 6. Availability of effective materials for learners

II. INITIAL SELECTION

The outcome of stage II will be: the identification of at least ten pieces of instructional material which, on first screening, appear compatible with learner requirements and which will be considered for further review. Identification of alternate materials for examination will facilitate final selection decisions on a comparative basis.

A. Search

(The items listed below encourage the user to investigate various potential materials information sources and to consider essential points when gathering information about materials.)

Yes No   NA

___ ___ ___ 1. Have you identified resources for materials which have potential use with the handicapped?

___ ___ ___ 2. Have materials been identified which may be appropriate for the learner characteristics of the handicapped?

___ ___ ___ 3. Have materials been identified which may be appropriate for the curricular needs of the handicapped?

B. Screen

(Under optimal conditions, a written product abstract or review will provide information pertaining to all of the items listed below, so that actual inspection of the product is not necessary. In the absence of thorough and accurate material descriptions, however, scrutiny of the material itself will be required.)

Yes No NA

___ ___ ___ 1. Is it a learner-use material?

___ ___ ___ 2. Is it an instructor-use material?

___ ___ ___ 3. Are all components of the material available?

___ ___ ___ 4. Does the material have potential for use with the handicapped?

___ ___ ___ 5. Is the material designed for use by the handicapped?

___ ___ ___ 6. Does the material appear to be practical to use with the handicapped?

___ ___ ___ 7. Does the material appear to be easily usable by the handicapped?

___ ___ ___ 8. Is the format of the material appropriate for the target handicapped audience?

___ ___ ___ 9. Is the material of acceptable technical quality?

___ ___ ___ 10. Does the material have instructional objectives?

___ ___ ___ 11. Does the material appear to meet the curricular needs of the handicapped target population?

___ ___ ___ 12. How does the cost of the material affect the accessibility to the material?

___ ___ ___ 13. Does the material appear to present any physical danger to the target handicapped audience?

III. REVIEW

The outcome of stage III will be: an in-depth analysis of an instructional material in order to match (section D) the material for use with a specific student based on section A, Learner Characteristics, section B, Teacher Requirements, and section C, Materials Characteristics. Implementation of this stage necessitates actual examination of the instructional material.

(Criteria continue on page 106)

A. Learner Characteristics

(The following outline is intended to serve as a guideline to the selector of instructional materials in identifying the characteristics and
educational requirements of the specific learner for whom material is
being sought.)

1. What are the possible modes of input?

    _____ auditory

    _____ visual

    _____ tactile

    _____ kinesthetic

2. What are the preferred modes of input?

    _____ auditory

    _____ visual

    _____ tactile

    _____ kinesthetic

    _____ multisensory

3. What are the possible modes of response?

    _____ verbal

    _____ written

    _____ gesture

4. _____ What is the learner's instructional level?

5. _____ What is the learner's interest level?

6. _____ What is the learner's reading level?

7. _____ What is the learner's interest areas?

8. What are the learner's interest/motivation requirements?

    a. _____ use of a game-type format

    b. _____ use of humor

    c. _____ use of a variety of stimuli

    d. _____ use of suspense

    e. _____ use of novelty

    f. _____ use of an interaction system of instantaneous feedback

    g. _____ use of cartoon format

h. _____ use of puppets

i. _____ use of characters

9. _____ What are the learner's entry level skills?

10. _____ What are the learner's reinforcement requirements?

B. Teacher Requirements

(The following outline is intended to serve as a guideline to the selector of instructional materials in identifying the requirements to allow a teacher/instructor to effectively use the material.)

1. _____ Are a teacher's manual and/or instructions provided?

2. If a teacher's manual and/or instructions are provided, does it include:

a. _____ philosophy and rationale

b. _____ statement of objectives

c. _____ statement of instructional and interest levels

d. _____ statement of reading level

e. _____ statement of prerequisite skills

f. _____ listing of material/program elements

g. _____ listing of required materials and equipment

h. _____ suggestions for teacher/instructor use

i. _____ suggestions for student/learner use

j. _____ suggestions for instructional alternatives

k. _____ suggestions for evaluation

l. _____ suggestions for additional resources

3. Instructor time requirements:

a. _____ training

b. _____ preparation

c. _____ use

d. _____ clean-up

4. What is the degree of instructor involvement?

a. _____ full-time teacher involvement is required during instructional period

b. _____ part-time teacher involvement required

(Criteria continue on page 108)

c. ____ no teacher involvement required

d. ____ full-time aide involvement required

e. ____ part-time aide involvement required

f. ____ no aide involvement required

g. ____ full-time parent involvement required

h. ____ part-time parent involvement required

i. ____ no parent involvement required

j. ____ full-time peer involvement required
k. ____ part-time peer involvement required

l. ____ no peer involvement required

m. ____ materials can be used independently by learners

5. Is the material practical?

Yes	No	NA		
___	___	___	a.	maneuverability
___	___	___	b.	ease of storage
___	___	___	c.	number of parts
___	___	___	d.	identification of parts
___	___	___	e.	size of parts
___	___	___	f.	storage/organization of parts
___	___	___	g.	durability of product and packaging
___	___	___	h.	replaceability of consumable and nonconsumable parts
___	___	___	i.	requires use of specialized equipment

6. Is the total cost reasonable?

Yes	No	NA		
___	___	___	a.	inservice training
___	___	___	b.	initial cost
___	___	___	c.	per use cost (replacement of consumables)
___	___	___	d.	required supplementary materials costs
___	___	___	e.	replacement cost (replacement of nonconsumables)

7. ___ ___ ___ Is the material appropriate for the curriculum?

8. ___ ___ ___ Has this material been field tested?

9. ___ ___ ___ If so, has it been found to be effective?

C. Materials Characteristics

(The following outline is intended to serve as a guideline to the selector of instructional materials in identifying specific characteristics a material requires to allow for communication with a learner.)

1. Technical quality

   a. Quality of auditory presentation: Acceptable Unacceptable

      (1) clarity (easily understood, recording quality good)   _____   _____

      (2) amplification   _____   _____

      (3) voice level   _____   _____

      (4) dialect/accent   _____   _____

      (5) voice speed   _____   _____

      (6) voice quality   _____   _____

      (7) sequence   _____   _____

      (8) quality of narration (reader style)   _____   _____

      (9) music/sound/voice mixing   _____   _____

   b. Quality of visual presentation: Acceptable Unacceptable

      (1) sharpness   _____   _____

      (2) color   _____   _____

      (3) distracting elements   _____   _____

      (4) complexity   _____   _____

      (5) size relationships   _____   _____

      (6) sequence   _____   _____

      (7) subjective angle (learner point of view)   _____   _____

      (8) objective angle (observer point of view)   _____   _____

      (9) composition (visual format, visual arrangement)   _____   _____

      (10) figure-ground definition   _____   _____

(Criteria continue on page 110)

c. Quality of print and graphic presentation:

	Acceptable	Unacceptable
(1) legibility (style and size)	____	____
(2) captioning (location and pacing)	____	____
(3) clarity of print (contrast)	____	____
(4) accuracy	____	____

d. Quality of tactile presentation:

	Acceptable	Unacceptable
(1) braille (clear and easily discriminable)	____	____
(2) tactile drawings (clear and easily discriminable)	____	____
(3) texture (clear and easily discriminable	____	____
(4) composition (physical format, physical arrangement)	____	____
(5) manipulables (discriminable, dimension, shape, mass)	____	____

2. Instructional quality

Yes No NA

____ ____ ____ a) Does the selection of subject matter facts adequately represent the content area?

____ ____ ____ b) Is the content presented in the material accurate?

____ ____ ____ c) Is the content logically sequenced?

____ ____ ____ d) Is the content organized for ease of study?

____ ____ ____ e) Are various points of view, including treatment of minorities, handicapped, ideologies, personal and social values, sex roles, etc., objectively represented?

____ ____ ____ f) Are the objectives of the material clearly stated?

____ ____ ____ g) Is the content of the material consistent with the objectives?

____ ____ ____ h) Are the prerequisite skills for use of the materials stated?

____ ____ ____ i) Are essential sub-skills required included in the instructional sequence?

___ ___ ___ j) Is the reading level of the material stated?

___ ___ ___ k) Is the vocabulary systematically introduced?

___ ___ ___ l) Is the vocabulary consistent with the stated reading level?

___ ___ ___ m) Is the instructional level stated?

___ ___ ___ n) Is the interest level stated?

___ ___ ___ o) Is the material self-pacing?

___ ___ ___ p) Does the material provide for frequent reinforcement of major concepts?

___ ___ ___ q) Does the material summarize and review major points?

___ ___ ___ r) Does the material provide frequent opportunities for active student involvement and response?

___ ___ ___ s) Does the material provide for evaluation of user performance?

___ ___ ___ t) Does the material provide criterion-referenced assessment?

___ ___ ___ u) Are all of the supplementary materials needed for instruction included in the materials package?

D. Matching Material to Learner

(The following questions require a synthesis of information gained from stage III, Review. The synthesis is essential before proceeding to stage IV, Decision.)

Yes No NA

___ ___ ___ 1. Are the characteristics of the material compatible with perceived learner characteristics?

___ ___ ___ 2. Are the characteristics of the material compatible with perceived teacher requirements?

___ ___ ___ 3. Have you checked the list of criteria in the TEACHER LEVEL, stage III, Review, section B, Matching Material to Learner?

(Criteria continue on page 112)

IV. DECISIONS

The outcome of stage IV will be: a final determination of material suitability for use in a specific learning situation. Individualization of the decision making, based on items of priority concern, is implicit in this process.

After the review process, it was found that the material was:

Yes	No	NI	
_____	_____	_____	needed by the learner
_____	_____	_____	usable with the learner
_____	_____	_____	usable by the instructor
_____	_____	_____	effective

Decisions to:

A. Use

B. Adapt

C. Field Test

can be made by identifying from the review data responsiveness of the material to learner need, usability with the learner, usability by the instructor, and effectiveness.

Directions: For each criterion met, place a "+" in the appropriate box. For each criterion not met, place a "-" in the appropriate box. If no information is available, place an "NI" in the appropriate box.

Needed	Usable with Learner	Usable by Teacher	Effective

Match your review summary with the decision matrix below:

D. Recommendations

N	UL	UT	E	Recommend for:
+	+	+	+	U = Use/make available for use/information dissemination
+	+	+	-	A = Adapt
+	+	+	NI	U/FT = Use/Field Test
+	+	-	+	R/A/D = Reject/Adapt/Develop
+	+	-	-	R/A/D = Reject/Adapt/Develop
+	-	-	-	R/A/D = Reject/Adapt/Develop
+	-	+	-	R/A/D = Reject/Adapt/Develop
+	-	+	+	R/A/D = Reject/Adapt/Develop
+	-	+	NI	R/A/D = Reject/Adapt/Develop
-	+	+	+	R = Reject/not acceptable
-	-	+	+	R = Reject/not acceptable
-	-	-	+	R = Reject/not acceptable
-	-	-	-	R = Reject/not acceptable
-	-	-	NI	R = Reject/not acceptable

V. EVALUATION

The outcome of stage V will be: a final judgment, either positive, negative, or inconclusive, as to the usefulness and effectiveness of the material with the learner in a given learning situation.

Yes   No   NA

___   ___   ___   1. Does this material meet the requirements of the teacher? (see teacher requirement section in review instrument)

___   ___   ___   2. Does this material meet the requirements of the learner? (see learner characteristics section in review instrument)

___   ___   ___   3. Does this material lead to the attainment of the specified objectives? (see instructional quality section in the review instrument)

___   ___   ___   4. Does the technical quality of the material meet the requirements of the learner? (see technical quality section in review instrument)

___   ___   ___   5. Do the instructional qualities of the material meet the requirements of the learner? (see instructional quality section of review instrument)

KEY ORGANIZATIONS

Evaluation Standards Project
Joint Committee on Standards for Educational Evaluation
c/o Evaluation Center
College of Education
Western Michigan University
Kalamazoo, MI 49908   (616) 383-8166

The Evaluation Standards Project is currently developing a set of 29 principles or constructive suggestions to follow in educational evaluations. While these do not encompass a particular view of what constitutes good education nor present specific criteria for judging educational programs, projects and materials, they do contain advice for dealing with these issues.

These findings, to be issued in 1980 as *Standards for Evaluations of Educational Programs, Projects and Materials*, are currently being prepared and revised by a Joint Committee of 17 members from 12 associations of educators, researchers, school officials and psychologists. In addition, the Committee hopes to issue a technical paper series and a casebook on topical issues and applications relating to these standards.

So far, the *Standards* identify four major desirable attributes in an evaluation: accuracy, utility, propriety and feasibility. The Committee has located 29 standards that help define these attributes.

KEY PUBLICATIONS

Consumer's Guide to Evaluation of Training Materials Developed by Educational Laboratories and R & D Centers, by Daniel Antonplis, et al. Washington, DC, National Institute of Education, 1976. Paged in sections. $8.00pa. (From Evaluation Improvement Program, Educational Testing Service, Box 2845, Princeton, NJ 08541.)

This program evaluation tool uses detailed descriptions of 36 products developed and field tested by regional laboratories or R&D centers to teach different aspects of program evaluation.

Evaluating and Choosing Curriculum and Instructional Materials, by Louise L. Tyler, M. Frances Klein, and associates. Glennville, CA, Educational Resources Associates, 1977. 192p. $5.50. (From Educational Resources Associates, P.O. Box 245, Glennville, CA 93266.)

This book offers a systematized, organized set of criteria to "eliminate whim, fashion and irrelevance" in the decision-making processes of evaluating and choosing instructional materials.

The Evaluation of Instructional Materials, by William J. Webster. Washington, DC, Association for Educational Communications and Technology, 1976. 26p. $4.00pa. ($3.00 for members.)

This succinct paper, originally prepared for the ERIC Clearinghouse on Information Resources, provides a useful summary of and an excellent 60-item annotated bibliography on the rather complex conceptual approach of educational researchers and educational evaluators to evaluating instructional materials. Mr. Webster includes his own model for evaluating instructional materials, complete with a flow chart, graphic representations of the instructional development process, and an outline, with many subcategories, of the 19 "necessary steps in product evaluation." It includes a demonstration of how this model was applied in the Dallas School District to assess relative merits of instructional materials in 1971.

Ideabook: The Joint Dissemination Review Panel, by G. Kasten Tallmadge. Washington, DC, GPO, 1977. 113p. $3.00pa.

This *Ideabook*, prepared at the request of practitioners on an NIE contract by G. Kasten Tallmadge of RMC Research Corps, has two main purposes: 1) to illustrate a variety of ways to gather evidence of effectiveness and 2) to suggest forceful and effective ways to present such evidence.

Separate chapters deal with the function of the Joint Dissemination Review Panel and the essentials and hazards of evaluation, with chapters on each of six JDRP criteria:

● Did a change occur?

● Was the effect consistent enough and observed often enough to be statistically significant?

● Was the effect educationally significant?

● Can the intervention be implemented in another location with a reasonable expectation of comparable impact?

- How likely is it that the observed effects resulted from the intervention?
- Is the presented evidence believable and interpretable?

The JDRP believes that its review procedure (discussed in this book on pages 98-100) has resulted in improved submissions and products.

The Justification of Curriculum, by Leroi E. Daniels. New York, American Educational Research Association, 1971. 62p. (ED 050 160).
   Deals with perspectives from which curricula can be evaluated and examined. These include four major stages: verification, validation, vindication and rational choice. Ideally, consideration of these four should precede consideration of other constructs.

A Practical Guide to Measuring Project Impact on Student Achievement, by G. Kasten Tallmadge, et al. Washington, DC, GPO, 1977. 120p. $1.90pa. postpaid.
   Covers common hazards in evaluation and evaluation models, means of collecting data (testing and recording), analyzing and reporting data and other practical measures for assessing the effects of projects on student achievement.

Procedural Guide for Validating Achievement Gains in Educational Projects, by G. Kasten Tallmadge and Donald Horst. Washington, DC, GPO, 1976. 95p. $2.50pa. postpaid.
   Provides procedures for validating the effectiveness of education projects with existing evaluation data.

Recommendations for Curriculum and Instructional Materials, by Louise L. Tyler and M. Frances Klein. Los Angeles, University of California, Los Angeles, 1968. 15p.
   Prepared for the AERA Committee on Curriculum Evaluation as technical recommendations intended to parallel test standards developed by the American Psychological Association. The booklet systematically covers specifications, rationale, appropriateness, effectiveness, conditions and practicality.
   Tyler and Klein raise some interesting questions—not yet answered. Their belief is that producers should provide documentation on the values and sources of formulated objectives and should describe how and why organizing elements are selected, whether these are derived from learner, society or subject matter. Why, for instance, is it important to understand the structures of various disciplines? Why does a physics curriculum typically include the topics of time, space, matter, light and motion?

Selecting a Curriculum Program: Balancing Requirements and Costs, by Rodney J. Ball, Michael D. Marvin, and Sanford Temkin. Philadelphia, Research for Better Schools, 1975. paged in sections. $8.50.
   This handbook-workbook is designed to help school district personnel select new programs on the basis of costs and other considerations they consider significant.
   The process presented here (divided into four units) entails: determining the requirements for a new program, identifying at least three suitable programs,

establishing specific criteria for selection, gathering cost and requirements information for each, comparing and analyzing these programs, selecting the most appropriate program, and documenting the selection process. The method is simple, clear and self-teaching.

The "Trouble-Shooting" Checklist (TSC) for School-Based Settings (Manual and Instrument), by B. A. Manning. Austin, TX, University of Texas Research and Development Center for Teacher Education, 1976. 46p. $1.50. (Also available as ED 126 095).

This checklist is designed to measure an organization's potential for success in adopting or implementing particular educational innovations. It bases a profile on seven variables: school communication pattern, innovative experience, staff, central administration, community relations, organization climate and students.

FOR FURTHER READING

*Items marked with an asterisk include other criteria checklists.
+Items marked with a plus include further lists of references.

This bibliography provides a brief survey of evaluation viewpoints—comprehensive but not exhaustive. There are some excellent bibliographies in the books listed as Key Publications (see page 114), especially in William Webster's *The Evaluation of Instructional Methods.*

*Abt, C. "An Evaluation Model: How to Compare Curriculum Materials," *Nation's Schools*, vol. 86 (July 1970), pp. 21-28.

+Alkin, M. C., and J. Wingard. *User Oriented Product Evaluation.* Los Angeles, Center for the Study of Evaluation, 1972. (CSE Report 81).

*+Armstrong, Jenny R. *Minimum Guidelines Used in Consumer Information Analysis.* Madison, WI, University of Wisconsin, 1976.

*+Armstrong, Jenny R. *Sourcebook for the Evaluation of Instructional Materials.* Madison, WI, Special Education Instructional Materials Center, 1973. (ED 107 050).

*Bleil, G. "Evaluating Educational Materials," *Journal of Learning Disabilities*, vol. 8, no. 1 (Jan. 1975), pp. 12-19.

Borich, Gary D., ed. *Evaluating Educational Programs and Products.* Englewood Cliffs, NJ, Educational Technology, 1974.

*"Checklist for Selecting Programs," *NSPI Journal*, vol. 2 (July 1963), p. 4.

*Eash, Maurice J. "Assessing Curriculum Materials: A Preliminary Instrument," *Educational Product Report*, vol. 2, no. 5 (1969), pp. 18-24.

*Fetter, Wayne R. "An Evaluation Instrument for Instructional Materials," *Educational Technology*, vol. 18, no. 10 (Oct. 1978), pp. 55-56.

*+Hood, Paul. *Evaluation of Instructional Materials for Educational RDD & E Content Areas.* San Francisco, Far West Laboratory for Educational Research and Development, July 1973.

+House, Ernest R. "Assumptions Underlying Evaluation Models," *Educational Researcher*, vol. 7, no. 3 (March 1978), pp. 4-12.

*+*How to Evaluate Education Programs: A Monthly Guide to Methods and Ideas That Work.* Washington, DC, Capitol Publications, Sept. 1977. Monthly. $35.00/yr.

*Klein, Susan. *NIE Product Rating Form.* Washington, DC, National Institute of Education, 1975.

*+Klein, Susan. *Toward Consensus on Minimum Criteria for Educational Products.* San Francisco, AERA Annual Meeting, April 1976. (Available from Dr. Susan S. Klein, National Institute of Education, 1200 19th St., NW,. Washington, DC 20208.)

*+Niedermeyer, Fred C., and M. H. Moncrief. "Guidelines for Selecting Effective Instructional Products," *The Elementary School Journal*, vol. 76 (Dec. 1975), pp. 127-31.

Sanders, J. R., and D. J. Cunningham. "A Structure for Formative Evaluation in Product Development," *Review of Educational Research*, vol. 43, no. 2 (Spring 1973), pp. 217-36.

Sawin, Enoch I. "Curriculum Evaluation or Descriptive Inquiry?" *Studies in Educational Evaluation*, vol. 2, no. 1 (Spring 1976), pp. 41-51.

+Scriven, Michael. "The Methodology of Evaluation," *American Educational Research Association Monograph Series on Curriculum Evaluation*, no. 1 (1967), pp. 39-83.

*+Tyler, Louise L., and Mary Frances Klein. "Caveat Emptor: Let the (Educational) Buyer Beware," *Educational Technology*, vol. 2, no. 4 (April 1973), pp. 52-54.

Walton, W. W., B. F. Esser, M. G. Epstein, E. H. Margoshes, and W. Schrader. *Selection of Exemplary Products.* Princeton, Educational Testing Service, April 1973.

LEARNER VERIFICATION AND REVISION (LVR)

Learner Verification and Revision (LVR), now legally required in at least two states, is the brainchild of Ken Komoski of EPIE. Essentially it is a means of ensuring some feedback from some students on instructional materials.

As a "learner-based process," LVR utilizes systematic feedback from learners (and presumably nonlearners) who have used these materials. With this process, producers and publishers must decide whether or how to revise their materials on the basis of data from students. This information may be collected from different sources:

- directly from students
- from teachers who report their perceptions of their students
- from staff members of publishing companies
- from other observers

Ways of collection may include:

- classroom observations
- interviews with students (individual or collective)
- interviews with teachers
- structured questionnaires (for students and/or teachers)
- criterion-referenced tests

An expensive process, LVR panicked a number of publishers when the concept first arose. However, it has probably provided a valuable function in nudging educational publishers to rationalize and consolidate their research components so that these can provide real help to publishers revising and developing educational programs. Most major publishers now have Learner Verification Departments, which naturally vary in effectiveness.

LVR, in itself, is no guarantee of quality. I have seen some "Learner Verified" versions of particular workbooks that were less coherent and logical than the original versions. Other materials, subjected to LVR, appear—like the camel—to be designed by a committee.

Carl A. Utberg, who directs Silver Burdett's outstanding Evaluation and Professional Development Department, was kind enough to write me a detailed letter on the implications of Learner Verification for publishers. Utberg feels that "Most of the improvements that have been made in the last six years in all our major educational programs have come as a result of the data that we have tabulated and analyzed." He finds it almost impossible to hazard a guess on the number of hours that go into original writing and production as a result of Learner Verification: "Authors spend time in revising their materials. Editors suggest content and pedagogical changes in approaches. . . . These major changes take considerable time and effort on the part of many unsung heroes from typists to typesetters and from printers to editors and authors."

While publishers differ in what they verify, the items below are the ones that Silver Burdett checked most closely at the time of writing:

- Readability of materials
- Understandability of materials
- Fair treatment of women and minorities
- Content
- The helpfulness of the teachers' edition
- Whether or not the illustrations help teach concepts
- The versatility of the program for urban, suburban, and rural areas
- The versatility of the program for above-average, average and below-average students

All of these seem to be valuable considerations for producers and selectors.

While LVR is not a panacea that guarantees instructional materials will bring about precise and predictable results, it can be most helpful for materials with specific instructional intents. Generally, it is not suited for open-ended materials of educational value nor for works of art—in any medium—used in education. It is appropriate for textbooks, for example, not trade books. For example, though *Macbeth* is taught in many U.S. high schools, LVR would not be appropriate for *Macbeth* though it could be used with a teachers' guide to *Macbeth*.

Whether or not learning can be verified, whether or not statutes are in force, educational producers for major basal texts and programs undoubtedly should have some student input. Selectors appraising major purchases should ask producers:

- what means the producers have used to involve children and teachers in developing these particular materials
- what means the producers intend to use to involve students and teachers in improving and revising these particular materials.

The Joint Dissemination Review Panel *Ideabook* (cited on page 114) has other good approaches for assessing effectiveness.

These guidelines on Learner Verification and Revision (LVR) are reprinted with permission from *Pilot Guidelines for Improving Instructional Materials through the Process of Learner Verification and Revision* by the National LVR Task Force, sponsored by EPIE Institute, New York, 1975.

GUIDELINES FOR REPORTING AND ASSESSING LVR ACTIVITIES

The purpose of a report on LVR activities is to enable the publisher of instructional materials to provide educators with evidence that a particular product has been—or soon will be—put through the LVR Process as part of a continuing effort to improve its effectiveness with learners. Although a publisher can fashion various LVR models and yet conform to the basic objective of the LVR Process, certain elements in every model are essential. These essential elements, which taken together operationally define the process, are asterisked below and should be addressed in every LVR Report. What is offered below, then, is not an inviolable *form* that all publishers must use or that purchasers demand be used; rather, it should be viewed as a flexible *format* which constitutes a set of guidelines to the publisher for preparing a LVR Report and to educators for reading and assessing such a report.

(Continues on page 120)

Descriptive Information on Product

[The publisher should provide "catalog" information on the product, such as title, authors, copyright, medium or media involved, kinds of supplementary components, and so on. The "product" is any kind of material offered for adoption consideration as an instructional material. It should be described as it normally is when submitted to an adoption/selection committee, that is, a six-year textbook series, for example, or a multicomponent (and perhaps multimedia) "system" being considered as one product.]

*Instructional Design

[The "instructional design" of a curriculum product can be thought of as the overall learning plan for the product. The design should be described and the underlying rationale for that design should be stated.

[It is to be expected that a product with integrity of design—a product whose instructional elements are well integrated—will easily be put through a well designed LVR effort. Conversely, a product without an apparent instructional design cannot easily, if at all, be subjected to a cycle of the LVR Process.]

*Intended Learner Outcomes To Be Investigated

[This should be a statement of what the publisher intends the product to accomplish when used with integrity with learners. If such a statement appears in the product itself or in accompanying promotional pieces, a reference may be made to where it can be found.

[It may be that at a particular time the publisher wants to investigate only certain outcomes within the larger scope of intended learner outcomes, in which case this intention should be stated. It may be also that a publisher of a six-year textbook series (with various attendant materials), for example, may investigate selected outcomes of an exemplary portion of the entire program and use the resultant data to guide revisions of other portions of the program; if so, this should be made clear.]

*Conditions of Use of Product

[The publisher should specify the overall instructional setting intended for the product. Basically, this includes a description of what is termed the "target population" and a noting of the kinds and extent of "teacher preparation." The target population is simply the kinds of learners the product is intended for. Characteristics which may or may not be relevant are: grades students are assigned to because of their maturity, not achievement, levels; actual grade levels, particularly with respect to reading achievement; ethnic backgrounds; family and community socioeconomic level; and so on. Teacher preparation involves such teacher-related matters as supplementary teacher materials, inservice teacher education, and classroom preparation.]

*Techniques for Gathering Feedback

[Techniques for gathering feedback from learners may include, but are not limited to, individual learner and classroom observations, interviews, questionnaires, and criterion-referenced tests. These techniques should be designed to gather data both on direct-learning effects and on affective reactions of learners.

[Techniques used in large-scale, field-test validation attempts are not to be confused with techniques used for gathering learner feedback for the LVR Process. Similarly, techniques used to elicit product testimonials for promotional purposes ("I like this textbook very much and so does my class")—as opposed to reactions gathered as a result of questionnaires or interviews, which may be used in promotion pieces—are inappropriate for the LVR Process.]

*Description of Learners Used in LVR Process

[The selection of learners for the LVR Process is not to be confused with a scientifically drawn "national sample" of students required for the validation of standardized tests and for attempts at validation of other materials. Such a "sample" will perforce involve thousands of students. A LVR selection—because the aim of LVR is to identify trouble spots in order to improve materials, not to prove how well materials work—may comprise a handful of learners from the target population or a handful of classes. In fact, in some instances—and the publisher should justify the use of this procedure—a few students might be taken through the LVR Process in the offices of the publisher, unless there are certain conditions of a classroom setting which are necessary and which cannot be approximated in the offices.

[The factor of conditions of a classroom setting suggests the relevant factor of two interrelated bases of product performance subject to LVR improvements, which can be conveniently distinguished as "textual" and "contextual" characteristics. Textual characteristics are characteristics of the materials themselves which learners use (goals and objectives; scope and sequence; provisions for evaluation; and so on); contextual characteristics are characteristics of the setting the materials are used in (the presence of absence of teacher's editions or manuals, or certain other supplementary resources; the teaching/management plan; and so on). Students might be taken to the publisher's office if textual improvements are being sought by the publisher, but they probably should not be if contextual improvements are being sought.

[In summation, the publisher should report: (1) the procedure for selecting learners, (2) the relevant characteristics of these learners, and (3) the rationale for this step.

[Those charged with the responsibility of assessing LVR Reports are urged not to get involved in a "numbers game"—that is, ranking publishers according to the number of learners used in a publisher's LVR activity—because such a ranking is at best unproductive, at worst grossly misleading.]

*Analysis of Findings

[After assessing the extent to which a product is and is not as effective as it might be with a selection of learners and after gathering data, the publisher analyzes the data. It is desirable that the publisher make known the analysis of the findings in a LVR Report. It may be, however, that the publisher would consider such information to be proprietary, because revealing it could give competing publishers an advantage; in such cases, the publisher may explain the reasons for keeping the findings and the analysis of the findings confidential, and, with this condition accepted by an adoption committee, release the information only on request. It may be also that the publisher states in a LVR Report a justification for not releasing any information whatsoever on findings, in which case the publisher should also describe—with as much specificity as prudence allows—the kinds of trouble spots identified both within the materials used by learners and in the overall teaching/management plan.

[Here too, those charged with the responsibility for assessing LVR Reports should understand the competitive nature of educational publishing, and they should be influenced by the reasonableness of the report that the publisher does provide.]

*Specific Improvements Made

[The analysis of findings enables the publisher to identify exactly where specific changes should be made, both textual and contextual changes. Improvements can involve aspects relating to learner materials (textual), such as verbal or visual communications, manageability, appeal to learners, goals and objectives, scope and sequence, various kinds of bias, motivational elements, directions to learners, activities for learners, and the congruence of product elements. Improvements can relate to teaching aspects (contextual), such as classroom preparation, record-keeping provisions, teaching design, and inservice education.

[As an ideal component of a LVR Report, the very in-house record of changes compiled by the publisher—including, perhaps, an annotated version of the product used with the selection of learners—might be made available by the publisher, on special request, for examination by an adoption committee.

(Continued on page 122)

*Specific Improvements Made (cont'd)

[Once again, however, the proprietary nature of changes made may constrain a publisher, in which case the reasonableness of what the publisher does report is itself a factor in assessment. Here, though, even more is involved than what was noted above. A publisher may fear that citing a large number of changes might be an adverse reflection on the product and the publisher. Then, too, an unscrupulous publisher might be tempted to develop an intentionally shoddy product to demonstrate, through the LVR Process, a substantial quantity of improvements.

[It is, therefore, up to those assessing LVR Reports to be conscious of realities constraining—and of apprehensions cautioning—a responsible publisher, and to be mindful of trickery tempting an irresponsible publisher.]

Background and Future of Product

[The publisher should briefly describe any part of the product's history that might be relevant and helpful to a full understanding of the publisher's LVR efforts with the product. Also, the publisher may want to describe plans for future LVR efforts with the product, although the publisher would want to consider that a premature revelation of plans might give competitors an advantage.]

Person to Contact for Clarification, More Detail, or Updated Information:

Name _____   Position _____

Company _____   Division _____

Address _____

Telephone _____

GUIDELINES FOR SCHOOLS PARTICIPATING IN LVR PROGRAMS

1. **Orientation**
   - School representatives should meet with media producer.
   - Purposes of procedures should be understood.
   - Type, nature, and placement of materials should be detailed.
   - Teacher and student role in using materials should be clarified.

2. **Class Identification**
   - Select class (or classes) and teacher(s) for whom materials are most suitable.

3. **Methods of Using Materials**
   - Teachers should become familiar with materials.
   - Teachers should discuss intended uses of materials with producer's representative.
   - Teachers should determine how best to use materials, for example, with individual students, small, or class-sized groups.

4. **Method of Recording Student Reactions**
   - Producer's representative may provide data collection materials.
   - Some procedure is needed to enable students to record their reactions to content which is unclear, ambiguous, not understood, too quickly presented, too simple, etc.

FOR FURTHER READING

*Items marked with an asterisk include criteria.
+Items marked with a plus have further references.

*California State Legislature. *Assembly Bill AB531*, Chapter 929, 1972.
  The California law states that "Learner Verification means the continuous and thorough evaluation of instructional materials for their effectiveness with pupils."

Dole, Phyllis W. *The Product Improvement Process.* Santa Ana, CA, Doubleday Multimedia, 1975. 28p. (Also available in microfiche, ED 101 692.)
  Paper presented at the 16th annual meeting of the National Audio-Visual Association, January 13, 1975. Describes how LVR is used as a product development procedure technique at this firm.

*EPIE Institute. *Pilot Guidelines for Improving Instructional Materials through the Process of Learner Verification and Revision.* New York, Educational Products Information Exchange Institute, 1975. (Available free from the Institute, Box 620, Stony Brook, NY 11790.)
  This study is particularly useful since the appendices include names of persons in agencies and industries who would be working with this procedure.

Florida State Senate. *Bill S492*, Chapter 74-337, June 27, 1974, pp. 24-25.
  Bill states that publishers must "submit written proof of learner verification and revision process during prepublication development and post-publication revision of the materials in question."

Klein, M. Frances. *A Perspective on Improving the Effectiveness of Curriculum Materials.* Las Vegas, NV, 1975. 13p. (ED 107 218).
  Paper presented at the 16th annual meeting of the National Audio-Visual Association, Las Vegas, January 1975. Analyzes LVR as one of several possible methods.

Komoski, P. Kenneth. "Statement to the U.S. House of Representatives. Committee on Education and Labor." In *Hearings to Establish a National Institute of Education*, 92nd Congress, First Session. Washington, GPO, 1971.
  Also reprinted as: Komoski, P. Kenneth. *Statement Before Select Subcommittee on Education.* New York, Educational Products Information Exchange Institute, 1971. 48p.

Lawyers Committee for Civil Rights Under the Law. Model Legislation Project. *Alternative Model Learner Verification and Revision Statutes to Require or Encourage the Utilization of Learner Performance Information in the Prepublication Development and Post-publication Revision of Instructional Materials Used in the Public Education System.* Washington, The Committee, 1975. (ED 122 390).
  A project funded by NIE, designed as model legislation and sent to every legislature in the country.

+"Quality Control for Instructional Materials: Legislative Mandates of Learner
    Verification and Implications for Public Education," *Harvard Journal of
    Legislation*, vol. 12, no. 4 (June 1975), pp. 511-62.
    This scholarly analytic study criticizes the effect of LVR legislation
presently enacted in California and Florida if translated to other states without substantial modification. To avoid rigidity in education, it suggests care and research
before drafting further legislation.

THINKING ABOUT THINKING
Selection Criteria for Cognition and Creativity

"Learning without thinking is labor lost; thinking without learning is perilous."
—Confucius

"By doubting, we learn to inquire; by inquiry, we learn the truth."
—Abelard

"There is nothing in the intellect that was not first in the senses."
—Aristotle

■ ■ ■

This chapter provides some models of intelligence and some applications of cognitive taxonomies to use in selecting instructional materials across subject boundaries.

Cognitive criteria, as such, are relatively neglected in current selection procedures, except by remedial teachers, special educators and teachers of the gifted. Special educators and remedial educators generally start from an awareness of student limitations and individual development; teachers of the gifted recognize that gifted children require intellectual challenge. Normal children's intellectual needs, aptitudes and interests—if considered at all—tend to be considered within the contexts of particular subject matters, such as "scope and sequence" or "individual differences." Little attention is paid to cognitive skills, per se, from grades one through twelve, though early childhood educators tend to have a cognitive-developmental outlook.

In the last few years, multicultural educators have started to look tentatively at differences in cognitive styles among U.S. ethnic groups, considering the hypothesis that intelligence may develop differently in different groups or that cognitive modalities may be culturally determined in part. Ultimately, they hope to develop or extend curricula that are appropriate for all types of learners: scanners and focusers, deductive thinkers as well as inductive, independent and dependent learners, theoretical and practical types, visualizers, verbalizers, and the mathematically oriented.

In times past, educators, backed by faculty psychology, focused on training minds. Today, both teaching methods and materials tend to stress subject matter mastery in two modes: memorization, and—to a lesser extent—comprehension. This approach is reinforced by machine-graded tests, which similarly test for memory and recognition.

Our curriculum however still includes subjects, such as languages and mathematics, originally taught largely because of their supposed capacity to train young minds. This may be the sole remaining educational justification for some of our high school mathematics courses, even though they are not generally taught as if this were their goal.

While almost all subject areas involve thinking skills (successful reading for instance, depends upon series of inferences), thinking skills and processes are rarely considered separately from subject matter. For example, reading skills and processes can also be generalized for problem-solving:

- selecting main ideas
- making inferences
- constructing sequences
- following directions for simple and complex choices
- reading maps, graphs, and pictures

Similarly, other subjects—such as new math, new science, new social studies—deal with, respectively, thinking skills, science process skills, and problem-solving skills. Most often, however, these are tied to subject matter and to related objectives rather than being considered as independent values or variables. Undoubtedly any encouragement of thinking is better than none.

Critical reading skills, incidentally, are important not only to students but also to educators selecting instructional materials. Appropriate skills for these might include:

- recognizing stereotypes and cliches
- recognizing bias
- recognizing underlying assumptions
- identifying central issues
- recognizing valid data
- evaluating evidence of authority
- determining whether facts support a generalization
- drawing warranted conclusions

Some teaching approaches, again, tend to support cognitive instruction. Open education is thought to encourage independence, resourcefulness, initiative, creativity and self-reliance. Individualization and contract learning may encourage the same traits and can—in some cases—result in rather impressive student productions. Learning centers ideally include materials from a wide variety of learning modalities and levels of difficulty.

Even teachers whose actions or materials encourage thinking do not usually spend much time considering cognitive aspects which can add an important dimension to every curriculum area from physical education to drama.

In this chapter I have tried to isolate some cognitive factors to help materials selectors improve both the intellectual and the pedagogical qualities of instructional materials. In the world of future shock, with changing work habits, altered environments, increasing computerized technology and huge increments in information, our abilities to think and to learn may be considerably more important than our tested stores of up-to-date or outdated knowledge.

COGNITIVE TAXONOMIES

There are several cognitive theories and one taxonomy of knowledge that can serve as overall frameworks for educators selecting materials for cognitive qualities. Bloom's *Taxonomy of Educational Objectives: Cognitive Domain* (New York, David McKay, 1956) is a simple, logical, two-dimensional model well-known to generations of educators. This *Taxonomy* is a hierarchical classification scheme for cognitive objectives whose stages describe relatively simple to relatively complex cognitive elements of understanding and mastery. As a taxonomy, rather than a psychological theory, it is based on reason and logic rather than on psychological research.

The two figures (below and on page 128) show two approaches for applying Bloom's taxonomy to educational materials selection. One approach adapts it into a checklist. The other indicates particular verbs in activities and questions that can provide quick clues to taxonomic levels.

SAMPLE COGNITIVE CRITERIA FOR MATERIALS ANALYSIS

	Poor				Excellent
	1	2	3	4	5
The materials offer opportunities to recall specific information.					
The materials offer ways and means of dealing with specifics.					
The materials offer uses, abstractions, ideas, generalized concepts, theories.					
The materials provide opportunities for students to translate ideas from one form to another.					
The materials help students understand and work with similarities and differences, cause and effect.					
The materials offer opportunities to follow directions.					
The materials offer students opportunities to choose processes.					
The materials offer students opportunities to understand the relationships and interaction of elements within specific processes and situations.					
The materials offer students opportunities to formulate hypotheses.					
The materials offer students opportunities to classify and/or to devise classification schemes.					
The materials offer students opportunities to evaluate on the basis of empirical evidence or previously established criteria.					

The Florida Taxonomy of Cognitive Behavior is more fully described in an article by J. N. Webb, "Taxonomy of Cognitive Behavior: A System for the Analysis of Intellectual Process," in *Journal of Research and Development in Education*, v.4, no.1 (Fall 1970), pp. 23-33.

VERBAL CLUES TO COGNITIVE LEVELS
(Based on Bloom's Taxonomy)

Action verbs in the *questions and activities* sections of instructional materials often provide valuable clues to the levels of abstractions.

The verbs below frequently correspond to particular areas in *Bloom's Taxonomy of Cognitive Objectives.* The list of process verbs is based on one developed by Sally Patton, Curriculum Consultant for the Gifted Resource Center in San Mateo County.

Area of Taxonomy	Teacher Activity	Student Activity	Related Process Verbs
Knowledge (recall specific bits of information)	Directs Examines Shows Tells	Absorbs Recognizes Remembers Responds	observe ask fill in label list
Comprehension (understanding of communicated materials, not related to other materials)	Compares Contrasts Demonstrates Examines Listens Questions	Demonstrates Explains Interprets Translates	identify locate match paraphrase research write
Application (using methods, concepts, principles or theories in new situations)	Criticizes Facilitates Observes Shows	Constructs Demonstrates Solves	apply diagram experiment draw, sketch interview illustrate list, paint record simulate
Analysis (breaking a communication into constituent elements)	Guides Observes Probes Serves as resource	Differentiates Discusses Dissects Lists Uncovers	analyze categorize classify compare contrast separate survey
Synthesis (combining parts into a whole)	Combines Extends Reflects	Abstracts Discusses Generalizes Relates	create design estimate hypothesize imagine invent produce synthesize
Evaluation (judging values, applying standards and criteria)	Accepts Harmonizes Recommends	Disputes Judges	compare conclude debate decide defend determine editorialize judge predict project suppose value

PSYCHOLOGICAL THEORIES

Psychologists whose theories offer frameworks for considering intelligence and cognitive factors in relationship to materials include Montessori, Piaget, Thurstone and Guilford. Montessori and Piaget, in particular, were both concerned with the use of specific materials for intellectual ends and are, respectively, important for early childhood education and for math and science. While Thurstone and Guilford did not develop or extend their theories to the selection of materials, their models can serve as usable frames of reference for such purposes, particularly for fulfilling the objectives of developing intellectual functions. Guilford himself has advocated that his structure-of-intellect model be used for this purpose.

Maria Montessori (1870-1952) is also discussed in my chapter on early childhood development (see page 353). Her materials were first experimentally developed for severely retarded children and then validated on young children in the slums of Italy. Essentially, these ingenious materials introduced highly abstract concepts in concrete ways through strongly visual kinesthetic devices so that children could explore them through sensorimotor experiences. They offer children both symbols and means of exploring the world in more differentiated ways.

They are congruent with her developmental scheme, which holds that certain conditions are required for normal development. She sees development as a complex process directed by inner drives that succeed one another at certain periods of life, and involve sequences of development as well as external reality. (Since development takes place within society, cultural values help define its form.) If materials are provided at the right time, they will be experienced as something the child can master. As Montessori put it:

> Children have an inner need to know themselves and their world; to develop their intelligence and other mental functions through purposeful activity, to develop control of their movements through the use of their bodies in specific structured situations, to organize the contents of their experience according to the order they perceive in the world, and, finally, through an acquaintance with the properties of things, to grow familiar with their own environment and their own capacities in order to become independent.

Her theories were based upon careful empirical observation of children in specific situations and have been validated by years of worldwide practice. For the most part this process has occurred outside the educational mainstream, but most early childhood education and materials owe a great deal to Montessori.

The sensory channels that Montessori emphasizes correspond to the "figural" component of Guilford's structure of intellect. Guilford, in a recent letter, noted that,

> this is a very natural approach, since everything that a person knows, in any informational content, goes back ultimately to sensory input. It requires translations from one informational content to another.

Her belief was that learning was a dynamic process in which the whole personality of the child must be involved (i.e., active rather than passive learning), that free choice in materials and activities is important to foster independence and to confront children with alternatives.

Though materials are basic to Montessori's practices and theories, her approach unfortunately is not one that lends itself easily to abbreviation or schematic representation. I can only recommend exposure to Montessori's materials as highly beneficial to anyone selecting materials for thought processes. Her materials themselves were constructed to foster indirect preparations for functions that will later become manifest and were designed to appeal to inner needs and to coordinate different functions. At the same time, each specific piece of equipment represents one particular objective quality or abstract concept and is set up to provide feedback as to whether or not it is being used correctly. Appropriate relations to these objects (materials) are supposed to promote both inner and outer development.

Jean Piaget (born 1896), who headed the Swiss Montessori movement in his early years, is a Swiss developmental psychologist. His major concerns have been research into the development of cognitive structure (and its description in mathematical and logical language) and the development of theories on intelligence and intellectual stages of development.

Like Montessori, he believes that thought grows best from actions, that knowledge is best discovered and constructed through activities, and that children are continually remaking their inner structures to deal with the external world.

To Piaget, children's mental development is influenced by four interrelated factors: 1) *maturation* (especially physical maturation and maturation of the nervous system), 2) *experience* with objects, 3) *social interaction* and 4) *equilibration*, the process of bringing these into balance.

He believes that developmental stages occur in a fixed sequence that is the same for all children, although different children may function in two stages simultaneously. The three stages of mental development which are most significant for teachers are:

Intuitive stage (about 4 to 7 years). Children are dependent upon superficial perceptions and form ideas impressionalistically. This stage is part of the *pre-operations* period from about 2 to 7.

Concrete operations stage (about 7 to 11 years). Children develop concepts of numbers, relations and classes in terms of their own experiences, while thought processes are becoming systematized and internally logical. Children generally will experience difficulty with abstract concepts.

Formal operations stage (about 11 to 15 years). Children can use abstractions, distinguish between possible and actual, and reason hypothetically in the absence of concrete evidence.

These theories are influential in mathematics, science and values curricula—notably in the fine British Nuffield science and math materials—and they provide a great deal of insight into children's thinking processes. As contrasted with Montessori and Guilford, Piaget's theories—as applied in some classrooms—tend to be used to impose ceilings upon children's abilities.

His actual recommendations for classroom structure and activities are quite congruent with those of Montessori. Educationally and developmentally, however, Montessori placed more importance on the significance of appropriate materials in a "prepared" environment, while stressing the long process of inner development that takes place before particular qualities or abilities become manifest in action. In that sense, her approach to development is rather less hierarchical.

L. L. Thurstone (1887-1955) is best known in education for his work in psychometrics, his hypothesis of primary mental ability and the development of multiple-factor analysis. His theory of primary mental ability (as contrasted to theories of general intelligence) postulates separate intelligence factors or primary mental abilities.

In *Can Intelligence Be Taught?* (Bloomington, IN, Phi Delta Kappa Educational Foundation, 1973. Fastback 29.) Thomas G. Sexton and Donald G. Poling report a successful experiment in raising intelligence from an average IQ score of 116 to average scores of 141 with ten weeks of summer training using special curricula based on Thurstone's intelligence factors (with the addition of creativity).

IQ RAISING BASED ON THURSTONE'S THEORY OF INTELLIGENCE

Intelligence Factors	IQ Raising Curricula
Verbal comprehension	Vocabulary building (3700 words)
Word fluency	
Number fluency	Math skills
Memory	
Visualization and spatial ability	
Perceptual speed	Rapid reading
Induction, or logic	

They recommend especially teaching rapid reading and rapid calculation.

The Los Angeles school district also used Thurstone's intelligence factors as a basis of a curriculum for improving skills for disadvantaged gifted students. Lessons in critical thinking, vocabulary enrichment and problem solving were combined with manipulative and fine arts curricula. To increase their self-confidence and self-esteem the children were exposed to a wide variety of creative and social experiences. The program also de-emphasized anxiety, time, grading and "correct" answers

J. P. Guilford's (born 1897) Structure of Intellect model (SOI or SI) reproduced on page 132, is at first glance more complex than the two-dimensional models of Bloom and Thurstone, but for that very reason it is perhaps a more appropriate model for selecting materials on several dimensions. (It resembles Greg Kearsley's Who-What-How Model of Instructional Dimensions on pages 23-24.)

While the (learning) *operations* are quite similar to the taxonomic areas in Bloom, the *products* dimension (explained below) provides another dimension for analyzing materials for complexity, difficulty or balance. The *contents* categories, as Guilford points out, are often similar to student interests (visual, figural, semantic, symbolic) or preferred learning modes and can be related to types of media. In Guilford's classification, each cell formed by the model represents an intellectual ability defined by these three dimensions.

GUILFORD'S STRUCTURE OF INTELLECT MODEL

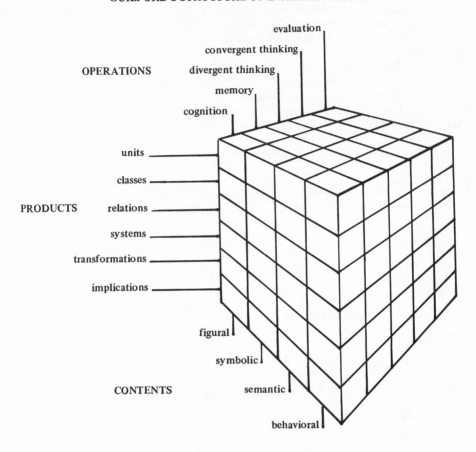

Contents categories are:

- figural (perceived, subdivided on sensory lines)
- symbolic (language and mathematics)
- semantic (imageless thoughts)
- behavioral (mental states)

For all contents, there are particular *products* (in order of increasing complexity):

- Units of information (such as a perceived visual object, printed word, concept or observed attitude)
- Classes (ideas underlying a set of similar units)
- Relations (specifiable connections between two units, such as a mirror image, fraction, antonym)

- Systems (complex relations, such as an algebraic equation, mechanical device, story plot)

- Transformations (changes of some kind, such as reversal, rearrangement, substitution, redefinition)

- Implications (one item implies another, as smoke implies fire or a smile implies a particular attitude)

Categories of learning *operations* are:

- Cognition (knowing or understanding)

- Memory (committing to memory)

- Divergent thinking (searching or scanning memory store broadly for logical alternatives to meet a need)

- Convergent thinking (searching pointedly to find an item that fulfills particular specifications)

- Evaluation (comparing and judging items of information for relevant or logical criteria)

The Structure of Intellect, or informational psychology, is a comprehensive and well-developed theory, based on what we learn (content) as well as how we learn. It uses information processing as an operational model to cover all intellectual aspects of behavior as well as psychomotor learning. The informational analogy represents Guilford's belief that we react not to the real world but to representations of that world that we construct ourselves. The SOI can therefore be used categorically to select materials for all cognitive areas and to assure that all children are given opportunities to sample or attempt all types of mental activities—to learn what they like, what they can do well or where they need help.

The SOI is also a useful model for individualization. SOI diagnostic profiles are particularly valuable in locating areas of strength in retarded children and areas of weaknesses for more capable children. In addition, it has been used extensively to diagnose intelligence. And in Japan and in the United States, at least, it has been used as a basis for developing materials. The SOI Institute in El Segundo, California (see page 138) uses the SOI model for diagnosis and for specific skill workbooks. In Japan, the Learned Society of Intelligence Education (see page 138) similarly uses the SOI model for diagnosis and has been developing instructional materials for children under 12, based on 90 of Guilford's 120 intellectual factors (excluding the 30 behavioral factors). Since September 1965 they have educated more than 1,000 children with these methods; currently they note an average IQ increase of almost 20 points per year.

Guilford's theory, like those of Piaget and Montessori, is based on research and validated by experience. One reason I prefer it to Thurstone or to Bloom's *Taxonomy* is that it includes a place for creativity within the cognitive structure through combining behavioral with cognitive factors and assigning specific categories for Divergent Thinking and Transformation.

Dr. Frank E. Williams' *Classroom Ideas for Encouraging Thinking and Feeling* (Buffalo, NY: D.O.K. Publishers, Inc., 1971) uses the Williams variation of the SOI cube to locate classroom exercises according to subject content, teaching strategy, or pupil behavior. This model was part of a National Schools Project productive thinking curriculum based on interpretations of Guilford, Torrance, Bloom and Piaget. I used it as an analytic device to select materials for gifted students, looking for well-reviewed materials that included at least two curricular areas and many cognitive-affective components.

WILLIAMS' MODEL FOR IMPLEMENTING COGNITIVE-AFFECTIVE BEHAVIORS

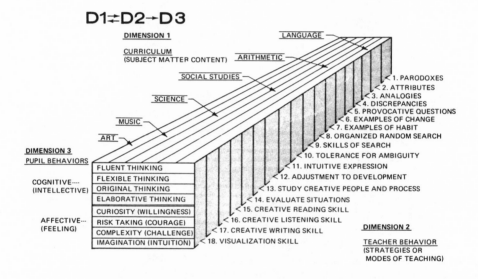

BRAIN RESEARCH

Our knowledge of left-brain and right-brain functions, derived from neurological research, provides still another viewpoint or model for considering cognitive factors in materials, one that emphasizes visual factors and creativity.

According to modern brain researchers, the two halves of our brains have slightly different functions and specialties. According to current theory, they are usually presented like this:

The Left	The Right
sequential	simultaneous
linear	spatial
analytic	synthetic
verbal processes	metaphoric
rational	intuitive
explicit	tacit
logical	holistic

The left half seems to perform the intellectual functions while the creative functions are performed by the right half. Some educators believe that curricula that concentrate on right-brain functions should also stimulate creativity (with its accompanying over-achievement).

Arthur Koestler's *Act of Creation* (New York, Dell, 1966) assembles the statements of men and women of genius who discuss the origins of their creative breakthroughs. Such geniuses as Einstein, Coleridge, Lise Meitner, Faraday and others received their breakthrough ideas not from logic but from kinesthetic or visual imagery. All of them describe intuitive leaps or discoveries which followed their immersion in the logical, factual backgrounds of problems. They returned, again, to logical processes to verify their insights and images.

Most students of creativity consider it a four-.or five-step process, involving:

- preparation (acquisition of skills, techniques and information)
- concentrated effort (to find solution or suitable form)
- withdrawal from the problem
- insight or illumination
- verification, evaluation or elaboration

In reality, of course, there is often a great deal of back-and-forth movement with changes of pace between experience and insight, involving immersion in data and requiring free access to a wide variety of materials as well as unstructured time flow within a structure of demands. Essentially, it is a process not suited to time slots except, possibly, for deadlines.

FOSTERING CREATIVITY

Though creative children—even in school situations—tend to have higher achievements than their IQ's would suggest, most school situations and most instructional materials are not well designed for fostering creativity. The atmosphere and materials should, optimally, provide for:

(List appears on page 136)

- flexibility (going beyond tradition)
- fluency (many answers or responses)
- elaboration (detailed answers)
- toleration of ambiguity (truth *and* beauty)
- originality (divergent thinking)
- breadth of interest (broad meanings and implications)
- sensitivity (to life, to oneself and to others)
- curiosity (openness to new ideas)
- independence (self-reliance and forcefulness)
- reflection (ability to consider and reconsider; implies adequate time)
- concentration and persistence
- commitment (deep involvement)
- expression of total personality
- sense of humor

In essence, creativity combines cognitive with affective and visual factors.

For creativity, a certain amount of open-endedness is necessary. Children need opportunities

- to determine questions to be answered
- to select specific facts for their solutions
- to choose an appropriate process for the solution.

Children also need experience both with problems that include unnecessary data and with those that have insufficient data. Individuals selecting materials that teach thinking and creativity should be thoughtful and creative in their search. The best or more interesting materials are not necessarily issued by educational producers. In general, trade books are apt to be more original and thoughtful than educational texts. Puzzles designed for fun are apt to be more interesting than didactic puzzles produced by educators.

Appropriate materials would be creative works in any media (open-ended, imaginative, motivating materials; quite possibly produced by students themselves). Posters, trade books, original art, blank tapes and reels, open-ended work books or task cards and carefully assembled junk are probably the cheapest materials. Libraries, toy stores and art stores are good hunting grounds for materials.

(MOSTLY) INFORMAL MATERIALS FOR COGNITIVE SKILLS

Cognitive Skills	Appropriate Materials	
Visual motor skills	mazes origami paper sculpture model cars	manipulatives stunts maps mobiles
Vocabulary development	word puzzles word games crossword puzzles guessing games creative writing materials	theater games poetry thesauri dictionaries
Verbal reasoning	similes, comparisons, metaphors outlining exercises puns charades riddle books	
Arithmetic reasoning	mental math math puzzles space puzzles	math estimation card games Monopoly
Problem solving and concentration	detective stories mysteries codes ciphers	card games task cards contract learning
Listening skills	old radio programs aural materials mental math problems oral readings games based on aural clues	
Visual discrimination	space puzzles junk art projects automobile identification games based on visual clues	

CLASSROOM CHECKLIST FOR
INTELLECTUAL SKILLS AND CREATIVE TRAITS

Intellectual skills and creative traits should be simultaneously fostered by teaching approaches, educational goals and objectives, school assignments and related tests as well as by appropriate curricular materials.

Directions: Note whether your materials, approaches, etc., *encourage, allow*, or *discourage* these traits and processes.

TRAITS AND PROCESSES	TEACHING APPROACH	CURRICULAR MATERIALS	SPECIFIC OBJECTIVES	ASSIGNMENTS	TESTS
Active learning manipulation					
Perception					
Concentration					
Application					
Extrapolation					
Analysis					
Contrast and comparison					
Generalization					
Definition					
Evaluation					
Visualization					
Verbalization					
Quantification					
Sensitivity to problems					
Flexibility					
Fluency					
Originality					
Self-instruction					

KEY ORGANIZATIONS

Learned Society of Intelligence Education
5-22-2 Sendayaya, Shibuya-ku, Tokyo
Japan   (03) 352-4321

The Learned Society (founded in 1972) is an outgrowth of the Research Institute of Education for Brilliant Children, founded by Professor Takeya Fushumi in July 1965. Both employ Guilford's model of intelligence. The purpose of the Society is to collect and perform research on education for development of intelligence, to prepare curricula on education for intelligence and to train researchers and instructors in this area.

It has designed its own tests—most recently the Chiken Diagnostic Method for Developmental Structure of Intelligence: Individual Intelligence Scale for All Contents. Its course for stimulating intelligence factors for children under 12 is a

26-month course which stimulates one factor twice each week, so that 40 intelligence factors are covered each year and 90 are covered in the complete course. A small-scale correspondence course is available.

SOI Institute
214 Main Street
El Segundo, CA 90245   (213) 322-5995
        The SOI focuses on intellectual abilities needed for learning rather than on subject matter, using Guilford's and Piaget's theories in its diagnostic and curricular materials.
        Its SOI Learning Abilities Test measures separate intellectual abilities rather than general intelligence. It assesses strengths and weaknesses in 24 separate abilities including those essential for reading, mathematics and creativity. It also uses templates to make curriculum prescriptions on the basis of IQ tests converted to SOI abilities. Its curriculum materials are similarly based on SOI abilities, and can be prescribed through individual profiles.
        Dr. Mary Meeker, who heads the Institute, has designed a classification to describe characteristics of normal children.

Synectics Education System (SES)
121 Brattel St.
Cambridge, MA 02138   (617) 868-5747
        SES is a private educational publishing house founded by William J. J. Gordon, creator of synectics and also author of *Making It Strange and Familiar*. Gordon's synectic theory of creativity is based on associational psychology, with an emphasis on metaphorical association.
        Gordon himself is a formidably creative individual who has achieved a long string of patents, an equally long list of educational publications and a few awards for creative fiction.
        SES sells publications almost exclusively on synectics, and provides workshops on the SES approach to learning and problem solving.

COGNITIVELY ORIENTED CURRICULA AND MATERIALS

        These are samples of a few intentional cognitive curricula. Other curricula concerned with thinking skills can be selected through indexes (such as those of NICSEM and NCEMMH) listed in the Special Education chapter (see page 293ff) and through some of the computer indexes treated in Commercial Retrieval Systems (see page 326ff). Computers are excellent for logic and linear analysis.

Classroom Ideas for Encouraging Thinking and Feeling, by Frank E. Williams.
        Buffalo, NY, D.O.K. Publications, 1971. $7.50. (From 71 Radcliff Rd.,
        Buffalo, NY 14214.)
        Categorizes 387 classroom ideas by subject matter and learning strategies. Designed to encourage fluent thinking, flexible thinking, original thinking and elaborate thinking, as well as curiosity, risk-taking, complexity in general thinking and emergent feeling, and imagination. A highly stimulating book that teachers can use to design and extend their own programs.

Cognitive Learning and Instruction (Teaching 2), by Wesley C. Becker and Don R. Thomas. Palo Alto, CA, Science Research Associates, 1975. 306p. $7.95. (Instructor's Guide $2.00).

This practical book for teachers provides a basis for understanding cognitive development and how to facilitate it.

Damn the School System: Full Speed Ahead!, by Vearl G. McBride. Jericho, NY, Exposition Press, 1973. 160p. $6.00.

This book, recommended by Sexton and Poling, provides methods for training for rapid reading Braille and print, spelling mastery, and rapid arithmetic, with specific classroom teaching hints interspersed with denunciations of our current teaching system.

Deal Me In! The Use of Card Games as Learning Tools, by Margie Golick. New York, Norton Publishers, 1973. 100p. $6.95.

This book is by a psychologist in a hospital learning center who finds that card games are invaluable in developing motor skills, rhythm, sequence, a sense of direction and number concepts, as well as verbal, visual, intellectual and social skills. "In these 52 pieces of pasteboard are innumerable opportunities for developing manual dexterity, visual efficiency, concepts of time, space and number, principles of sorting and grouping, and the forethought, logic, planning ability and mental alertness needed to handle many intellectual tasks." This book includes a convincing introduction plus the rules and learning benefits of 80 card games, which are tabulated according to the skills they teach.

Making It Strange Series, by William J. J. Gordon and T. Poze. Evanston, IL, Harper and Row, 1968. $6.75 each; $3.75 each for more than 5.

This series of workbooks was designed for children in grades three to six, with open-ended exercises to increase students' creative writing skills. They are based on synectics theory of connections.

Mind & Math Cassette Kits. $26.95 for 4 cassette sets, $59.25 for 10.

(From Educational Resource Associates, Box 415, Glennville, CA 93226.)

These cassette sets provide experience with mental math for all grades from two to adult. The program is designed to build students' confidence in their own abilities to do math mentally, starting with math fundamentals and progressing to problems with fractions, decimals and percentages.

Each problem is heard only once, requiring complete attention and concentration. This concentrated effort is intended to help extend mental keenness and agility to all areas of thinking.

Productive Thinking Program, by Richard S. Crutchfield and Martin V. Covington, et al. 2nd ed. New York, Merrill, 1977. 15v. $150.00 set.

This program is carefully designed to develop and reinforce higher-order problem-solving skills and strategies in children. The materials, separate books of about 150 pages each, include mysteries in comic-book format to be solved by and with the main characters (two children and their uncle). Self-administered lessons last about one hour each.

Skills in this program include: problem recognition and formulation, organization of information, idea generation, testing of hypotheses, and positive affect towards thinking and problem solving.

Solve It: A Basic Approach to Problem-Solving, by Thomas C. O'Brien. 5 books. $5.25 each; $24.75 set. (From Educational Teaching Aids, 159 West Kinzie St., Chicago, IL 60610.)

Each of these books includes about 100 pages of classroom-tested problems for grades four to eight, which can be solved variously by individuals, small groups, or the whole class. Some are open-ended; others are based on real-life situations; most emphasize the process of thinking more than correct answers.

The Strange and Familiar Series, by William J. J. Gordon and T. Poze. Cambridge, MA, Porpoise Books, 1976. $6.75 each; $3.75 each for more than 5.

These workbooks contain exercises in science, social studies, hypothesis formation, and values clarification. Students using these workbooks learn how to make their own connections and how to use these connections to express their understandings. Visual aids, like the printed materials, are both strange and familiar.

The Thinking Book, edited by Susan Dalziel. Cortland, NY, Project Change, State University of New York, 1973. 84p. $4.50. (From Cortland, NY 13045.)

Games, materials and activities focuses on thinking, emphasizing teacher-made materials based on scrounged and recycled items classified by Piaget concepts. This booklet is based on the creative collective thinking of participants in the Summer Institute of Open Education, 1973. Includes some traditional thinking games, ways to vary games and a bibliography of related sources.

Activities deal with attributes, matrix puzzles, sender-receiver games, seriation, probability, spatial transformation, senses, visual thinking, numerical progressions, classification, patterning, estimation, matching, sending and receiving, and conservation.

Workjobs: Activity-Centered Learning for Early Childhood Education, by Mary Baratta Lorton. Menlo Park, CA, Addison-Wesley, 1972. 255p. $7.00.

Conceptually organized activities for early childhood education use inexpensive, readily-available materials to develop skills in perception, matching, classification, sounds and letters, and mathematical skills involving sets, number sequences, combining and separating, and relationships. All are clearly presented and illustrated with photographs. It includes an afterword explaining the concepts of activity-centered learning and is well indexed for accessibility.

FOR FURTHER READING

This is an extremely short list of materials for a complex topic, and leans heavily on simple, clear expositions rather than original reports or research.

*Items marked with an asterisk include criteria.
+Items marked with a plus have substantial lists of references.

Adams, James L. *Conceptual Blockbusting: A Guide to Better Ideas.* San Francisco, W. H. Freeman, 1974.

Aschner, Mary Jane, and Charles E. Bish. *Productive Thinking in Education.* Washington, National Education Association, 1968.

+Beyer, Barry K., and Anthony N. Penna, eds. *Concepts in the Social Studies.* Washington, National Council for the Social Studies, 1971. (Bulletin 45.) Very thoughtful discussion of the what, how and why of teaching concepts.

Bloom, Benjamin S. *Taxonomy of Educational Objectives: Cognitive Domain.* New York, David McKay, 1956.

Bruner, Jerome S. *Toward a Theory of Instruction.* Cambridge, MA, Harvard University Press, 1966.

Charles, C. M. *Teacher's Petit Piaget.* Belmont, CA, Fearon, 1974. This concise key to Piagetian theory includes two interesting appendixes: "Children's Ideas about Causes" and "Mental Readiness for Arithmetic."

Covington, M. V. "Some Experimental Evidence on Teaching for Creative Understanding," *The Reading Teacher*, vol. 20, no. 5 (Feb. 1967), pp. 390-96.

Dale, Edgar. *The Good Mind.* Bloomington, IN, Phi Delta Kappa Educational Foundation, 1978. (Fastback 105.)

Eberle, Bob. "Problem-Solving Modes of Classroom Instruction," *Educational Leadership*, vol. 30, no. 8 (May 1973), pp. 726-28.

Formanek, Ruth. *Charting Intellectual Development: A Practical Guide to Piagetian Tasks.* Springfield, IL, C. C. Thomas, 1976.

Gordon, William J. J. "Some Source Material in Discovery by Analogy," *Journal of Creative Behavior*, vol. 8, no. 4 (Fall 1974), pp. 239-57.

Grady, Michael P., and Emily A. Luecke. *Education and the Brain.* Bloomington, IN, Phi Delta Kappa Educational Foundation, 1978. (Fastback 108.)

Guilford, J. P. "Education with an Informational Psychology," *Education*, vol. 98, no. 1 (Fall 1977), pp. 3-16.

Harrison, Alton. *Cognitive Learning in Children: Theories and Strategies.* New York, Academic Press, 1976.

Inhelder, G., and J. Piaget. *The Growth of Thinking from Childhood to Adolescence.* New York, Basic Books, 1958.

Kagan, J. "Impulsive and Reflective Children . . . Significance of Conceptual Tempo," in *Learning and the Educational Process*, by J. D. Krumbottz. Chicago, Rand McNally, 1965.

Koestler, Arthur. *Act of Creation.* New York, Dell, 1966.

*+Kurfman, Dana G., ed. *Developing Decision-Making Skills.* Arlington, VA, National Council for the Social Studies, 1977. (47th Yearbook.) Includes evaluation charts and many references.

Montessori, Maria. *The Montessori Elementary Material.* New York, Schocken, 1973.

Montessori, Maria. *The Montessori Method: Education of Children from Three to Six.* New York, Bentley, 1964.

Montessori, Maria. *Spontaneous Activity in Education.* New York, Schocken, 1965.

Piaget, Jean. *The Origins of Intelligence in Children.* New York, International Universities Press, 1966.

Piaget, Jean. *The Psychology of Intelligence.* Totowa, NJ, Littlefield, 1976. (Reprint of 1969.)

Polya, George. "On Learning, Teaching, and Learning Teaching," *American Mathematical Monthly*, vol. 70, no. 6 (June-July 1963), pp. 605-619.

Rubin, Louis J., ed. *Life Skills in Schools and Society.* Washington, Association for Supervision and Curriculum Development, 1969.

Scriven, Michael. *Reasoning.* New York, McGraw-Hill, 1976.

+Sexton, Thomas G., and Donald R. Poling. *Can Intelligence Be Taught?* Bloomington, IN, Phi Delta Kappa Educational Foundation, 1973. (Fastback 29.)

Suydam, Marilyn. *Classroom Ideas from Research on Computational Skills.* National Council of Teachers of Mathematics, 1976.

Webb, J. N. "Taxonomy of Cognitive Behavior," *Journal of Research and Development in Education*, vol. 4, no. 1 (Fall 1970), pp. 23-33.

Winter, David G., A. J. Stewart, and D. C. McClelland. "Grading the Effects of a Liberal Education," *Psychology Today*, vol. 12, no. 4 (Sept. 1978), pp. 68-73.

APPRAISING MATERIALS FOR READABILITY

"Word lists must be based on the vocabularies of children."
    —Dale Johnson

"Readability formulas are perhaps more comparable to probability statements than to scientific formulas."
    —Mary Monteith

■ ■ ■

Since written materials need to be read and comprehended to serve their educational functions, educators selecting instructional materials are naturally concerned with the readability of written materials they are examining. This chapter covers outlines of reading behaviors, readability formulas, vocabulary lists and other common means of determining the readability and/or reading level of instructional materials, as well as some means of evaluating the accuracy and applicability of the tools themselves.

INFORMATION SOURCES ON READABILITY

For text books and similar materials, reading level is generally provided or assigned in publishers' descriptions. Many librarians' catalogs also supply this information. Similarly, most distributors and wholesalers (87 percent) supply reading-level or grade-level figures for media materials and trade books in their catalogs. According to AASL's (*Survey of Marketing, Selection, and Acquisition of Materials*, see pages 28-29), 20 out of 46 catalogs examined included information on reading levels; 23 out of 46 (exactly one-half) included information on grade level, a related though not identical concept. These reading or grade levels may be assigned on the basis of guesswork, intuition or subjective judgment; more often they are determined through one or another readability formula. (Dale-Chall is popular with educators; Spache with librarians.) The reading levels of some textbooks are still determined through vocabulary control based on more or less obsolete or valid vocabulary lists.

Increasingly, librarians' catalogs, like the *Elementary School Library Collection*, include readability, according to a formula, along with their usual interest-maturity placement. The latter may be the more valuable of the two, but the combination is good. Generally, librarians' catalogs describe which formulas they use and why.

Though such reading formulas and vocabulary lists tend to assign a satisfyingly specific single number to grade levels, such figures in themselves may not be valid (though they do correlate fairly well with each other). They are also no indication that students at this particular grade level will find these materials comprehensible and/or interesting and worth reading. Reading formulas do serve as an index of vocabulary difficulty and sentence length—two factors that affect but do not determine readability. Vocabulary lists, at best, are an indication of word familiarity or frequency, generally not word comprehension. Many who research these formulas and measures question how well they succeed in predicting who will be able to understand which particular written works.

WORD LISTS

Around the turn of the century—in the era of John Dewey—studies of readability stressed the importance of meaning vocabulary, that is, word and concept identification. Subsequently research moved out to qualitative and quantitative studies attempting to identify both specific words used by specific groups and the kinds and numbers of words that children and adults might be expected to know at different stages of maturity. It was a short step from these studies to vocabulary lists specifying and assigning (often widely different) levels of difficulty to particular words according to their usage or, more often, their frequency of use.

In the twenties, thirties and forties, when word lists flourished, they were used to study the growth of children's vocabularies, as a source of curricula (assigning words to be learned) and as a means of analyzing passages for difficulty. Though these lists were often accused of lacking broadness and validity, they were widely used by authors and textbook publishers to determine the vocabulary of grade level textbooks.

There is and was an incestuous and self-perpetuating quality to these lists, especially lists compiled from textbooks (like basal readers) which were originally composed on the basis of words supplied by earlier vocabulary lists derived from previous textbooks. Even though creative geniuses like Dr. Seuss are able to create worthwhile publications with limited vocabularies, such restricted vocabularies have, overall, imparted a repetitive, unappealing quality to textbooks (especially elementary textbooks). This tends to create inattention and boredom rather than comprehension. Certainly, as old lists—of dubious validity—are perpetuated in new texts, they move further away from meaningful contact with children's lives outside classrooms.

Vocabulary lists are most valuable when they are based on words in children's current speaking and listening (including television and radio) vocabularies, and when the reading vocabularies are chosen from children's magazines, popular library books or trade books rather than school texts.

With today's computer technology, it is relatively painless to compile lists of words and to tabulate their frequency. Too often, however, computer-created lists fail to include definitions of meaning for the terms listed "in order of frequency." Since English is, notoriously, a language of homonyms, slang and ambiguity, we cannot tell from such lists even in what senses simple words like "run" or "saw" are most commonly used. These ambiguities and double meanings may often be sources of miscomprehension of seemingly innocuous, common words. For instance, several detailed studies of the old (1921 and 1931) Thorndike lists indicated that students often had more difficulties with non-technical terms on the list than with scientific terms excluded from the lists.

Since spoken vocabulary from television is less easily searched by computer, current computer-created word lists are probably not fair samples of terms that today's youngsters hear most frequently. Such lists often do not distinguish between words that are merely recognized (that is, students have heard or seen them before) and those whose meaning and usage is fully understood. Even if such lists are accurate and represent a fair national cross section, they still may not be well chosen for children in a particular school, in a particular place, in a particular time.

READABILITY FORMULAS

Readability formulas are considered more modern, though they, too, date back to the 1920s. Over the years they have been a persistent educational enterprise. Reviewers have noted the creation of about 30 predictive formulas in the last 45 years. Spache, Lorge and Dale-Chall are among the most used today. Those that correlate word difficulty with inclusion on a specified word list are extensions of the old vocabulary lists.

The Dale-Chall formula, for instance, considered one of the more valid lists, uses Dale's 2,000-word list to ascertain difficulty of words encountered in reading passages. Others attempt to measure difficulty of words through the number of syllables or the number of letters, whether a word is abstract or concrete, or whether it is a (noun or verb) content word. Sentence complexity may be measured simply by the number of words, the number of clauses and prepositional phrases, the kind and number of punctuation marks, and/or by other means.

The related concept of idea density is similarly measured by the proportion of nouns and verbs, or abstract versus concrete words and phrases. Even interest may be measured by the number of personal pronouns(!).

To estimate readability, passages (of different lengths, depending upon formula) are analyzed, coded and then manipulated to produce a single figure that is supposed to represent grade-level placement. Of necessity, these formulas omit less tangible factors that make for clarity, comprehensiveness or memorability—such things as accurate vocabulary, sentence rhythm, overall organization, typography, concept development, logical sequence, fuzzy language, precision, etc. They can provide a starting place for the analysis of language, but overall may be more valuable for educators preparing professional papers than for those appraising the readability or intelligibility of materials for students.

Fry's Readability Graph

Edward B. Fry's readability graph is a simplified readability formula often found attached to district selection policies. In essence, it is a do-it-yourself model that determines grade level by plotting the number of sentences in 100 words against the number of syllables in 100 words and finding their spot on Fry's readability graph. (Three representative passages of 100 words each are recommended per book.) Despite its simplistic nature, Fry's figures correlate relatively well with those supplied by more complex and seemingly rational formulas. It is popular with librarians and classroom teachers who want to test the readability of unlabeled instructional materials. It can, in a pinch, be done by upper elementary students.

It may, however, be just as easy to ask representative students to read these representative passages and comment on their difficulties and problems, to underline or circle words they do not know or are unsure of. Fry himself suggests that students can probably handle passages if they do not meet more than one unfamiliar word in 20 words. One old educational standard is "no more than two new words per page." Librarians tend to accept five new words per page—in books that children *want* to read.

Cloze Procedure

The cloze procedure, developed by Wilson Taylor in 1953, is another rather simple do-it-yourself procedure involving students, who are asked to fill in or complete a passage in which every fifth word has been deleted. The percentage of items correctly "clozed" by the students is compared to a criterion scale. Essentially, this measure is a test of idea density or comprehension and is recommended for concept materials like science and social studies. "Maze," a modification of cloze, is recommended for elementary materials.

Difficulty and Maturity Levels

Another approach is that of the Center for Children's Books in Chicago, which assigns a difficulty level based on a thorough reading of the book, considering such factors as:

- length and complexity of sentences
- kinds of words used
- difficulties of concepts and ideas
- clarity of presentation of concepts and ideas
- organization of materials

They feel this rather subjective grading is usually more satisfactory than readability formulas which basically test only sentence length and familiarity of individual words. At the easy-book level, the Center uses a combination of the Spache formula and the Stone Word List.

Maturity levels, also assigned to books, are based on a combination of difficulty and interest. A book listed as fourth-to-seventh grades, for instance, would be interesting to children in all these grades, though it might be difficult for children in fourth grade, easy for those in sixth and seventh grades, and just right for a fifth grader. Despite the difficulty, younger children might want to read this book because of its popularity or interest.

Of the formulas, Spache and Lorge tend to be favored by librarians and Dale-Chall by educators, while Fry and Cloze are used for convenience by both. The Swinburne Readability Laboratories in East Norwich, New York, use Spache formula for primary grades (ages six to eight) and the Dale-Chall formula for grades four and up (over age nine). Other formulas also have their adherents.

The informed opinion of librarians seems to test out rather well as a criterion of readability. Their consensus has been rather consistent in cross-country checks, more consistent than that of teachers (whose classes, of course, might differ considerably for the same grade).

Since children, particularly at the upper grade levels, have widely different abilities even within the same classroom, a single grade level figure might, in reality, be less accurate than a placement-range figure that considers children's interests in assigning levels.

STUDYING COMPREHENSION

A rather lengthy approach to the attempt to assay readability is to review materials against the processes thought to be involved in reading comprehension (using the concepts of one's choice).

Theodore Clymer does an excellent job of presenting several important concepts of reading and reading comprehension in "What Is Reading?: Some Current Concepts," in *Innovation and Change in Reading Instruction* (Part II of the 67th *Yearbook of the National Society for the Study of Education*). In this article Clymer summarizes the concepts of Ruth Strang, J. P. Guilford, George D. Spache, Lee Deighton, Constance McCullough, Donald Cleland, William S. Gray and Helen M. Robinson, among others.

Thomas Barrett's interesting Taxonomy of Reading Comprehension is one concept reprinted here. This taxonomy, based to a large extent on Bloom's *Taxonomy*, includes cognitive and affective aspects and could be a workable taxonomy for selection. The full taxonomy, with commentary, is presented on pages 19-23 of the 67th *Yearbook*.

BARRETT TAXONOMY OF READING COMPREHENSION

Literal Comprehension

- Recognition
  of details
  of main ideas
  of a sequence
  of comparisons
  of cause and effect relationships
  of character traits

- Recall
  of details
  of main ideas
  of a sequence
  of comparisons
  of cause and effect relationships
  of character traits

Reorganization

- classifying
- outlining
- summarizing
- synthesizing

(Continued on page 149)

BARRETT TAXONOMY OF READING COMPREHENSION (cont'd)

Inferential Comprehension

- inferring supporting details
- inferring main ideas
- inferring sequence
- inferring comparisons
- inferring cause and effect relationships
- inferring character traits
- predicting outcomes
- interpreting figurative language

Evaluation

- judgments of reality or fantasy
- judgments of fact or opinion
- judgments of adequacy or validity
- judgments of appropriateness
- judgments of worth, desirability and acceptability

Appreciation

- emotional response to the content
- identification with characters or incidents
- reactions to author's use of language
- imagery

In *Toward Better Reading* (Champaign, IL, Garrard Publishing Co., 1963), George D. Spache demonstrated a method of applying Guilford's Structure of Intellect Model (see page 132) to reading behavior. His model (shown on page 150), while not a selection device, does provide an inclusive view of processes and behaviors that take place in reading comprehension, and suggests appropriate questions and exercises to determine comprehension.

In *Good Reading for Poor Readers*, also published by Garrard (Springfield, IL, 1974), Spache discusses the readability of instructional materials in relation to children's reading abilities, as determined by his and other reading formulas.

In "Research in Comprehension in Reading" (*Reading Research Quarterly*, vol. 3, no. 4, pp. 499-545), F. B. Davis presents still another outline of the discrete processes involved in reading. According to Davis, these include:

- recalling word meaning

- understanding concepts and questions explicit or implicit in the content

- integrating ("weaving together" ideas in the content)

- drawing inferences from the content

- recognizing purpose, attitude, tone and mood

Even the best readability formulas and vocabulary lists cannot indicate whether books are sufficiently well written to aid these processes. Educators and librarians, attempting to determine the true readability of materials need detailed stylistic analysis and/or some forms of student feedback for a more accurate appraisal of comprehensibility. Ideally the student input should be as near as possible to point of use and selection.

PROCESSES AND BEHAVIORS IN READING COMPREHENSION

(Reprinted by permission of George D. Spache and Garrard Publishing Co.)

	UNIT	CLASS	RELATIONS	SYSTEMS	TRANS-FORMATIONS	IMPLICATIONS
Cognition (recognition of information)	Recognition that word has meaning	Recognition of sentence as complete thought	Recognition of paragraph meaning (literal idea of paragraph)	Recognition of types of relationships within structure of paragraph	Underline key words of paragraph	Recognize that there are implications in author's main idea
Memory (retention of information)	Recall specific word meanings	Recall of thoughts of sentence (reverberations)	Comprehend main idea as summation of sentences (reverberation)	Summarize facts of paragraph in own words with due attention to structure	Combine recall with own associations	Choose possible implications from given alternates
Divergent Production (logical, creative ideas)	Meaning from context by inference	Selecting implied meaning of sentence	Choosing implied main idea	Analyze author's reasons for structure	Construct rebus of paragraph: offer new titles for paragraph	Amplify author's implications and ideas in free association
Convergent Production (conclusions, inductive thinking)	Meaning from structure of context, (i.e., appositive sentence)	Combining ideas into literal meaning of sentence	Evolving main idea as extension of topic sentence	Categorize structure of paragraph; outline it	Choose among alternate titles or statements of main idea	Suggest future applications of author's ideas
Evaluation (critical thinking)	Acceptance or rejection of author's diction	Acceptance or rejection of meaning of sentence, as fact-opinion	Acceptance or rejection of main idea as fact or opinion; check author's sources; compare with own experiences and beliefs	Look for fallacies in logic, appeals to reader's emotions, overgeneralizations, omissions, distortions	Identify author's viewpoint and purpose; compare with other viewpoints; explore the ultimate outcomes of acceptance of author's viewpoint	Check author's background as basis for viewpoint; react to author's value judgments; examine author's basic assumptions and inferences from these

One book that is very helpful in pointing out the range of reading difficulties in different content areas is James Laffey's *Reading in the Content Areas*, an IRA monograph, which summarizes reading research for each of the content areas and points out problems apt to be encountered in each. I would strongly recommend that selectors review appropriate chapters of this book sometime in the course of selection.

KEY PUBLICATIONS

Fry Readability Scale, by Edward B. Fry. Providence, RI, Jamestown Publishers, 1978. slide-rule. $2.00 + $0.25 handling charge. (From Dept. EY-9, P.O. Box 6734, Providence, RI 02940.)

This extended scale version of the Fry readability formula is a convenient device to use in applying the Fry formula. When sentence length and syllable count are aligned on the scale, the grade level appears in the window.

An Introduction to the Cloze Procedure, compiled by Richard D. Robinson. Newark, DE, International Reading Association, 1972. 12p. $0.75; $0.50 for members.

This annotated bibliography covers cloze as a measure of readability and as a teaching strategy.

Reading in the Content Areas, edited by James L. Laffey. Newark, DE, International Reading Association, 1972. 236p. $6.00pa.; $4.00 for members.

Reviews, analyzes and synthesizes the findings of two decades of research on reading in the content areas, including literature, mathematics, the sciences, social studies and mass media. The discussions for each area are quite pertinent to selection; they include appraisals of difficulties students have and problems likely to be encountered in, say, understanding poetry or mathematics problems, etc., and with the vocabulary, study or reading skills most needed for particular content areas. It can help selectors focus their attention on parts of texts (or other materials) that need to be scrutinized carefully in each subject area.

FOR FURTHER READING

*Items marked with an asterisk include criteria.
+Items marked with a plus have substantial lists of references.

+Calhane, J. W. "Cloze Procedures and Comprehension," *Reading Teacher*, v. 23, no. 5 (Feb. 1970), pp. 410-13.

*+Chall, Jeanne S. *Readability: An Appraisal of Research and Applications.* Columbus, OH, Ohio State University, 1958. (Bureau of Educational Research Monograph B4.)

Clymer, Theodore. "What Is Reading?: Some Current Concepts," pp. 11ff. in *Innovation and Change in Reading Instruction*, Part II of 67th *Yearbook of the National Society for the Study of Education* (Chicago, NSSE, 1968).

*Dale, Edgar, and Jeanne S. Chall. "A Formula for Predicting Readability," *Educational Research Bulletin*, v. 27, no. 1 (Jan. 21, 1948), pp. 11-20, 28.

+Davis, F. B. "Research in Comprehension in Reading," *Reading Research Quarterly*, v. 3, no. 4 (Summer 1968), pp. 499-545.

+De Rocher, James, et al. *The Counting of Words: A Review . . . with Annotated Bibliography.* New York, Syracuse University Research Corp., 1973. (ED 098 814).

*Flesch, Rudolph. *How to Test Readability.* New York, Harper and Brothers, 1951.

*Fry, Edward B. "A Readability Graph for Librarians, Part I," *School Libraries*, v. 19, no. 1 (Fall 1969), pp. 13-16.

+Gilliland, John. *Readability.* Newark, DE, International Reading Association, 1972.
Reviews published research on practical implications of readability.

Griffin, Peg, ed. *Assessing Comprehension in a School Setting.* Arlington, VA, Center for Applied Linguistics, 1978.
Considers the relevance of ongoing activities of children and teachers to comprehension.

Guilford, Joy P. "Frontiers in Thinking That Teachers Should Know About," *Reading Teacher*, v. 13, no. 5 (Feb. 1960), pp. 176-82.

Guilford, Joy P. "Three Faces of Intellect," *American Psychologist*, v. 14, no. 8 (August 1959), pp. 469-79.

*Johnson, Dale D. "A Basic Vocabulary for Beginning Reading," *Elementary School Journal*, v. 72, no. 11 (Oct. 1971), pp. 29-34.

Johnson, Dale D. "Word Lists That Make Sense—And Those That Don't," *Learning Magazine*, v. 4, no. 3 (Nov. 1975), pp. 60-61.

*Klare, George R. "Assessing Readability," *Reading Research Quarterly*, v. 10, no. 1 (1974-5), pp. 62-102.

Laubach, Robert S., and Kay Koschnick. *Using Readability: Formulas for Easy Adult Materials.* Syracuse, NY, New Readers Press, 1977.

+Monteith, Mary K. "Readability Formulas," *Journal of Reading*, v. 19, no. 7 (April 1976), pp. 604-607.

+Monteith, Mary K. "A Whole Word List Catalog," *Reading Teacher*, v. 29, no. 8 (May 1976), pp. 844-47.

+Seels, Barbara, and Edgar Dale. *Readability and Reading: An Annotated Bibliography.* Newark, DE, International Reading Association, 1971. (ED 075 759).

Spache, George D. *Toward Better Reading.* Champaign, IL, Garrard Publishing Co., 1963.

Wanat, Stanley, ed. *Language and Reading Comprehension.* Arlington, VA, Center for Applied Linguistics, 1977.

FAIRNESS AND BIAS

"Let your heart feel for the affliction and distress of everyone."
—George Washington

"Guideline 17
    Materials should treat with fairness and balance human diversity with respect to: sex, race, handicapping conditions, ethnic heritage, age, socio-economic status, attitudes, interests, values, philosophies, religions, political preferences and social customs."
                    —Jenny Armstrong, *Minimum Guidelines Used in Consumer Information Analysis*, 1976 (reprinted on pages 82-85)

"School readers must assume their responsibility in directing the subliminal learning process to more psychologically constructive ends."
                    —Women on Words and Images, *Dick and Jane as Victims*, 1975

"Hundreds of voices are calling for our attention and demanding fair and accurate portrayal in the educational materials we prepare. Each voice supplies its own definition of fair and its own definition of accurate."
                    —Barbara Thompson Howell (Senior Vice-President, Silver Burdett)—*Presentation to New Jersey Association of School Administrators*, Atlantic City, NJ, May 12, 1977

"Textbook adoption procedures must be broadened to allow teachers to select other teaching materials, at state expense, in addition to or in lieu of textbooks from state adoption lists."
                    —Richard L. Simms, "Bias in Textbooks: Not Yet Corrected," *Phi Delta Kappan*, November 1975

"Any writer who follows anyone else's guidelines ought to be in advertising."
                    —Nat Hentoff, *School Library Journal*, November 1977

■ ■ ■

At the present time, American educational communities seem extremely well supplied with guidelines and criteria relating to racial, ethnic and sexist bias—to the point where this chapter might be redundant.

While minority groups have long had criteria and content analysis checklists for sexism and racism, such criteria are now being incorporated in state laws, constitutions and Textbook Committee guidelines; promulgated by professional organizations, teachers' groups, parents' groups and resource centers; and issued prolifically by publishers as guidance for their staff and authors. Almost all supply objective criteria that must be applied subjectively.

Despite these proliferating criteria—probably the most common in American instructional materials selection—just about every published study evaluating our instructional materials from any perspective seems to conclude that the materials examined (particularly texts) exhibit bias of one sort or another—or fail, somehow, to meet the standards set by the evaluators.

Historically a similar dichotomy pervades American schooling: our school books have had great difficulties escaping their early New England Protestant origins. In the melting-pot era, American schools, despite flaws, offered remarkable opportunities overall to native- and foreign-born, rich and poor children, using textbooks that were sometimes inspirational but often steeped in cultural, racial and religious (anti-Catholic) bias.

While individuals like Jane Addams (in 1908) and the Anti-Defamation League of B'nai B'rith (founded in 1913) attempted to promote intercultural understanding and combat discrimination in educational materials, this viewpoint had little noticeable influence on American education until the 1940s, when the Committee on the Study of Teaching Materials in Intergroup Relations of the American Council on Education published its study, *Intergroup Relations in Teaching Materials* (Washington, 1947).

This ACE study concluded that American teaching materials as they related to intergroup relations were ineffective, inadequate and—often—damaging. A 1961 follow-up study by Lloyd Marcus, *The Treatment of Minorities in Secondary School Textbooks* for the Anti-Defamation League (ADL) of B'nai B'rith, had a similar conclusion (New York, ADL, 1961). Ten years later, Michael Kane (again for the ADL) surveyed *Minorities in Textbooks: A Study of Their Treatment in Social Studies Texts* (Chicago, Quadrangle, 1970) to find, despite "uneven improvement," that a significant number of texts continued to represent a "white, Protestant, Anglo-Saxon view of America's past and present" that ignored the problems and nature of minorities. (The Council on Interracial Books for Children still has similar findings in its current assessments, though misrepresentation seems considerably less blatant.)

Since the Anti-Defamation League of B'nai B'rith has a substantial history of assessing discriminatory presentations in instructional materials—long before such assessments were fashionable—its criteria—which seem to hold up rather well—are worth presenting, if only for historic reasons. Their seven basic (essentially critiquing) criteria (compressed and over-simplified) are:

- inclusion (all relevant facts)
- validity (accuracy)
- balance (both good and bad)
- concreteness (as opposed to generalizations)
- comprehensiveness (range of characteristics)
- unity (materials presented in graspable contexts, not dissipated or diffused through texts)
- realism (honest presentations of social evils)

In the 1950s, 1960s, and 1970s, the civil rights movement, assisted by parents and committees of educators, finally succeeded in calling attention to pervasive ethnic and racial stereotypes and misrepresentations, with—for awhile—rather modest results. Faces in basic readers gradually began turning tan and darker, but the middle class ethos still prevailed in these readers, and historical treatments were superficial, at best. (Subsequently other ethnic groups demanded fair representation.)

Meanwhile, the stories in these same readers, attempting to teach Johnny to read, presented overwhelmingly boys and men leading relatively interesting lives, while women were shrouded in aprons and girls assigned the role of admirers of their adventurous older brothers.

Though Amelia Earhart had complained about the dearth of girls' adventure stories in the 1920s, and Mary Beard had documented women's role in history in the 1930s and 1940s, it was not until the late 1960s and early 1970s that feminist scholars, women's organizations and local committees of women began to research school learning materials in depth and to call attention to their findings; results were discouraging. As Allene Dietrich of the Committee to Study Sex Discrimination in the Kalamazoo Public Schools put it: "Textbooks of all content areas consistently separate people into two rigidly defined molds which provide unfair and distorted stereotyped role models for both boys and girls."

Dick and Jane as Victims (1975) was one capable, well-documented work by Women on Words and Images (WOWI) which called attention to the extent of sex stereotyping in children's readers. WOWI's *Help Wanted* (1976) and *Sexism in Foreign Language Textbooks* (1975) showed sex stereotyping to be equally pervasive in foreign-language texts and career education materials.

According to Allene Dietrich's committee in Kalamazoo, sex-role stereotyping was possibly more extensive in math and science materials where women's roles seemed limited to household shopping and making change. Groups like the Kalamazoo study group spent hundreds and thousands of hours in detailed and thoughtful analysis of texts, looking for ways to combat the misrepresentation and omission of women. They also looked actively for materials that treated women in nondemeaning ways, and they established guidelines for locating and selecting such materials.

Contents analysis found sexism in common children's encyclopedias and other reference books and—to a lesser extent—in library collections in general. At this point, individuals and groups concerned with words—English teachers and publishers—began to study the sexism inherent in the English language. Two frequently-used guidelines are the *Guidelines for Nonsexist Use of Language in NCTE Publications* prepared by the National Council of Teachers of English in 1974 and the *Guidelines for Equal Treatment of the Sexes* developed by McGraw-Hill. And in 1977 a panel for the Women's Educational Equity Communications Network even reviewed the indexing terminology of the *ERIC Thesaurus* to determine whether it was appropriate and adequate to incorporate guidance, research and programatic materials on women in education.

While the educational community gradually began to adopt some criteria for ethnic, racial and sexual slurs, the Far West Laboratory, in its *Perspectives on School Print Materials*, extended four of ADL's criteria—validity, balance, unity and realism—to four minority groups, as well as to blue collar workers, the aged, non-Christians, and followers of alternative life styles.

In 1978 the California State Board of Education, which may not be unique, adopted its own standards on age discrimination stereotypes in textbooks. As Marion Marshall of the California State Education Department put it: "Students should learn that aging is a normal part of the life cycle." These new standards require that older persons "must be suitably depicted" in educational materials and "show the social involvement, contributions and problems of all age groups, including older persons." Similar provisions on religious portrayal exist in many states.

More detailed *Guidelines for the Representation of Exceptional Persons in Educational Materials* were developed by a consortium that included the National Center on Educational Media and Materials for the Handicapped, the Council for Exceptional Children, and faculty from the University of Pittsburg. These *Guidelines* (reprinted on pages 167-69) address the problem of achieving fair, balanced and positive representations of persons with exceptionalities in educational materials— where they have certainly been excluded, though they can be found frequently enough in literature.

While the Far West Laboratory, elderly activists and advocates for the handicapped were extending the boundaries of fairness to encompass more groups, the Council on Interracial Books for Children redefined and extended its "human values" criteria to oppose all materials guilty of espousing elitism, materialism, ageism, conformism, escapism, individualism and "other negative values." In its *Bulletin* and other publications, the Council reviews both textbooks and trade books for conformity to its values. Nat Hentoff, viewing the CIBC, believes that these "slippery" guidelines promote a new kind of conformity and censorship.

To me, also, these particular guidelines seem to narrow rather than extend presentations of individuality and diversity among human attributes, values and philosophies. Guidelines that offer general directions and goals seem preferable to those that create rigid structures of their own.

While the contents analysis instruments developed using the techniques of propaganda analysis have been very useful in calling the attention of publishers and users to extensive misrepresentations and bias in existing materials, I am personally ambivalent about these lists. I find them stimulating to read but difficult to apply accurately, despite extensive experience in selection. Some, again, are more misleading than others.

Though I object to the CIBC's negative stance on individualism and escapism, its reviews of textbooks are still worth consulting for their format and, more particularly, for documenting many instances of historic misrepresentation. CIBC has several useful categories for evaluating coverage that could be applied to evaluate the treatment of any group:

- incorrect information
- no information
- omits this period
- limited information
- full information

Since texts are, in most cases, mandatory reading, they should probably be closely scrutinized for accuracy and full representation in history and social studies. Similarly, it seems unfair that stories in our elementary readers have three males to one female. Again, textbooks in science, math and career education need to move beyond the white male world in their problems, illustrations and examples.

For a fuller representation of diversity and a more accurate view of the real world, however, we must move beyond textbooks to trade books and media materials. When students have a wide range of materials we can look for balance and choice in their total exposure. We need not attempt to assure that every item is perfect. If our history texts, for example, minimize women's roles, as most do, we need not ban them if we have supplementary materials that provide insight and information on women's multifaceted role in history. If our budget reduces us to one text per course, we are being poorly educated, no matter how excellent the text.

In the aggregate, trade books and media materials provide a far greater range of the human condition than can ever be included in even the best text. Library tools and bibliographies are essential finding devices. My chapter on ethnic materials in *Media and Curriculum* provides some guides for locating accurate, high-quality materials in this area, while the chapter on the feeling domain in the same volume includes many tools to help locate moving and effective representations of such groups as women, ethnic minorities, aged and handicapped. Biographies of women or other groups can be located through biographical indexes like *Her Way* (by Mary E. Kulkin, Chicago, ALA, 1976). Even library card catalogs are useful finding devices if you start with terms like "Women" and "Japanese Americans."

There are also, increasingly, indexes to media materials in ethnic studies, women's studies and mental health—all covered elsewhere in this guide and locatable through the index. The chapter on special education (see pages 293ff) also has some sources. School or district media centers also issue their own classified, annotated bibliographies of recommended, non-stereotyped print and nonprint materials. Kalamazoo's Media Center's *200 Plus—A Framework for Non-Stereotyped Human Roles in Elementary Media Center Materials*, for example, is issued annually.

Commercial television, too, can be immensely effective. Despite their faults, the television docu-dramas of *Roots* and *Holocaust* presented the history and outcomes of prejudice far more effectively than any text I know.

The optimum approach, perhaps, would be to teach children to be aware of the extent and kind of bias and prejudice they encounter in instructional materials and real life situations.

The instruments that follow are a miniscule share of those available. The Key Publications and For Further Reading lists lead to further criteria and studies.

Many groups have prepared suitable discussion outlines and lesson plans on bias and prejudice. Four major criteria are presented in *Perspectives on School Print Materials: Ethnic, Non-Sexist and Others*, coordinated by Dr. Wayne E. Rosenoff (San Francisco, Far West Laboratory for Educational Research and Development, October 1975) (ED 114 213): *validity, balance, unity* and *realism*. These criteria have been further developed for four minority groups (native American, Mexican American, black American, Chinese American) and for blue collar workers, the aged, non-Christians, and for those with alternative life styles.

SAMPLE CRITERIA FOR FAIRNESS

Validity of Information
a. Information is accurate.
b. Stereotypes are not perpetuated.

Balance
a. A set of values in one culture is not described in such a way as to make them appear inferior in comparison to values in another culture.

(Criteria continue on page 158)

Balance (cont'd)

b. The distinctive cultural characteristics of an ethnic group or groups are presented in a positive and comprehensive manner.
c. Members of an ethnic group are shown as engaged in a broad range of social and professional activities, and the contributions of many elements within the group are included (e.g., most or all Chicanos are not portrayed as blue-collar or migrant workers).
d. The text acknowledges the existence of different social classes and values within the ethnic group (e.g., it is made clear that a particular individual or community presented in the text does not necessarily represent all others of the group).

Unity

a. All points of view concerning historical events or issues are included (e.g., is only the Anglo point of view emphasized? Other points of view should be emphasized as well).
b. The text presents the full range of events when discussing historical events.
c. The text includes the contribution and involvement of the ethnic group(s) at all points where it is appropriate and meaningful to do so.

Realism

a. Erroneous impressions are not created by citing selected facts and omitting others about an ethnic group.
b. Individuals and groups are portrayed in true-to-life fashion.
c. The language of the text, its tone, and its illustrations (if any) combine to give an overall impression of recognizable people.
d. The text does not provide woodenly literal or stilted translations.

The School Division of the Committee on Social Issues of the Association of American Publishers has also provided educators with general guidelines for evaluating bias in content, illustrations and language. The AAP guidelines—like all of the criteria discussed or presented in this chapter—are readily available. They were first issued in *Statement on Bias-Free Materials* (1976) and are available from the AAP office.

AAP GUIDELINES
(Reprinted by permission)

CONTENT: Individuals of all ages and ethnic groups have much to gain from the elimination of stereotypes. Bias-free educational materials more accurately represent reality, encourage tolerance for individual differences, and allow more freedom for children to discover and express their needs, interests, and abilities.

Specifically, bias-free educational materials are those that:

* represent different groups of people in varied activities and vocations, including positions of leadership, and show children aspiring to a variety of careers.
* represent fairly and accurately the historic and current achievements of people, especially women and members of minorities, and include a fair proportion of materials about, and written or executed by, women and minority people.
* use material that honestly conveys the exploitation of people and the real hardships imposed on people through such exploitation.
* depict all men and women as having the full range of human emotions and behavior, and finding for themselves attributes that lead to self-esteem and success.
* represent minority and majority groups in varied communities—urban, suburban, and rural; and all ranges of socio-economic levels.

ILLUSTRATIONS: Illustrations in educational materials, by virtue of their visual immediacy, may carry an even stronger message than the text they illustrate. Pictures may leave a lasting impression about the tone of a book; the array of illustrations in a book is a strong projection of its intent.
Specifically, bias-free illustrations should:

AAP GUIDELINES (cont'd)

- reflect a fair and reasonable balance of representation with regard to race, religions, ethnic groups, age, economic levels, sex and national origin.

- provide positive role models for students of different ethnic and racial backgrounds and of both sexes.

- avoid stereotypes and caricatures of individuals and groups to offer a realistic and broad view of physical features.

- promote opportunities for placing women and minority group members in positions of prominence, leadership and centrality.

LANGUAGE: Bias-free language is language that includes all people and treats them with equal dignity and respect, whatever their race, sex, age, religion or national and ethnic origin. Bias-free language deals with people as individuals, not as members of stereotyped groups. It minimizes the cultural differences on which prejudice is often based, avoids insults and derogatory connotations, and does not trivialize or patronize, slight or slander, mock or deride whole classes of people. It is language of equal opportunity.

Specifically, bias-free language is language that:

- seeks to encompass members of both sexes by 1) avoiding the use of *man* and its derivatives to denote the average person or the human race; and 2)

designating occupations by the work performed, not only by the gender of the worker.

- avoids excluding women by the use of the generic pronoun *he* by pluralizing, shifting to *one, you,* or *we;* rephrasing to eliminate gender pronouns altogether, or balancing *he* with *she.*

- understands generic terms such as *doctor, lawyer, teacher, secretary,* and *poet,* as applying to both sexes and to all races or ethnic groups.

- uses parallel language to give equal treatment to various persons and groups through the use of equivalent terms and construction. Parallel style in names means that the style employed for one individual is used for all and does not vary depending on the sex, race, or social or marital status of the persons named. Parallelism in descriptions calls for an emphasis on pertinent information and an avoidance of role stereotypes.

- reflects our cultural diversity by including a variety of ethnic names as well as the more common Anglo-Saxon ones.

- avoids loaded words, biased connotations, and prejudiced assumptions. Particularly it expresses critical or negative judgments with words not associated with a particular race or sex, as, *an evil heart rather than a black heart, affected mannerisms rather than effeminate mannerisms.*

Similarly, the Task Force for the Evaluation of Instructional Materials, a voluntary organization of representatives from ethnic, women's and community groups, has approached the problem of bias (of all kinds) by composing general evaluation guidelines. These guidelines are reprinted below with permission from *A Guide to Text Book Evaluation* (P.O. Box 4003, Palo Alto, CA 94305, 1974).

SUGGESTED GENERAL GUIDELINES FOR THE EVALUATION OF INSTRUCTIONAL MATERIALS

OMISSIONS

1. Do the materials include the contributions and roles of both men and women, American Indians, black Americans, Mexican Americans, Asian Americans, Jews and other cultural and ethnic groups?

2. Are all socioeconomic levels and settings (urban, suburban, rural, etc.) included?

3. Is diversity in terms of religion, cultures (e.g., African and Asian as well as European), family structures, etc. included?

4. Are all the ethnic groups represented among the authors?

PORTRAYALS

1. Do the materials provide for accurate information and portrayal of the contributions and roles of the above?

2. Do the materials portray the diverse groups from a multiracial, multicultural perspective without predominant values and attitudes of one group?

(Guidelines continue on page 160)

PORTRAYALS (cont'd)

3. Do materials portray different religious orientations without being patronizing or sectarian?

4. Do content, approach and illustrations provide for factual accuracy in the presentation of root cultures and subcultures? Do they avoid Eurocentrism?

STEREOTYPES

1. Are generalizations made about the behavior, physical appearance, dress, values, customs, etc. of a group of people or sex without regard to factual accuracy?

2. Do these generalizations perpetuate stereotyping and acquisition of misinformation?

3. Are there any negative portrayals of individuals or groups from which it would be logical to conclude that the individual was representative of a whole group (either by content, approach or by virtue of the fact that a diversity of other stories or articles are not presented serving to illustrate that diversity exists in such groups or among such individuals)?

4. Could a minority child in a classroom be subject to ridicule as a result of the way in which that child's group or a member of that child's group is portrayed?

5. Is the image of diversity developed in such a way as to portray a total human being with strengths and weaknesses and an ability to respond to a contemporary (or historically appropriate time) situation, which includes multiracial, multicultural interaction?

ILLUSTRATIONS

1. Do illustrations perpetuate stereotypes and myths of various groups, etc.? Do illustrations infer obvious or subtle cultural attitudes and values, e.g., the treatment of beauty?

2. Is there only tokenism (e.g., tinting of faces rather than actual minority features)?

CHARACTERIZATIONS

1. Do the main characters help children in identifying positively with respective heritage and culture?

2. Are minority people and women portrayed as central characters or in the main roles?

3. Are there situations in which minority children are presented in settings in which caucasian children appear as well as in settings in which most of the children are minority?

4. Are there situations in which minority children and girls are shown in leadership positions in relationship to caucasian children and boys?

5. Are non-whites and women depicted in a variety of occupations including an ample number in the area of the professions?

SITUATIONS DEALING WITH PREJUDICE

1. Is it implied that being "different" is a negative attribute? The norm often used is that of trimness, caucasian, Anglo-Saxon, Christian, middle class, tall, etc. Hence, any deviation from any one or a combination of those areas would be regarded as a reason for rejection or persecution.

2. Do characters behave towards one another in a hostile, negative manner due to differences based on race, color, creed, physical appearance, handicaps, etc.? In such stories is it implied that prejudice based on color, etc., is a natural and acceptable way of behaving by omitting certain facts or not providing an adequate explanation of prejudice?

3. Are persecutors or perpetrators of prejudice held accountable for their behavior?

4. Must minority and/or female characters demonstrate extraordinary skills or talents in order to "compensate" for differences in order to be "accepted" by their non-minority and/or male peers? Is it therefore implied that in order to be "acceptable" a person of difference must possess extraordinary skills or talents?

MINORITY PEOPLE AS AMERICANS

1. Do content, approach or illustrations portray minority people as being less American or not American? (Some situations and stories imply that non-whites are not Americans, whereas whites or Europeans are. Other stories imply a degree of Americanism. For example, an Indian youngster may be introduced as an Indian and a white youngster as an American in a story. Later on, in an incidental sort of way, a statement may be made to the effect that the Indian is *also* an American.)

2. Do content, approach or illustrations provide for a distinction between root cultures (i.e., those of another country) and American subcultures? In other words, stories about Asian Americans should be included in addition to those about Asians, or Mexican Americans should be included in addition to those about Mexicans.

GREAT LITERARY WORKS

1. Some people become upset when the works of persons whom they greatly admire and respect are shown to be biased or racist. In their unwavering devotion to such writers, some people fail to acknowledge the fact that writers, too, are humans possessing the same frailties as others and subject to the prevailing sociologic forces of the time. Moreover, such "revelations" should not detract from the literary contributions such persons have made. Furthermore, it should be recognized when applicable that some such authors were ahead of their time albeit not up to measure using today's standards.

2. The questions which must be satisfactorily answered in terms of biased sexist and racist inclusions in literature are the following:

   a. Is there assurance that students will be provided with sufficient background in order that they will be able to understand the author's perspective and the historicity of the inclusion?

   b. Are the children sufficiently mature to understand the historical context of the biased or racist inclusion?

   c. How will students regard persons in the classroom or in society whose group is portrayed?

GENERAL

1. Is the color black or the concept of darkness used in a negative context? Many sociologists feel that this concept lies at the heart of racial prejudice and until people come to grips with it racial strife will exist. Are other colors such as red and yellow also used in negative stereotypic ways?

2. Are opinions stated as fact or value judgments made inappropriately?

3. Are questions asked of students regarding cultures or minority groups which could not be answered on the basis of information provided students or teacher? Such questions often result in students drawing erroneous conclusions based on insufficient information and cultural bias.

4. Are inclusions accurate when appropriate?

In general, stories, articles, and illustrations should be portrayed in a manner which will help minority children and girls develop a sense of pride in their cultural ancestry and at the same time contribute to the education of caucasian children with respect to acquiring a greater knowledge and appreciation of other races, cultures, etc.

Max Rosenberg's generalized criteria for evaluating the treatment of minorities in curriculum materials have been widely used (as far as Australia). They are reprinted with the permission of the originators—The Michigan Association for Supervision and Curriculum Development.

The November 1972 issue of *Audiovisual Instruction* (vol. 17, no. 9, pp. 21-22) has reprinted these criteria with a position paper by Dr. Max Rosenberg of the Detroit Public Schools.

ROSENBERG'S EVALUATION CRITERIA

Does this textbook or curriculum:

1. Evidence on the part of writers, artists, and editors a sensitivity to prejudice, to stereotypes, to the use of material which would be offensive to any minority group?

2. Suggest, by omission or commission, or by over-emphasis or under-emphasis, that any racial, religious, or ethnic segment of our population is more or less worthy, more or less capable, more or less important in the mainstream of American life?

3. Utilize numerous opportunities for full, fair, accurate, and balanced treatment of minority groups?

4. Provide abundant recognition of black people and other minority groups by placing them frequently in positions of leadership and centrality?

5. Depict both male and female adult members of minority groups in situations which exhibit them as fine and worthy examples of mature American types?

6. Present many instances of fully-integrated human groupings and settings to indicate equal status and non-segregated social relationships?

7. Make clearly apparent the group presentation of the individuals—Caucasian, Afro-American, Indian, Chinese, Mexican-American, etc.—and not seek to avoid identification by such means as smudging some color over Caucasian facial features?

8. Give comprehensive, broadly ranging, and well planned representation to the minority groups—in art and science, in history and literature, and in all other areas of life and culture?

9. Delineate life in contemporary urban environments as well as in rural or sub-urban environments, so that today's city child can also find significant identification for himself, his problems, and his potential for life, liberty, and the pursuit of happiness?

10. Portray racial, religious, and ethnic groups in our society in such a way as to build positive images—mutual understanding and respect, full and unqualified acceptance, and commitment to insure equal opportunity for all?

11. Present social group differences in ways that will cause students to look upon the multi-cultural character of our nation as a value which we must esteem and treasure?

12. Assist students to recognize clearly the basic similarities among all members of the human race, and the uniqueness of every single individual?

13. Teach the great lesson that we must accept each other on the basis of individual worth, regardless of race or religion or socio-economic background?

14. Help students appreciate the many important contributions to our civilization made by members of the various human groups, emphasizing that every human group has its list of achievers, thinkers, writers, artists, scientists, builders, and statesmen?

15. Supply an accurate and sound balance in the matter of historical perspective, making it perfectly clear that all racial and religious and ethnic groups have mixed heritages, which can well serve as sources of both group pride and group humility?

16. Clarify the true historical forces and conditions which in the past have operated to the disadvantage of minority groups?

17. Clarify the true contemporary forces and conditions which at present operate to the disadvantage of minority groups?

18. Analyze intergroup tension and conflict fairly, frankly, objectively, and with emphasis upon resolving our social

ROSENBERG'S EVALUATION CRITERIA (cont'd)

problems in a spirit of fully implementing democratic values and goals in order to achieve the American dream for all Americans?

19. Seek to motivate students to examine their own attitudes and behaviors, and to comprehend their own duties and responsibilities as citizens in a pluralistic democracy—to demand freedom and justice and equal opportunity for every individual and for every group?

20. Help minority group (as well as majority group) students to identify more fully with the educational process by providing textual content and illustrations which give the student many opportunities for building a more positive self-image, pride in his group, worthy models to emulate, knowledge consistent with his experience; in sum, learning material which offers the student meaningful and relevant learning worthy of his best efforts and energies?

More specific guidelines have been formulated by groups concerned with bias toward particular groups. The Resource Center on Sex Roles in Education, for instance, provides procedures for dealing with biased materials as well as criteria for materials selection. Their emphasis is on training students, teachers, administrators, parents and community groups to recognize sexist material, but their criteria are readily adaptable to the evaluation of materials for racial bias as well. The *Guidelines for the Evaluation of Print and Non-Print Materials* (1973), adopted by Kalamazoo public schools, include specific sets of criteria for both sexism and racism. (These guidelines are readily available from the Instructional Media Department, Kalamazoo Public Schools, Kalamazoo, MI 49008.) In fact, the Kalamazoo school system established a Committee to Study Sex Discrimination which composed an analysis chart for ascertaining the percentages of male- and female-oriented items in any instructional materials. My chart, below, is adapted from theirs with permission. (Once again, these evaluative materials can be easily adapted to other groups.)

PERCENTAGES OF MALE- AND FEMALE-ORIENTED ITEMS

	Male	Female
Stories	____	____
Poems	____	____
Roles in Plays	____	____
Skills Lessons	____	____
Informational Articles	____	____
Fun and Games	____	____
Supplementary Materials	____	____
Biographies	____	____
Historical Figures Mentioned	____	____
Story Illustrations, Human	____	____
Story Illustrations, Animal	____	____
Occupations	____	____
Others	____	____

Dr. Jean D. Grambs has also provided specific criteria for evaluation of treatment of the sexes in instructional materials in *Teaching about Women in the Social Studies*. This outline below is reprinted with the permission of Dr. Grambs and the National Council of Social Studies. (*Teaching about Women* is annotated on page 177.)

TREATMENT OF SEXES IN INSTRUCTIONAL MATERIALS

Criteria for the Evaluation of Instructional Materials

I. Visibility of Males and Females
    A. Male-centered episodes to female-centered episodes
    B. Male main characters to female main characters
    C. Balance of males and females in pictures
    D. Conspicuousness of males and females in pictures

II. Role Models: Male and Female
    A. Kinds of occupations in which males and females are engaged
    B. Variety and breadth of occupations for each sex
    C. Portrayal of life styles for males and females

III. Behavior
    A. Active Mastery
        1. Ingenuity, Cleverness, Creativity, Resourcefulness
        2. Perseverance, Industry, Initiative
        3. Heroism, Strength, Bravery
        4. Competitiveness and Use of Power
        5. Exploration, Mobility, Imaginative Play
        6. Autonomy, Assertiveness
        7. Friendship
        8. Morality
        9. Achievement Motivation
        10. Leadership
    B. Dependence Themes
        1. Passivity, Docility, Real and Pseudo-dependency
        2. Incompetency and Mishaps
        3. Victimization and Humiliation
        4. Fear, Insecurity
        5. Aimless Activity
        6. Expression of Emotion
        7. Goal Constriction
        8. Servitude, Pleasing

IV. Language
        1. Pronouns
        2. Occupational terms
        3. Use of man-words
        4. Demeaning language
        5. Descriptions of men and women
        6. Patronizing tone
        7. Sexist assumptions and stereotypes

V. Parallel Treatment
        1. Equivalent terms for men and women
        2. Names
        3. Titles
        4. Linking pronouns and occupations.

CHECKLIST

Go through each book you are planning to use for the points listed below.

	MALE	FEMALE
1. Number of stories where main character is:		
2. Number of illustrations of:		
3. Number of times children are shown to be—		
—in active play		
—using initiative		
—independent		
—solving problems		
—earning money		
—receiving recognition		
—inventive		
—involved in sports		
—passive		
—fearful		
—helpless		
—receiving help		
—in quiet play		
4. Number of times adults are shown—		
—in different occupations		
—playing with children		
—taking children on outings		
—teaching skills		
—giving tenderness		
—scolding children		

5. Ask these questions:

	YES	NO
—Are boys allowed to show emotion?		
—Are girls rewarded for intelligence rather than for beauty?		
—Are there any derogatory comments directed at girls in general?		
—Are mothers shown working outside the home? What kind of jobs?		
—Are there any stories about one-parent families? Families without children?		
— Are babysitters shown?		
—Are minority and ethnic groups treated naturally instead of stereotypically?		

This checklist was developed by Women on Words and Images, P.O. Box 2163, Princeton, NJ 08540. It may be reproduced without permission as long as credit is given.

The *Checklist on Sexism* of the Council on Interracial Books for Children promotes active combating against sexist materials. The criteria are reprinted below with permission from the Racism and Sexism Resource Center for Educators, a division of the CIBC (1841 Broadway, New York, NY, 10023) and are not to be reprinted further without written permission. A free catalog of materials is available from the council.

CURRICULUM	Yes, always	Sometimes	Rarely	No, never
Are instructional materials as anti-sexist as possible?	A	B	C	D
When ideal materials cannot be found, are teachers trained to detect—and to guide their students to detect—both overt and subtle manifestations of sexism?	A	B	C	D
Does a curriculum committee, composed of school professionals, parent representatives (including minority and feminist groups) and student representatives (age permitting), screen all instructional materials prior to purchase for sexist stereotyping, omissions and distortions?	A	B	C	D
If materials omit the contributions and struggles of women in our society, does the teacher supplement them with materials that provide this information?	A	B	C	D
Is literature by women authors, literature about women, and literature with women as central characters in non-stereotyped roles equally represented in the curriculum?	A	B	C	D
Do materials on classroom wall depict males and females in non-traditional non-stereotyped roles?	A	B	C	D
Is a conscious effort made to bring in outside people who counteract traditional sex roles? Female scientists, engineers, dentists and plumbers or male nurses, secretaries and house-husbands?	A	B	C	D
Does your library avoid special sections listed "especially for girls" or "especially for boys"?	A	B	C	D

And finally, believing that educational materials have failed to represent persons with exceptionalities, a Consortium for Appropriate Representation of Exceptional Persons in Educational Materials developed the following Guidelines for publishers. These guidelines are reprinted here by kind permission of the Council for Exceptional Children.

GUIDELINES

1 In print and nonprint educational materials, ten percent of the contents should include or represent children or adults with an exceptionality.

Do your educational materials reflect the fact that ten to fifteen percent of the population is composed of persons with exceptionalities?

If your materials do represent exceptional persons, have you limited the exceptionalities to deaf, blind, or physically handicapped?

Have any of your materials included the following conditions?

Behavioral Problems
Giftedness
Hearing Impairments
Learning Disabilities
Mental Retardation
Multiple Handicaps
Neurological Problems
Physical Handicaps
Serious Emotional Problems

2 Representation of persons with exceptionalities should be included in materials at all levels (early childhood through adult) and in all areas of study.

Do all of your efforts at representation focus on the elementary education market?

Have you made an effort to include persons with exceptionalities in such curriculum areas as:

Career Education
Guidance
Health Studies
Language Arts
Mathematics
Physical Education
Science
Social Studies
Vocational Education

3 The representation of persons with exceptionalities should be accurate and free from stereotypes.

Are you aware that each exceptionality has varying degrees of severity?

(Guidelines continue on page 168)

GUIDELINES (cont'd)

Have you represented the deaf as dumb; the blind as pitiful; the intellectual as bookwormish; the mentally retarded person as poorly groomed, as unkempt, or as the "fool"?

Have you stereotyped persons with exceptionalities as "the blind beggar," "the disfigured villain," or "the insane criminal"?

5 In describing persons with exceptionalities, the language used should be nondiscriminatory and free from value judgments.

Do you avoid the use of clichés and phrases that cast aspersions on persons with exceptionalities, such as: village idiot, deaf and dumb, spastic, egghead, four eyes, bookworm, gimp, retard, lamebrain?

Do your materials reflect attitudes of pity or condescension, such as "poor little cripple"?

4 Persons with exceptionalities should be shown in the least restrictive environment. They should be shown participating in activities in a manner that will include them as part of society.

Are all deaf persons shown only in the company of other deaf persons?

Are all retarded persons shown in institutions, or going places only in groups?

Does your material reflect the idea that persons with exceptionalities cannot function in the mainstream of society?

Does your material foster the attitude of "one of them" as opposed to "one of us"?

6 Persons with exceptionalities and persons without exceptionalities should be shown interacting in ways that are mutually beneficial.

Are the persons with exceptionalities always shown being helped by others rather than vice versa?

Have your materials shown positive interpersonal relationships between persons with and without exceptionalities?

Do your materials show how persons with and without exceptionalities can communicate naturally, without embarrassment or awkwardness?

GUIDELINES (cont'd)

7 Materials should provide a variety of appropriate role models of persons with exceptionalities.

Have you explored the full range of jobs that persons with exceptionalities do perform or have you limited yourself to a narrow range of occupations?

Have you ever depicted persons with exceptionalities as parents, community leaders, or business executives?

Do you depict the typical achiever, as well as the super achiever as a role model?

8 Emphasis should be on uniqueness and worth of all persons, rather than on the differences between persons with and without exceptionalities.

Does your use of labels set persons with exceptionalities unnecessarily apart from others, in a manner such as "Sally, Anne, and Robert, their blind friend"?

Do your materials foster the appreciation of similarities between persons with and without exceptionalities?

9 Tokenism should be avoided in the representation of persons with exceptionalities.

Is your idea of representation one child with a hearing aid in a full classroom?

Do you use persons with actual exceptionalities in your materials?

Do you attempt to go beyond the superficial or obvious in depicting the exceptionalities?

KEY ORGANIZATIONS

Anti-Defamation League of B'nai B'rith (ADL)
315 Lexington Ave.
New York, NY 10016   (212) 689-7400

The ADL, an early and leading human relations agency, was founded by volunteers in 1913 with the purpose of eradicating racial and religious prejudice against Jews and other minority groups. It is now a vast national agency with 26 regional offices—active in law, human relations, urban affairs, education and related areas.

Its educational productions include a wide variety of printed and audiovisual materials on racial and ethnic groups for general school use, most produced through educational grants. These include materials on Jews in America, Italians in America, blacks, Puerto Ricans and Mexican-Americans, and a bicentennial filmstrip, *West to Freedom*. Their simulation games use filmed situations and specially-developed manuals to assist school systems in recognizing and resolving classroom conflicts based on racial, ethnic or socio-economic tensions. Model programs for school systems faced with interracial or social tensions include in-service training for

for teachers, supervisors and administrators at all levels from kindergarten to college.

A recent ADL conference, "Pluralism in a Democratic Society," brought together nationally prominent educators and sociologists. Another ADL project— integrating studies of the Holocaust into established history and social studies courses—will be attempted nationwide. Current efforts, in part, are concerned with positive changes in texts dealing with Jews, Judaism and Israel.

As a result of a study on *Adolescent Prejudice*, ADL is developing a multi-media educational package on minorities for teachers and students as part of a process for helping teachers uncover their own negative attitudes as well as those of their students.

Clearinghouse on Women's Studies
c/o Feminist Press
SUNY College at Old Westbury
P.O. Box 334
Old Westbury, NY 11568   (516) 876-3086

Active since 1970, this clearinghouse is an educational project of the Feminist Press, publishers who direct much of their efforts toward schools. The clearinghouse collects, compiles and disseminates information about women's studies at all levels of education. At the college level, its information bank includes in-house information and syllabi from women's study courses and 100 programs on U.S. college campuses. It provides a similar information network and curriculum-gathering service for the elementary and secondary school levels, with a collection that includes curriculum outlines, course materials and instructional strategies.

The Council on Interracial Books for Children (CIBC)
1841 Broadway
New York, NY 10023   (212) 757-5339

The Council was founded in 1966 by writers, editors, illustrators, teachers and parents committed to effecting basic change in books and other media. Council programs are designed to promote learning materials that embody the concepts of cultural pluralism and apply procedures to this end.

Their *Bulletin* features critical analyses of racist and sexist stereotypes in children's books and instructional materials. It publishes the findings of Council studies and recommends materials that it believes will combat racism and sexism.

The Council itself conducts workshops and university courses for parents, publishers and educators, focusing on stereotypes, distortions and omissions found in children's trade books and textbooks and on criteria for analyzing instructional materials.

The Racism and Sexism Resource Center of the Council is a national resource and referral center which collects, adapts and publishes books, pamphlets, lesson plans and teaching strategies to encourage pluralism and to eliminate racism and sexism in education. Its publications include a frequently-used set: *Ten Quick Ways to Analyze Children's Books for Racism and Sexism* (10 copies for $1.00). Other publications are *Racism and Sexism in Children's Books* (10 articles for $2.50); *Sexism and Racism in Popular Basal Readers*, a feminist group report ($2.50); *Racism in Career Education Materials* ($2.50); *Little Black Sambo: A Closer Look*, by Phyllis J. Yuill ($2.50); *Stereotypes, Distortions and Omissions in U.S. History Textbooks*, including content analysis charts ($7.95); *Racism in the English Language*, including lesson plans ($2.00); *From Racism to Pluralism*, by Dr. Patricia M. Bidol, an 18-minute sound and color filmstrip with cassette or record and a group-process curriculum kit suitable for human relations workshops ($32.50); and *The Bulletin*, which reviews children's books and other learning materials for human value content (8 issues per year—$8.00 to individuals; $15.00 to institutions). A detailed catalog will be sent on request.

Project on Equal Education Rights (PEER)

1029 Vermont Ave., NW, Suite 800
Washington, DC 20005   (202) 332-7337

PEER, created in 1974, is an organization which monitors Title IX enforcement efforts of the U.S. Department of Health, Education, and Welfare in the Nation's public schools to bar discrimination against girls and women in education. PEER also provides information to educators and citizens trying to eliminate sex bias in schools. Some of their publications include:

An annotated bibliography, *Resources for Ending Sex Bias in the Schools* (single copies and small orders free; $6.00/100).

Selected reprints of articles such as "The Influence of Sexism on the Education of Handicapped Children" (single copy free), and "Vocational Preparation for Women: A Critical Analysis" (single copy free).

A four-page summary of Title IX regulations (single copy and small orders free; $5.00/100).

A report entitled *Stalled at the Start: Government Action on Sex Bias in the Schools* ($1.00), describing what has been done to enforce Title IX.

The quarterly newsletter, *Peer Perspective*, which includes developments in Washington, DC, the courts and local school districts, and lists resources. The newsletter can be received on a complimentary basis.

The Resource Center on Sex Roles in Education

National Foundation for the Improvement of Education
1201 Sixteenth St., NW
Washington, DC 20036   (202) 833-5426

The Resource Center on Sex Roles in Education is currently preparing materials for instructional staffs, administrators, Title IX coordinators, school board members, counselors, physical education personnel, vocational education personnel and community representatives to help overcome sex bias and sex discrimination in education.

Materials previously developed by the Resource Center are available on a prepaid basis. Specific publications include: *Biased Textbooks: A Research Perspective* ($1.00); *Student Guide to Title IX* ($1.50); and *Implementing Title IX: A Sample Workshop* ($5.00). A publication price list is available upon request.

KEY PUBLICATIONS

Asia in American Textbooks. New York, Asia Society, 1975. 37p. (Free from
    112 East 64th St., New York, NY 10021.)

This Ford Foundation study examined 306 texts used in 50 states in
1974-1975 and found a serious absence of Asian source materials and a failure to
present Asian life authentically. Appendixes include references and guidelines for
evaluating such textbooks as well as a list of texts examined.

The methods used in this survey are described in a related work: *Back-
grounder: Treatment of Asia Deficient in U.S. School Books*, published by the
Asia Society in 1976.

Being a Man: A Unit of Instruction and Activities on Male Role Stereotyping, by
    David Sadker. Washington, U.S. GPO, 1977. 64p. $2.10. (SIN-017-080-
    01777-6). (Single copy free from U.S. Office of Education).

The first section of this handbook for junior high school students provides
background information on male sex role stereotyping. The second section includes
classroom activities and lesson plans to help students identify, analyze and evaluate
sex role stereotyping. The emphasis on male role stereotypes is extremely hard to
find in educational materials.

Biased Textbooks: A Research Perspective, by Lenore J. Weitzman and Diane
    Rizzo. Washington, Resource Center on Sex Roles in Education, 1974.
    Unpaged. $1.00pa.

This brief, two-part guide includes a colorful documented guide to images
(i.e., illustrations) of males and females in elementary school texts (grades one to
six) in five subject areas—science, mathematics, reading, spelling and social
studies—based on samplings of widely-used texts.

Each illustration was categorized on 50 different dimensions, including sex,
race, expression, activity and occupation, for a systematic analysis whose results
were rather intriguing.

As expected, the world found was predominantly white (69 percent male),
and composed predominantly of children. Interestingly, there are fewer pictures
of women as students get older (32 percent in second grade, 20 percent in sixth).
While men were shown in 150 occupational roles, women were—almost exclusively—
housewives. While boys were active, girls were shown as watching for and waiting
for boys. There were more women in social studies than in science, and math texts
were loaded with dumb girl images. Reading series seemed to include about three
times as many stories about boys as about girls. In spelling, vowels were illustrated
with female images, consonants with males.

These categories and data should be helpful in themselves for anyone evaluating texts. The guide also includes a "What You Can Do about Biased Textbooks"
section.

Black Image: Education Copes with Color, edited by Jean D. Grambs, et al.
    Dubuque, IA, William Bowen Co., 1972. 202p. $3.95pa.

An incisive, provocative collection of essays on the impact of textbooks and
other books in their views and treatment of blacks. Some particularly interesting

essays are Jean Grambs' "Dick and Jane Go Slumming: Instructional Materials for the Inner-City Negro Child," J. Janis' "Education for Social Stupidity: History, Government and Sociology Textbooks" and "Their Own Thing: A Review of Seven Black History Guides Produced by School Systems," and J. C. Carr's "My Brother's Keeper: A View of Blacks in Secondary School Literature Anthologies."

Checklist: Rate Your School for Racism and Sexism, by the Racism and Sexism
    Resource Center for Educators. New York, Council on Interracial Books for
    Children, 1977. 11p. $2.50. (From 1841 Broadway, New York, NY 10023.)
    Includes a glossary, checklists on racism and sexism and examples of institutional sexism.

Classroom Treatment of the Right to Work, prepared by Concerned Educators
    Against Forced Unionism. Fairfax, VA, CEAFU, 1979. $1.00pa.
    (From 8316 Arlington Blvd., Suite 6000, Fairfax, VA 22038.)
    The CEAFU, an educational division of the National Right to Work Committee, has reviewed more than 200 classroom materials in high school history and government courses solely on the issue of the "right to work." According to their research, 81 works discussed this issue, 52 of them (or 64 percent) unfairly and/or inaccurately. This guide includes a point-by-point analysis of these texts in relation to the right to work issue. A title index lists the names of states that may have included particular texts on their state adoptions lists. A *Summary Edition* is also available.

Dick and Jane as Victims: Sex Stereotyping in Children's Readers, an Analysis, by
    Women on Words and Images. Princeton, NJ, WOWI, 1975. 57p. $2.00. (From
    P.O. Box 2163, Princeton, NJ 08540.)
    A definitive study of 134 school readers from 14 publishers, in which generally boys are found to be competent, curious, brave and independent, while girls are presented as passive, dependent, incompetent and fearful. In general the study found that boys are multidimensional while girls are severely limited and that stories are unrealistic with sex role stereotyping pervading even faraway times and places.

Eliminating Ethnic Bias in Instructional Materials: Comment and Bibliography,
    edited by Maxine Dunfee. Washington, Association for Supervision and
    Curriculum Development, 1974. 53p. $3.25pa.
    This five-chapter booklet, prepared under the auspices of an ASCD working committee, begins with a chapter providing a Rationale for a Pluralistic Society, and continues to produce evidence of ethnic bias, and documents efforts to change. It includes a 98-item bibliography of resources for educators by Maxine Dunfee, and reprints the same evaluation instrument by Max Rosenberg that is reprinted on 162-63 of this text. All chapters have concise, interesting introductions and substantial bibliographies.

*Help Wanted: Sexism in Career Education Materials. How to Detect It and How to
    Counteract Its Effects in the Classroom*, by Women on Words and Images.
    Princeton, NJ, WOWI, 1975. 51p. $2.50. (From P.O. Box 2163, Princeton,
    NJ 08540.)
    This report, commissioned by EPIE, is a four-part summary of research on

the extent of sex-role stereotyping in career education materials, advice to teachers and counselors on how to counteract sexism when it is necessary to use somewhat sexist materials, an activity list for enriching career opportunity awareness and a good resource list.

Her Way: Biographies of Women for Young People, by Mary Ellen Kulkin. Chicago, American Library Association, 1976. 480p. $25.00.

The first section of this enormously helpful book combines brief, interesting profiles of 260 significant women with detailed analysis, comments, ratings, and appropriate grade levels of bibliographies. The second section provides similar information on 300 collective biographies. The third section indexes about 800 women in these biographies by name, nationality and activity or profession (as abolitionist, actress, American civil rights worker, etc.).

How to Find and Measure Bias in Textbooks, by David Pratt. Englewood Cliffs, NJ, Educational Technology Publications, 1972. 50p. $3.95pa.

Describes and explains an "objective" method for determining bias in textbooks and other print materials, through the ECO Analysis instrument, "a relatively simple but sensitive method of analyzing the attitudes expressed towards any minority or other group in a textbook." The ECO (Evaluation Coefficient) Analysis is based upon content and propaganda analysis methods. Scores are determined by counting the frequency of "favorable" and "unfavorable" terms, mostly adjectives, interpreted by the analyst-scorer's value judgments (using Appendix III, an ECO Word List of about 350 words, as a guide). Once the number of favorable (F) and unfavorable (U) terms are counted, the coefficient of evaluation is determined by a formula:

$$\frac{100F}{F+U}$$

The book provides a complete description of the method, with examples, cautions and scoring sheets. Apparently it has been validated and is rather consistent among analysts.

Human (and Anti-Human) Values in Children's Books: A Content Rating Instrument for Educators and Concerned Parents: Guidelines for the Future, by the Council on Interracial Books for Children. New York, Racism and Sexism Resource Center for Educators, 1976. 280p. $7.95pa. (From Council on Interracial Books for Children, 1841 Broadway, New York, NY 10023.)

This book presents and demonstrates CIBC's compact matrix for analyzing children's books for racism, sexism, ageism, escapism, elitism, materialism, conformism and individualism, as well as for literary and artistic quality. The book includes discussions of language and terminology and the above terms. It applies the matrix and brief expository analytic reviews to 235 children's trade books (mostly published in 1975) and mostly recommended by their publishers as dealing with social concerns or feminist or minority themes—for preschool to teenage children. There is a topical grouping at the end which could be used to select books about girls and women, books including varied (specified) ethnic groups, and books dealing with issues like death, divorce, adoption, illness, drug abuse, old people or handicaps.

The CIBC, an advocacy group which admittedly seeks to impose its societal values through assessment of children's books, had to use many reviewers and discard many reviews in compiling this book, since reviewers were differentially sensitive to art and language which revealed the presence and direction of these various "isms."

The Image of the Middle East in Secondary School Textbooks, by William J.
Griswold. New York, Middle East Studies Association, 1975. 101p. $2.50
prepaid. (From MESA, Hagop Kevorkian Center for Near Eastern Studies,
New York University, 50 Washington Square South, New York, NY 10003.)
This thorough report by area experts evaluates the content of 50 American and 12 Canadian texts in world histories, social studies and geography in relation to 1) their treatment of Islamic history and cultures, and 2) their view of modern problems, especially stereotypes and biases related to Israel and Arab countries. It includes a list of recommended books, as well as two syllabi—one on the history and culture of Islam and the other on Arab-Israeli wars.

Measures of Educational Equity for Women prepared by Kathleen Williams, et al.
Palo Alto, CA, American Institutes for Research, September 1977. 3 looseleaf
volumes. $13.00 prepaid. (From P.O. Box 1113, Palo Alto, CA 94302.)
This package of evaluation resource materials is prepared under a contract of the Women's Educational Equity Act Program and is heavy on materials dealing with career education and women's roles. It does include a section on implementing Title IX as well as needs assessment questions which could be lifted or adapted.

Non-Sexist Education for Young Children, by Barbara Sprung. Englewood Cliffs,
NJ, Citation Press, 1975. 128p. $3.25pa.
This practical guide to combat sex stereotyping in the early learning years is loaded with teaching ideas and resource guides. The author, project director of Women's Action Alliance in New York City, suggests ways to create non-sexist environments in housekeeping, cooking, block and workshop areas and discusses how to make or where to buy block accessories, pictures, puzzles, games, records, books or filmscripts. Includes five units of study, field tested in four different preschool centers: Families, Jobs People Do, Human Body, Homemaking and Sports. It also includes useful bibliographies of non-sexist reading for adults and non-sexist picture books for children.

Perspectives on School Print Materials: Ethnic, Non-Sexist and Others, a Hand-
book, coordinated by Wayne E. Rosenoff; developed by STRIDE. San
Francisco, Far West Laboratory for Educational Research and Development,
1975. 82p. Out of print; microfiche. $4.43 + postage for paper copy.
(ED 114 213).
An anthology which includes 1) checklists and guidelines for evaluating and analyzing books and curriculum materials for racism and sexism, and 2) contributions which include perspectives on native Americans, black Americans and Chinese Americans, as well as a non-sexist perspective and an article which discusses some often overlooked viewpoints: blue collar workers, the aged, non-Christians and alternative life styles.

Resources in Women's Educational Equity—Non-Print Media and Materials, by
Aileen Wehren. Washington, GPO, 1978. 243p. $5.00.

This catalog, prepared for the Women's Educational Equity Communications
Network, describes and annotates about 350 items dealing with women in all kinds
of non-print media—films, filmstrips, tapes, transparencies, records and others,
based on a search of two machine data bases, NICEM and NIMIS, and such outside
sources as reviewers, commercial distributors and trade publications.

Materials chosen to coincide with the scope of the Women's Educational
Equity are categorized as follows: biographies and portraits of significant women
in American life; history of women; laws and legislation; equal rights; family and
life styles; sex roles and stereotypes; women and work. Most items have been produced since 1972.

Materials are tied together by a title index, and indexed by audience types
and levels; these range from preschool to adult and include parents, minority
women, teacher training and managers.

Their annotations, generally, provide fairly full mediographic descriptions,
as well as an abstract. The format, however, differs for materials from each source—
NICEM, NIMIS or other. (Source of information is included for each.)

School Desegregation and Cultural Pluralism: Perspectives on Progress, edited by
Jeanne L. Lance and Wayne E. Rosenoff. San Francisco, Far West Laboratory
for Educational Research and Development, 1975. 91p. $2.50pa.
(ED 121 865).

The nine papers in this book stem from a series of conferences held by
STRIDE (Service, Training and Research in Desegregated Education) during the
1974-1975 school year, dealing with community relations, cultural pluralism,
content analysis of print materials for multicultural suitability, and appropriate-
administrative strategies. These nine presentations selected for wider distribution
include three on the state of the art of cultural pluralism, four dealing with minority perspectives on curriculum (California Indians, Mexican Americans, Chinese
and black), an interesting article on constructive uses of school conflict by John
DeCecco and another by James Vasquez on the implications of locus of control
learning for educators.

Sex Discrimination in Education Newsletter. Ann Arbor, MI, University of Michigan Department of Psychology, 1977. Bi-monthly (six issues a year). $5.00
for individuals; $10.00 for institutions. (From Sex Discrimination News,
Department of Psychology, University of Michigan, Ann Arbor, MI 48109.)

This newsletter, edited by students at the University of Michigan, under the
supervision of Sara Lincoln and Robert Hefner, includes ongoing reviews and
information on such resources as books, periodicals, organizations and media dealing with education, affirmative action, language and sexism, and related topics.

Sexism and Racism in Popular Basal Readers, 1964-1976, by the Racism and Sexism
Resource Center for Educators. New York, Council on Interracial Books for
Children, 1976. 43p. $2.50. (From 1841 Broadway, New York, NY 10023.)

Very thorough and detailed analyses of several reading series published
between 1964 and 1974.

Stereotypes, Distortions and Omissions in U.S. History Textbooks, by Robert B.
    Moore, et al. New York, Council on Interracial Books for Children, 1977.
    143p. $7.95.

This publication examines thirteen current textbook series from ten major
publishers (all but one published since 1970) for sexist and racist stereotypes for six
important groups: women, African Americans, Asian Americans, Chicanos, native
Americans and Puerto Ricans.

It uses an interesting three-column format: quotations from the texts are
coupled with comments and authoritative references. It includes discussion, definitions, bibliographies and summaries as well as checklists for each of these groups.

Teaching about Women in the Social Studies: Concepts, Methods, and Materials,
    edited by Jean Dresden Grambs. Arlington, VA, National Council for the
    Social Studies, 1976. 117p. $5.95pa. (Bulletin 48).

An excellent, interesting and rational guide that provides practical assistance
in structuring concepts, locating and evaluating materials, and including women's
roles in all sorts of social studies materials. Patrick Ferguson and Lois Conley Smith
provide guidelines for evaluating the treatment of the sexes in instructional materials on pages 59-70. Carole A. Hahn has a critical assessment of materials for teaching about women on pages 71-101. Other chapters also include resources, checklists
and inventories.

Textbooks and the American Indian, by Jeannette Henry. Edited by Ruperto
    Costa. San Francisco, CA, American Indian Historical Society, 1969. 269p.
    $5.35. (From 1451 Masonic Ave., San Francisco, CA 94117.)

In a commentary on curriculum (page 245), Ms. Henry states that "the
Native American must be a living part of the study of American history, social
sciences, citizenship and world history from first grade on." In keeping with this
philosophy, Indian historians from the American Indian Historical Society have
examined textbooks in all these fields as well as the treatment of American Indians
in comprehensive resource books. The thoughtful, detailed studies of native Americans in state histories are particularly valuable. This book includes criteria for each
of these areas as well as a thorough examination of texts as of 1969; still interesting
and rewarding reading even though the texts are outdated, since many of their
successors show similar flaws.

*Today's Changing Roles: An Approach to Non-Sexist Teaching, Teacher Resources
    with Curriculum Activities,* developed by Educational Challenges, Inc. for
    Resource Center on Sex Roles in Education. Washington, National Educa-
    tion Association, 1974. 108p. $3.00pa.

This interesting curriculum for elementary, intermediate and secondary levels
helps students (and their teachers!) explore sex-role stereotyping, clarify their
perceptions and apply their learnings. This curriculum should be invaluable, particularly for teachers who are stuck with stereotyped materials.

Its well-structured yet open-ended social studies units are based on student
experiences and can be adapted to a variety of teaching approaches, from mini-
courses to learning centers.

FOR FURTHER READING

These references represent a fraction of those available and are chosen for breadth, for expression of various viewpoints and for clarity. Other, related references can be found in a companion to this book, *Selecting Materials for Instruction: Subject Areas and Implementation* (henceforth to be cited as *Subject Areas*), especially in the chapter on Ethnic Studies.

*Items marked with an asterisk include criteria of some sort.
+Items marked with a plus include other references.

Banks, James A. *Evaluation of an Instructional Program in Training Teachers to Analyze Educational Materials for Possible Racial Bias* (paper presented at annual meeting of the American Educational Research Association, April 1974). (ED 090 307).

+Brody, C. M. "Do Instructional Materials Reinforce Sex Stereotyping?," *Educational Leadership*, v. 31, no. 2 (Nov. 1973), pp. 119-22.

*Burr, E., S. Dunn, and N. Farquhar. *Guidelines for Equal Treatment of the Sexes in Social Studies Textbooks*. Los Angeles, Westside Women's Committee, 1973.

+Caliguri, J. P. "Teacher Bias in the Selection of Social Studies Textbooks," *Journal of Negro Education*, v. 40 (Fall 1971), pp. 322-29.

*+"Combating Stereotypes: A Symposium," *Elementary English*, v. 52 (May 1975), pp. 711-51.

*Detroit Public Schools Staff. "What about Us? Our Textbooks Do Not Meet Our Needs," *Educational Product Report*, v. 3, no. 2 (Nov. 1969), pp. 12-18.

+Dietrich, D. J. "Racism, Sexism, in Children's Literature," *The Reading Teacher*, v. 28 (Dec. 1974), pp. 346-49.

Fishman, Anne S. "A Criticism of Sexism in Elementary Readers," *Reading Teacher*, v. 29, (Feb. 1976), pp. 443-46.

Gough, Pauline B. "41 Ways to Teach about Sex Role Stereotyping," *Learning*, v. 5, no. 5 (Jan. 1977), p. 74.
    Presents numerous ideas on how to stimulate student interest in sex-role stereotyping. Aimed at elementary school teachers, but the 41 independent research projects and the classroom materials for sex-role study are easily adaptable for high school.

Gough, Pauline B. *Sexism: New Issue in American Education*. Bloomington, IN, Phi Delta Kappa Educational Foundation, 1976. (Fastback 81).

Gurule, Kay. "Truthful Textbooks and Mexican Americans," *Integrated Education*, v. 11 (March/April 1973), pp. 32-34.

Hata, Don, Jr., and Nadine Hata. *I Wonder Where the Yellow Went? Distortions and Omissions of Asian Americans in California Education* (paper presented at the annual meeting of the American Educational Research Association in Chicago, April 1974). (ED 093 747).

Hentoff, Nat. "Any Writer Who Follows Anyone Else's Guidelines Ought to Be in Advertising," *School Library Journal*, v. 24, no. 3 (Nov. 1977), pp. 27-29.

*+Johnson, Laura O. *Non-Sexist Curricular Materials for Elementary Schools*. Old Westbury, NY, Feminist Press, 1974.

+Kane, Michael. *Minorities in Textbooks: A Study of Their Treatment in Social Studies Texts*. Chicago, IL, Quadrangle Books, 1970.

Kraft, Linda. "Lost Herstory: The Treatment of Women in Children's Encyclopedias," *School Library Journal*, v. 19, no. 5 (Jan. 1973), pp. 26-35. Reprinted in *Sexism and Youth*.

*+National Education Association. *Combating Discrimination in the Schools: Legal Remedies and Guidelines*. Washington, NEA, 1973.

National Education Association. *How Fair Are Your Child's Textbooks?* Washington, NEA, n.d.

Quillen, James. *Textbook Improvement and International Understanding*. Washington, American Council on Education, 1948.

*+Rosenberg, Max. "Evaluate Your Textbooks for Racism, Sexism," *Educational Leadership*, v. 31, no. 2 (Nov. 1972), pp. 107-109.

+Saario, T. N., et al. "Sex Role Stereotyping in the Public Schools," *Harvard Educational Review*, v. 43 (Aug. 1973), pp. 386-416.

+Shelly, A. C. "Can We Find More Diverse Adult Sex Roles?" *Educational Leadership*, v. 31, no. 2 (Nov. 1973), pp. 114-18.

+Simms, Richard L. "Bias in Textbooks: Not Yet Corrected," *Phi Delta Kappan*, v. 57 (Nov. 1975), pp. 201-202.

*Trezise, Robert. *Michigan School Studies Textbook Study*. Lansing, MI, Michigan State Department of Education, 1974.
Fifty-four reviews of 18 elementary and secondary school social studies textbooks rate how adequately they reflect pluralistic American society.

+Turner, R. C., and J. A. Dewar. "Black History in Selected American History Textbooks," *Educational Leadership*, v. 6, no. 3 (Feb. 1973), pp. 441-44.

*Uribe, Oscar, Jr., and J. S. Martinez. *Analyzing Children's Books with a Chicano Perspective*, San Francisco, Far West Laboratory for Educational Research and Development, 1975.

Waite, R. R. "Further Attempts to Integrate and Urbanize First Grade Reading Textbooks: A Research Study," *Journal of Negro Education*, v. 37 (Winter 1978), pp. 62-69.

Weitzman, L. J., and D. Rizzo. "Sex Bias in Textbooks," *Today's Education*, v. 64, no. 1 (Jan.-Feb. 1975), pp. 49, 52.

Weston, Louise C., and Sandor L. Stein. "A Content Analysis of Publishers' Guidelines for the Elimination of Sex Stereotyping," *Educational Researcher*, v. 7, no. 1 (March 1978), pp. 13-14.

+"Women and Girls," *Elementary English*, v. 50, no. 7 (Oct. 1973), pp. 1019-1110.
Entire issue of 19 articles covers almost every imaginable aspect of women and girls and literature, mostly avoiding simplistic solutions and approaches. Includes methods of teaching, recommended titles and authors, and intelligent analyses.

*+Zimet, Sara. *Teaching Critical Reading Skills: A Guide for Analyzing Racial and Sexual Bias in Elementary Readers.* Washington, DC, Resource Center on Sex Roles in Education, 1976.

PART IV

SOME PARTICIPANT ROLES

PARENT AND COMMUNITY INVOLVEMENT
IN SELECTION

" . . . parents and teachers are natural enemies, predestined each for the discomfiture of the other. The chasm is frequently covered over, for neither parents nor teachers wish to admit to themselves the uncomfortable implications of their animosity . . .
. . . [Yet] if parents and teachers could meet often enough and intimately enough to develop primary attitudes towards each other, and if both parents and teachers might have their say unreservedly, such modifications of school practice and parental upbringing might take place as would revolutionize the life of children everywhere."

—Willard Walker, *The Sociology of Teaching*, 1932

"It appears vital that professional educators and boards of education acquire a better understanding of the value structure of their own community and make every effort to develop educational goals or alternative programs that recognize these values."

—Todd Clark

■ ■ ■

This chapter will explore several facets of parent-community involvement in the materials selection process as perceived from my particular equivocal perspective. While I am a practicing parent of three widely-spaced children and by temperment and conviction a civil libertarian, by long experience and training I am a selector and organizer of educational materials who prefers to have undisputed sway over those materials. On the other hand, as a citizen and parent dealing with my own children's schools, I, like many other parents, have experienced frustrations at every level.

The current parental demand for input into the materials selection process is, likely, a manifestation of a broader community movement directed at the schools: partly a taxpayers' revolt, partly an outgrowth of federal guidelines of the 1960s, but largely an overdue demand for some control over what transpires in schools, a demand that is treated defensively by educators, though parent goals, overall, seem eminently reasonable to me.

One extensive literature review of citizen-parent-community school evaluations from 1951 to 1974, by Robert Feldmesser and Esther Ann McCready, noted that parents—across the years and surveys—demonstrated a surprising unanimity in what they wanted in their children's schools. Parent groups—of widely varied incomes and political beliefs—all placed major importance on:

● adapting education to the individual child

● high standards of performance

● high achievements as measured by test scores

● small classes with favorable student-teacher ratios

● pleasant classroom atmosphere

● pleasant physical surroundings, plant and equipment

While teachers perceive groups of parents as potentially overbearing and frightening, parents often have a similar perception of teachers and schools. The federal guidelines of the 1960s, which required parental involvement in Head Start and ESEA Title I programs, served to promote a wider recognition of parental rights and roles in education (and affected the controversies over community control and centralization which remain with us today). But beyond specific suggestions or complaints, many parents and community groups still seem to share a common disillusionment with school bureaucracy and a perception of public education as an unresponsive monolith.

This viewpoint is aptly stated in an organization brochure of the National Committee for Citizens in Education (NCCE):

YOU WANT TO HELP YOUR CHILD IN SCHOOL . . . BUT

You are unsure of your rights under the law

You don't know how to get the information you need

You have little free time

You know you will meet resistance from school officials

You are afraid the effort will be costly

You have tried before and failed

You are afraid of reprisals against your child

You don't know how to organize the group support you will need

You feel overwhelmed by the "system" and powerless to change things or even to make yourself heard.

Still for good or ill, parental involvement (which educators fear more than the apathy they deplore) has strongly affected curricula and policies, especially in recent years. Often under the guise or plea of due process or discrimination, parents have sought a voice in controlling the education to which their children are exposed and have gained a right to access their children's records, programs and materials. Often they tackle issues which educators neglect or overlook, although too often through adversary action. Activist parents and groups that include parents are raising the consciousness of teachers and their communities. It was originally parental litigation, Gordon vs. Lau, that brought forth our bilingual education programs and some multicultural programs. Parents of handicapped children have served valiantly as pressure groups to win their children adequate educations, and parents of gifted children—considered nuisances in some school districts—are opening up educational options for all children. Black parents in Cleveland and Detroit helped desegregate and rewrite biased textbooks. Other pressure groups are now applying head counts to illustrations of males and females in textbooks. And pressure from parents and activist groups has opened many opportunities for girls.

Community and parent groups are demanding review roles in major adoptions of educational materials. These demands can take several forms, primarily those of individual parents for alternative materials for children. Litigation in regard to materials seems as often to be for access to materials as for limiting materials. For example, the case of Presidents Council, District No. 25 (New York City) vs. Community School Board No. 25 (1972) was a suit against restrictions on a book about Spanish Harlem. Minarcini vs. Strongsville City School District (Ohio) (1976) was successful in blocking a school board from removing books from a school library.

Successful litigation or agitation requires determination and energy, not necessarily power or prior influence. Sometimes one parent, with sufficient motivation and timely perceptions, can start a mass movement. It was junk food in the textbooks that got to Suzanne Barrera of Santa Rosa, California, who was outraged to find her daughter's third-grade arithmetic text loaded with practice problems involving Twinkies, Tootsie Rolls, Cracker Jacks and 55 other products and corporations. Her outrage led first to the formation of Vigilance in Public Education, then to a petition campaign, then to submitted legislation and a meeting with the state Curriculum Committee. Within a short time California had a brand new set of *State Guidelines for the Depiction of Brand Names, Corporate Logos and Specified Types of Food in Instructional Materials.*

In this particular concern, Vigilance in Public Education—itself largely composed of concerned parents—was joined in its anti-junk-food campaign by doctors, dentists, nutritionists and church groups, as well as by a California Citizens Action Group, a Children's Rights Group, the Committee on Children's TV, the Consumers Union and other groups. Some of these groups have gone on to try to remove junk food from school lunch rooms as well as from texts.

The issue of free advertising and industrial classroom promotions is now being pursued by Sheila Harty of the Center for the Study of Responsive Law in Washington, DC, and is more fully discussed in the chapter on free materials in *Media and Curriculum.*

At the national level, other parent-citizens groups have developed policy positions on parental roles in selecting instructional materials, beyond their demands that educators as a group learn to communicate with parents and community groups. My directory of key national parent organizations, starting on page 188, includes policy excerpts and lists selected publications.

Sometimes the federal government mandates parental involvement in development and selection. For example, one major precondition for refunding the Human Behavior Curriculum Project in 1976 was that its Advisory Board should include four parents to review units for community impact. As my chapter on the feeling domain (in *Subject Areas*) indicates, the psychologically-oriented advocates of affective education and education in psychology are acutely aware of the importance of community input. Similarly, Public Law 94-142, The Education for All Handicapped Children Act, validated the rights of parents of handicapped children to participate in planning and monitoring educational programs for their own handicapped children.

Parental rights are now recognized in national legislation like the Family Education Rights and Privacy Act of 1974, the Buckley Amendment, which provides parents greater access to children's school records, while restricting outsiders' access. The General Education Provisions Act, Section 439, similarly provides parental access to "all instructional materials, including teachers' manuals, films, tapes or other supplementary materials which will be used in connection with any research or experimentation program or project."

States too are increasingly recognizing parental rights; one comprehensive survey of states (*State Education Agencies and Parent Involvement*, by Daniel Safran. Oakland, CA, Center for the Study of Parent Involvement, 1974) indicated that, as of 1973, at least 14 states had legislation requiring or recommending some forms of parent involvement, while a larger number of state education agencies had policies and/or regulations promoting parent involvement in school processes. An increasing number of states, including Indiana, Maryland, California and Texas, require parents on textbook selection committees. The state law of Indiana, not too atypical, requires that at least 40 percent of textbook committee members be parents.

Unfortunately, according to Ralph Fuller, lay participation in materials selection does seem to invite conflict on either the state or the district level, since the majority of expressed reactions are negative. Moreover, the complaints are not uniform, and tend to come from the left as much as from the right. Kris McCough, reporting on Maryland's policy of community review in "Confessions of a Book-Burner" (*Social Education*, v. 41, no. 6, pp. 556-59), categorized recent Maryland citizen complaints and comments as follows: poor print and formats, religious and political bias, sexism, racism, inaccurate information, lack of citations or bibliographies, and invasion of privacy—certainly a wide spectrum.

Such comments or policies often are perceived as negative and treated defensively by teachers and school administrators who tend to retreat behind professionalism or academic freedom. But, neither professionalism nor academic freedom is at stake when, as is often the case, teachers and/or students have no choice in materials (or, for that matter, in schools) but must use whatever materials are assigned. Our broader democratic value of unhampered, critical, free search for truth is not readily apparent in most school selection methods nor in the materials that stem from these.

Teachers—especially high school teachers in English and social studies—have been sufficiently exposed on the firing line to earn their paranoia. Still, the educators' stereotype of parental involvement in selection as merely militant, redneck objection to courses in sex education and books by liberal authors is, at best, a partial truth.

If public schooling is, as is generally agreed, a means of teaching values, parental values seem as appropriate as those of educators. Certainly parents are ultimately responsible for the guidance of their own children, even though society has delegated part of that guidance role to professional educators.

Since parents, like teachers or students, are diverse individuals, with diverse values, interests, perspectives and talents, parental and lay involvement in the selection process comes from a variety of perspectives and takes place in a variety of forms at different levels. As Vigilance in Public Education demonstrates, the state level is often one where parents can be rapidly effective. Still, parents may be most valuable at local school and district levels. As community representatives, parents can provide insights into community concerns and attitudes that are different from those of educators. Often they have more or wider contacts with community groups than these educators.

Todd Clark, in "Community Participation: A Two Way Street" (*Social Education*, v. 41, no. 6, pp. 557-58), recommends a careful analysis of the community to locate individuals or groups particularly concerned about instructional materials. He would like a representative group to examine and critique materials and provide insight to educators on the degree of support that might be expected for traditional or innovative materials. He believes such a committee could humanize curricula and build understanding between educators and their adult constituents. Kris

McCough similarly thinks that such an enlightened committee could be "enormously helpful" to teachers with a limited amount of time for reviewing. Suzanne Barrera of Vigilance in Public Education would like to see citizen reviewing a continuing process independent of adoption schedules.

I personally would like to see parent and community input on an ad hoc basis, with community experts brought in to advise on particular programs and materials. For example, employment development people could consult on career and vocational materials; park rangers and environmental groups could offer expert advice on environmental education and local facilities; ethnic groups could be helpful in bilingual or multicultural education. In general, all community resource groups—especially public libraries and museums—and adjacent school districts should be continuously consulted to arrange for maximum supplementation rather than duplication.

As parents rather than materials experts, the best parental role in the selection process might be to assess their own community and student bodies and to establish learning and budget priorities. Parents know what they want their children to learn. In reviewing materials, as Barbara Howell of Silver Burdett points out, many parents do tend to look for materials similar to those they used as children, or expect all materials to reinforce reading, writing and mathematics. Still, whatever their knowledge gaps on current teaching methodologies or subject matter, parents can provide valuable insight to their own children. They have an intimate knowledge of their own children and, unlike some teachers, tend to see them as whole individuals with a whole range of concerns.

In *The Censorship Game and How to Play It* (Bulletin 50 of the National Council for the Social Studies), C. Benjamin Cox provides a model of a professional/community dialogue that can be used in selecting instructional materials to meet both professional standards and community concerns. This model is discussed in detail in his book and is reprinted (page 187) with the permission of C. Benjamin Cox and the National Council of Social Studies.

Parents often are advocates of fuller, more adequate budgets for instructional materials. In some school jurisdictions this has been of major concern to parents. Particularly in rural areas, parents and parent groups are often donors, above and beyond their taxes, of textbooks, library materials, games and equipment.

Schools can expect increasing involvement of parent groups in many aspects and levels of materials selection. The selection process will undoubtedly be improved if the school staff is sensitive to the educational expectations of parents and keeps communication channels open. Shared decision-making may lead to well honed, realistic goals, backed by instructional materials adequate in kind and number to meet these goals.

CRITERIAL/CONTEXT STRUCTURE OF A PROFESSIONAL/COMMUNITY
RATIONAL DIALOGUE

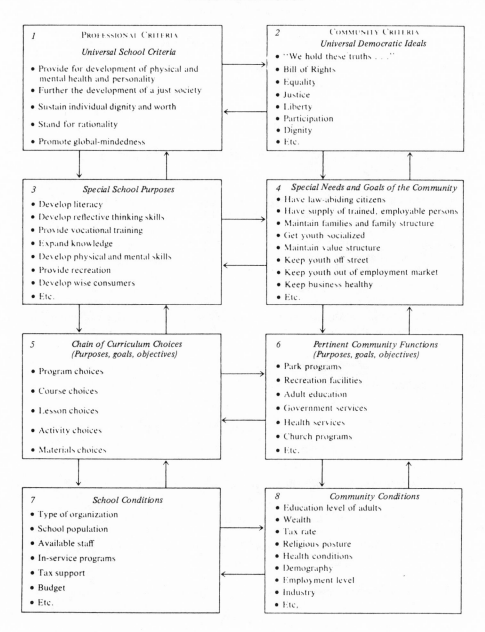

1	PROFESSIONAL CRITERIA

Universal School Criteria

- Provide for development of physical and mental health and personality
- Further the development of a just society
- Sustain individual dignity and worth
- Stand for rationality
- Promote global-mindedness

2	COMMUNITY CRITERIA

Universal Democratic Ideals

- "We hold these truths . . ."
- Bill of Rights
- Equality
- Justice
- Liberty
- Participation
- Dignity
- Etc.

3	Special School Purposes

- Develop literacy
- Develop reflective thinking skills
- Provide vocational training
- Expand knowledge
- Develop physical and mental skills
- Provide recreation
- Develop wise consumers
- Etc.

4	Special Needs and Goals of the Community

- Have law-abiding citizens
- Have supply of trained, employable persons
- Maintain families and family structure
- Get youth socialized
- Maintain value structure
- Keep youth off street
- Keep youth out of employment market
- Keep business healthy
- Etc.

5	Chain of Curriculum Choices

(Purposes, goals, objectives)

- Program choices
- Course choices
- Lesson choices
- Activity choices
- Materials choices

6	Pertinent Community Functions

(Purposes, goals, objectives)

- Park programs
- Recreation facilities
- Adult education
- Government services
- Health services
- Church programs
- Etc.

7	School Conditions

- Type of organization
- School population
- Available staff
- In-service programs
- Tax support
- Budget
- Etc.

8	Community Conditions

- Education level of adults
- Wealth
- Tax rate
- Religious posture
- Health conditions
- Demography
- Employment level
- Industry
- Etc.

KEY ORGANIZATIONS

Two disparate groups of organizations are included here: parents' groups and public opinion surveying groups, both valuable sources of information on public response to education that have been largely overlooked by the educational community. Descriptions of the parents' groups provide information on programs, policies and publications related to the concerns of this chapter. Information on public opinion groups includes information on their addresses, data banks and publications that report public opinion.

National Parents' Groups

Center for the Study of Parent Involvement (CSPI)
5240 Boyd Street
Oakland, CA 94618 (415) 658-7557

More study-oriented than activist, CSPI, which began in 1973, has drawn up position papers on various aspects of parent involvement in 1976 and 1977. Like the National PTA and the Institute for Responsive Education, CSPI suggests that parents and other lay groups should have roles in school planning. CSPI, like the National PTA, believes that such groups should actively design, implement and evaluate teacher training activities.

In a thoughtful, well-documented position paper by Daniel Safran, *Preparing Teachers for Parent Involvement* (1974, 26p. $3.00), CSPI advocates that teacher training include role-playing situations and supervised field work with individual parents and groups of parents to assure that teachers can work effectively with parents to:

- maximize values of meetings with parents

- achieve good parent-teacher conferences

- deal effectively with angry or passive parents

- encourage parents to perform specific educational tasks with children

- encourage parents to participate in school and community functions

- work with parents in joint ventures

- deal with their own anxieties about parents

Such training, Safran believes, would result in more humane and productive education that would better serve the needs of parents, students, teachers and communities.

Proceedings of the 1976 conference, *Parent Involvement: An Inalienable Right*, are available from CSPI for $10.00 (prepaid).

Institute for Responsive Education (IRE)
70 Commonwealth Avenue
Boston, MA 02215 (617) 353-3309

This group is interested in citizen involvement in educational decision-making—possibly more in curriculum evaluation than in the specifics of programs or instructional materials per se. They advocate, in general, decentralized decision-making with a sensible system of checks and balances to emphasize collaboration more than competition or confrontation. School councils are the mechanism of choice.

Don Davies, IRE director, suggests that school councils should have the responsibility of assessing community, school and facility needs; setting goals and priorities for schools; setting school budget priorities; improving community support for schools; investigating student or parent complaints or problems; participating in selection of principal and teachers; reviewing new school programs, curricula and student activities; and communicating school needs to area or district councils.

Members of these councils should be democratically elected, should cooperate with other existing groups, should represent a cross section of the community and should include a majority of parents along with teachers, students and residents.

He sees this decentralized approach as providing more diverse school programs and greater choices for parents and children, within individual schools and within districts. Essentially he advocates many local strategies rather than one national strategy.

Publications (Partial List)

Burges, Bill. *Facts for a Change: Citizen Action Research for Better Schools.* 1976. 192p. $5.00.
This introduction to locating educational facts for community action can be used by citizen groups, school officials, teachers, students and community leaders; it could also be used as a text for urban affairs or civic education at the secondary and post-secondary levels.

Citizen Action in Education. $5.00/yr.
Quarterly news magazine includes new models and ideas for citizen involvement in schools.

Clasby, Miriam, and JoAnne Lema. *Together: Schools and Communities.* 1975. 334p. $4.00.
This handbook and resource directory, developed from a Massachusetts project, includes suggestions for advisory councils, organizations and schools, and community people interested in shared decision-making.

Davies, Don, ed. *Schools Where Parents Make a Difference.* 1976. 164p. $3.95.
Accounts of schools in urban and rural settings in California, Boston and Tennessee.

Ferreira, Joseph, and Bill Burges. *Collecting Evidence: A Layman's Guide to Participant Observation.* 1976. 24p. $2.00.
This guide can help citizen groups and students investigating schools.

The National PTA
700 North Rush Street
Chicago, IL 60611   (312) 787-0977
This membership organization, established as the National Congress of

Parents and Teachers back in 1897, is one of the largest (quasi?) voluntary organizations in the nation, with 6.5 million members in about 31,000 local parent-teacher associations. Its dual concerns are parent education and child welfare. Traditionally, it has acted as interface between schools and parents—interpreting schools' objectives to parents, acting to make parents' needs understood by school administrators, and facilitating programs for parents and families.

It has been active in media evaluation since 1910 (when it directed its attention to movies and vaudeville) and recently has been concerned with television. The National PTA Television Action Center, a project now actively engaged in evaluating (mostly) network television offerings, is discussed in the chapter on television in *Media and the Curriculum*.

At its recent annual meeting (in Atlanta) in June 1978, the PTA adopted as a priority item the amendment of state and federal education legislation to assure that PTAs can be used as school advisory councils when legislation requires such councils. The PTA is also working on establishing parent training centers to help parents develop the skills they need to represent their children's educational interests.

Earlier—in September 1977—the National PTA Board of Directors adopted two statements that are relevant to this book: one on teacher preparation and staff development the other on the role of PTAs in reviewing instructional materials. The statement on teacher preparation suggests that teacher education should provide skills in evaluating programs and materials and a basis for developing self-evaluative skills. It further recommends that preservice and in-service programs be closely related to curriculum, to the classroom and to student and parent interests. It suggests also that teachers should learn respect for students as persons, respect for teachers who may use differing teaching styles, and confidence in developing approaches for different student needs. Finally, the statement suggests these criteria for preservice and in-service programs (reprinted with the permission of the PTA):

- opportunity for teachers to identify their own strengths and needs for help as a base for planning their professional education
- involvement of direct classroom experience
- opportunity for learning to plan curriculum with other teachers and with use of community resources
- planning teams representing school and community interests
- continuity in program development
- periodic follow-up of specific efforts
- stress on respect for the student as a person and for the need to provide the student with understanding of skills and awareness of life options
- encouragement for teachers to recognize when they cannot help and should refer a particular student to other resources
- assistance to teachers in identifying additional resources for students
- respect for the enthusiasm of teachers
- support for teachers in feeling comfortable in the community and some skill development to help them make parents feel comfortable in the school
- provision for adequate and ongoing evaluation of pre-service and in-service programs
- systematic in-service development of teacher education faculties

The policy on PTA reviewing of instructional materials confirms the parental role in the reviewing process while recognizing that different criteria might be used to determine the appropriateness of required textbooks as compared to nonrequired materials. It suggests that PTAs become informed on procedures for selecting instructional materials in their own states and urges boards of education to provide a process involving input of lay citizens in regard to their appropriateness for the larger community. In states where such procedures cannot be implemented, PTAs are urged to try to change state laws.

Publications (Partial List)

The National PTA has a substantial publication program (about 40 inexpensive publications, 15 films and filmstrips) with two on-going publications, *PTA Today* and *PTA Communiqué* ($3.50/yr. for both). *PTA Today* (9 issues $2.50), which has won several awards, includes information on research, development, health and safety as well as information on PTA activities. *PTA Communiqué* reports on PTA locally, at the state level and nationally, with information on policies and procedures, activities and organization.

What's Happening in Washington ($3.00/yr.) is a rather inexpensive intermittent newsletter reporting on federal legislation relating to PTA priority concerns.

A few of their publications relevant to this book are:

Looking in on Your School: Questions to Guide PTA Fact Finders. 42p. $0.20. (100 copies for $16.00).

Reviews aims, practices and resources, with a "Quick Quiz on School Quality," which includes evaluation of materials.

The Fine Art of Parenting: A PTA Priority. 4p. Single copy free. (100 copies $4.00).

Suggests that parenting education should be an integral part of the public school curriculum and sets out what to include in a comprehensive program on parenthood education.

How to Help Your Child Select a Career. 4p. Single copy free. (100 copies $4.00).

Defines career education and explains why it should be integrated into each school's total curriculum for all students at all levels of education.

Mass Media and the PTA—Television—Radio—Comic Books—Movies—Pornography. (1970, 1962). 49p. $0.25.

This early effort includes action plans and worksheets for evaluating the mass media and a variety of suggestions for individual and PTA action to affect the trends and quality of mass media "in the direction of becoming the rich resources they might be."

Put an S in Your PTA. 12p. $0.15. (100 copies $12.00).

Suggests ways to include students in the work of the PTSA, with discussion of education programs that involved youth successfully.

The School Board and the PTA: Partners in Education. rp. $0.05. (100 copies
$4.00).
Describes responsibilities of parental involvement in school decision-making
with common-sense tips on maintaining good relations with school boards.

A complete list of publications is available on request from the PTA headquarters office.

The Parenting Materials Information Center (PMIC)
Southwest Educational Development Laboratory
211 East 7th Street
Austin, TX 78701   (512) 476-6861
The Parenting Materials Information Center, part of the Early Childhood Program of the Southwest Educational Development Laboratory, is an information
center for materials on parenting that includes about 4,000 items on all aspects of
parenting, indexed in 200 categories. Its current bibliography, *Parenting in 1977*
($5.00, prepaid), lists 3,700 items (print and nonprint) dealing with some aspects
of parenting, parent involvement, and/or parent education. It also offers a free
literature search for individuals looking for specific kinds of materials on parenting.

Parents' Network
National Committee for Citizens in Education (NCCE)
410 Wilde Lake Village Green
Columbia, MD 21044   800-NETWORK
An outgrowth of the National Committee for the Support of the Public
Schools (founded by Agnes Meyer in 1962), NCCE is now an information network
for the benefit of parents, designed to help parents and citizens deal effectively
with public school issues and problems. Membership at $15/yr. includes *Network*,
a monthly publication during the school year ($8.00/yr. to non-members), and two
publications of NCCE, as well as a citizen hotline (800-NETWORK).
As of early 1978, Parents' Network included 305 groups, representing 200,000
individuals in 40 states, whose members can get legal contacts, technical assistance,
and NCCE publications at reduced prices, while retaining autonomy. Members are
eligible to attend NCCE's Citizens Training Institutes which are held monthly at
different locations and which teach practical skills for working with school systems.
Since NCCE recommends parent participation in legislation affecting children, its services include legislative guidance, periodic surveys (public opinion
polls) on citizen participation issues and liaisons with other groups. Their productions include a substantial number of handbooks and filmstrips on topics like
parents' rights, organizing and *Materials Used in the Schools.* (This particular publication is currently being revised and should sell for around $1.50 when issued.)

Publications (Partial List)

Parents Organizing to Improve Schools. 1976. 52p. $2.00.
Provides step-by-step guides for organizing and running parent groups in
schools with the purpose of upgrading the quality of education through parental
involvement. Available in Spanish.

Schimmel, David, and Louis Fischer. *The Rights of Parents in the Education of Their Children.* 1977. 162p. $2.95 + $0.55 postage and handling.

This best seller—by parents who are lawyers and professors of education—discusses the legal rights of parents to make decisions about their children's education in the public schools, with descriptions of state and federal laws and court decisions which affect discipline, freedom of expression, racial and sexual discrimination, student rights and the rights of parents in the educational process. There are many implications for materials.

NCCE accomplishments include bringing the issue of school records to a national audience and supplying information incorporated into the Family Educational Rights and Privacy Act of 1974. It also convened the first national conference of Title I parents with other parents.

Vigilance in Public Education (VPE)
P.O. Box 4575
Santa Rosa, CA 95402   (707) 544-0437

This California pressure group, founded by a parent in 1976, developed a network of 2,000 citizens and liaisons with numerous other groups as it mobilized public opinion and pursued both research and legal means to oppose the use of commercial examples and the promotion of junk foods in mathematical problems.

Suzanne Barrera, the founder and coordinator, believes that parents are not only concerned, but responsible for the materials presented to children in public schools. VPE is active in establishing on-going committees to review textbooks displayed in California Public Schools Display Centers and is also concerned with corporate advertisements in free instructional materials.

Major Public Opinion Organizations

Gallup Organization, Inc.
53 Bank Street
Princeton, NJ 08540   (609) 924-9600

The easiest access to the current Gallup polls on contemporary issues is Gallup's expensive semi-weekly publication, *Gallup Opinion Index—Political, Social and Economic Trends* ($90.00/yr.), which tabulates results of polls and discusses their significance.

Phi Delta Kappa Educational Foundation has yearly reprints of the Gallup poll on education in *Phi Delta Kappan* and has published two books on public attitudes toward education revealed in the Gallup poll.

National Opinion Research Center (NORC)
6030 South Ellis Ave.
Chicago, IL 60637   (312) 753-1300

NORC surveys, unlike Gallup polls, tend to focus on single topics. These include relevant areas like public education, community problems, health, welfare and politics. NORC issues a *Newsletter* as well as a *Publications Bibliography.* As of early 1978, it had completed more than 200 comprehensive studies on a wide range of current-interest and/or opinion topics; reprints of surveys are available for many of these.

Roper Center, Inc.
Yale University Center
Box 1732, Yale Station
New Haven, CT 06520

The Roper Center serves as an international depository for survey data (in machine-readable form) from commercial market research firms and from academic public opinion polling organizations. Currently a total of nearly 15,000 files of social survey and related data are on file. Many of these files are accessible through the Roper Center. Its monthly publication, *Public Opinion* ($45.00/yr.), tabulates and discusses survey results of its own polls, as well as the Gallup Poll, the Harris Survey, the California Poll, Wallace's Farmer Opinion Poll and other significant polls.

KEY PUBLICATIONS

The works listed below were chosen for their potential value in providing community and parental input in educational and curricular issues, including the selection of instructional materials. Relevant materials issued by parent groups are incorporated into the parents'-group list which starts on page 188.

The Censorship Game and How to Play It, by C. Benjamin Cox. Arlington, VA, National Council for the Social Studies, 1977. (Bulletin 50). 48p. $3.95pa.
Suggests a rationale for a method of incorporating community concerns into materials selection and similar curriculum decision-making activities. His context implies respect for students, teachers and community. The method is a means of analyzing and balancing out values (assuming mutual goodwill). The appendix includes NCSS position papers on censorship and academic freedom.

How to Recognize a Good School, by Neil Postman and Charles Weingartner. Bloomington, IN, Phi Delta Kappa Educational Foundation, 1973. (Fastback 30). 42p. $0.75.
A useful starting place for actions and discussion for parent groups that include both parents and educators.

Know Your Schools. Washington, League of Women Voters, 1974. 31p. $1.00.
(From 1730 M St., NW, Washington, DC 20036.)
A compact and useful outline for a citizen study of local educational systems, with well-organized sample questions and how-to information. Covers program and systems, including ways to study special programs, community, teachers, facilities, etc.

Parental Involvement in Title I ESEA: Why? What? How? Washington, U.S. Office of Education, 1972. 12p. $0.45. (Single copy free from U.S. Office of Education.)

Explains the provisions of Public Law 91-230, mandating district-wide councils, with duties, roles and information needs of parent councils.

Parents and Schools, compiled by Clara Pederson. Grand Forks, ND, Center for Teaching and Learning, 1976. 51p. $2.20 including postage. (From Center for Teaching and Learning, University of North Dakota, Grand Forks, ND 58201.)
Selections which have been found useful in parent-teacher interactions include ways to use parents and community in the schools. Other sections provide guidelines and summaries of parent interviews and conferences.

Parents' Choice: A Review of Children's Media. Waban, MA, Parents' Choice Foundation, 1978- . 6 issues/yr. $7.00. (From Box 185, Waban, MA 02168.)
A professional publication written from a parental perspective, with perceptive and entertaining reviews and think pieces. Covers books, television, advertising, films, records, toys and games.

Surveying Your Community: An Approach to Community Involvement in Schools, by Beatrice Cromwell and Suzanne Root. Philadelphia, Research for Better Schools, 1976. Paged in sections. $8.00.
This guide—for school staffs rather than grass-roots parents' groups—is a well-structured, self-teaching workbook which provides thorough coverage of the tasks involved in a community survey. These include: defining the purpose, developing questions, deciding on methods, developing materials, conducting the survey, processing data, interpreting data and/or preparing a report.

What People Think about Their Schools: Gallup's Findings. Bloomington, IN, Phi Delta Kappa Educational Foundation, 1977. (Fastback 94). 66p. $0.75. (From Box 789, Bloomington, IN 47401.)
Very interesting summary and analysis of eight Gallup polls on attitudes toward public education, with a guide for those who would like to conduct local polls. The questions cover citizens' willingness to participate in education, as well as parental priorities in many areas.
Gallup polls on education are reported each year in *Phi Delta Kappan*'s November issue. Reprints are available from *Phi Delta Kappan*.

FOR FURTHER READING

*Items marked with an asterisk include criteria.
+Items marked with a plus have extensive references.

Carlson, Ken. "Censorship Should Be a Public, Not a Professional Decision," *Social Education*, v. 42, no. 3 (Feb. 1978), pp. 118-22.

Clark, Todd. "Community Participation: A Two-Way Street," *Social Education*, v. 41, no. 6 (Oct. 1977), pp. 557-58.
Community participation in the selection of curriculum materials is vital to the health of American education.

Clark, Todd. "The West Virginia Textbook Controversy: A Personal Account," *Social Education*, v. 39, no. 4 (April 1975), pp. 216-19.

Contreras, Angel D., and Oscar Uribe, Jr. *Communicating with Ethnically Different Parents.* San Francisco, Far West Laboratory for Educational Research and Development, 1974.

*Feldmesser, Robert A., and Esther Ann McCready. *Information for Parents on School Evaluation.* Princeton, NJ, ERIC Clearinghouse on Tests, Measurement, & Evaluation, Dec. 1974. (TM Report 42).

Fuller, Ralph N. "Textbook Selection: Burning Issue?," *Compact*, v. 9, no. 3 (June 1975), pp. 6-8.

Lurie, E. *How to Change the Schools: A Parents' Action Handbook on How to Fight the System.* New York, Random House, 1970.

McGough, Kris. "Confessions of a Book Burner," *Social Education*, v. 41, no. 6 (Oct. 1977), pp. 556-58.
Reports on Maryland's review policy.

*+Munger, Richard, and Mark M. Ravlin. *Furthering the Development of Children in Schools: The Role of Community Mental Health in the Synthesis of Cognitive and Affective Learning.* Ann Arbor, MI, Behavioral Science Education Project, 1977.

Naylor, David T. "Censorship in Our Schools: The Need for a Democratic Perspective," *Social Education*, v. 42, no. 3 (Feb. 1978), pp. 119-22.

Van Geel, Tyll. "Parental Preferences and the Politics of Spending Public Educational Funds," *Teachers College Record*, v. 79, no. 3 (Feb. 1978), pp. 339-64.

Webb, Kenneth W., and Harry P. Hatry. *Obtaining Citizen Feedback: The Application of Citizen Surveys to Local Government.* Washington, Urban Institute, 1973.

TEACHERS' ROLES IN SELECTION

"The whole art of teaching is only the art of awakening the natural curiosity of young minds for the purpose of satisfying it afterwards."
—Anatole France

"Today's teacher is becoming more of a manager and less of a wisdom dispenser... If teachers are to carry out this expanded role as selectors of materials, they must learn how to discriminate which materials will be appropriate for the desired results."
—Gordon Bleil, "Evaluating Educational Materials,"
Journal of Learning Disabilities, January 1975

"Flooding teachers with information is the flaw in a curriculum resource center which is no more than a storehouse of the 'validated products' from which teachers can select new goodies. What teachers need is supportive, constructively critical help in importing new ideas to their own classrooms. This almost always involves some adaptation or even substantial reinvention of the curriculum materials."
—Kathleen Devaney, "Surveying Teachers' Centers,"
Teachers' Center Exchange, Occasional Papers,
April 1977

"It is proposed, therefore, when teachers are asked to provide data about their experience with instructional materials, that they be assured their responses, and those of their peers, will be routed back to them in a way that will aid them in their task of selecting appropriate materials for their instructional needs."
—Glenn Latham, "Measuring Teacher Responses to
Instructional Materials," *Educational Technology*,
December 1974

■ ■ ■

Teachers—who spend almost as much time as students (maybe more!) with instructional materials, are in an equivocal position in relation to selecting these materials, hampered by censorship on one hand, feelings of inadequacy on the other, and possibly by boredom over the entire process.

The National Education Association, our largest professional organization, states that "the decision on which school learning experiences will develop a student's talents are best made by a teacher who knows the learner." A strong advocate of teacher input into selection and teacher selection without censorship, the NEA believes that materials selection policies are a suitable topic for contract negotiations.

While the NEA is attempting to assert and protect teachers' roles in selection, at least one parent organization—the National PTA—has policy statements demanding that teachers receive training in selecting materials for individual students, and asking them to accept alternative approaches to learning. Similarly, EPIE, while it deplores teachers' minimal role in selection, also notes that few teachers are trained for the task—a fact confirmed by the American Association of Colleges for Teacher Education, which, in answer to my request, was unable to locate a single college-level course in selection. (I later managed to locate a few.) Still, according to repeated surveys at teachers' centers and the National Needs

Assessment (for materials for the handicapped), teachers overwhelmingly expressed a need for workshops or training in selecting materials—particularly in selecting materials for individual students.

Among all these groups there seems to be an implicit consensus that the most appropriate selection role (for most teachers most of the time) is in selecting materials for their own students and for their own classrooms. In the main, teachers' strengths in assessing materials seem to derive from their knowledge of the teaching process, their sensitivity to practical difficulties in materials, and their intimate knowledge of the children they teach.

Though teachers are not always skilled at selecting materials, the *Michigan Cost-Effectiveness Study* (Washington, Turnkey Systems, 1976) indicated that the proportion of materials selected by the teacher is an important factor in reading achievement: the higher the fraction selected by teachers, the higher the reading results. The 1977 *California School Effectiveness Study* agreed with this finding while it stressed a sheer variety of materials as most important to reading success. If or when teachers were encouraged or given time to share their expertise (personal interests, specific teaching approaches, subject matter materials), teacher selection could be even more beneficial for their students.

Unfortunately, teachers selecting materials for their own classes are often not aware of the full range of available materials, nor of how to locate information. Their assets are their knowledgeability about students' ability levels, awareness of reading vocabulary and potential difficulties, a feel for whether or not the materials will integrate well with the rest of the curriculum and, perhaps most importantly, whether or not materials are likely to appeal to specific children.

To draw upon these strengths teachers should have some discretionary funds to spend through the year for specific needs and specific children, as well as easy access to at least one good, well-stocked, current library/media collection. Too often, when selection is done in advance, teachers have to select materials for next year's class of unknown children or for children in different schools or different programs.

For many teachers, selecting materials for their own students is a largely intuitive task. To develop their skills, teachers should be encouraged to articulate their own values and those of their school, their own best teaching styles and classroom objectives and priorities as well as those aspects of classroom arrangement, people patterns and time organization that affect materials. They should be encouraged to use or design simple records and evaluation systems that have room for comments on materials. Above all, teachers need to consider many factors simultaneously to choose materials with contents appropriate for their styles, curriculum goals, and their particular classroom mix.

While principals in EPIE'S NSAIM tended to perceive teachers as playing a significant role in selection, 45 percent of teachers surveyed claimed no role whatever in selecting materials, while 30 percent spend less than one hour per year on selection and 25 percent spend an average of 10 hours per year on the process. Despite this relative lack of choice, the survey indicated that the majority of teachers said they were fairly satisfied with or at least adapted to the materials they were assigned to use.

Nonetheless, repeated assessments of teachers' perceived needs have found teachers wanting help in individualization and in selecting materials, particularly where the two intersect. For example, Peter Martin, surveying teachers in nine rural towns in east-central Connecticut found that "a materials-based center would be most successful, initially, at least."

This survey, reported in *Teachers' Center Exchange*, revealed that some important teacher priorities are: individualizing instruction, locating free or inexpensive materials, motivating slow learners and gifted students, creating and introducing learning centers, developing metrics curricula, and updating or creating guides and materials for career education, science, social studies and language arts. Other materials-related needs are organizing audiovisual materials, making media programs and establishing a teacher-resource center.

Dr. Carol A. Vale of Educational Testing Service, who conducted the National Needs Assessment (for handicapped children) discussed on page 299, also found that the greatest learning priority of these teachers as a group (almost 90 percent) is learning how to select materials for individual learning needs. A very high proportion of teachers working with special-education children wanted help in the following specific areas: selecting media according to pupil function (88.5 percent), designing or adapting media according to functional levels (88.1 percent), adapting materials for specific learning objectives (81 percent), selecting according to pupil interest levels (77 percent), evaluating effectiveness of selection (70 percent). Of the teachers surveyed, a consistent 69 percent (of different teachers) wanted help in selecting materials for 1) specific learning objectives, 2) language and speech, 3) social and personal development, 4) cognitive development, and 5) academic development.

Similarly, when I was part of a California State panel preparing a directory for educators of the gifted, our first section was a guide and directory to sources of materials.

Even though they want to learn selection sources and to improve their skill in selection, teachers—almost universally—dislike filling out existing evaluation forms. In a series of interviews with teachers at all levels of the public school system, G. Latham found that teachers considered these forms too long, too irrelevant and a bother. I myself know teachers who would have been willing to pay in order not to fill out Vale's competent, lengthy, and—to me—interesting National Needs Assessment form. Despite this teacher preference, I am including some forms on pages 202-213 and 217-219 for teachers to review to help them develop and refine their own selection criteria. (Other recommended forms are noted in the asterisked [*] items in For Further Reading.)

Other teacher assessments have similar findings. The predominant emphasis on selecting for individuals and small groups or topics—as well as the hostility to standard evaluations—implies, in my opinion, a recognition that teachers and learners are not static and that materials may not be universally applicable. An excellent teaching tool in one teacher-student or teacher-class combination can be educationally valueless in another situation.

Unfortunately, in the real world of educational planning and educational materials, provisions are rarely made for the real differences that exist among teachers (or students) in interests, knowledge, experience and expertise. Teachers are treated as if they all were equally competent in all subject fields and in all media and methods of instruction. Textbooks and teachers' manuals are set up for some least common denominator of teacher and student competence. As a result, they can be difficult for some while boringly obvious to others.

Unfortunately, again, teachers who spend most of their school time in one classroom with one group of children have few opportunities to develop expertise on materials. A great deal of teacher energy is devoted merely to keeping school going and to getting through the day, with little time left for activities to improve educational practices and materials.

In an isolated classroom it is hard to know just what is going on. One study by Gene Hall and his colleagues at the Research and Development Center for Teacher Education at the University of Texas (reported by Joseph Schneider) found that 20 percent of teachers in innovative schools were not individualizing instruction, while 49 percent of the teachers at "traditional" schools were individualizing their classes.

Since most school staffs function in relative isolation from other schools, teachers tend to be classroom rulers rather than team members. There may be limited sharing of ideas and expertise within each school. There are few mechanisms, except for selection and curriculum committees, teacher centers and extension courses, for sharing creative ideas, instructional approaches and instructional materials with other teachers in other schools, programs or districts. Except for resource teachers and experienced substitute teachers, few teachers in any district have wide experiences with a variety of materials. With declining budgets for materials, libraries and media centers, many schools, particularly elementary schools, have very few supplementary or individualized materials available for enrichment and for particular student needs.

Many teachers themselves have somewhat ambivalent attitudes toward materials, or at least materials budgets. "They don't think about school libraries until they close," according to the Sacramento office of the California Teachers Association. I would not be surprised if some teachers who complained loudly about closed libraries and the dearth of materials had advocated these particular cuts for resolving California's educational budget crisis. Still, most teachers—or at least most teacher members of the National Education Association—spend a fair amount of money from their own pockets buying materials for their classrooms. According to NEA's Research Division, 66.9 percent of classroom teachers spent some personal funds on instructional materials in the six-month period between July 1975 and January 1976; 25.7 percent spent from $1.00 to $25.00; 20.1 percent spent from $26.00 to $50.00; 12.4 percent spent between $51.00 and $100.00; while 8.6 percent spent more than $100.00 each. Assuming 1.8 million members of the NEA, this would add up to about $31.6 million.

Certainly every big city has Teachers Exchanges and educational supply stores that sell most of their materials directly to teachers buying for their own students. The very existence of such stores—and similar resource and display institutions such as textbook display centers, libraries, and math laboratories—can be a positive force for selection by increasing teachers' awareness of materials and helping them become more sophisticated in choosing. Often teachers tend to become more choosey, eclectic and original.

Gordon Bleil has some good advice for teachers selecting materials at such centers, with their own or district money: "Don't shop on an empty stomach!" Materials too often are marketed for teacher appeal rather than student performance. He believes that teachers should make (and keep handy) an ongoing list of needs and suggests that a short evaluation list is better than a massive screening process that is too cumbersome to be used. He believes, too, that teachers should attempt to buy materials that help multiply their own effectiveness (since you cannot be everywhere at once), and should not expect any materials to replace teachers in managing or even in motivating kids.

While some materials are intrinsically interesting and attractive to children, teachers may have to choose other materials which have learning strengths (such as logic, sequence or clarity), and set up the motivation for use outside the materials themselves. Bleil, who works mostly with teachers of exceptional children, feels that, for these groups at least, built-in clues are important for students—particularly verbal or visual clues. He believes materials should supply data on what they attempt to do and that this data can be structured to be part of the motivation, or structured so that children can chart their own process of reaching goals.

I feel myself that if materials are interesting to children and organized for self-instruction, teachers can choose to supply their own data or charts for learning goals and activities.

Bleil's advice is, in a sense, almost a form of consumer education for teachers: Be wary of superlatives, magic solutions and fad words. (For whom is "high-interest/low-vocabulary" interesting?) Specifics, too, may be meaningless; a grade-level label, for instance, labels a structure, not any particular student who happens to be in that grade. A less specific range may be more apt to be appropriate.

He feels that teachers need to become aware of why they buy, and be able to identify the elements that make them decide for or against specific items. For improving selection, I would heartily recommend an informal teacher self-assessment that covers classroom environment, children's strengths and needs, and an awareness of the teacher's own strengths, weaknesses and preferences. (Some of the materials reproduced in the chapter entitled "Needs Assessments," see page 45, may prove helpful in these assessments.)

Another approach is that of James D. Raths, who, in "Teaching without Specific Objectives," sets up some criteria that can be quite helpful in identifying educational activities that are truly educational. He believes activities or materials are apt to be inherently worthwhile if they:

- permit or encourage children to make informed choices
- employ active rather than passive learning roles
- engage students in inquiry into ideas, personal or social problems, or applications of intellectual processes
- involve children with real objects or realia
- can be completed successfully by children of different abilities
- explore *in a new setting* something studied earlier
- examine important topics or issues, largely ignored by our society or communication media
- involve a risk or success or failure
- require students to rewrite, rehearse or polish initial efforts
- involve students in the mastery of meaningful rules, standards or disciplines
- allow children to share responsibilities for planning or carrying plans through
- relate to expressed purposes of students

These criteria establish a baseline which teachers can use to estimate the learning potentials of materials, as do the cognitive criteria in the chapter entitled "Thinking about Thinking" (see page 125).

More pragmatic desiderata for materials are that they:

- fulfill a need not currently met by available materials

- are reasonable in cost

- are appropriate to the location, structure and physical environment of the classroom

- allow a reasonable amount of time for completion in relation to the time available for a skill or subject

Other criteria for teachers can be found in the chapter on individualization starting on page 272, as well as chapters on particular media and subject areas. The criteria for curricular guides and workbooks are in the chapter entitled "Selecting Basic Learning Materials" (see pages 257-258). Teachers selecting textbooks should review this chapter carefully; it has a fairly complete exposition of criteria and the role of the selection committee. Learning activities can be scanned with the criteria for workbooks on pages 259-260 and on the criteria above.

As a means of coding materials, the *Strategy Notebook* (San Francisco, Interaction Associates, 1972) provides the following instructional strategies which may also serve as a checklist for selection. (The *Notebook* is available for $3.50 plus $1.00 handling, from Interaction Associates, 149 Ninth St., San Francisco, CA 94103.) This outline is reprinted with their permission.

1. Master Strategies
   a. Build up
   b. Eliminate
   c. Work forwards
   d. Work backwards

2. Strategies for Set Manipulation
   a. Associate
   b. Classify
   c. Generalize
   d. Exemplify
   e. Compare
   f. Relate

3. Strategies for Involvement
   a. Commit
   b. Defer
   c. Leap in
   d. Hold back
   e. Focus
   f. Release
   g. Force
   h. Relax
   i. Dream
   j. Imagine
   k. Purge
   l. Incubate

4. Strategies for Manipulating Information
   a. Display
   b. Organize
   c. List
   d. Check
   e. Diagram
   f. Chart
   g. Verbalize
   h. Visualize

5. Strategies for Information Retrieval
   a. Memorize
   b. Recall
   c. Record
   d. Retrieve
   e. Search
   f. Select

6. Strategies for Dealing with the Future
   a. Plan
   b. Predict
   c. Assume
   d. Question
   e. Hypothesize
   f. Guess

(Item 6. continues on page 203)

6.	Strategies for Dealing with the Future (cont'd)	7.	Strategies for Physical Manipulation
	g. Define		a. Play
	h. Symbolize		b. Manipulate
	i. Simulate		c. Copy
	j. Test		d. Interpret
			e. Transform

The Open Education Assessment for the Corridor Schools in New York City started out with a provision for assessing materials in their statement on the planning and preparation of the classroom environment:

> Provide appropriate materials characterized by richness and variety, attractively arranged and accessible to children, in a planned environment that allows for social interaction of children, for individual differences in learning, for continuity of the learning and for a variety of interactions (teacher with individual child, with whole class and with the corridor community).

This teacher's diagnostic instrument was designed by Elli Ohringer and Agnese Violensis of the Advisory Service of the Workshop for Open Education, 6 Shepard Hall, City College, New York City, NY 10031. This portion is reprinted from *Evaluation Reconsidered: A Position Paper* (1973).

To aid in this assessment forms like the one reproduced below can be adapted for reporting the results back to teachers. They can, of course, be prepared for all subjects and for all kinds of materials.

TEACHER RESPONSE FORM
INSTRUCTIONAL MATERIALS NEEDS ASSESSMENT

LANGUAGE ARTS

Return to your curriculum) committee at
            selection)   by

I   Rank the following curriculum areas in terms of your priority needs for materials. (Use 1 for most important.)

Your grade level:

English
Reading
Mathematics
Literature
Handwriting
Social Studies
Spelling
Health
Other

II   Do your current language arts materials meet your students' needs?

Yes   No   To a degree

Are there any specific materials you would prefer?

(Questionnaire continues on page 204)

II   (cont'd)

What approaches do you prefer?

Individualized   Comments:
Basal
Language experience
Programmed

Which English approaches do you prefer?

Eclectic   Thematic
Language analysis   Language mechanics
Oral language   Creative writing
Programmed   Traditional
Composition   Transformational
Listening   Other

Comments:

Do the current materials meet your needs?

Yes   No   To a degree

Are there any specific materials you would prefer?

This Teacher Opinionnaire (page 205) reprinted with permission of Association for Educational Communications and Technology from *Evaluating Media Programs: District and School*, evaluates the adequacy of the media center and program in relationship to teacher needs. (This material is not to be reproduced further without permission.)

TEACHER OPINIONNAIRE

Subject _____

Grade _____

Always
Frequently
Occasionally
Seldom
Never

1. I can easily find relevant materials in the media center . . . . ☐ ☐ ☐ ☐ ☐

2. I use instructional materials in my classes. . . . . ☐ ☐ ☐ ☐ ☐

3. My requests for assistance from the media center staff are promptly, adequately, and conveniently filled. . . . . ☐ ☐ ☐ ☐ ☐

4. Lack of resources affects my use of the media center . . . . ☐ ☐ ☐ ☐ ☐

5. Indifference to my requests affects my use of the media center . . . . ☐ ☐ ☐ ☐ ☐

6. Inadequate staffing prevents my fullest use of the media center . . . . ☐ ☐ ☐ ☐ ☐

7. The professional materials collection is up-to-date and relevant . . . . ☐ ☐ ☐ ☐ ☐

8. I use the professional materials collection. . . . . ☐ ☐ ☐ ☐ ☐

9. I am asked to participate in the selection of new materials. . . . . ☐ ☐ ☐ ☐ ☐

10. I do participate in the selection of new materials . . . . ☐ ☐ ☐ ☐ ☐

11. My requests for new materials are honored equally with other requests as budgetary limitations permit . . . . ☐ ☐ ☐ ☐ ☐

12. My requests for new equipment are honored equally with other requests as budgetary limitations permit . . . . ☐ ☐ ☐ ☐ ☐

13. I participate actively in media in-service workshops as offered . . . . . ☐ ☐ ☐ ☐ ☐

14. The media center staff offers a wide variety of media in-service workshops during the school year. . . . . ☐ ☐ ☐ ☐ ☐

15. I make media items for instructing my classes . . . . ☐ ☐ ☐ ☐ ☐

16. I have the media center produce materials for my teaching . . . . ☐ ☐ ☐ ☐ ☐

17. My students produce original media materials . . . . ☐ ☐ ☐ ☐ ☐

18. I utilize types of television as follows:
    (a) commercial television. . . . . ☐ ☐ ☐ ☐ ☐
    (b) educational and instructional television . . . . ☐ ☐ ☐ ☐ ☐
    (c) programs produced by the school . . . . ☐ ☐ ☐ ☐ ☐
    (d) videotaping of teacher and student self-evaluation . . . . ☐ ☐ ☐ ☐ ☐

19. My students make independent use of media . . . . ☐ ☐ ☐ ☐ ☐

20. My students successfully locate materials in the media center collection. . . . . ☐ ☐ ☐ ☐ ☐

21. Time is available to preview instructional media . . . . ☐ ☐ ☐ ☐ ☐

22. The principal supports the media center staff in providing a full array of media services . . . . ☐ ☐ ☐ ☐ ☐

23. The superintendent recognizes the need for and supports quality and variety of media services needed for an effective instructional program. . . . . ☐ ☐ ☐ ☐ ☐

24. The Board of Education recognizes the need for and supports the quality and variety of media services needed for an effective instructional program . . . . ☐ ☐ ☐ ☐ ☐

These *Standard Criteria for the Selection and Evaluation of Instructional Material*—which, unfortunately, are now out of print—were developed by NCEMMH for teachers selecting materials for individual students—to be more precise, individual handicapped students. They stem from a lengthy ten-year project and seem appropriate for teacher selection in many teaching-learning situations.

NCEMMH CRITERIA FOR MATERIALS SELECTION AND EVALUATION AT THE TEACHER LEVEL

I. IDENTIFICATION OF NEEDS

The outcome of stage I will be: a definition of the target learner and the learning environment prior to any selection of suitable instructional materials.

A. Learner Characteristics

(The following outline is intended to serve as a guideline to the selector of instructional materials in identifying the characteristics and educational requirements of the specific learner for whom material is being sought.)

1. Has an assessment of the learner occurred, and does the resulting data specify:

a. demographic information about the learner, including:

Yes No NA

___ ___ ___   (1) age

___ ___ ___   (2) sex

___ ___ ___   (3) instructional/developmental level

___ ___ ___   (4) language development or preference

___ ___ ___   (5) interest level

___ ___ ___   b. limiting conditions (medical/physical factors, etc.)

___ ___ ___   c. behavioral/affective characteristics

___ ___ ___   d. preferred modalities

___ ___ ___   e. strength areas

___ ___ ___   f. deficit areas

2. Has an educational plan been developed, based on learner assessment data, which specifies:

___ ___ ___   a. needed skill area

___ ___ ___   b. short and long-term instructional objectives

___ ___ ___   c. instructional strategies, including:

___ ___ ___   (1) sequencing

___ ___ ___   (2) reinforcement

___ ___ ___   (3) modalities (input/output)

___ ___ ___   (4) monitoring

(Text continues on page 212)

Yes No NA

          d.   recommendations for:

— — —   (1) general instructional areas

— — —   (2) specific materials

— — —   (3) related activities

B. Program Characteristics

(The following outline is intended to serve as a guideline to the selector of instructional materials in identifying the overall program considerations with the specific learner(s) and learning requirements in mind.)

    1. Have provisions been made for integration of the individual educational plan into the total instructional program:

— — —   a. content

— — —   b. curricular compatibility

— — —   c. format/alternatives

    2. Would implementation of the educational plan be affected by any of the following environmental constraints:

— — —   a. time/cost/physical considerations

— — —   b. grouping

— — —   c. equipment

— — —   d. personnel

— — —   e. teacher skill

II. INITIAL SELECTION

The outcome of stage II will be: the identification of at least two pieces of instructional material which, on first screening, appear compatible with learner requirements and which will be considered for further review. Identification of alternative materials for examination will facilitate final selection decisions on a comparative basis.

A. Search

(The items listed below outline the most common information resources available to the selector of instructional materials. The intent of this section is to

(Checklist continues on page 208)

encourage the user to investigate various potential materials information sources.)

1. Have you located resources which might provide information about materials:

_____ a. colleagues

_____ b. commercial

_____ c. materials bibliographies

_____ d. journals

_____ e. curriculum libraries and centers (colleges, schools for handicapped, learning resource centers)

_____ f. professional organizations

_____ g. governmental agencies
(national network, audio-visual center, etc.)

_____ h. information systems (NIMIS, EPIE, ERIC, etc.)

2. As a result of the above process, have you identified at least two instructional materials which appear to address the learner's needs?

B. Screen

(Under optimal conditions, a written product abstract or review will provide information pertaining to all of the items listed below, so that actual inspection of the product is not necessary. In the absence of thorough and accurate material descriptions, however, scrutiny of the material itself will be required. A secondary intent of this section is to educate both material users and material abstractors (including commercial publishers) about desirable elements to be included in product reviews.)

1. Does the material information resource provide information about the identified instructional product(s), such as:

Yes No   NA

___ ___ ___ a. instructional level

___ ___ ___ b. language level

___ ___ ___ c. interest level

___ ___ ___ d. sensory input and output modalities

___ ___ ___ e. educational subject/skill content

Yes   No   NA

___ ___ ___   f.   format

___ ___ ___   g.   cost

___ ___ ___   h.   grouping requirement(s)

___ ___ ___   i.   required equipment

      2.   On the basis of the available information, does the identified instructional material appear compatible with:

___ ___ ___   a.   learner characteristics

      (1)   the learner assessment

      (2)   the learner educational plan

___ ___ ___   b.   program characteristics

      (1)   the total instructional program considerations

      (2)   the identified environmental constraints

III. REVIEW

The outcome of stage III will be: an in-depth analysis of an instructional material in order to define the material's characteristics and match these characteristics to previously defined learner requirements. Implementation of this stage necessitates actual examination of the instructional material.

A. Analysis of Material

(This section includes recommended questions for determining the intrinsic qualities of the material(s) independent of specific learner characteristics and program requirements.)

___ ___ ___ 1.   Are objectives in behavioral terms (specifying what the student task is, under what conditions, and level of performance expected)?

___ ___ ___ 2.   Are techniques of instruction for each lesson either clearly specified or self-evident?

___ ___ ___ 3.   Are facts, concepts, and principles ordered in a logical manner (e.g., chronologically, easy to difficult, etc.)?

___ ___ ___ 4.   Does the material contain appropriate supplementary or alternative activities that contribute to or extend proposed learning?

___ ___ ___ 5.   Is repetition and review of content material systematic and appropriately spaced?

(Checklist continues on page 210)

Yes No NA

___ ___ ___ 6. Does the content appear accurate?

___ ___ ___ 7. Does the material avoid content which betrays prejudice, perpetuates stereotypes, or neglects the talents, contributions, or aspirations of any segment of the population?

___ ___ ___ 8. Can the material be readily adapted to meet individual learner differences in abilities and interests?

___ ___ ___ 9. Can pacing of the material be adapted to variations in learner rate of mastery?

___ ___ ___ 10. Is provision made for adapting, altering, or combining input and response modalities according to learner variations?

___ ___ ___ 11. Does the material incorporate evaluation items and procedures which are compatible with program objectives?

___ ___ ___ 12. Are there sufficient evaluative items to accurately assess student progress?

___ ___ ___ 13. Is performance assessed frequently enough to allow accurate assessment of student progress and continuous feedback to learner?

___ ___ ___ 14. Is the format uncluttered, grammatically correct, and free of typographical errors?

___ ___ ___ 15. Are illustrations and photographs clear, attractive, and appropriate to content?

___ ___ ___ 16. Are auditory components of adequate clarity and amplification?

___ ___ ___ 17. Are all necessary components either provided with the material or readily and inexpensively available?

___ ___ ___ 18. Can consumable portions of material be easily and inexpensively replaced or legally reproduced?

___ ___ ___ 19. Is cost reasonable in comparison with similar commercial materials or homemade alternatives?

___ ___ ___ 20. Does the publisher clearly state the rationale for selection of program elements, content, and methodology (e.g., choice may be based on tradition, survey of other materials, logic of subject matter, experimental evidence, unvalidated theory)?

___ ___ ___ 21. Are testimonials, research, and publisher claims clearly differentiated?

___ ___ ___ 22. Are reinforcement procedures and schedules clearly indicated?

___ ___ ___ 23. Is a variety of cuing and prompting techniques used?

B. Matching Material to Learner

(This section involves the integration of the identified learner needs with the analyzed material characteristics to determine compatibility for instructional purposes.)

Yes No NA

___ ___ ___ 1. Are stated objectives and scope of the material compatible with learner's need?

___ ___ ___ 2. Are prerequisite student skills/abilities needed to work comfortably and successfully with the material specified and compatible with the learner's characteristics?

___ ___ ___ 3. Are the skills and abilities needed by the instructor to work effectively with the material specified and compatible with instructor's expertise?

___ ___ ___ 4. Are levels of interest, abstraction, vocabulary, and sentence structure compatible with characteristics of the learner?

___ ___ ___ 5. Is the degree of required teacher involvement (constant interaction, supportive or monitoring role, largely student directed, variable) compatible with teacher resources and learner characteristics?

___ ___ ___ 6. Does the material incorporate motivational devices to sustain student interest which are appropriate to the learner's characteristics?

___ ___ ___ 7. Are input and output modalities (visual, auditory, motor, tactile) compatible with learner characteristics?

___ ___ ___ 8. Is the demonstration of task mastery (e.g., written test, performance test, oral test) compatible with or adaptable to intended learner's characteristics?

___ ___ ___ 9. Is the format of the material (e.g., game, book, filmstrip, etc.) compatible with the learner's mental and physical abilities?

___ ___ ___ 10. Is the durability and safety of the material adequate for the learner?

___ ___ ___ 11. Is information provided indicating (successful) field testing of the material with students similar in learning characteristics and interests to those of the learner?

IV. DECISION MAKING

The outcome of stage IV will be: a final determination of material suitability for use in a specific learning situation. Individualization of the decision making, based on items of priority concern, is implicit in this process.

(Checklist continues on page 212)

A. As a result of the review process, which questions have you identified as (most) critical to you in deciding to utilize the material with the learner?

B. On the basis of those critical priority concerns, is the material appropriate for specified learning requirements?

_____ Yes   (implies accept)

_____ No   (implies reject)

_____ Unsure   (requires more analysis)

C. If unsure of appropriateness, are there other less critical questions which could be considered in making the decision to utilize the material?

D. On the basis of those additional considerations, is the material now deemed appropriate for specified learning requirements?

_____ Yes

_____ Unsure

E. If still unsure of appropriateness of the material, will comparison with other previewed material(s), in relation to critical questions, help identify the material which most closely approximates the specified learning requirements?

F. If still unsure of the appropriateness of the material, would modifications of the material render it usable?

1. Do you have access to resources for required modification?

G. If no:

1. Return to search process. Re-examine sources of material identification and information in locating other potential materials.

2. Review learner characteristics in an effort to modify requirements for material.

John A. McLaughlin and Jack S. Trlica's *Instructional Materials Evaluation Form* (shown on page 213) for teachers of exceptional children can be completed in 10 to 12 minutes and is machine-readable for rapid analysis. This form is reprinted from *Educational Technology* (March 1976) with the permission of the authors and the publisher.

The Teachers National Field Task Force on the Improvement and Reform of American Education, in their *Final Report* in 1974, strongly recommended teachers' centers as a major instrument for curriculum reform. Kathleen Devaney, who heads the Teachers' Center Exchange, commented extensively on teachers' center roles vis-à-vis curriculum materials in the April 1977 issue of *Teachers' Centers Exchange*.

According to Ms. Devaney, "the basic stock in trade of many teachers' centers is a 'make-it-and-take-it' workshop," where teachers construct some child-appealing lessons to bring back to their classrooms:

(Quote appears on page 214)

INSTRUCTIONAL MATERIALS EVALUATION FORM

Title_____

Terminal objectives_____

I.

   +   N A

1. ▯ ▯ ▯ Fits existing terminal objectives
2. ▯ ▯ ▯ Can be extended to other phases of curriculum
3. ▯ ▯ ▯ Helps accomplish objectives of curriculum
4. ▯ ▯ ▯ Organized for sequential development of concepts/skills
5. ▯ ▯ ▯ Enables student to practice and maintain concepts/skills
6. ▯ ▯ ▯ Provision made to evaluate progress
7. ▯ ▯ ▯ Enables student exploration, problem solving, discovery
8. ▯ ▯ ▯ Allows flexibility, provides for individual differences
9. ▯ ▯ ▯ Motivating to student
10. ▯ ▯ ▯ Multi-sensory in approach
11. ▯ ▯ ▯ Content
12. ▯ ▯ ▯ Interest level
13. ▯ ▯ ▯ Reading level
14. ▯ ▯ ▯ Vocabulary
15. ▯ ▯ ▯ Graphic illustrations
16. ▯ ▯ ▯ Instructions for student clear, concise, easily understood
17. ▯ ▯ ▯ Instructions for teacher easily followed, appropriate
18. ▯ ▯ ▯ Allows independent use by student
19. ▯ ▯ ▯ Format
20. ▯ ▯ ▯ Type size, material used in construction
21. ▯ ▯ ▯ Size, number of parts, storage factor, portability
22. ▯ ▯ ▯ Durability
23. ▯ ▯ ▯ Requires in-service training for users
24. ▯ ▯ ▯ Teaching value justifies its cost
25. ▯ ▯ ▯ Requires adaptation for present purposes
26. ▯ ▯ ▯ Can be used with bilingual children

II. Number of pupils for whom material requested: 1 ▯ 2–5 ▯ 6+ ▯

III. Capacity in which you serve exceptional children:

▯ Special class teacher   ▯ Regular class teacher

▯ Resource teacher   ▯ Speech therapist

▯ Educational diagnostician   ▯ Hearing therapist

▯ Bilingual educator   ▯ Student

▯ Other (specify)_____

IV. With what type of child will material be used:

▯ EMR   ▯ TMR

▯ L/LD   ▯ PMR

▯ Blind   ▯ Deaf

▯ Physically handicapped   ▯ Multiply handicapped

▯ Special health problems   ▯ Speech impaired

▯ Emotionally disturbed   ▯ Minimally brain-injured

▯ Partially sighted   ▯ Hard-of-hearing

▯ Regular class   ▯ Other_____

V. Educational level of material desired:

▯ Pre-school   ▯ 6–7 years

▯ 8–9 years   ▯ 10–11 years

▯ 12–13 years   ▯ 14–15 years

▯ 16–17 years   ▯ 18–up

VI. Current location of instructional program:

▯ Regular class   ▯ Special class

▯ Resource room   ▮ Homebound

▯ Other_____

PLEASE USE THE REVERSE SIDE FOR CRITICAL COMMENTS

> In their ongoing emphasis on concrete curriculum materials, teachers' centers
> hark back to the voices in the curriculum development movement of the '60s
> who called for hands-on, "real-life," lesson material with which to teach the
> 3 R's, science, and social studies. These materials, easily adaptable to students
> of differing achievement levels, could be used with heterogeneous as well as
> homogeneous groups of students. Many teachers' centers are led by first- or
> second-generation leaders of those curriculum projects. These people still con-
> centrate on inventing or adapting curriculum materials *with* teachers, and help-
> ing teachers make use of the potent learning experiences in nature, homes, and
> communities. In the teachers' centers' perspective, the curriculum development
> task is never-ending and must be teacher-involving, especially where there are
> schools operating under social mandates for desegregation, "mainstreaming"
> mentally retarded into regular classrooms, or other forms of mixed-ability
> grouping. Such mandates create a multiplicity of learning backgrounds and
> styles among students, which in turn demand that a teacher continually collect,
> adapt, or concoct new curriculum materials to fit particular children and to help
> children understand and value each other. . . .
>
> Communicating over curriculum—literally choosing, adapting or develop-
> ing materials—is a way of "diagnosing" what teachers need (page 4).

This way of diagnosis is one that Ms. Devaney considers more accurate than needs
assessment.

Ms. Devaney believes that teachers' center strategy, organization and pedagogical styles—if applied to some "critical, but not overwhelming mass of
teachers"—might energize teachers to invest themselves in new ideas. Applied to
curriculum and materials, it could:

> Gain teachers involvement in tailoring curriculum for their own classroom and
> students, using an expansive, beyond-the-classroom-walls definition of what are
> appropriate learning materials and experiences. Help teachers tie informal,
> student-appealing learning episodes to formal concepts and skills, so that
> students' experience of the wider community and natural environment as part
> of schoolwork are at a thinking level deeper than show-and-tell (page 7).

Teachers' centers as they now exist are probably a major information source
for teachers on materials and programs, whether or not they are about to call forth
an educational utopia. They themselves are an invaluable information source on
the felt needs of teachers. They are set up for in-service training and have often
developed curricula for local needs (though they are not always aware of the
existence of comparable commercial materials). Often they are experts on making
inexpensive equipment and using recyclables. Individual teachers' centers have put
out more or less substantial bibliographies and lists of materials, including a now-
out-of-print *Catalog of Self-Published Learning Materials* compiled by Berkeley's
Center for Open Learning and Teaching.

The National Education Association, which also wants teachers to be major
selectors of instructional materials, works on three fronts—opposition to censorship, a demand that selection policies be part of contract negotiation and some
modest recommendations for selection training through its project on Utilization
of In-Service Education. But, whether teachers' exclusive rights to determine content and method are actually protected by the First Amendment is a subject for
heated controversy, even court action. I have discussed a few aspects in my chapter
on parent/community involvement.

So long as instructional materials are selected for legitimate school objectives and curricula and are appropriate to the age of the students, who should have some sort of choice in alternative materials, teachers probably are covered by the First Amendment. However, the demand for absolute autonomy, like the demand for settling selection policies by negotiations between the school administration and a teachers' organization, seems to indicate some insensitivity to or fear of the community. Clearly it is hard to draw a fast line between selection and censorship. (I select, you censor.)

Unfortunately the English teachers, librarians and social studies teachers who are most apt to run aground on censorship issues include many individuals who are capable of choosing materials extremely well but who do not include selection as a dimension of community relations. For selection, particularly of large basal programs, I would like to see some community input and alternatives as well as teacher input.

Overall, the quest for increased teacher choice in selection is, I believe, healthy. If teachers have more choice in materials for their own classrooms, they are likely to become supporters of adequate budgets for these materials. The main problem in teacher selection for individual classrooms is excessive duplication or possessiveness within a school or a district. Teamed buying, central catalogs or inventories, materials workshops, and other means of sharing materials or information may minimize this flaw. If teachers can work closely with librarians and media specialists in selecting enrichment or supplementary materials, or check out their own orders from a common source, the problem will be negligible.

Ideally, teachers making selections should be assisted by competent reviews, recommendations, source lists and possibly summaries of evaluations; they should move beyond their traditional methods of selecting from publishers' catalogs, informational flyers, magazine advertisements and chance encounters at meetings. Rather, an intelligent selection of source guides from the subject and media sources recommended in this book and in such works as Mary Sive's *Selecting Instructional Media* should be available somewhere nearby in each district.

The NEA is quite realistic on the need for released time in selecting instructional materials, whether for individual selection or for selection by committee. Many teachers would like released time or free time in preservice orientations to study the range of materials available to them. If released time is given during the school years, teachers can look for materials as needs arise during the course of instruction and can evaluate materials with particular problem areas in mind. When I worked at the Gifted Resource Center in San Mateo County—a now-defunct resource consultation center for gifted students in Northern California—teachers, especially those from remote counties, would spend days browsing, writing down comments, and selecting materials.

In-service training and staff orientation should be used to apprise teachers of sources and facilities in their own districts that can facilitate their choice of material. Teachers should be made aware of the existence of services and facilities like central inventories, computer catalogs or instructional materials centers. These organizations, in turn, need to make an effort to inform teachers of their services by materials workshops and other means.

Teachers often could use training in use of materials by curriculum experts (for textbooks and subject matter materials) and librarians (on the range of possibilities in trade books and media). Essentially, teachers select materials by valid, if usually unarticulated criteria. They can improve their selection skills by broadening and extending their individualized or programmatic criteria. This is particularly important for teachers in early childhood education, special education, open education and individualized education.

Teachers need a great deal of exposure to the range of materials available. They need time (and sometimes support) to incorporate new materials into instructional patterns, and they can benefit from training in selecting instructional materials. In fact, teachers, especially reading teachers, flock to resource classes and classes on children's literature.

Since textbook publishers—to a degree—depend more than other publishers on quasi-district monopolies and geographic clusters, increased teacher involvement in selection might slightly increase the cost of individual textbooks and make publisher assistance more costly as programs become geographically dispersed. This would probably not occur if teacher involvement resulted in larger materials budgets.

A greater teacher involvement in selection could make the task of major educational publishers and producers more difficult, but it would open up opportunities for smaller and more innovative publishers. District-wide teacher involvement in selection also allows opportunities for in-depth assessment of alternative programs and materials. If districts or schools elect to stay with one text or one text series, full teacher involvement in selection will assure that teachers know the virtues and defects of the text they are using.

The forms designed by Masako Tanaka seem well suited for this purpose. This screening instrument was designed to help teachers in Berkeley, California, choose the most suitable social studies text for their students from texts already screened by the state of California. Since Berkeley is a multi-racial, politically-conscious area, social fairness was considered first priority. Each book was evaluated by 14 teacher-reviewers, with a cutoff point assigned for the first category. The books which passed this screening procedure were routed to all schools and reaction sheets were made available.

SELECTION GUIDE
Social Science Textbook Screening

Name of Textbook _____ Grade _____ Date _____

Publisher _____ Reviewer _____

Author _____ School _____

	Check one					
	Excellent	Good	Fair	Poor	No Opinion	Category* Scores
	3	2	1	0	0	
A. Racism and Sexism: Group 1						
1. Illustrations (examples)						
a. stereotypes_____						
b. lifestyle_____						
c. tokenism_____						
2. Storyline_____						
a. relationships_____						
b. standard for success_____						
c. viewpoint_____						
d. sexism_____						
3. Self-Image/Self-Esteem_____						
4. Author/Illustrator's Qualifications_____						
5. & 7. Copyright Date_____						
6. Determine the Author's Perspective_____						
8. Illustrations (pictorial)_____						
9. Loaded Words_____						
10. Heroes and Heroines_____						
B. Authenticity						
1. Accuracy of Facts/Appropriate to Context_____						
2. Impartiality of presentation _____						
3. Up-to-date Information_____						

*Category Scores: For each category (A-G) total the number of points by counting checks in each column and multiply by appropriate weighing points, e.g., 3 checks in "Excellent" = 9 points.

(Form continues on page 218)

SELECTION GUIDE (cont'd)

	Excellent	Good	Fair	Poor	No Opinion	Category Scores
Check one						
	3	2	1	0	0	
C. Appropriateness						
1. Contribution to the program objectives_____						
2. Vocabulary level_____						
3. Style of writing and presentation _____						
4. Provision for individual differences_____						
D. Scope						
1. Coverage of subject matter ___						
2. Concept development_____						
3. Skills development (map-reading, use of graphs, etc.) ___						
4. Process development (e.g., problem solving)___						
E. Interest						
1. Relationship to user's experience___						
2. Intellectual challenge ___						
3. Appeal to students ___						
4. Up-to-date illustrations and content ___						
5. Provision of concrete activities___						
F. Organization						
1. Sequential development of concepts___						
2. Match with District sequences___						
G. Special Features						
1. Teachers and/or users guide ___						
2. References & footnotes ___						
3. Identification of resources ___						
4. Table of Contents, glossary, index ___						

SELECTION GUIDE (cont'd)

	Excellent	Good	Fair	Poor	No Opinion	Category Scores
Check one						
	3	2	1	0	0	
H. Physical Characteristics						
1. Use of pictures and illustrations ____						
2. Use of graphs, charts, and maps____						
3. Cover and page layouts ____						
4. Type face and spacing ____						
5. Construction and binding ____						
6. Paper quality____						
TOTALS ____						
WEIGHTING POINTS ____	3	2	1	0	0	
SUBSCORES						

TOTAL SCORE = _____

POSSIBLE RANGE =   0-123

In another attempt to involve teachers in selection this simple teacher reaction sheet accompanied three prescreened social studies series textbooks on display at Berkeley elementary schools. It allows room for comments and reactions.

SOCIAL SCIENCE TEXTBOOK SELECTION
TEACHER REACTION SHEET

Please indicate your general rating of the following textbooks using a scale as follows:

3	2	1	0
Highest	**Middle**	**Lowest**	**No Opinion**
Recommend adoption	Recommend adoption with revisions	Adoption *not* recommended	

Please note that you may assign several textbooks the same rating.

NAME OF TEXTBOOK	Cost	Rating (Write in 0-3)	REASONS Please explain all items rated "2" in previous column

KEY ORGANIZATIONS

National Education Association (NEA)
1201 16th Street, NW
Washington, DC 20036   (202) 833-4000

The NEA, the major organization for educators, first established in 1857, has had a very long history of concern relating to instructional materials. A Joint Committee of the National Educational Association and the American Textbook Publishers Institute was organized in 1959 to deal with issues relating to printed materials (especially textbooks) in such areas as censorship, selection, distribution, quality and uses. During its existence this joint committee produced several basic guidelines for the selection process, including *Guidelines for Textbook Selection* in 1963 and 1968 and a thoughtful *Guidelines for an Adequate Investment in Instructional Materials* in 1967. They currently advocate five percent of the on-going budget.

Though the Joint Committee no longer exists as an operating unit, publishers and educators are still collaborating through the NEA and the School Division of the Association of American Publishers (AAP). Their most recent collaboration is *Instructional Materials: Selection and Purchase*, revised in 1976, a book that deals with the process of selection rather than with specific criteria.

Basically, the NEA believes in local selection (primarily by teachers) and in a multiplicity of options to meet local conditions. Its activities in and publications on selection reflect this view.

The NEA advocates that policy governing the selection of instructional materials is a legitimate topic for collective bargaining negotiations and suggests that it can clarify details of the selection process and help mobilize the interest and energies of teachers in providing instructional materials.

The NEA believes that standards for educational programs should be established in consultation with the majority teachers' organization and that such programs should guarantee adequate resources for materials and staffing. The Association also believes that state-mandated standards should set only broad, general curricular guidelines (and should not be based on student achievement). The NEA urges its state affiliates to seek the removal of laws and regulations that limit educators in selecting materials or that restrict the selection of diversified materials.

The NEA has also been quite active in recent years in boosting legislation establishing teacher centers under policy boards governed by (a majority of) classroom teachers. Such teachers' centers might provide more teachers access to a greater variety of learning materials, as well as in-service education courses designed by teachers, and would be more likely to cover materials selection in programs designed to meet the needs of teachers.

The NEA also recommends that educators should adopt and use only those basal texts and other materials that include accurate portraits of the roles of ethnic minorities.

NEA publications include many that are helpful—in one way or another—in selecting materials. Some of their publications include *Biased Textbooks* (1974), *Sex Role Stereotyping Factsheets* (duplicating masters) and *A Child's Right to Equal Reading* (1973).

Teachers' Center Exchange
Far West Laboratory for Educational Research
  and Development
1855 Folsom Street
San Francisco, CA 94103   (415) 565-3097
  This Exchange, funded since 1975 by the National Institute of Education
(School Capacity for Problem Solving Group), is an information and referral cen-
ter for a national network of teachers' centers practitioners—both experienced and
neophyte. The network operates on a voluntary, give-and-take basis on the premise
that curriculum development and staff development programs should be designed
on the basis of teachers' identification of their own needs and interests.
  Its newsletter, *Teachers' Centers Exchange*, is free on request. Kathleen
Devaney's *Essays on Teachers' Centers* sells for $6.00; the two *Teachers' Centers
Exchange Directories* are listed under Key Publications.

KEY PUBLICATIONS

For the Love of Teaching, by Jeannette Veatch. Encino, CA, International Center
    for Educational Development, 1972. 103p. $2.50pa.
    Concrete suggestions for ways to implement direct teaching, intrinsic learn-
ing, pupil choice, individualized instruction and other teaching approaches which
lead to positive (joyful) and meaningful interactions between children and teachers.

The Integrated Day in an American School, by Betsye Sargent. Boston, National
    Association of Independent Schools, 1972. 80p. $2.50pa.
    This detailed primary curriculum demonstrates one teacher's methods for
selecting, developing and reporting both activities and materials. Much of curriculum was shown to flow from, as well as be implemented by, activities.

Teach and Reach: An Alternative Guide to Resources for the Classroom, by Ellen
    Barnes, Bill Eyman, and Maddy Bragar. Syracuse, NY, Human Policy Press,
    1977. $4.50 + $0.50 postage and handling.
    Written by teachers for teachers, this book is a mixture of specific things to
do with children and a listing of resources for teachers. It is a why-to as well as a
how-to book and includes ways to teach and learn about differences, ways to
humanize classrooms and ways to meet the needs of children of varied interests
and abilities. Chapters include: alternative curriculum ideas, values, a guide to
special education, classroom space, community resources and more.

Teachers' Centers Exchange Directory, by Jeanne Lance and Ruth Kreitzman. San
    Francisco, Far West Laboratory for Educational Research and Development,
    1977. 207p. $6.50pa. *Supplement*, 1978. 112p. $6.00pa.
    This is a directory of teachers' centers and similar in-service programs in
communication with the Teachers' Centers Exchange at Far West Laboratory for
Educational Research and Development in San Francisco, an exchange which operates as an informational, referral and assistance agency for teachers' centers.
    The major section of the directory provides descriptions of 28 centers in 25
states, with information on each center's program, resources, staff, setting,

participation, fees and credit, affiliation, support, decision-making and origin. These are arranged alphabetically by state, city and name of center.

The last section is an annotated list of curriculum publications and materials produced by the center staff and by teachers who work closely with centers. It is a useful and unique guide to teachers' center materials which provides insight to educational needs experienced by teachers.

The recently-issued *Supplement* provides similar program information on 55 additional centers in contact with the exchange. A 12-page update on 1977 centers is also available from the Order Department, Far West Laboratory.

Teacher's Choice: Catalogue of Curriculum Materials, edited by Peter Dublin.
 Cambridge, MA, Institute of Open Education, 1976. 168p. $4.00pa. (From
 133 Mt. Auburn Street, Cambridge, MA 02138.)
  This catalog includes teachers' reviews of somewhat more than 100 educational items—books, games and simulations, manipulatives and media kits. Reviews, largely based on classroom experience, are intelligently grouped into large classes, such as math, social studies, early childhood, affective and miscellaneous. Each review includes source, price, level, grouping, one or more well-chosen illustrations, and sections devoted to description and use. Though the individual annotations vary considerably in quality, the format is generally helpful. The book also includes 20 activities for classroom use and two tear-out feedback sheets.

  Though this book was intended as an alternative to publishers' catalogs, it seems to be unaware of existing alternatives, such as EPIE or *Curriculum Review*, or other relevant items in this guide. There are no common criteria for critiquing nor any expressed criteria for selection, except for classroom use by teachers known to Mr. Dublin. As a consequence, the user often has to guess at the identity, setting or philosophy of the teacher-reviewer and his or her class or school.

FOR FURTHER READING

Some other bibliographies, particularly those in the chapters on special education and individualizing, include many entries related to the concepts in this chapter.

*Items marked with an asterisk include criteria of some sort.
+Items marked with a plus include further lists of references.

*Bleil, Gordon. "Evaluating Educational Materials," *Journal of Learning Disabilities*, v. 8, no. 1 (Jan. 1975), pp. 12-19.

Bogatz, B. E. "An Investigation of Teacher Expectations of Instructional Materials," *Exceptional Children*, v. 38, no. 3 (Nov. 1971), pp. 233-36.

*+Brown, Bob Barton, and Jeaninne N. Webb. *The Use of Classroom Observation Techniques in the Evaluation of Educational Programs.* Princeton, NJ, ERIC Clearinghouse on Tests, Measurement and Evaluation, 1975. (TM Report 49).

Bussis, Ann M., et al. *Beyond Surface Curriculum: An Interview Study of Teachers' Understandings.* Boulder, CO, Westview Press, 1976.

*Carini, Patricia F. *Observation and Description: An Alternative Methodology for the Investigation of Human Phenomena.* Grand Forks, ND, University of North Dakota, 1975.
    Suggests several ways for observers to note and code student interactions with materials.

*Eash, Maurice, et al. *Evaluation Designs for Practitioners.* Princeton, NJ, ERIC Clearinghouse on Tests, Measurement and Evaluation, 1974. (TM Report 35).

Kaplan, Sandra. *Teacher's Choice: Ideas and Activities for Teaching Basic Skills.* Santa Monica, CA, Goodyear, 1978.

Katz, Lillian. *Second Collection of Papers for Teachers.* Urbana, IL, ERIC Clearinghouse in Early Childhood Education, 1975.
    Four papers deal in various ways with the need to respect both teacher and learners as learners; one deals with mistaking excitement for education in the classroom; another contrasts the use of overstatements in American educational information dissemination as contrasted with more sedate British reporting.

*Klein, Susan. *Teacher(s)' Product Rating Form.* Washington, DC, National Institute of Education, 1975.
    A teacher-tested product-evaluation form whose major criteria are desirability, intrinsic quality, practicality and effectiveness.

Latham, Glenn. "Measuring Teacher Responses to Instructional Materials," *Educational Technology*, v. 14, no. 12 (Dec. 1974), pp. 11-15.

*Lawson, Tom E. *Formative Instructional Product Evaluation: Instruments and Strategies.* Englewood Cliffs, NJ, Educational Technology, 1974.
    A sourcebook of instruments usable by teachers.

Lortie, Dan C. *Schoolteacher: A Sociological Study.* Chicago, University of Chicago Press, 1975.
    A long-overdue sociological study of American teachers that uses interviews, surveys, historical reviews and insight for a factual, descriptive and continually interesting portrait of teachers as they are—based on data from the early 1960s to early 1970s. The book as a whole addresses the central characteristics of teachers and teaching in conventional school situations. Chapter 9, which includes speculation on the process of change, should be required reading for all change agents.

*+McLaughlin, John A., and Jack S. Trlica. "Teacher Evaluation of Instructional Materials," *Educational Technology*, 16, no. 3 (March 1976), pp. 51-54.

+National Education Association. *Selection of Instructional Materials and Equipment by Teachers.* Washington, NEA, 1970.
    Survey of teacher role in selection.

*Patton, Michael Quinn. *Alternative Evaluation Research Paradigm.* Grand Forks, ND, Center for Teaching and Learning, University of North Dakota, 1975. (North Dakota Study Group on Evaluation Series.)
    Suggests that practitioner evaluations need to include contexts, treatments and outcomes of specific programs. Within this context, analyzes and suggests evaluation using sets of continua, such as qualitative or quantitative, holistic or component, process or outcome, closeness to or distance from data.

*Project Change, compiler. *A Plentiful Packet of Practical Procedures for Record Keeping.* Cortland, NY, Project Change, State University at Cortland, 1973. (Separate items in folder.)

Many practical suggestions for classroom record keeping, often for materials as well as procedures and processes, with many means of keeping systematic records on individual children.

*Raths, James D. "Teaching without Specific Objectives," *Educational Leadership*, v. 28, no. 7 (April 1971), pp. 714-20.

+Reavis, Charles A. *Teacher Improvement through Clinical Supervision.* Blooming-ton, IN, Phi Delta Kappa Educational Foundation, 1978. (Fastback 111).

*Schneider, E. Joseph. "Teachers Determine Success of Innovations," *Educational R&D Report*, v. 1, no. 1 (undated), pp. 2-5.

Teachers National Field Task Force on the Improvement and Reform of American Education. *Inside-Out: The Final Report and Recommendations.* Washing-ton, GPO, 1974.

Report of a teachers' task force, involving 10,000 educators, on educational reform and improvement. Strongly recommends autonomous teacher-controlled teacher centers as a major instrument, with recommendations of evaluations related to needs of teacher, means of including teachers in research, and specific guidelines for federal funds.

*Tyler, Louise L., M. Frances Klein, and Ruby Takanishi. *Inner Teaching: Mastery in Selecting Classroom Materials.* Glennville, CA, Educational Resource Associates, 1977.

Discusses 15 evaluation criteria most relevant to teachers including facilities, care of materials, learning opportunities, teacher skills and content, as well as means of using these criteria in selection.

*Winsor, Charlotte, ed. *Experimental Schools Revisited.* New York, Agathon, 1973.

Discusses the work of the Bureau of Educational Experiments in assessing children's growth through record keeping methods.

STUDENT INPUT INTO SELECTION

"Of the various functions of schools, the crucial one is what they do with the human resources with which they deal. No society can afford to waste talent or destroy potential."

–Edward Kifer, "The Impact of Success and Failure Upon the Learner," *Evaluation in Education*, 1977

"The common practice of establishing an entire year's course of study before any students have entered the building is unreasonable if teachers accept the fact that student interest and involvement are at least as important to consider as the content and reading difficulty of the materials used."

–Peter Hasselriis, "Reading in Literature: Student Involvement Is Just the Beginning," in *Reading in the Content Areas*, 1972

"A Pawn is a person who feels that someone other than himself is in control of what he does."

–Richard deCharms, "Students Need Not Be Pawns," *Theory into Practice*, April 1976

"Schools should . . . take steps to prevent education from being a one-way process where children watch and listen."

–Barbara Grant, " 'Cold' Media Victims," *Theory into Practice*, April 1976

■ ■ ■

This chapter will briefly consider student input into the process of selecting instructional materials. Other aspects of student involvement are treated elsewhere in this book, especially in the chapters on individualization, special education, commercial retrieval systems, cognitive and affective criteria and teachers' roles in selection, all of which tend to consider the needs of particular students. Learner Verification and Revision (see page 118) is a formalized means of incorporating the input of many "learners" for particular materials. The former methods generally use educators' judgments of student interests, class and achievement. LVR, whose input can affect the development of materials, seems in practice to affect mainly reading levels, understandability, versatility of programs for different types of populations, and choice of illustrations.

In learning centers, independent study, contract education and in school and public libraries, students often have some choice in selecting from pre-selected materials. Both school and public librarians, depending upon budgets and policies, tend to choose a certain proportion of materials based on the expressed interests of students, as do teachers who are allowed to choose their own materials.

Despite these exceptions, students in general are treated as passive recipients of education rather than experts on their own interests and concerns or as individuals who have had a great deal of experience with various sorts of learning materials. As Todd Clark points out, student opinions and attitudes are quite accessible. Informal and indirect indicators such as these are readily available to educators:

- Which textbooks are most frequently lost?
- Which ones are most apt to be mutilated and damaged?

  or, conversely,
- Which books or topics are most frequently checked out of the library?
- Which ones are most frequently stolen?

Student assessments can be simple or complex and can be arranged to elicit indications of satisfaction as well as dissatisfaction. In a 15-minute Friday afternoon writing break, for example, students could list and discuss such topics as:

- the three most interesting occurrences during the week
- the textbook or section of text they enjoyed the most
- the most/least interesting film seen so far during the year

Students, or at least selected students, can also be asked to supply more extensive information on:

- the specifics or difficulties of materials being selected or used
- the order in which they would like to use these materials
- their goals, interests and objectives
- their preferences in learning materials
- what they would like to learn

On the last item, they are far more expert than any teacher.

In the *Biological Sciences Curriculum Studies Journal* (April 1978), Norris Ross reported one interesting study of the substantial gap between the actual preferences of adolescent students and predictions made by perceptive, experienced teachers. Though this study is based on the Human Sciences Program, it is almost certainly indicative. Certainly Daniel Fader (in *The New Hooked on Books*, 1977), came to the same conclusion.

Encouragingly, the BSCS study showed that all students wanted to learn and study something. All had questions they wanted answered. Their questions were "tremendously varied and diverse," yet few could be answered with information from only one discipline. Most questions were quite different from those adults would have predicted or expected.

If students (possibly selected students) are not engaged actively in selecting materials, they need to know that there is a selection policy and to learn the basis on which textbooks, library materials and other learning materials are chosen to meet their needs.

For standard teaching materials such as texts and workbooks, students should be consulted on organization and clarity and asked to review such things as indexes, summaries and tables of contents, as well as to assess both the comprehensibility and the innate value of student activities and instructions. Students particularly should review glossaries to see if they are easy to use and the definitions clear. Live students probably are as good as any formula for determining readability. It is a good idea to ask a wide range of students just how long homework assignments and activities actually take to complete and whether the questions make sense to them.

Students should also be included somewhere in the review process for expensive items like films—either as members of preview panels or as trial audiences. In my own experience in an introductory journalism class, I found students extremely capable in assessing the learning content of films and in indicating where or whether they should be used in the courses. Typically, I had detailed and helpful answers from students on whether particular films were better for introduction or review and suggestions on the optimum order for showing these films.

Even at the elementary level, student comments, though often unsophisticated ("It's boring" or "It's too complicated") are often correct and should be considered in selection. I found elementary students useful in evaluating student appeal of media items (mostly filmstrips)—even in pointing out learning values that I had overlooked.

In school libraries, I have found student comments and questions provide excellent guidance in book selection, with consequent high circulation. While I have always felt free to disagree with or veto student suggestions, in the main they have helped me refine and improve selection. Selections based on student preferences are apt to be more used and more successful.

According to research, "learner-controlled" learning systems—at levels from preschool to graduate school—also tend to reduce the time needed for learning without reducing performance. While these systems are most effective for motivated students and students who have good retrieval skills, their use may serve to increase motivation and retrieval skills for other students.

These research experiences are completely consistent with three principles or "laws of learning" that George Polya extracted from a psychological study of learning theory:

- Learning should be active: for efficient learning the learner should be actively involved, and discover for himself as large a fraction of the materials to be learned *as is feasible under the given circumstances.*

- The best motivation is intrinsic motivation (implying interest in the materials to be learned and pleasure in the activity of learning).

- Learning occurs in consecutive phases from *exploration* (action and perception) to *formalization* (words and concepts) and then to *assimilation* (desirable mental habits). Good education, then, would promote desirable mental habits.

Choosing materials in accordance with these postulates—to support active learning, intrinsic motivation and desirable mental habits—can have far-reaching implications on the kinds of materials that are selected. Educators would have to consider such questions as whether following a text page by page encourages active learning, whether tests and grades provide intrinsic motivation and whether programmed instruction promotes good mental habits.

Ideal selection procedures should include some systematic methods for student input into the goals and objectives they are required to learn. Most materials, in actuality, fail to state or indicate these goals clearly for students. Even assuming that schools and authorities should be the arbiters of overall content, I believe that learning materials selection would be improved if students were consulted (or at least informed) on:

- what they believe they are expected to be able to do when they have completed their study or use of a particular work
- the kinds of tasks, procedures and skills expected of them
- attitudes and behavior required for learning these materials
- the extent of congruence with student abilities, interests and educational expectations

James McPartland, in *Student Participation in High School Decisions* (1970), outlined some other dimensions of student choice on academic *content* (for example, which English class, which unit, which course), on academic *obligations* (difficulties and standards) and *time allocations* (pace and sequencing). Other non-materials choices were of teachers and grading methods. He found that requiring students to make their own choices forced both teachers and students to pay more attention to the long- and short-run consequences of education. Some consequences of choice he noted were reduction in friction, student improvement in attention, greater happiness with courses and students' tendency to maximize their strengths and minimize their weaknesses.

Similarly, the Coleman report found that students' sense of control and self-concept (measured in the ninth and twelfth grades) were highly correlated with achievement.

Another desirable mental habit often developed through student selection is responsibility. Students who have chosen their own learning materials are often more committed to learning with these materials or to finding usable substitutes if the materials do not work out. Student Project Records (below) help students rationalize their resource selection.

STUDENT PROJECT RECORD

Name   Date

Teacher

Project or problem

Specific goals

Planning procedure

Resources to be used   Why were these chosen?

Experiences and activities   What is (are) their purpose(s)?

Product: (Presentation, Organization, Record)

Evaluation (Include evaluation of resources, experiences and products)

These records should be designed to include appropriate available resources and materials selected by teachers or students. Librarians, resource teachers and media personnel can also provide consultation and advice on materials for student projects for both individuals and groups.

Access to materials is an important part of student selection and is, of course, impossible if materials are nonexistent or unavailable. Access requires, in addition to good collections in the library and classroom, freedom to use these materials.

As the San Francisco Public Library put it in a *Children's Rights* flyer:

You have the right

- to gain information about yourself

- to discover the world around you

- to explore other worlds

- to pursue experiences through many media

- to be able to choose from a wide and varied collection of the best available materials

- to have a comfortable environment which reflects your needs

- to be free to pursue your own interests, at your own pace, in your own way

In many school situations, whether or not libraries or media centers are well stocked, well staffed and well arranged, their contents often are not accessible to students because of limited hours, early-departing buses, arbitrary limitations on number of titles and pass systems required for using libraries and media centers. Again, students need to develop their skills in locating materials within these centers or libraries.

Facilities, too, need to be designed to allow a variety of learning activities to take place simultaneously. A quick accessibility analysis of any collection might include considerations like those in the chart below.

ACCESS CHART

	Poor 1	2	3	4	Excellent 5
Appropriate materials are accessible in many media					
Materials are logically arranged and well indexed for use					
Materials are accessible at convenient times					
Instructional materials personnel are available as needed					
Users are provided information on all materials including new materials					
Location(s) is (are) convenient and adequate in size					
Supportive equipment is available and well maintained					

If students are active or actively consulted in materials selection, we can probably expect, because of individual interests and learning modes, to have a greater variety of materials and more variation in modes. We may need, for example, to have the same or comparable materials in tape, filmstrips and printed versions.

We may have a bigger budget for materials, but a higher proportion of materials will be used.

Some of the rhetoric for basic education ascribes our acknowledged student decline in traditional academic skills to permissiveness or to the intervention of the federal government in education. (Interestingly, this 15-year decline parallels a decline in budgets for instructional materials and, since 1970, an increasing proportion of children living in conditions of poverty.) Still, according to the voluminous *Wirtz Report* which studied the SAT decline thoroughly, there are no discernible "causal relationships between experimental teaching methods and SAT score decline." A similar study by the American Institutes for Research could find no substantial or consistent association between student achievement and the level of innovation. A detailed study in mathematics (discussed more extensively in *Subject Areas and Implementation* indicates that students learn just about as well (or as poorly) with new math as they do with old math materials (though they learn better with manipulatives).

On available evidence, high school students' academic achievements have declined overall during the last 15 years, though the decline is inconsistent. (Some schools and some states have not declined, while others have improved.)

One facet of the general decline, according to the *Wirtz Report* investigators, could be related to high school texts' lowered expectations in reading comprehension and willingness to meet challenge. While passages in the SAT test are generally written at the eleventh to twelfth grade levels (sometimes at thirteenth or fourteenth), most eleventh grade texts are now written at what is considered to be a ninth to tenth grade level. Since student tests, in textbooks and out, are primarily objective, students have fewer occasions to write or to develop their thinking skills.

Interestingly, even though current student achievement rates and attitudes toward school are depressingly low overall, students have considerably more favorable attitudes toward learning itself and toward specific subject areas. (For example, student attitudes toward literature and music are overwhelmingly favorable, even though neither student performances nor achievement are high.)

I believe our best path to increasing student achievement is through tapping these latent student interests and involving students in their own education. This could include not only their assessment of materials, but also an ongoing collection of information on the interaction between students, materials and programs. The instrument reproduced below is a preliminary design for collecting such information, based loosely on a collection instrument used by Richard Watkins and C. Lynn Jenks of the Far West Laboratory for Educational Research and Development.

DESIGN FOR COLLECTING INFORMATION
RELATED TO STUDENT SATISFACTION AND ACHIEVEMENT
WITH PROGRAM AND MATERIALS

Questions	Information Source	Collection Timing
How effective are the program and materials in meeting personal objectives in learning goals?	student opinion teacher opinion	ongoing "
How effective are materials and program in affecting aca- demic skills and knowledge?	student tests teacher and student opinion	"
How effective are programs and materials in affecting atti- tude toward learning?	student opinion	beginning and end of program
Is program effectiveness related to or dependent upon materials?	teacher- student opinion	middle and end of program
Is program differentially effec- tive at different grades or for students of different backgrounds or capabilities?	records files	beginning, end of program
Does program effectiveness increase with increased uses of materials?	usage count tests student	ongoing and end
Does program effectiveness increase with increased use of other resources?	"	"
How do the teachers feel about the program and materials?	teacher opinion	ongoing end
How do the parents perceive the program and materials?	parent opinion	end of program

INFORMATION SOURCES ON CHILDREN'S PREFERENCES

Though there are advocates of student input on materials, there are few systematic means of collecting such information, except for LVR. The Children's Book Council issues one yearly list of child-tested books. The American Library Association and its divisions dealing with children and young adults have probably, collectively, assembled the most information on student interests. The filmstrips reviewed in the *Elementary School Library Collection* have also been selected with a fair amount of student input, and the Media Center for Children and, to an extent, the Educational Film Library Association, discussed in the chapter on films in *Media and Curriculum*, both have student input on the films they review. Library reviewers too, if they are practicing librarians, usually are rather well tuned to children's expressed likes and dislikes. At local levels, some schools— through libraries or English teachers—systematically ask for student reviews and help in selection.

Some information on topics that students find particularly interesting is also available. These include, besides sex (universal) and motor vehicles (male), environmental studies and mental and physical health.

Still, overall, there is less information than desirable. Typically, student input into selection is conceived as collecting information *about* students. Since students are often the best information sources on themselves, I would prefer, if possible, to collect information *from* students.

Some information about students that may aid selection includes:

- Demographic information
  age distribution
  race distribution
  sex distribution
  cultural/community factors
  school stability

- Student perception of school situations
  perception of materials and materials access
  attitude toward school
  attitude toward learning

- Learning characteristics
  ranges of abilities
  learning styles
  major successes and failures in school
  cognitive preferences and abilities
  mastery of subject-matter skills

- Life experiences
  affecting attitudes toward school and learning
  exposure to learning in school situations
  exposure to wider resources

- Aptitudes
  in school situations
  outside interests

- Preferences, priorities

- Handicaps related to learning

While teachers and librarians should probably consider all these factors in selection, the criterion of *interest* may be the one that is most meaningful for individual selection. An excellent practice in selecting materials for classroom collections is consciously to identify one or more areas of concern for each child and to select materials accordingly (naturally considering other factors at the same time). It is *not* necessary to let each child know which items you have chosen for him or her!

My own belief is that children should have *some* voice in determining the goals and values of their own education. At a minimum, they should be free to hold their own values. Both materials and classroom practices should be chosen to permit and encourage students to formulate and develop their own impressions, feelings, values, ideas and conclusions within a school setting.

KEY ORGANIZATIONS

National Assessment of Educational Progress (NAEP)
300 Lincoln Tower
1860 Lincoln Street
Denver, CO 80295   (303) 861-4917

National Assessment, federally funded by the National Center for Education Statistics, gathers and disseminates comprehensive information on the educational attainments—knowledge, abilities and attitudes—of a representative cross section of students at the ages of 9, 13 and 17, and of young adults between 26 and 35 years of age. Ten subject areas are currently under assessment, two each year on a revolving plan. With this information, NAEP is the basic information source on students' educational achievements and achievement trends. The December issue of the free *NAEP Newsletter* is apt to contain a useful summary of the previous year's trends and surveys.

Group and national reports on results in such fields as science, political science, citizenship, writing and reading are available from NAEP and the Government Printing Office. The data are also available on computer tape for statistical studies or analyses. An NAEP leaflet, *User Studies*, provides fuller information on these tapes' applications.

The NAEP survey questions are based on stated educational objectives and can be used singly or in groups. About one-half of the questions asked in each assessment are in the public domain and can be used by state and local school systems assessing their own programs. One such assessment is explained in detail in *Using National Assessment for Program Evaluation* (1975). *How to Use the Findings from National Assessment* (1974) provides general guidelines.

KEY PUBLICATIONS

Classroom Choices for 1977: Books Chosen by Children, compiled by the International Reading Association—Children's Book Council Joint Committee. New York, Children's Book Council, 1978. Reproduced from *The Reading Teacher* (Oct. 1977). Single copies free upon request with a $0.24 stamped envelope. (From Children's Book Council, 67 Irving Place, New York, NY 10003.)

The books in this annual list represent a selection of trade books field-tested with about 5,000 children in classrooms across the country. The books in the 1977 list are those voted as favorites by children from about 500 trade books preselected for quality and diversity by educators and experts in children's literature. About 90 books, grouped in broad classes, are annotated here, with annotations which sometimes detail children's reactions and/or classroom applications. Interestingly, most of these favored books were found applicable for a broad variety of grades.

These lists, valuable for currency and children's evaluations, could be improved by including prices and an index.

Elementary School Evaluative Criteria: A Guide for School Improvement. Arlington, VA, National Study of School Evaluation, 1973. 152p. $6.00. (From NSSE, Arlington, VA 22201.)

Includes a good section (B) for studying the characteristics of pupils as individuals, as subgroups and as part of community groups to help determine what programs and learning experiences can best promote the progress of all students. One aspect, omitted from some studies, is a chart studying the stability of student population, by recording in numbers and percentages the time in years that students have attended their particular schools.

The National Study of Secondary School Evaluation has produced similarly valuable *Evaluative Criteria for Junior High Schools* (Washington, DC, 1963).

Media and the Young Adult: A Selected Bibliography, 1950-1972, by Young Adult Services Division, Research Committee. Chicago, American Library Association, 1977. 154p. $5.00pa.

This 400-item annotated bibliography is a rather interesting exploration of adolescent attitudes relating to information needs, with many references on access to and impact of media, media content, media use and information-seeking behavior, as well as teaching strategies and library adaptations that may better meet these information needs. Some specific topics are: reading interests, career needs, consumer behavior and use of libraries/media centers.

Though this overview is not current, it could be helpful to both teachers and librarians.

Pupil Perceived Needs Assessment Package, by Hsuan DeLorme and others. Philadelphia, Research for Better Schools, 1974. 6 units. $15.00.

This six-unit package gives a systematic procedure for identifying educational needs as students perceive them. The units detail how to plan a Pupil Perceived Needs Assessment project, how to develop a Pupil Perceived Needs indicator, how to administer the indicator, how to process the data and how to analyze and report the data.

FOR FURTHER READING

*Items marked with an asterisk have criteria for selection.
+Items marked with a plus have extensive lists of references.

Ahmann, J. Stanley. *How Much Are Our Young People Learning? The Story of National Assessment.* Bloomington, IN, Phi Delta Kappa Educational Foundation, 1976. (Fastback 68).

+Barron, Daniel D. "A Review of Selected Research in School Librarianship, 1972-1976," *School Media Quarterly,* v. 5, no. 4 (Summer 1977), pp. 271-88.

+Bieland, Hunter M. *The SAT Score Decline: A Summary of Related Research.* New York, College Entrance Examination Board, 1976.

Byler, Ruth, et al. *Teach Us What We Want to Know.* New York, Mental Health Materials Center, 1969.

*+Conte, Joseph M., and George H. Grimes. *Media and the Culturally Different Learner.* Washington, National Education Association, 1969.

deCharms, Richard. "Students Need Not Be Pawns," *Theory into Practice,* v. 16, no. 4 (Oct. 1977), pp. 296-301.
The entire issue deals with active student roles in education.

Grant, Barbara M. " 'Cold' Media Victims," *Theory into Practice,* v. 15, no. 2 (April 1976), pp. 120-25.

Harnischfeger, Annegret, and David Wiley. *Achievement Test Score Decline: Do We Need to Worry?* St. Louis, CEMREL Inc., 1977.

+Kifer, Edward. "The Impact of Success and Failure on the Learner," *Evaluation in Education: International Progress,* v. 1, no. 4 (1977), pp. 281-359.

Lickona, Thomas. "The Psychology of Choice in Learning," in *Open Education: Increasing Alternatives for Teachers and Children.* Cortland, NY, Open Education Foundation, 1973.

McPartland, James. *Student Participation in High School Decisions: A Study of Students and Teachers in Fourteen Urban High Schools.* Johns Hopkins University Center for Social Organization of Schools, 1970. (Report 25).

Marcus, Stuart Paul, and Paul Jeffrey Richman. "A Proposal to Revise the Secondary School Cirriculum in Economics," *Social Education,* v. 42, no. 1 (Jan. 1978), pp. 76-77. From "The Other Side of the Desk: A Column of Student Opinion" (ongoing in *Social Education*).
This particular column includes extremely cogent, specific suggestions for improving economics instruction.

+Mayeske, George W., and Albert E. Beeton, Jr. *Special Studies of Our Nation's Students.* Washington, GPO (U.S. Office of Education), 1975. 197p. $3.95pa.
Contains the results of a number of investigations of earlier studies, among them an assessment of achievement and motivation for different geographic and socio-cultural groups; extensively explores the role played by school factors, sometimes using new or seldom-used analytic models.

+Mayeske, George W., et al. *Study of the Attitude toward Life of Our Nation's Students.* Washington, GPO (U.S. Office of Education), 1973. 92p. $2.15pa.
Documents the nature of the relationship between student motivation, achievement and family background for students from different ethnic, regional and sex groups as baseline data for program planning for the federal, state and local school district levels.

Michael, James J. "Children's Freedom and the Public Library: An Interview," *Journal of Clinical Child Psychology*, v. 1, no. 1 (Winter 1971-1972), pp. 12-15.

National Council of Organizations for Children and Youth. *America's Children: 1976: A Bicentennial Survey.* Washington, National Council of Organizations for Children and Youth, 1976.

Polya, George. "On Learning, Teaching and Learning Teaching," *American Mathematical Monthly*, v. 70, no. 6 (June-July 1963), pp. 605-619.

Ross, Norris M. "Learning and Liking: Predicting Student Interests," *Biological Sciences Curriculum Study Journal*, v. 1, no. 3 (April 1978), pp. 21-22.

+Sherman, Thomas M. *Normative Student Evaluation of Instruction.* Princeton, NJ, Educational Testing Service, 1975. (TM Report 46).

Thomas, Donald. "Five Clues to a Good School," *American School Board Journal*, v. 158 (Dec. 1970), pp. 23-25.
Major clues for Thomas are self-concept of children, communication methods, alternatives in learning opportunities, respect for the students and student enjoyment of school experiences.

*+Tyler, Louise. "Materials as Persons," *Theory into Practice*, v. 16, no. 4 (Oct. 1977), pp. 231-37.

*Watkins, Richard W., and C. Lynn Jenks. *Values and Information: An Approach to Evaluation Planning.* San Francisco, Far West Laboratory for Educational Research and Development, 1976.

PART V

AREAS AND ISSUES

SELECTING BASIC LEARNING MATERIALS
(Textbooks, Workbooks, Curriculum Guides)

"Mold the textbook and you can mold the mind."
—Allan J. Dyson, "Ripping Off Young Minds,"
Wilson Library Bulletin, Nov. 1971

"Whenever a book is written of real educational worth, you may be quite certain that some reviewer will say that it will be difficult to teach from it."
—Alfred North Whitehead

"The basal reader, in practice, is a crutch for the teacher and the administrator rather than an aid to the child. It assures administrators that even the poorest teacher in their classrooms will 'get through' some semblance of the curriculum for that grade."
—Martin Mayer, *The Schools*, 1961

"Now we are being asked to put everything a child needs to know within the covers of a single textbook. Today it is not unusual to find textbooks that include not only the basic content but developmental activities, motivational techniques, slow-learner techniques, extension exercises, enrichment activities and activities for reinforcement and review. In addition, we are being asked to provide teachers editions that have grown from a page or two of introduction to actual teacher training for any given grade level in any given discipline."
—Barbara Howell (Vice-President, Silver Burdett),
Presentation to New Jersey Association of School
Administrators, Atlantic City, NJ, May 12, 1977

"Unfortunately, education is a political question, and like other political questions, it is usually paraded forth in the full paraphernalia of intellectual dishonesty."
—Martin Mayer, *The Schools*, 1971

" . . . much of the pressure on American textbooks lies in the nature of textbooks and how they are used. If they are balanced, they are bland or inconsistent; if not, someone will justifiably accuse them of bias."
—Allan J. Dyson, "Ripping Off Young Minds"

■ ■ ■

This chapter, in part historical, concentrates on methods and criteria—real and ideal—for selecting our basic standardized instructional materials—that is, materials consciously designed for instruction in basic programs. While I use the term "textbooks," in this chapter it refers not only to individual textbooks but to basal texts, comprehensive series and textbook programs. Some of these textbook programs now include, in addition to basic texts, a variety of worksheets, workbooks, supplementary readers and audiovisual materials in many formats. As a result, it is becoming increasingly difficult to distinguish absolutely between textbook programs supplemented by media and media programs supplemented by printed materials. Textbooks, however, with or without back-up, are still our basic instructional tools.

Other intentional instructional materials considered briefly in this chapter are workbooks, curriculum guides, and activity books—all exclusively designed for educational use.

A chart on pages 274-275 indicates some characteristics of structured instruction as contrasted with individualized curricula.

The Key Publications and Key Organizations listed at the end of this chapter provide wide coverage of instructional materials—especially of intentional and structured instructional materials.

Textbooks, of some sort, have been the major staple of American education since the advent of the *New England Primer* ("In Adam's Fall, We Sinned All"), a religious abecedarius that provided a complete curriculum and combined value education (then religious values) with the ABCs. Though a complete curriculum today now takes years rather than four to six months, we still place similar demands on our textbooks. We attempt to inculcate basic skills in a setting congruent with the dominant values of our society.

American textbooks became a major commercial enterprise during our Revolutionary War when an English blockade cut off shipments of books from Britain. Noah Webster's response, the "Bluebacked Speller" of 1792, mingled patriotism and commerce in a well-developed text. After writing this text, Webster campaigned state by state to establish copyright laws to protect his right to sole publication. He was correct in believing the copyright valuable. In 1880, almost 100 years and four editions later, the speller was still in use after selling more than one-million copies per year for 40 years; except for the Bible, it was our national best seller. McGuffey's textbooks, which flourished from the 1830s to the 1920s (and are now revived), had formidable, though not quite equal sales, and were important in creating national values of thrift, hard work and patriotism.

Though current textbook authors may lack the stature of Webster, textbook publishing can be enormously profitable for both authors and publishers. Mabel O'Donnell, of Texas, unknown to literary critics, or indeed to most educators, is said to have reached 300 million children over 30 years with her two series, *Janet and Mark* and *Alice and Jerry*, and to have cleared $270,000 in royalties from her efforts. As a form of publication, textbooks are geared to huge sales in large markets, while each book has a rather low margin of profit.

Though the first free texts apparently date back at least as far as 1818 in Philadelphia, it was not until the early 1920s—more than 100 years later—that schools nationwide took responsibility for supplying all students with free texts.

In the subsequent years between the 1920s and the 1970s, we have seen vast changes in the types, varieties and sources of instructional materials, which were limited almost exclusively to textbooks and blocks in the 1920s. We added teachers' manuals and workbooks in the 1930s. The 1940s brought filmstrips and movies; the 1950s programmed instruction and substantial funds for television. The injection of federal monies for materials in the 1960s helped stock school libraries and built up stores of all kinds of learning materials and audiovisuals, including boxes, kits, filmstrips, games and records. The 1960s also saw a fairly substantial amount of federal monies devoted to developing textbooks. Of the $200 million distributed by the National Science Foundation, a sizeable proportion went to textbook development. The Biological Science Curriculum Study, for instance, spent four years and $8 million writing and testing the BSCS textbook series (deploying 110 high school and university teachers as writers and testing the book on 150,000 students in 1,000 schools in 47 states). The BSCS textbooks, subsequently published by three commercial firms, were eventually used by more than one-half the biology students in United States schools, while the remainder used books modeled on or affected by BSCS.

By the end of the free-spending 1960s, many textbook publishing firms had been taken over by technology and communications giants such as IBM, Xerox, Bell and Howell, ITT, the New York Times, and Litton, possibly on the assumption that the federal government would continue its large subsidies for instructional materials and computer-assisted instruction. If these were their hopes, they were not realized.

Ironically enough, the 1970s have been a period of increasing austerity for instructional materials budgets. Despite technological advances and resources, a significant number of school districts are returning to basics with the basic (expanded) textbook. In the twenties our expenditures for instructional materials (essentially texts) averaged around 2.2 percent of instructional budgets (considerably higher in some states in some years). Textbooks today, despite their major role in education, account for less than 0.7 percent of our instructional budgets ($640 million in 1976-1977), a decline from 1.6 percent in 1965.

The textbook firms that succeed in making money in this declining market seem to owe their success to luck, timing and/or marketing know-how rather than to educational worth. One survey indicated that seven firms (out of 150 textbook publishers) earn 57 percent of the revenues. Similarly, EPIE's National Survey (NSAIM) of four areas—reading, math, science and social studies—showed that 20 companies produced the 120 most frequently used materials with only six publishers responsible for 62 percent of the items.

Interestingly, EPIE's detailed assessment of the most-used and least-used materials revealed that these two groups were remarkably similar. Either EPIE's meticulous assessment instruments somehow failed to reveal genuine differences *or* the most-used materials were selected on some basis other than quality.

Whatever the range of quality, our expenditures for texts are exceedingly low considering their function in American education and the time consumed in their use. One estimate is that during elementary and high school years each student will read—or at least be exposed to—more than 32,000 textbook pages—excluding supplementary reading. EPIE established that 62.5 percent of *classroom* time—*exclusive* of homework—is spent on printed materials—textbooks to a large extent.

According to Robert Leeper's *Strategies for Curriculum Change* (Washington, Association for Supervision and Curriculum Development, 1965), 85 percent of classroom teachers honestly believe the textbook adoption process to be the major means through which curriculum content is determined.

Principals too, according to an NEA survey (*The Principals Look at the Schools*, Washington, National Education Association, 1972), rated textbooks as their most useful resource for teaching programs—as compared to national groups, professional organizations, state courses of studies, local materials and educational foundations. Another more recent study of textbooks, summarized in Daniel Barron's "Review of Selected Research in School Librarianship," noted that, though textbooks are ranked the "least desirable" media by teachers, they are used the most.

Whether popular or not, textbooks are our major means of conveying curriculum content and standardizing by grade level. Since standardized tests are correlated with textbooks, our basic concepts of student mastery and achievement are similarly standardized through our textbooks.

Textbook publishers, at least in print, assert that textbooks are a major repository of knowledge and have a unifying role in our large, pluralistic nation. They do, undoubtedly, supply a very large proportion of the knowledge on which children are tested.

At their best, textbooks offer comprehensive, sequential, orderly presentations of commonly-accepted knowledge correlated to a commonly-accepted curriculum most often prepared for a national market and selected largely by groups of educators. As such, they omit the specific, the regional, the particular, the immediate and—as much as possible—materials that could possibly stir up community opposition.

Their virtues, in short, imply possible defects. As materials intentionally devised for a national market, textbooks cannot afford to be original or innovative, but must adhere to approaches that have worked (or been purchased) before. In their attempts to meet the cumulative requirements and group needs of states and school districts, they are subject to group-think in their very origin.

Many of the criteria designed for textbooks and other large basal programs fail to come to grips with the problems of textbooks that stem from their marketing approaches and from their very virtues of comprehensiveness, sequence and inclusion of teacher methodology. The flaws and problem areas listed below seem common to textbooks as a genre. (I do not imply that every textbook or textbook series suffers from each or any of these problems.)

Some basic textbook problem areas are:

- Textbooks are written for knowledge, not thinking.

- Textbooks test for memory rather than understanding.

- Their breadth precludes depth.

- They are, of necessity, aimed at the lowest common denominator of ability for both teachers and students.

- As a group effort, they are assembled, rather than written.

- They lose originality in attempting to be universally accepted.

- They limit good, original teachers.

- They do not meet the range of abilities or knowledge present in any classroom.

- They contain hidden value systems.

- They present commonly-accepted knowledge that may not be accurate.

- At our present growth rate in knowledge, texts become obsolete before they are adopted or when still in use.

- Because of high investment costs, publishers cannot afford to abandon programs or to experiment without special funding.

- Curriculum easily becomes reduced to reading the text.

(List continues on page 242)

- Major texts resemble each other strongly.

- Texts are selected on the basis of familiarity and marketing skill rather than educational worth.

- Textbooks rarely exceed minimal standards.

According to one study of texts in relation to achievement, these minimal standards for texts may have a role in our declining student achievement (SAT scores). The Wirtz Report, *On Further Examination*, explored the reason for our 15-year decline by allowing Jeanne Chall to look at the history and reading textbooks of students who took the SAT examinations in 1947, 1955, 1967, 1972 and 1975. Ms. Chall found, over the years, 1) a decline in reading level, difficulty and challenge, 2) greater space taken up by pictures, larger print and wider margins, 3) shorter sentences, words and paragraphs, 4) less exposition and 5) more narrative.

The textbooks commonly used in eleventh grade were found to be written at a ninth or tenth grade level, while student tests—in or out of textbooks—became increasingly objective. Similarly, textbook assignments in most recent history, reading and literature texts require only underlining, circling and filling in single words, rather than writing or thinking.

While these watered-down texts are neither challenging nor diversified, it is hard to tell whether they are a cause of—or a response to—decreasing literacy. If they continue to be used as our exclusive teaching tools, they will probably contribute further to the vicious cycle.

In most eyes, the major defect of textbooks is that they tend to impose conformity upon the curriculum, teachers and students. A prescribed curriculum, of necessity, ignores current, unexpected, educationally relevant materials and events. The built-in support system that textbooks supply for poor or insecure teachers stifles gifted or above-average teachers and limits those who can do better than the book on any particular occasion. The grade level assigned to texts can be almost beside the point, particularly for older children. In every grade above the sixth, pupils vary from four to seven grades in reading and ability levels. A typical textbook will be too hard for one-fourth to one-third of the students and too simple for or boring to a comparable number. As teaching devices, they are most successful for children who combine good work habits and intelligence that is on the low end of the normal range.

Again, though some publishers opt for originality on some occasions, the market research programs of many publishers tend to increase conformity or unintentional plagiarism by picking up the features that are most successful or appealing in other (possibly more original) texts.

Textbook publishers are early selectors of instructional materials, both for in-house publications and for those prepared by outside authors. Though large publishers generally base and design their own books, small publishers often solicit teachers for ideas (and ask their prospective authors to fill out detailed descriptive analyses of their prospective works). The selection process begins as the publisher reviews the author's description of the target audience, the components, the planned organization and the educational applications of the proposed text. And in large publishing houses—which often provide the impetus for proposed texts—publishers may even help define the parameters of the proposed material by, for instance, providing their solicited author with collaborators.

These publishers recognize that a complex interaction arises between the contents and the function of textbooks, whose societal role is to teach (captive) groups. Unlike trade books, produced and sold to (aggregates of) individuals, textbooks aim at mass sales to large groups. Textbooks are not selected *by* their ultimate users, or even *for* their ultimate users in the same sense as library books (which essentially are selected for users' tastes and interests). State laws, political climates, earlier curricula, established policies and miscellaneous traditions all play a far greater role in textbook selection.

MARKETING PRACTICES

Even during the nineteenth century, while textbooks consistently preached honesty and thrift, the textbook industry had a goodly share of scandals involving anti-trust trials, charges of monopoly and bribery and accounts of moonlighting by teachers and pressure tactics by textbook salesmen.

Efforts to avoid corruption included gentlemen's agreements among the more scrupulous publishers, evaluation standards promulgated and developed by school administrators and other educators, quality mandates by educational jurisdictions and, perhaps most importantly, a crazy patchwork of state laws and state adoption policies and practices designed to improve materials and curriculum.

Many of the laws that affect current selection policies and content arose from experiences that have little relevancy today. California's complex procedures, for example, stem in part from a 90-year-old "Know-Nothing" constitutional amendment, and a suspicion of railroads and Eastern publishers that may have had some historic justification. Our state practice of printing textbooks, in turn, stems from the days when our legislature met only on alternate years and our state printer needed something to occupy his idle presses. As a consequence, the California state printer was still printing some textbooks as of 1978, and California's process for evaluating texts is most cumbersome, if thorough.

STATE ROLES IN SELECTION

While state roles in textbook adoption are generally in the form of adoption policies, all states—whether or not they have such policies—have many laws that influence or determine curriculum, most often in the fields of health, safety, alcohol, narcotics, cultural pluralism, women's studies and other science and social-science areas. One or more states actually forbid the teaching of such topics as evolution and human reproduction, and most forbid the use of religious denominational literature. State requirements for accountability and competency and state-wide examinations such as New York's Regents' Examinations also influence selection. Roy H. Millenson's *Selected Federal and State Book Program Information* provides current information on state textbook adoption agencies.

Twenty-two states, with about 40 percent of the school population, have state adoption policies of varying degrees of complexity that tend overall to lengthen the time of selection. The chart on page 244 is a survey of state policies, current as of 1977.

STATE TEXTBOOK ADOPTION POLICIES–1977

LOCAL SELECTION STATES

Alaska	Massachusetts	Ohio
+*Colorado	*Michigan	Pennsylvania
R Connecticut	*Minnesota	*Rhode Island
*Delaware	Missouri	C South Dakota
*District of Columbia	Montana	Vermont
Illinois	*Nebraska	R Washington
*Iowa	New Hampshire	Wisconsin
Kansas	New Jersey	+ Wyoming
Maine	*New York	
*Maryland	R North Dakota	

LOCAL CHOICE FROM STATE LISTS

*Florida	Nevada
*Hawaii	Virginia

DUAL SELECTION (elementary from a state list; upper grades local)

*California (divided K-8 and 9-12)
West Virginia (divided K-6 and 7-12)

STATE ADOPTIONS

Alabama	Kentucky	Oregon
Arizona	*Louisiana	*South Carolina
Arkansas	Mississippi	Tennessee
*Georgia	New Mexico	*Texas
*Idaho	*North Carolina	*Utah
Indiana	Oklahoma	

KEY

*   Guidelines for selection/adoption of instructional materials as of April 1976.

R   Requires local policy, or state can recommend.

C   County textbook committee selects.

+   State board prohibited from prescribing textbooks.

Typically, textbooks are selected on a revolving schedule which is made specific by annual schedules of events. Publishers try to time their texts so that copyright dates on new editions will coincide with adoption cycles in big states like California (which is the source of these schedules) and Texas.

INSTRUCTIONAL MATERIALS ADOPTION CYCLES
1979-1996

Academic Year → / Subject Area ↓	79/80	80/81	81/82	82/83	83/84	84/85	85/86	86/87	87/88	88/89	89/90	90/91	91/92	92/93	93/94	94/95	95/96
SOCIAL SCIENCE / MUSIC	F	a		A		a	F	a		A		a	F	a		A	
BILINGUAL/BICULTURAL (Including ESL) / FOREIGN LANGUAGES	a	F	a		A		a	F	a		A		a	F	a		A
SCIENCE / HEALTH		a	F	a		A		a	F	a		A		a	F	a	
ENGLISH & RELATED SUBJECTS / ART	A		a	F	a		A		a	F	a		A		a	F	a
MATH		A		a	F	a		A		a	F	a		A		a	F
READING / LITERATURE	a		A		a	F	a		A		a	F	a		A		a

A = Major adoption
a = Minor adoption
F = Framework/Criteria revision development (distribution in following year)

(Approved by State Board of Education, March 11, 1977)
Rev. 1/2/79

SCHEDULE OF EVENTS
for the
1979-80 ADOPTION

Distribution of "Invitation to Submit Materials"	March 5, 1979
Receipt of submission lists and samples (c. 1979 or before) by the State Department of Education (SDE)	May 9, 1979
Distribution of notices to publishers of where to send additional samples	July 13, 1979
Receipt of all additional samples by Display Centers and receipt of samples (c. 1980) by SDE	September 26, 1979
Distribution of request for bids	January 28, 1980
Receipt by SDE of formal bids	March 7, 1980
Completion of Legal Compliance reviews	March 12, 1980
Completion of educational content reviews	April 4, 1980
Completion of Legal Compliance Appeals (1st level)	April 28, 1980
Completion of Legal Compliance Appeals (2nd level)	May 28, 1980
Curriculum Commission's recommended list	June, 1980
State Board of Education adopts	September, 1980

From a marketing perspective, states with and those without state policies are considered adoption territory and open territory, respectively. To complicate matters further, adoption territory includes not only adoption states but city and county enclaves within free states that have their own adoption policies (such as Seattle, New York City, Washington County, Maryland). Parochial schools also have varying open and adoption policies that tend to follow diocesan borders.

In areas with adoption policies, the adoption process generally begins with a call from an agency (such as the state department of education) announcing the need for a new adoption. Then a committee, typically an Adoption Committee or a Textbook Committee, is selected to evaluate and recommend textbooks from among those offered in bids by educational publishers. After the committee—usually composed of experts and/or citizens—recommends its choices to the state board of education, the state board may change, accept or reject the committee's recommendations. As a final step—after two to eight months or more—the state board officially approves and announces the list. Throughout this period, the publisher must meet numerous rigid deadlines. After this approval, those publishers whose texts are included are free to call on local jurisdictions.

States with adoption policies require that texts be available to them for periods of three to eight years (most often five years) usually at a fixed price over that period. The publisher generally is not supposed to substitute any other edition for the approved edition—a provision that almost guarantees obsolescence for the user and increased inventory and accounting costs for the publisher (who has to print and store sufficient texts to meet his obligations). Pricing amid increased costs for paper and warehousing in a period of inflation is particularly difficult.

Aside from the printed criteria of adoption states, textbook manufacturers have to fill in forms that include bid deposits and bid guarantees, statements that materials meet the manufacturing standards of the National Association of State Textbook Administrators, indications of readability levels, and proof of conformance with learner verification statutes—all with their own deadlines.

While this extended process used to lead to single basal adoptions, almost all states now practice multi-list adoption. Many states approve hundreds or thousands of titles; this provides schools with a variety of materials from which to choose and returns the ultimate selection process back to the local jurisdictions.

The state and local criteria on which sales and adoption depend vary considerably in structure and complexity, even though most agencies are concerned with questions of content and quality. A few state agencies have simple one-page lists of points to be considered; others prepare massive proclamations. Some require ratings or scores, or analyses according to a template; others are limited to checklists or comments. Some states merely require that local educational jurisdictions work out their own standards. In turn, some city and county standards are far more extensive than some state standards.

Most textbook publishers, in self-defense, have one or more employees whose sole task is to screen books for compliance with these assorted codes.

State criteria (mostly) are summarized in the chapter on selection policies and Susan Klein's criteria clusters are reproduced in the chapter entitled "Using Evaluation Criteria in Selecting Instructional Materials" (see page 92). Educational Research Service's (ERS) *Procedures for Textbook and Instructional Materials Selection*, cited as a Key Publication in this chapter, is a survey of district practices in 44 districts in 33 states, with reprints of some representative policies. ERS notes that 61 percent of these districts have general statements or criteria for selection, while about 14 percent have no written criteria for selection. Most districts have no written criteria for testing materials or verifying producers' statements.

In some states, state evaluators are expected to grade items for their compliance with state mandates and requirements. In California, a state with a complicated adoption process, a Legal Compliance Committee looks at the social content of textbooks to see whether their treatment corresponds to particular sections of California code law on the treatment of male and female roles, entrepreneur and labor, ethnic and cultural groups, ecology and environment, dangerous substances (i.e., tobacco, narcotics and alcohol) and religion. Essentially, these value questions imposed on texts are answered, not by trained analysts or literary critics, but by educators who resort to such methods as head counts in illustrations to arrive at appraisals of fairness and balance. Other committees review materials for educational excellence and conformity to California educational frameworks. This lengthy process is then—to a great degree—repeated in local jurisdictions.

Overall, it is unclear whether textbooks and instructional materials are any better or different in states that adopt, evaluate or supply textbooks. Certainly the selection policy is more complex. In some cases, state textbook subsidies correlate with exceedingly low district-level instructional budgets. Again, it is hard to say if this correlation indicates a cause-effect relation or, if so, which is cause and which effect.

Adoption states, generally, do have longer time spans between adoptions. Procedural requirements (such as posting bonds and negotiating) are apt to be more restrictive, as are regulations on content. Some people believe that some states' adoption policies inadvertently provide a disproportionate amount of influence to unqualified individuals, especially in Texas, where 15 individuals are responsible for choosing up to five books per subject. Historically, books have been changed or deselected because of the supposed political affiliation of authors. Other textbooks have been partially rewritten to get sales or acceptance in major states.

This state adoption process can result in handy guides or structured comparisons issued by states. If and when display centers are set up to aid the process of selection, a higher proportion of teachers become aware of the possibilities of new offerings. State adoption periods are also natural times for statewide or districtwide in-service training on selecting and evaluation principles. Whether these gains are worth the effort is anybody's guess.

SELECTION COMMITTEES

The establishment of a district selection committee close to local needs with responsibility for selecting local materials has been strongly advocated by the Joint Committee of the National Education Association and the American Textbook Publishers' Institute (a group founded in 1959 to deal with textbook issues like censorship, selection, distribution, quality and usage).

The Joint Committee's 1963 *Guidelines for Textbook Selection* attempted to provide an orderly adoption and selection process for textbooks through a sort of flow chart of educational roles, with thoughtful comments and recommendations on roles for superintendents and selection committees and generalizations on state adoption. Its basic purposes seem to be to provide a voice for teachers while guaranteeing major textbook publishers fair and equal access to educational markets.

Since the Joint Committee recommendations still provide the most comprehensive overview to date, I have summarized some of their suggestions and recommendations below:

- Since education is a state function, individual states can delegate responsibilities for selection to state or local agencies, often school boards.

- In practice most school boards delegate responsibilities to the professional staffs of their schools.

- Each school board should be guided by a set of written policies for evaluation, selection and adoption.

- Such policies should define the responsibilities of the board itself, classroom teachers, parents and an administrative officer.

- Policy statements (approved by the board) should be made available to administrators and teachers, to textbook publishers and their representatives—and, upon request, to any member of the school community.

- Prime responsibilities for selections, recommendations and adoption should be placed upon those who have to guarantee the quality of instruction and use of the materials—administrators, supervisors and classroom teachers.

- Teachers, parents and citizen groups should have opportunities to transmit their views on content to the authorities who have power to adopt the books.

Comments on Textbook Adoption

- Every textbook should be considered for replacement every four to five years— one part each year.

- Adoption schedules should be systematically reviewed.

- Adoption systems should be publicized.

Recommendations on Role of Superintendent

The Superintendent should
- provide leadership to the Textbook Committee

- choose and name the committee (with advice from principals or administrators if desired)

- delegate a Chairman or ask the Committee to choose its own

- define and sharpen goals

- set the tone for evaluation and selection

- provide ground rules

- allow administrative time

- set rules for contacts with publishers' representatives

- make public the names of Committee members

Recommendations for Textbook Selection Committee

The Committee should
- review, evaluate and make recommendations to the Superintendent
- include classroom teachers, administrative personnel, curriculum specialists, and school librarians
- include approximately 7 to 11 people, depending upon what is being evaluated (series, text, single grade)

(List continues on page 250)

- include teachers from affected grades, as well as from grade above and grade below

- work during school hours

- have secretarial help as needed

- have regularly-scheduled, well-spaced meetings at consistent times

The selected work flow of the Selection Committee should be as follows:

- decide on goals

- formulate temporary criteria which can be revised but which should include course of study, curriculum and educational philosophy

- obtain evaluations by users

- sort out books to be considered

- list them, make lists available, ask for comments

- send criteria to publishers

- consider comments

- rate and rank books

Education Research Service's recent survey would seem to indicate that most of these *Guidelines* are not being followed in many schools, even though some sort of selection committee appears to function in about three out of four districts returning the questionnaire. While they do provide some helpful common sense procedures, they fail to come to grips with some of the major problems in adoption and selection. One problem area is the appalling duplication that occurs as hundreds or thousands of individuals and committees across counties and states all review and assess the same items. We badly need some ongoing means to exchange information with state-level selectors and with other districts looking at comparable materials.

Overall, selection committees are widely representative groups that may include (rarely) school board members, research personnel, superintendents or assistant superintendents; (usually) principals, curriculum and instructional specialists; (some of the time) media center personnel and assistant principals; parents (rather frequently), students (occasionally) and (always) teachers and/or their union representatives. But few single districts have this wide a spectrum, and even fewer adequately represent either special education or gifted education. While teacher representatives on these committees are apt to be attuned to the student learning difficulties that might affect materials, these groups rarely include members who select for student strengths and potentials.

I am also somewhat doubtful about the practice of choosing union representatives for teacher members of selection committees. While their abilities in handling grievances and controversies can be helpful in assuring teachers a voice in selection, teachers with expertise in or sensitivity toward materials should have priority. In most districts, experienced substitute teachers, resource teachers, and early retirement teachers probably have the most relevant experience and the most time for service.

Similarly, the NEA position that selection policies should be subject to contract negotiations (see chapter entitled "Teachers' Roles in Selection," page 197) can politicize the selection process and might tend to narrow participation to teachers and administrators. It could also be helpful in providing released time or compensatory time for educator members of selection committees.

According to ERS' survey, in about one-half the districts surveyed (45.8 percent) teachers are *not* given time off for time-consuming meetings which can easily run from September to March. Despite the work and effort spent in meetings, in about one-half of the cases the committee's role is only advisory. In 72 percent of the districts surveyed, the district selection committee differs from the district curriculum committee, though obviously their work overlaps extensively— or should.

District policies vary considerably from the Joint Committee's stated ideal of who should be on the committee. In some cases there is no policy. Most committee members—whatever their status—have no training for the task of selection, through either courses or in-service training (though EPIE is now reaching a number of selection committees with its training programs). So far as I can tell, there is no provision—anywhere—that selection committees should include even one person with some background or experience in selection.

The *Joint Committee Guidelines* also failed to clarify the purpose and function of the selection committee—which should be to select materials for particular district needs rather than to evaluate materials in general. Selection—with or without a selection committee—ideally should start with a thorough assessment of what is available in the district, an evaluation of how district selections have worked out in the past, a knowledge of the strengths, preferences and needs of students and teachers, of relevant problem areas in the district (such as morale and teacher-community communication) and a thorough understanding of programs and long-range goals.

Committees should use a systematic standardized form to compile information from publishers and state sources. They should also take advantage of printed reviews and analyses, such as those compiled by the Key Organizations and Key Publications listed at the end of this chapter.

Since committee selection is rather slow, committees should select only major instructional items (though they can suggest items that correlate with these). They should delegate other selection primarily to individual schools and their teachers, librarians and principals. Through workshops and print they should let these selectors know how they assess district needs, what they have purchased for the district and why.

The questions listed on page 252 are typical of those which should be considered by a selection committee and by individual selectors.

- Are there students who are not being served by present instructional materials?
- Are there curricular goals which are not being met for:
    student body as a whole?
    groups of students?
    individual students?
- Should some successful materials be supplemented/replaced?
- Are some materials especially well adapted to meet particular learning processes?
- To what extent do the instructional materials consider, utilize, build on or negate existing resources, approaches and materials?
- Should all children in the same grade or learning the same subject use the same materials?
- Should the district adapt its courses to textbooks or adopt textbooks for the courses?
- Can these material(s) be linked to existing programs?
- Should material(s) be linked to existing programs?
- Do we have appropriate materials and long-range plans for new programs? What is an appropriate budget?
- Do these materials impose any limitations upon the school's organization and programs?
- Do they add flexibility?
- Can these materials be adapted to
    individualized instruction?
    independent study?
    large-group presentation?
    laboratory experiences?
    small groups?
    other teaching methods in the school?
- Can these materials be used in interdisciplinary or multi-disciplinary approaches?
- If these materials meet immediate needs, are they consistent with long-range goals?
- How often might it be necessary to replace consumable parts of the materials?
- How convenient and costly is it to replace damaged or used parts of the materials?

Committees should also use the strengths and specialties of committee members and the local staff far more effectively than is current practice. For example, teachers might assess the teachers' guides with the local staff against local conditions; a librarian could work up lists—with costs—of desirable supplementary materials for each text or program; media experts could look for supporting media in their collections; curriculum consultants could consider the long-term values and useful life expectancy of each text; parents might appraise community impact;

and, above all, representative students should comment directly on interest, relevance and difficulties.

OBJECTIVE CRITERIA AND ANALYSES FOR TEXTBOOKS

According to a 1931 survey reported in *The Use of Score Cards in Evaluating Textbooks* (*Yearbook of the National Society of the Study of Education*), some large school districts had used score cards for objective evaluation of textbooks since 1913, while most city school superintendents approved their use as of 1930.

According to this article, such score cards allowed schools to set up criteria for analyzing textbooks that forwarded the objectives of the school system and reduced the selection of textbooks to a scientific (quantitative) procedure. The forms used then, like the forms presented in the educational journals of the period and in Clement's 1942 *Manual for Analyzing and Selecting Textbooks*, seem amazingly like those advocated today, exhibiting a wide range of detailed questions (some optional) and an interesting combination of value judgments with quantitative standards.

A math text, for example, could score a maximum of 450 points, divided into:

Authorship, Personnel and Point of View	75
Content, Organization and Methodology	225
Instructional Aids and Other Helps	100
Physical and Mechanical Features including Typography	50
TOTAL POSSIBLE POINTS	450

State and district criteria use variations of the same categories and questions today, except for an increased emphasis upon fairness and bias (discussed in the chapter entitled "Fairness and Bias").

Many of the criteria included in the chapters on policy and evaluation are objective analytic criteria appropriate for large, all-encompassing programs such as textbooks. EPIE and educational evaluators are proponents of a detailed analytic approach.

Such detailed analyses can be exceedingly expensive. The Far West Laboratory, for example, spent $220,000 to produce an *Elementary Science Information Unit* comparing six elementary science programs on histories, rationale, objectives and goals, educational processes, requirements for implementation, effectiveness and evaluation in a parallel format. Even simple, inexpensive checklists can cost a great deal in time to consider for local levels.

James Brown's workbook, *The AV Instructional Materials Manual* (McGraw Hill, 1969), includes a practical textbook analysis chart, reprinted on page 254 with permission of McGraw-Hill Book Company and not to be reprinted without written permission.

TEXTBOOK ANALYSIS CHART

BASIC CONSIDERATIONS IN EVALUATING SCHOOL TEXTBOOKS	Names of texts			
CONTENT				
Is the author (or authors) regarded as competent in the field? (Check the writer's background in a reference such as *Who's Who in America*.)				
Does the text interpret the curricular objectives of the subject as prescribed by the course of study? (Select a subject area in the text and compare information given in the book with the objectives set up in a course of study for a similar subject.)				
Does it contain biased views on controversial issues? (Read a section in the book dealing with the point of controversy, i.e., in a social studies text—public versus private development of power resources.)				
Does the subject matter appear to promote sound moral values and contain writing of literary merit? (Read several random paragraphs and as you read note such features as sentence structure, use and choice of colorful words, objectionable slang expressions, etc.)				
TREATMENT OF CONTENT				
Is the style adapted to the age level of the students? (Check such items as the length of sentences, length of paragraphs, logical and suitable comparisons.)				
Is the vocabulary suitable for the grade it is intended for? (Check the words used on two or three pages with a basic word list for the grade for which book is intended.)				
Does the material adapt itself to individual differences? (Examples: Will the material appeal to girls and to boys? Are helps included for slow readers? Are there extra challenges for superior students?)				
ARRANGEMENT OF CONTENT				
Are the index and table of contents complete and easy to use? (Note the subjects mentioned on one or more pages in the text. Check these subjects with the entries in the index. If the index is to be really useful, most of the subjects should be included in the alphabetic arrangement.)				
Are difficult and unusual words included in a glossary?				
Are illustrations, maps, sketches, tables, graphs used to supplement the printed matter? (Select any ten pages in the text and tabulate the number of pages that have no illustrations, only one, more than one.)				
Do the visual aids add interest to the textual matter? (Check for such factors as reality in color, artistic page arrangement, size ample for good perception, minimum of irrelevant details.)				
Are the suggested related activities practical and do they add information not given in the text? (Analyze the activities to determine amount of time, special facilities, out-of-school resources, etc., needed to carry out the activity.)				
Do well-organized summaries and reviews appear at the end of chapters and units?				
Do the bibliographies include the most up-to-date materials, both printed and audiovisual?				
MECHANICAL STANDARDS				
Is the type clear and plain?				
Is there enough leading or spacing between lines to make the text easy to read? (Four inches of vertical space should include no more lines than number indicated for each age level: under 7 years, 10 lines; 7 to 9, 20; 9 to 12, 22; and above 12, 24 lines.)				
Are the lines of proper length for easy reading (not more than 4 inches nor less than 3 inches in length)?				
Is the paper of good weight and durability?				
Is the binding reinforced so that the book is held firmly in the cover?				
Are the pages planned for easy readability? (Check the following factors: pages inked evenly, ample margins, nonsmear ink, etc.)				

Though no reviewing purpose is apt to require all 29 criteria on the exhaustive and slightly redundant list printed on page 255, selection committees and reviewers can use this list to consider which criteria are most appropriate for their purposes, and to set priorities among relevant criteria. This list is reprinted from *A Survey and Analysis of Educational Product Review Activities*, prepared for the

School Practice and Service Program of the National Institute of Education by Diana Schermer under the direction of Susan Klein. (Washington, National Institute of Education, 1975, 96+8p.)

POSSIBLE PRODUCT REVIEWING CRITERIA

	Include?	Priority Item	Suggested Weight
Need			
1. priority of the needs addressed			
2. how well the goals address the need			
3. appropriateness to users			
4. cumulative effects			
5. product uniqueness			
6. social acceptability			
7. marketability			
Intrinsic Quality			
8. social fairness			
a. sex d. religion			
b. race e. socio-economic class			
c. ethnic f. age			
9. choice and accuracy of contents			
10. technical quality			
11. instructional quality			
12. product appeal and learner satisfaction			
13. adequacy of development process			
Practicality			
14. costs—initial, ongoing, and competitive			
15. staff effort needed			
16. acceptability to users			
17. adaptability: exportability, flexibility, and manageability			
Effectiveness			
18. strength of effect			
19. long-term effects			
20. comprehensiveness or number of effects			
21. scope of the effect			
22. comparative effectiveness			
23. efficiency in use of learners' time			
24. side effects			
Credibility of the Evidence			
25. relevance and completeness			
26. quality of the evidence			
27. generalizability			
28. comparative evidence			
29. difficulty of obtaining evidence			

Both materials and programs can be scored on appropriate criteria using the four factors of compatibility (from acceptable to unacceptable) taken from C. Lynn Jenks' *Guide to Adoptions and Implementation Decisions: A Workbook for Decision Makers: Experience-Based Career Education* (San Francisco, Far West Laboratory for Education Research and Development, 1977).

ASSESSING MATERIALS FOR COMPATIBILITY

	Acceptable	Minor Problems	Major Problems	Unacceptable	Total
PHILOSOPHY_____					
SCOPE_____					
CONTENT_____					
ORGANIZATION_____					
ORGANIZATION OF LEARNING_____					
STUDENT FACTORS_____					
LEARNING FACTORS_____					
SUPPLEMENTARY MATERIALS_____					
COSTS					

CRITERIA FOR SELECTING WORKBOOKS

Few standards or criteria have been designed for the ubiquitous workbooks, whose costs tend to be buried in a "consumable supplies" category along with pencils, paper and rabbit food. Even though their costs are difficult to determine in local school districts, they often account for more of current budgets than do more long-lasting library books and media materials; sometimes they cost more than textbooks. Though the initial costs are relatively low, their consumable nature almost guarantees repeated expenditures, which are often undertaken without much thought.

By definition, workbooks are study or learning guides for pupils, often related to a particular textbook or to several textbooks. Generally, they include outlines for studying a subject, along with exercises, problems, practice materials, questions to be answered, items to be checked and/or blanks to be filled in. Usually, they include written instructions; sometimes diagrams, maps or other graphics, and means of evaluating the work done. In their most recent manifestations, many resemble programmed instruction.

One of the few individuals to provide an approach to evaluating workbooks is Edgar Dale, in *Audiovisual Methods in Teaching* (New York, Holt, Rinehart & Winston, 1969. 3rd ed.). Many of the criteria below are based on page 582 of that book. As he points out, the main issue in the use of workbooks is whether they do in fact promote the learning they are supposed to develop. In many cases their major functions seem to be to fill time and, possibly, to promote good work habits in students. Their use also saves teacher time, sometimes beneficially. But whatever their purpose, workbooks, in particular, should be field tested (or at least tried out on a few students) before being purchased the first time. Certainly, if or when they are considered for repurchase, student comments and reactions and possibly student achievement should be a significant factor in any decision to re-order.

(The questions listed below are also appropriate in evaluating spirit masters, learning exercises developed by local teachers, and other items that compete with or supplement workbooks and textbooks.)

QUESTIONS TO CONSIDER IN EVALUATING WORKBOOKS
AND SIMILAR EXERCISES

	Rating				
	1	2	3	4	5

Is this workbook an interesting experience for most children or a time-consuming chore?

How much time would the average assignment take to do well? Is this time reasonable?

Would use of this workbook take time from more beneficial activities?

Does this workbook supplement text(s) in carefully planned ways, or render text(s) unnecessary? Is this desirable for this particular subject in this particular teaching situation?

Does this workbook provide for individual differences or must all children do all the exercises, whatever their variations in abilities, knowledge and skills?

Is this workbook diagnostic?

Is this workbook self-instructional or does it require extra explanations by the teacher? Are these explanations valuable learning experiences?

Does this workbook provide clear, well-written explanations *before exercises* so that children engage in meaningful practice?

Does this workbook tend to encourage thinking or to promote unreflective behavior?

Can a child do the exercises correctly and still not learn what s/he is supposed to be learning?

Could use of this workbook displace or limit writing experiences?

Has the material in this workbook been experimentally validated or field tested?

How would your own students evaluate this workbook?

How would local teachers evaluate this workbook?

CURRICULUM GUIDES AND TEACHERS' GUIDES

Curriculum guides, which cover the whole spectrum of curricula, should be evaluated—rather like textbooks—on philosophy and objectives, content, instructional methods and practicality. These guides are important teaching tools that should be carefully evaluated by classroom teachers.

One evaluation checklist for curriculum guides is included on pages 153-57 of James Laffey's *Source Book of Evaluation Techniques for Reading* (cited in the chapter on Reading and Language Arts Materials in *Subject Areas*). This *Source Book* as a whole has many suggestions for evaluation that are useful for all textbooks.

Other usable criteria can be extracted from *Packaging Your Educational Program* by Fred Rosenau and Diane H. McIntyre (San Francisco, Far West Laboratory for Educational Research and Development, 1977). They suggest, for example, that classroom manuals should contain information in the following areas:

- *Overviews*

  Provide a *brief* overview of major aspects of a program, including: basic philosophy, goals and objectives, student characteristics, organizational arrangements, staffing arrangements and required experience, facilities used, materials and equipment required, and instructional characteristics.

- *Materials/Equipment*

  Outline materials used and their costs (including any teacher-made materials), and the size of teacher-controlled budgets.

- *Classroom/Course Activities*

  Should include information on: diagnosing student needs, selecting and scheduling students, teachers' responsibilities for instructional programs and classroom management requirements.

- *Community/School Relationships*

  Include information on teachers' roles as well as the specialized training and evaluation procedures required.

- *Learner Activities*

  For each activity (or group of activities) provide information on purpose, goal, for whom it is useful and why, how it is intended to be used; specify *materials* and *directions*, follow-up, variations and evaluations.

In one survey of the use of guides, about one-half the teachers surveyed claimed they followed guides closely—less in some subjects, more in others. About 85 percent of elementary teachers followed guides supplied with reading materials.

Media specialists queried on the value of media guides differed among themselves; 16 percent thought them essential, 65 percent helpful, 13 percent of little use, 6 percent of no use. (On the surface, since media materials are more difficult to scan than printed materials, such guides would seem to be more important for media.)

Whatever the value of individual guides, their excessive use can limit learning opportunities for both students and teachers. The existence of built-in guides is one factor that causes certain publishers to minimize their revision of books. Rather than making changes that might interfere with teachers' work habits, they limit themselves to inserting current details and statistics.

ACTIVITIES BOOKS

Since I have not been able to locate any checklists or criteria for activities books, I have designed this checklist, borrowing rather freely from Dr. Thorum's recommendations and criteria for curriculum guides on pages 164-85 of *Instructional Materials for the Handicapped* (reviewed on pages 320-21). His book includes an extensive annotated listing of activities books.

ACTIVITIES BOOKS CHECKLIST AND EVALUATION FORM

Directions: Please fill in _____ to the best of your ability.
     0 = Omits   P = Poor   A = Adequate   E = Excellent

CONTENTS CHECKLIST

_____   Includes developmental age range of _____

_____   Purposes and/or objectives are supplied or apparent.
          (Please circle word that applies.)

_____   Estimated overall quality of activities

     _____   appeal to children   Comments:

     _____   learning value

     _____   correlated with suggested developmental levels

     _____   correlated with appropriate subject matter and/or
               skills (Please circle terms that apply.)

_____   Provides clearly-written procedures and directions for_____

_____   Provides suggested variations

_____   Is helpfully open ended

_____   Encourages _____

_____   Can be easily adapted for special needs

_____   Specifies equipment and materials required

     _____   includes sources, approximate costs, precise
               dimensions and materials for activities and for
               patterns of games, toys, equipment
               (Please circle appropriate terms.)

(Checklist continues on page 260)

ACTIVITIES BOOKS CHECKLIST AND EVALUATION FORM (cont'd)

_____ Provides bibliographies/directories of additional sources for students, teachers, parents, or _____. (Please circle appropriate terms.)

_____ Has an adequate table of contents

_____ Includes adequate location devices: index(es), index table(s), _____

_____ Easy to use

_____ Overall appraisal of contents

CONTENTS COMMENTS

How would you rate this book overall?

What are its strengths?

What are its weaknesses?

How does it compare with others?

PHYSICAL FORMAT CHECKLIST AND COMMENTS

_____ Ease of use (Comments:

_____ Construction (Comments:

_____

_____ Secured pages or loose patterns, Ditto masters, etc. (Comments:

_____ Attractiveness (Comments:

_____ Overall appraisal of physical format

_____ Could it be easily improved or adapted? Suggestions:

APPLICABILITY COMMENTS

For whom would you recommend this activity book?

For whom would you not recommend this activity book?

Is it applicable for your school or class? For anywhere else in this district?

Are there any particular materials or type of materials that would be better for your needs? Specify:

If so, do you know where or how to obtain these items?

ACTIVITIES BOOKS CHECKLIST AND EVALUATION FORM (cont'd)

RECOMMENDATIONS

Please check and fill in appropriate boxes

_____   Do not purchase

_____   Purchase _____ copies by the date specified below
                    (number)
          _____ for the following classes

          _____

          _____

_____   Consider for purchase again at date specified below

          _____

FOLLOW THROUGH.

KEY ORGANIZATIONS

Association for Supervision and Curriculum Development (ASCD)
225 North Washington Street
Alexandria, VA 22314   (703) 549-9110
     A membership organization, in existence since 1921, largely concerned with improving instruction and curriculum. It has a substantial publication program (audiocassette and print) in its areas of interest and expertise: curriculum, supervision, school and society, teaching and learning, multicultural education, middle school/high school, particular subject areas, assessment, evaluation, and accountability.
     Its publications range from around $1.50. A few particularly helpful for selection are:

> *About Learning Materials*, by M. Frances Klein. 1978. 45p. $4.50pa.

> *Criteria for Theories of Instruction*, by Ira J. Gordon. 1968. 56p. $2.00pa.

> *Curriculum Theory*, by Alex Molnar and John A. Zahorik. 1977. 135p. $7.00pa.

> *Needs Assessment: A Focus for Curriculum Development*, by Fenwick English and Roger Kaufman. 1975. 73p. $4.00.

> *Selecting Learning Experiences: Linking Theory and Practice*, by Bruce R. Joyce. 1978. 55p. $4.75.

> *What Are the Sources of the Curriculum?*, by Robert Leeper. 1962. 86p. $1.50.

     Audiotape cassettes, that might be useful in aiding selection, include an interview with James Block on "Mastery Learning" (1976, $6.50) and another with Elliot W. Eisner on "Educational Connoisseurship and Educational Criticism, A New Evaluation Approach," 1978. 55 min. $0.60.

For the past four years, ASCD's National Curriculum Study Institutes, which combine outstanding scholars and well-designed take-home packets, have tackled some topics related to selection such as Learning/Teaching Styles, Curriculum Evaluation, Instructional Media and Design.

Curriculum Advisory Service (CAS)

500 South Clinton St.

Chicago, IL 60607   (312) 939-1333

For the past 17 years (since 1961), Curriculum Advisory Service has issued successive publications that reviewed traditional curriculum materials. Its current publication, *Curriculum Review*, revised and refurbished as of 1976, includes excellent reviews. Items covered are mainly textbooks, supplements and multi-media kits for grades K-12; however, other items—tradebooks, games, kits and particular media items—are often reviewed.

Curriculum Review is a well-indexed, well-organized periodical with five issues (about 400 pages) a year for $35.00. (Single back issues are available at $5.00 each.) Each issue combines the basic subject-area reviews (in language arts, mathematics, science and social studies) with one or two special themes or features. These have included women, metrics, mainstreaming, consumer education, values and media. Other feature articles tackle educational trends and issues related to curriculum and instructional materials—for example, open classrooms, readability scales, or the future of the textbook. "Cluster reviews," a new feature, groups together trade books and other materials on related topics. These are excellent for comparative reviewing, for searching interdisciplinary subjects and for individualized selection. Other materials may be described in brief annotations, announcements or overview articles.

CAS has a staff of about 150 reviewers nationwide, mostly subject specialists who are active classroom teachers or professors. Their one- or two-page reviews of texts and basal programs are competent, almost always evaluative and relatively compact.

Compared to *EPIE Materials Reports* (discussed below under EPIE), *Curriculum Review* is more current and covers more items, though it provides somewhat less depth for the items it covers.

Materials are selected for review—on the basis of newness as well as instructional value—from publishers' catalogs and press releases, convention exhibits and ads in professional journals. CAS additionally receives review copies of many basal programs directly from publishers.

CAS has had a long no-advertising policy, but in 1978 began to include advertisements in *Curriculum Review*—a change that does not appear to have affected the objectivity of its reviews and appraisals.

CAS's excellent indexes make it easy to locate relevant reviews and evaluations through good cross references, multiple listings, indication of grade levels, and separate indexes by topic, by sequence, and by type of material.

Text/Kit Guidelines (reprint begins on page 263), presented by CAS as instructions to reviewers, provide an idea of what one experienced group of reviewers considers most significant in textbooks. These guidelines, reprinted by permission of the editors of *Curriculum Review*, are copyrighted ©1978 by the Curriculum Advisory Service.

TEXT/KIT GUIDELINES:
Instructions to Reviewers for *Curriculum Review*

Content Emphasis

Characterize program. What makes it different, unusual? What is its major purpose in the classroom? What is its major source of appeal? What is the target audience? This paragraph should let the reader know immediately whether or not to go on.

If this is a revised edition, how does it differ from the previous one?

For a multimedia (kit) program, this is the place to list briefly the components of the kit. Try to help the reader understand the kit's physical scope and what type of activities it emphasizes.

Reading Level

Identify specific reading level range, and the scale you used to determine it (Fry, Fog, Spache, Dale-Chall). This information should be included in the evaluation of any major text program, whatever the subject area. Do not rely on the publisher's opinion. (If you are unfamiliar with reading level analyses, you should be able to obtain one of the briefer versions from your English/Language Arts Department. It should not take longer than a half hour to do. If your school cannot supply this information, CR will mail you a copy of the Fry scale.)

Does the actual reading level differ from the publisher's designation? What is the relationship between reading and interest level? Is the reading level appropriate for this type of material? Must any provisions be made for technical vocabulary (glossary available)? Any remedial uses?

Rationale

What education philosophy or approach underlies the program? Is the emphasis on discovery? deduction? cognitive learning? values clarification? individualized pacing? group interaction? other? In other words, what assumptions does the author make about the teaching/learning process?

What long-range learning goals is the material designed to accomplish? Is the text material consistent with this rationale? Will it achieve the goals implicit in its design?

Objectives

What specific learning objectives does the program identify? Are these implicit or explicit? Where and how are they specified--as student unit goals, or as lesson objectives in the teacher's guide? Give a few brief examples. Are the objectives stated in strict behavioral terms, or are they simply desired learnings?

(Guidelines continue on page 264)

TEXT/KIT GUIDELINES (cont'd)

Organization

Describe format of presentation of the materials. Is there a scope and sequence chart provided? Is the sequence self-evident?

Identify the major topics covered. It may be useful to list unit titles; however, do not list all chapter titles--a representative sampling is sufficient. How long will it take to cover the material? Are some topics or segments optional? Are some segments self-contained?

Additional Material

Comment on the availability of manuals, workbooks, filmstrips, tapes, or wall charts. (List available tests, but save their discussion for "Evaluation" section of the review.) Are there bilingual versions of the material available? Other supportive but not essential materials?

Instructional Method

Describe the suggested (or most appropriate) teaching approach. What is the teacher's role? The student's role? (Teacher-directed, inquiry-oriented, teacher-as-resource-person, discussion-based, paper-and-pencil?) What teaching devices are built into the program?

How flexible is the material? How much room is there for a variety of instructional modes? Is the program better suited to individual, small-group, or whole-class use? What kinds of learning activities are emphasized? What type of teacher preparation is necessary?

Student Evaluation

How does the program determine student progress? Are there devices for immediate student feedback? (Quizzes, chapter tests, etc.?) Are there pretests or diagnostic inventories available? Are there mastery tests?

Does the material "teach to test" or teach ways to use the information in a variety of contexts? Is evaluation an integral part of the program? Are the evaluation procedures or outcomes affected by the level of reading skills?

Field Testing

This section may include publishers' data on field-testing; however, publishers' comments often lack both specificity and objectivity. (Some objective field test data may be available on federally funded curriculum projects like BSCS, SCIS, etc.)

TEXT/KIT GUIDELINES (cont'd)

Since reliable field-testing statistics are rarely available on brand-new programs, reviewers are encouraged to try these materials in their own classes and comment on students' reactions. Please identify general type of school and students involved in your test situation.

Physical Features

Discuss quality of type, type size, binding durability, error frequency, quality of illustrations, use of color, visual appeal—comment only on those points which are significant or unusual.

Note the inclusion of photographs, diagrams, maps, charts and tables, index, glossary, bibliography.

In the case of multimedia programs, comment in a non-technical way on film color, sound clarity and synchronization, tape quality, voice and music reproduction, durability of manipulative devices, etc. Is the general package design functional as well as eye-catching?

Recommendations

Is this program good, bad, indifferent, or the best thing you've seen in years? Would you recommend that your own school purchase it? What are its major strengths and weaknesses?

Can it stand on its own, or would it be best used in conjunction with another program? What are its interdisciplinary possibilities? What type of student would benefit most from this type of material? Does it reveal any cultural biases? any sexual, racial, or ethnic stereotyping? any basic inaccuracies of content?

Please remember to back up serious criticisms with specific examples from the text. Are there ways the teacher can compensate for serious drawbacks? If possible, end with a strong rather than a weak point.

Educational Materials Review Center (EDMARC)

(U.S. Office of Education)
Room 1127, 400 Maryland Ave., SW
Washington, DC 20202   (202) 245-8439 or 245-8437

EDMARC is the closest approach to a central collection, evaluation and review center for those who select or purchase textbooks and tradebooks for classroom use. It houses a large proportion of current textbooks, many recently-released tradebooks, a working collection of older, well-reviewed tradebooks and a wide assortment of other instructional and curriculum materials used in schools.

It was originally established cooperatively in 1953 as a joint venture of textbook publishers, the Department of State, and the Office of Education, so that foreign educators could see American textbooks. It added children's books in 1958 when the Children's Book Council joined the venture. Subsequently it acquired a historical collection of old texts and children's books, and changed its focus primarily to help American educators. It is now part of the Information and Materials Branch of the Office of Education, Administrative Services Division.

More than 200 publishers provide EDMARC with approximately 2,500 current textbooks, tradebooks and professional titles each year by making available review copies on a permanent loan basis. EDMARC's collection now includes approximately 7,000 K-12 textbooks, 8,000 tradebooks, 800 professional books, 100 educational periodicals and a historical collection of 8,000 volumes.

Reviews of children's books (from five major reviewing media) are summarized on cards (along with information on prices, etc.) to provide concise but complete information on books in the collection. Trade books are displayed for one year, after which the best are selected for inclusion in the permanent collection. These well-reviewed books often end up in EDMARC bibliographies.

Textbooks are retained indefinitely, but are transferred to the permanent collection after revision, replacement or three years. These textbooks are filed by a well-designed *Textbook Classification Scheme*, available free from the Office of Education.

The EDMARC collection is the basis of bibliographies compiled by the EDMARC staff alone, or cooperatively with other institutions. The Children's Book Committee of the Library of Congress, for example, uses EDMARC to produce its annual annotated list of 200 best books, *Children's Books*.

The EDMARC staff has produced the *Aids to Media Selection* (cited in *Media and Curriculum* and will update this when time permits. Other staff bibliographies are *Dealing in Futures* (annotated in *Subject Areas*) and *Coping* (annotated in the same volume).

The EDMARC staff is also reviving an old service of planning and conducting seminars on the development, selection and use of educational materials and on the organization and maintenance of materials centers.

Educational Products Information Exchange (EPIE Institute)
P.O. Box 620
Stony Brook, NY 11790   (516) 246-8664

EPIE West Coast
1018 Keith Avenue
Berkeley, CA 94708   (415) 525-1451

EPIE, a non-profit, membership organization, was established in 1967 as a sort of consumers' union for educational products. An independent agency, without commercial sponsorship, EPIE's income is entirely derived from fees paid by educational consumers, and from occasional grants from public agencies and private foundations.

Its proclaimed objective is to "provide educational consumers with information and evaluative services that enable them to select educational products which best meet the needs of learners." To achieve this goal, EPIE attempts to work with most groups that have roles in selecting materials, including parents, teachers, students, administrators and school board members. (To this date, EPIE has not worked extensively with librarians.) EPIE is currently active in approximately ten percent of the nation's school districts. Since 1974—through workshops and in-service programs—it has trained teachers in its systematic approach to analyzing instructional materials. It has been offering three-day sessions on selecting instructional materials since 1977.

EPIE is the originator of Learner Verification and Revision (LVR) treated on pages 118-24 of this book. Its basic approach to analysis is presented in the chapter on evaluation criteria (pages 92-117). Its current media evaluation program is discussed more extensively in the chapter on audiovisual materials.

EPIE uses a variety of means to review and report on educational products—through commissioned product reviews, careful examination and analysis of producers' claims, and through feedback from a rather broad sample of users.

As part of its membership it issues eight *EPIE Reports* ($20.00 each if purchased separately), one-half on equipment and one-half (*EPIE Materials Reports*) on materials. Its newsletter, *EPIEgram*, similarly devotes 18 issues to materials and 18 to equipment. Subscription to the whole package is $100.00 ($50.00 for materials only). Non-members can purchase individual issues of the *EPIE Reports*.

Individual issues of *EPIE Materials Reports* have had titles like "Selector's Guide for Elementary School Social Studies," "Selector's Guide for Elementary School Reading Programs," and the like. These "Selector's Guides" are usually written by task forces or workshops (acknowledged in the preface) and aim to provide a comprehensive view of a currently important subject field.

EPIE basically uses analytic comparisons in a concrete format rather than reviews. Their reports are apt to be long and detailed (occasionally 27 pages or so on a single item) and sometimes hard to read. The most interesting reading is generally found under "Remarks" or "Other Considerations."

Since EPIE appraisals are so lengthy and detailed, they are best suited to major programs and texts, for which they provide a plethora of information.

As compared with, say, *Curriculum Review*, these reports are not well or consistently indexed (some issues have no internal indexing). However, recent "Selector's Guides" are mostly arranged by publisher with an author-title index at the back. Over the last ten years, the Reports had several titles, including *EPIE Educational Product Report, Educational Product Report* and *EPIE Forum*. Unfortunately, since each issue has a single theme, individual titles are not well indexed in either *Current Index to Journals in Education* (CIJE) or *Education Index*.

KEY PUBLICATIONS

Publications dealing with particular subject areas are listed in appropriate chapters. The topic "fairness" is treated in the chapter entitled "Fairness and Bias," pages 153-80.

Curriculum Development Library (CDL). Belmont, CA, Fearon-Pitman Publishers, 1978. 1,644 microfiche in 3 boxes. 6 vol. index. Complete collection $1,495.00. Indexes $72.50 complete set; $15.00 each. Complete set includes microfiche, storage boxes and three sets of the Indexes. (Portable microfiche reader available for $100.00).

This new *Curriculum Development Library* by Fearon-Pitman is planned as the first of an annual series of curriculum guides in 20 subject categories, arranged and indexed for easy use, intended as a research tool for school district people developing curricula.

The 900 curriculum guides and similar documents included here were selected by a team of doctoral students in education at Stanford—serving as a substantive model for others planning curricula in specific subject areas. There was "definitely a bias toward documents which appeared to contain the results of some real and original work by teachers on a district level, although some overall guideline documents from state agencies were also included to show general approaches currently mandated or suggested by these agencies." Almost all documents included were compiled in 1975 or later.

While there is considerable variation in the guides, almost all have goals, objectives, suggested teaching strategies and some ideas for variations. Many have games, worksheets, activities and/or tests, and some are teacher-to-teacher resource books.

Subject categories are Bilingual/Bicultural Education, Business Education, Consumer Education, Early Childhood Education, English/Language Arts, Environment/Ecology, Fine Arts/Music, Foreign Languages, Guidance/Career Education, Health/Safety, History/Geography, Home Economics, Mathematics, Miscellaneous/Unique, Physical Education, Science, Social Studies/Social Sciences, Special Education, Systems Management/Administration and Vocational Education/Industrial Arts. Within these alphabetical categories, materials are arranged by grade level in ascending order. The six indexes group related topics together and are broken down into smaller keyword categories for quick indexing. Brief instructional abstracts analyze contents, provide comments and indicate characteristics.

Educational Marketer Yellow Pages, edited by Danita Quirk. 4th ed. White Plains, NY, Knowledge Industry Publications, 1978. $17.95.

This annual, now in its fourth edition, lists companies that produce instructional materials or provide services for producers of instructional materials. By their definition, instructional materials include textbooks, print materials, audiovisual software, tests, multimedia kits, manipulatives and teacher training materials. The support services include art, consulting, tape-duplicating, editorial assistance, as well as printers and distributors. Under each state, entries are arranged alphabetically by name, with current addresses, names of officers and/or sales representatives and their phone numbers. The information is compiled by the editors of *The Educational Marketer*, a newsletter concerned with marketing aspects of educational materials and equipment.

El-Hi Textbooks in Print: Subject Index, Author Index, Title Index, Series Index.
New York, R.R. Bowker, 1979. 703p. $32.50, postpaid. (quantity discounts).

Revised annually in the spring, this useful index covers more than 31,000 textbooks and "pedagogical" books for elementary, junior high and senior high, including information on supplementary readers.

Materials are arranged by curriculum area with author, title, grade level, publication date, price, publisher and related teaching materials. The book has indexes to textbook series, as well as the usual author-title indexes and publishers' directories.

Preparation of Textbooks in the Mother Tongue, by Constance M. McCullogh.
Newark, DE, International Reading Association, 1968. 126p. $8.00; $5.00
for members.
Guide for those who write and evaluate textbooks in any language.

Procedures for Textbook and Instructional Materials Selection, conducted and
reported by Linda H. Kunder. Arlington, VA, Educational Research Service,
Inc., 1976. 129p. $10.00pa.
This is a report on an April 1976 survey of review and selection procedures
for textbooks and instructional materials in school districts in 33 states where selection takes place at the local system level. Its findings are based on a survey sent to
district administrators in 1,275 selected school districts in 33 states and the
District of Columbia, using returns from 414 school systems in these areas.

While there is some discussion of the findings, the bulk of the book consists
of well-chosen reprints and excerpts of selection policies and procedures in 16
school districts and one state. These excerpts cover criteria for selecting—general,
evaluative and pilot testing; provisions for representing minorities and avoiding sex
stereotyping; procedures for handling challenged materials; and factors germane to
the selection committee itself.

Twelve charts provide analytic and statistical information on the structure,
location, methods, and composition of textbook selection committees. Six charts
deal with other facets of selection: challenges, criteria, minority representation
and methods of selection by state.

This is a useful compilation of real data (as opposed to theory) on the
selection process—focusing on structure and function of selection committee, with
a back-up bibliography of 113 items.

FOR FURTHER READING

*Items marked with an asterisk include criteria.
+Items marked with a plus have substantial lists of references.

*Barron, Daniel D. "Review of Selected Research in School Librarianship," *School
Media Quarterly,* v. 5, no. 4 (Summer 1977), pp. 271-88.

Benthul, Herman F. "The Textbook: Past and Future," *Curriculum Review,* v. 17,
no. 1 (Feb. 1978), pp. 5-8.

Black, Hillel. *The American Schoolbook.* New York, William Morrow, 1967.

Bowler, Michael. "The Making of a Textbook," *Learning,* v. 6, no. 7 (March
1978), pp. 38-43.

Bowler, Michael. "Selling the 3 R's: How Textbooks Get into Classrooms," in *The
Ford Fellows in Educational Journalism,* edited by Diane Brundage. Washington, George Washington University, 1977.

Broudy, E. "The Trouble with Textbooks," *Teachers College Record,* v. 77,
no. 1 (Sept. 1975), pp. 13-34.

Chall, Jeanne S., et al. *An Analysis of Textbooks in Relation to Declining S.A.T. Scores.* Princeton, NJ, College Entrance Examination Board, 1977.

*Clement, John Addison. *Manual for Analyzing and Selecting Textbooks.* Champaign, IL, Garrard Press, 1942.

*Committee on the Study of Teaching Materials in Intergroup Relations. *Intergroup Relations in Teaching Materials.* Washington, American Council on Education, 1947.

Crane, Barbara. "The 'California Effect' on Textbook Adoptions," *Educational Leadership*, v. 32, no. 4 (Jan. 1975), pp. 283-85.

*Davidson, Dorothy, comp. "Trends in Curriculum Guides: (Evaluating Curriculum Guides)," *English Journal*, v. 57, no. 6 (Sept. 1968), pp. 890-97.

+Dyson, Allen J. "Ripping Off Young Minds: Textbooks, Propaganda, and Librarians," *Wilson Library Bulletin*, v. 46, no. 3 (Nov. 1971), pp. 260-67.

*Educational Product Information Exchange. *Selecting among Textbooks: A Special Report for UNESCO.* New York, EPIE, 1974.

+Leeper, Robert R., ed. *Strategies for Curriculum Change.* Washington, Association for Supervision and Curriculum Development, 1965.

*+Loveridge, A. J., et al., eds. *Preparing Textbook Manuscripts: A Guide for Authors in Developing Countries.* Paris, United Nations Educational Scientific and Cultural Organization, 1970.

A simple but systematic overview of the functions of textbooks, particularly in underdeveloped countries. It covers the rights and responsibilities of authors and how to plan, develop, print and distribute textbooks. Its sets of criteria for authors and pupils are quite relevant for most learning materials.

McCloud, Paul L. "A Survey of State Textbook Practices," *Educational Leadership*, v. 31, no. 5 (Feb. 1974), pp. 438-41.

Mayer, Martin. *The Schools.* New York, Doubleday, 1961.

*+Maxwell, C. R. "The Textbook in American Education," in *30th Yearbook for the Study of Education.* Chicago, National Society for the Study of Education, 1931.

+Millenson, Roy H. *Selected Federal and State Book Program Information.* New York, Association of American Publishers, 1978.

*Miller, Richard I. *Selecting New Aids to Teaching.* Washington, Association of Supervision and Curriculum Development, 1971.

Moore, J., ed. *Instructional Materials Adoption Data File.* White Plains, NY, Knowledge Industry Publications, 1975.

*+National Education Association. *Instructional Materials: Selection and Purchase.* Washington, NEA, 1976.

+National Education Association. *The Principals Look at the Schools.* Washington, NEA, 1962.

National Science Foundation (prepared by BCMA Associates). *Commercial Curriculum Development and Implementation in the United States.* Washington, NSF, 1971. Reprinted in a *Report* by the House Committee on Science and Technology (94th Congress, 1st Session), Nov. 1975.

Pritt, David. *How to Find and Measure Bias in Textbooks.* Englewood Cliffs, NJ, Educational Technology, 1977.

Reynolds, John C., Jr. "American Textbooks: The First 200 Years," *Educational Leadership*, v. 33, no. 4 (Jan. 1976), pp. 274-76.

+Sikorski, Linda. *Factors Influencing School Change: Science, Mathematics, Social Science.* San Francisco, Far West Laboratory for Educational Research and Development, 1976.

Simms, Richard L. "Bias in Textbooks: Not Yet Corrected," *Phi Delta Kappan*, v. 57, no. 3 (Nov. 1975), pp. 201-202.

"A Survey of Textbook Purchasing Practices," *School Management*, v. 10 (March 1966), pp. 138-66.

Taskforce for the Evaluation of Instructional Materials. *A Guide to Text Book Evaluation.* Palo Alto, CA, Task Force, 1974.

+"Textbooks," *Education Libraries*, v. 3, no. 2 (Winter 1978), pp. 44-56 [+ scattered pages].
Eight brief but well-written articles by four education librarians cover review sources, marketing practices, publishers' guidelines, textbook collections and more. I have borrowed heavily from two articles in this issue: Earl R. Shaffer's "Sources of Textbook Reviews," pages 51-52, and Guest Perry's "This Little Book Went to Market," pages 54-55.

SELECTING "INDIVIDUALIZED" MATERIALS

"A lesson plan is a teacher's plan. Therefore, it cannot meet the learning needs of even one learner. It cannot assist one learner in the process of growth which of its nature is personal and therefore based on his needs. *Any plan for learning must of necessity be initiated and implemented by the learner; otherwise 'learning' remains mere short-term and superficial memorization of information.*"
— Sister Marie Schuster, *The Library-Centered Approach to Learning*, 1977

"The lesson plan denies the learner the right to learn how to learn."
— Sister Marie Schuster, Ibid.

"In guiding the educational development of the young, schools have made too little use of personal information about the individual student; the accumulation, interpretation, and utilization of such data should be emphasized in subsequent reforms."
— Louis Rubin, *Curriculum Handbook*, 1977

"When a teacher is concerned with the facilitation of learning rather than with the function of teaching, he organizes his time and efforts very differently than the conventional teacher—he concentrates on providing all kinds of resources which will give his students experiential learning relevant to their needs."
— Carl Rogers

"No specific system or approach ever invented can possibly be advocated for all types of learners, though eclectic systems that combine numerous, diverse approaches seem likelier to succeed than systems of limited variety."
— Robert H. Anderson, "Individualization—the Unfulfilled Goal" (Editorial), *Educational Leadership*, Feb. 1977

"Once you allow anyone freedom, you reduce your ability to predict precisely what the person will do. If the power of final decision rests with the child, you can't be sure he will choose to do what you want him to do, to learn all the things you want him to learn."
— Thomas Lickona, "The Psychology of Choice in Learning," 1973

■ ■ ■

Individualized learning, recently surfaced as mastery learning, is based on the premise that children learn best when attention is given to their individual learning styles, rates of learning, special needs and interests. Benjamin Bloom, in fact, declares (in *Human Characteristics and School Learning*) that it is possible—with favorable learning conditions—for 95 percent of students to learn all that the school has to offer, at or near the same mastery level—if the kind and quality of instruction and the amount of time allowed for instruction are made appropriate to the characteristics and needs of each learner.

This recent text by Benjamin Bloom is merely one of a series of works advocating individualized teaching and learning. Historically, these go back at least as far as Comenius, Pestalozzi and Montessori. In the United States this approach has had its advocates for at least 100 years. The 1925 *Yearbook* of the

National Society for the Study of Education, *Adapting the Schools to Individual Differences*, was one eloquent presentation that still could serve as a useful guide to individualization, as could their more recent (1962) NSSE *Yearbook, Individualizing Instruction.*

Despite the long advocacy and convincing arguments, individualization has never really taken hold in American education because it tends to bypass both standard textbooks and the cherished didactic skills of teachers, who are asked to assume the new task of "learning facilitator" and to learn new skills of locating and identifying appropriate materials.

If districts have chosen relatively flexible, open-ended texts and have a good variety of supplementary materials, many teachers can achieve a modest degree of individualization. With rigid or limited materials, individualization—except possibly for remedial purposes—is considerably more difficult. Successful individualization seems to require a fair proportion of materials to be cooperatively selected specifically for local schools and classrooms, near the time of use, by teachers, school librarians and students.

If students are encouraged to articulate their own interests and needs while teachers sharpen their skills in observation and diagnosis, librarians and media specialists can contribute their knowledge of materials. The particular skills of librarians in matching materials to users has a natural outlet in individualization.

I am a strong advocate of individualization because of personal experience. I was fortunate enough to encounter, in the era of progressive education, two elementary school teachers who practiced their own variations of individualization. I still recall vividly my second grade class in Bemidji, Minnesota, where I learned more than in the next four years of basically adequate schooling. Again, a seventh grade "individual progress class" in Brooklyn, New York, which was backed by the Dalton Plan, brought a spurt in personal development that benefitted me for life. While my classmates in Brooklyn were largely "gifted" learners, the class in Bemidji was a catch-all in a near-rural community. Both were superb learning situations for all.

Within individualization today, there are divergent trends that affect selection approaches and policies. At one end we find student choice, perhaps best propounded in Fader's *New Hooked on Books* approach. The other end of the continuum is the rather programmed instructional model exemplified by Individually Guided Education (IGE). This particular approach is more congenial to instructional managers and to research-and-development specialists; it has engendered a great deal of recent literature.

In the chart that follows, I have tried to isolate the basic features of an individualized curriculum by contrasting the features of structured and individualized curricula. Few individualized curricula will exhibit all these features.

This outline was suggested by a chart, "Characteristics of a Structured vs. a Developmental Curriculum," in Alan Gartner and Frank Riessman's *How to Individualize Learning* (1977).

STRUCTURED INSTRUCTION	INDIVIDUALIZED CURRICULUM

Coverage

comprehensive	in-depth with possible gaps
predictable	unpredictable
not integrated with outside experiences	timely
unrelated to student interests or prior knowledge	flows from life experiences and student interests

Content

set boundaries	open boundaries
logically developed in relation to course	piecemeal development or inner logic
course related	problems and issues related
focuses on facts and skills	focuses on student interests (which may be facts and skills)
directed toward fixed objectives and ends	open-ended, developmentally appropriate
sometimes cognitive	experiential and cognitive

Pace

standardized pace (usually adjusted toward a low common denominator)	self paced; allows for periodical fluctuations in learning readiness and interests
prescribed time period	time dependent upon interest and ability; varied time for mastery

Teacher Role

directive leader with guidance from lesson plan or teachers' manual that determines content, pace, goals	facilitator, enabler may venture into areas where s/he lacks expertise

Grouping and Staffing

age and/or ability groupings	ability, interest, needs, purpose groupings; may be large or individual
classroom unit with one teacher	flexible staffing and flexible units with more resource experts

Process

teacher-directed or text-dominated	eclectic, student- or group-initiated
imposed standards	negotiated contract
conformist	risk-taking
imposed or set learning style	flexible individual learning style
extrinsic motivation	intrinsic motivation
focused on mastery of content	emphasizes learning to learn
deductive learning	primarily inductive learning

Appropriate Materials

sequential materials based on standard curriculum	area- or interest-related materials based on student interest and available resources
textbooks	trade books
programmed learning	media (for best modality)

STRUCTURED INSTRUCTION (cont'd)	INDIVIDUALIZED CURRICULUM (cont'd)

Appropriate Materials (cont'd)

workbooks	task cards
reinforcement	role playing and simulation games
(selected to conform to curriculum outlines)	(selected to illuminate various aspects of subject and to provide a wide first-hand exposure to relevant concepts and experiences)

STUDENT VARIATIONS

The basic rationale for individualized education—in all its forms—is that students learn best in their own unique, individual ways and in their own particular styles, even when learning the same materials. For instance, children who succeed quite well in learning to read or in solving math problems—through standard teaching materials—may have mastered these processes in quite different ways, with or without teacher intervention. If they are able to follow their own interests, they may learn even more.

In typical school situations, students—especially elementary students—whatever their individual characteristics, tend to be placed in age-graded classes where they are expected to reach the same imposed instructional objectives by studying the same basic textbooks and, usually, the same supplementary materials for the same time period. Evaluations of abilities and achievement are most typically used for grading and categorizing students rather than for diagnosing their needs for targeted instruction. Many schools have insufficient provisions for observing or working with differences in rates of learning, learning styles and other characteristics. Most educators, when they consider differences, consider only learning orientation, measurable abilities and achievement, and sometimes demographic data. Rather less thought is given to individual, personal or social development. Parents, often, are justly concerned that their children are not treated as individuals—a complaint that runs through parent-community surveys, policies and grievances. In reality, the standard achievement standards used as norms may have very little relation to individual competence or individual potential. Similarly, many variations on individualization merely adjust the path or the pace to a set goal, without questioning whether or not particular goals are appropriate for particular students.

Media people, who advocate media for individualization, tend to see learners as primarily either visually, aurally or tactually oriented and as capable of either synthesizing material or only of making quantitative judgments. (These learning approaches and capabilities, of course, may be combined in many different proportions.) Media specialists also perceive individuals as differing in reasoning approaches, in their predispositions toward certain types of symbolic forms, and in the meanings they attach to these symbols. They believe in providing appropriate media for learners who work well in particular modes or at different rates.

Montessori stressed the importance of timing in relation to materials. She believed that children have an inner need to learn and found that with adequate help and appropriate materials, they respond with intense concentration and thereby perform tasks more fully. She proposed self-selection (of prepared materials that have been well thought through) and believed the child's own response in interest and concentration could inform the teacher of the right approach.

While educators naturally tend to concentrate on measurable achievement and abilities, other individual factors besides learning modality, intelligence, interests and background knowledge may be equally important. Children who learn by slow incremental stages need materials with sufficient repetition to enable them to interact and feed back. Children who learn visually need visual materials as well as materials to improve their ability to learn through words, logic and other means. Children who learn holistically should not be bored to death with seemingly endless repetition or extra homework problems at the same level.

Other factors on the personal-social development continuum include such things as a child's confidence in his or her own learning abilities, his or her initiative and courage to accept challenges despite prior failures or too-easy successes, whether or not a child can ask for help or accept help, and whether or not s/he prefers to please or annoy adults.

Children who work best independently include inner-directed, competitive or self-reliant children, as well as children with strong abilities or interests. Some other personal factors could be the ability to persevere, impulse control, and the ability to choose appropriate learning strategies and to modify these as necessary. And, of course, the ability to locate needed information through library or media skills or other means can also vary.

Children who flourish in small groups and make them possible for other children are those who are cooperative and sensitive to others, who can communicate ideas and/or feelings and whose defense and/or offense mechanisms are limited or appropriate. Teachers who wish to design effective working groups may select children with independent-learning or group skills in order to allow for balanced interaction.

While most of the student characteristics discussed above must be judged subjectively, teachers can take advantage of existing data in individualizing. The individualization checklist on page 277 is based on records that are available somewhere in most schools. This chart was suggested by one in *Source Book of Evaluation Techniques for Reading*, by James Laffey and Carl B. Smith, University of Indiana.

MEDIA FACTORS

While particular media may be appropriate for particular children, certain media seem more suited than others for individualized instruction (see chart on page 278). Desirable physical factors include flexibility, portability, time flexibility, low individual costs, control of pace and built-in review or feedback mechanisms. Content factors include the extent, breadth, depth, and number of materials available in each medium. Portability and content may be the most important of these factors. If materials are portable, children can carry them around, can decide when to use them, when to stop and which parts to use and can even use them at home. But if too few materials are available in a particular medium to meet the needs of

INDIVIDUALIZATION CHECKLIST

	Yes	No
Have you used the following school records in planning programs and selecting materials for individual children?		
Home information		
Vision test		
Hearing test		
Interest inventory		
Indication of mental capacity		
Diagnostic reports on reading skills and abilities		
Information on the child's preferred learning styles		
Are your records current or useful?		
Do you use pre-tests to discover each child's strengths, weaknesses and knowledge of ground to be covered?		
Do you keep notes on individual strengths and problems to know which areas need attention?		
Are materials and programs directed to children's interests and strengths as well as to areas of deficiency?		
Do children have an opportunity to learn at their own rates?		
Do children keep their own records so that they are aware of what things they are trying to learn and how they are progressing?		
Do children who need help receive help from a teacher, tutor and/or instructional aide?		
Are there opportunities for students to discuss their individual progress during individual conferences on a regular basis?		
Is materials selection correlated with the needs, strengths and interests of the students?		
Do the school and the teachers provide money for learning materials on many levels of difficulty covering a wide range of interests?		
Do these materials provide depth as well as scope?		

a wide variety of students, the medium is of limited use, whatever its theoretical attributes. Questions to ask in selecting media are:

- Which media seem most appropriate in light of the student's individual characteristics?

- What alternative media are there that provide opportunities for student knowledge and interaction on this particular topic or concept?

- What evidence is there that the student(s) will learn from this particular medium?

MEDIA FACTORS IN INDIVIDUALIZATION

0 = none   1 = slight   2 = fair   3 = good   4 = excellent

INSTRUCTIONAL MEDIUM	CONTENT EXTENT	ACCESS	PORTA-BILITY	FLEXIBLE TIME	PACE CONTROL	BUILT-IN REVIEW OR FEEDBACK
Television	2	3	0	0	0	1
Radio	1	4	4	0	0	0
Films	2 or 1	2	2	3	1	0
Filmstrip Slides	2	3	3	3	3	1
Audio	3	3	3	2	2	1
Photographs Pictures	2	2	3	4	4	0
Games Simulations	2	2	3	3	4	1
Computer	1	1	0	2	4	3
Printed Materials						
Texts Workbooks	2	4	4	2	2	3
Trade books Magazines	4	4	4	4	4	1

NOTE: These figures are overall estimates, which may not be accurate for the range of instructional media in any particular school.

Programmed learning approaches are useful when goals are measurable and definable, when skills and behaviors can be easily categorized, when course content is definable, and when appropriate teaching strategies are clearly indicated. For changing knowledge, complex skills or mixed school populations, programmed learning approaches will be inadequate for individualization, even with built-in feedback.

INDIVIDUALIZED EDUCATION APPROACHES AND METHODS

There are, of course, many approaches to individualizing curricula. In open education, for instance, the teacher is able to select and/or create his or her own materials in a way that insures some orderly progress and gain. Means of provisioning are discussed often in the literature and are cited at the end of the chapter.

Another approach is provided by Individually Guided Education, a behaviorally-oriented system developed by the University of Wisconsin Research and Development Center for Cognitive Learning. IGE is a rather programmed approach to making the school program more responsive to the needs of individual children. Its instructional programming model starts with the assessment of each child's entry skills and proceeds by the use of criterion-referenced tests, observation schedules and a plan for monitoring each child's progress. But since there are relatively few IGE materials, teachers must select commercially-available materials to fit into this plan.

Learning stations or learning centers are used often with intermediate-age children who have developed basic skills and have attained some abilities for self-directed learning. With these stations, students can work in pairs, small groups, or individually, toward common objectives and/or their own goals. Learning stations with a common core provide some commonality for classrooms while allowing for differences in interests and learning styles. These stations or centers should include a wide variety of materials on common themes, at different reading levels emphasizing different learning processes.

Media centers and libraries (both school and public) are good sources of these materials. Library reviewing tools (or library consultation) can be useful in setting up particular learning centers. Bibliographies and comparative reviews are particularly helpful. For example, the Cluster Reviews in *Curriculum Review* (see the annotation for CAS on page 262) group together books and other materials on particular topics to "adapt to individual differences, cope with several reading levels, develop student interest, display a variety of points of view, and add a personalized dimension to the selection of learning materials." With a variety of materials, children will also have an opportunity to develop critical reading and reasoning skills by comparing and evaluating materials.

The center should include materials appropriate for each student who will use it. The materials should be in a variety of media, including games, simulations and tactile materials as well as printed materials and the more portable audiovisual media. In addition, effective centers usually include strong visual components such as eye-catching posters or photographs. In general, teachers faced with this variety of materials will have to supply their own objectives, questions and assignments, though open-ended assignments can be appropriate for many learning centers. Cognitive criteria can be used to develop assignments and to select materials.

At lower levels individualization may be achieved by organizing small groups, which may use different materials, or the same materials at different paces. Minicourses or separable modules serve the same needs at upper levels. If instruction is individualized, children should be able to choose at least the order or method of mastery. This requires materials with built-in alternatives or small modules to be assigned as needed. Bloom suggests learning tasks of from one to ten hours that integrate well with existing courses.

Teachers who like to work with structured instructional objectives may prefer to approach individualization through selecting instructional objectives from such cluster banks of instructional objectives as the Instructional Objectives Exchange (IOX) or the Instructional Based Appraisal System (IBAS) of Edmark. Others may like to use UNIPACS or other learning packages. References to such sources are included in Key Organizations and Key Publications.

James Raths, whose criteria are excerpted in the chapter on teacher roles in selection (see page 201), makes a good case for "Teaching without Specific Objectives," in *Educational Leadership* (April 1971).

While few schools would turn all students loose in a library/media center to educate themselves, this method is probably appropriate to some children most of the time, and to all children some of the time. Library-based methods of individualization are particularly appropriate for students with good research and reasoning skills (the ability to analyze and synthesize), with an adequate mastery of previous courses, and with ability to persevere. Cline, who believes in individualizing social studies through reading, recommends a library "saturation" and reading one supplementary book for each unit taught, particularly carefully-chosen novels for history and social studies. The library/media center, of course, needs to be adequately stocked with current materials related to the school curriculum and to children's interests. Levels should be appropriate for the full spectrum of children in the school (with a program that meets the standards suggested in the chapter on media programs in *Media and Curriculum*). Book selection tools suggested in the chapter on printed materials (in *Media and Curriculum*) can be used to select and locate materials.

Research on individualized reading (as summarized in Duker) indicates that students who choose their own reading materials perform at least as well on language and literature objectives as comparable students in structured courses. In addition, they enjoy reading more and consider it a source of information and understanding. It grants them a sense of the value of self-development and vicarious experience, of being stimulated to think and to realize new ideas, and of literature itself.

Some teachers prefer to garner materials into a classroom collection to avoid the frustrations inherent in insufficient, lost, missing or circulating library materials. This technique is probably preferable if library/media centers are absent, poorly stocked or poorly maintained.

By requiring individualized programs for mildly and moderately handicapped children in regular classrooms, special education may possibly increase and extend the range of individualization to all children in such classes. As of September 1980, the Education for All Handicapped Children Act requires Individualized Education Plans (IEPs) for all handicapped children between the ages of 3 and 21 as well as placing such children in an educational environment that is "most appropriate" and "least restrictive." IEPs are supposed to provide handicapped children full services based on each child's needs. They require participatory planning starting at the classroom level, involving parents and treating all levels and disciplines.

The process, the materials and the learning involved may be useful for all teachers, who may have to develop something of the expertise of the special education teacher in matching materials to children. These materials themselves may well be adaptable to individualized education. To illustrate, the figure on page 281 establishes marked parallels between an IEP and the Individualized Programming Model developed by the University of Wisconsin. This figure is reprinted with the permission of the Wisconsin Research and Development Center for Individualized Schooling from their newsletter.

William Schipper of the National Association of State Directors of Special Education, who has examined the problems implicit in IEPs, notes that many teachers are having difficulties in projecting goals and objectives for specific periods of time and matching these goals to appropriate materials, though teachers trained in diagnostic prescriptive techniques find it relatively easy to work with IEP concepts. He notes that IEPs require teachers to change their perceptions of their roles to

IPM	IEP
1. Set educational objectives to be attained by the student population. 2. Estimate the range of objectives for subgroups of students.	
3. Assess the level of achievement, learning style, and motivation level of each student.	1. Specify the present levels of educational performance of each child.
4. Set instructional objectives for each student to attain over a short period of time.	2. Specify annual goals, including short-term instructional objectives.
5. Plan and implement an instructional program suitable for each student.	3. Specify the specific educational services to be provided and the extent to which he/she will be able to participate in regular programs. 4a. Specify date for initiation and duration of such services.
6. Assess students for attainment of initial objectives. 7a. If objectives are attained, implement next sequence of the program or take other action as determined by the staff. 7b. If objectives are not attained, reassess student's characteristics, or take other action as determined by the staff.	4b. Specify criteria and evaluation procedures and schedules for determining whether instructional objectives are being achieved.

encompass the role of provisioner or resource person, and that teachers require help in dealing with complicated and unwieldy resource systems.

Individualization through IEPs works best when administrators and administrative systems use standardized forms, provide teachers with support through information assessment systems, cross-reference educational materials to objectives, provide consultants (possibly materials consultants) and on-going assessments, and encourage teacher feedback to administrators. Teachers need carefully-planned administrative support to work with formal and informal assessments, to develop annual goals and short-term objectives, and to communicate with parents, students and each other. These administrative structures and habit patterns can be used to further individualization for non-handicapped children.

INFORMATION SOURCES FOR INDIVIDUALIZING

The special education sources most useful for individualizing include the NCEMMH and NICSEM data banks discussed in the chapter on special education (see pages 306-308), and commercial retrieval systems treated on pages 328-32. According to David Elliott of EPIE, the vast majority of materials (about 80 to 90 percent) in the original NCEMMH-NIMIS data bank are materials designed to be used or capable of being used in standard classrooms. In fact, they are cross-referenced and indexed to topic and modality.

Each chapter on subject-matter materials includes materials that can be used for particular topics. Cognitive criteria (see chapter entitled "Thinking about Thinking" on pages 125-43) can help in broadening selection for individuals. The chapter on printed materials (in *Media and Curriculum*) also includes many resources. The chapters on language arts and the feeling domain (in *Subject Areas*) include sources for selecting materials that correspond to personal interests and problems.

APPROACHES TO SELECTION

Successful individualized selection depends upon adult-child cooperation in the presence of a wide variety of materials. In practice, materials can be selected by students, parents, teachers, library/media personnel, curriculum consultants, principals and district personnel. It would seem logical that individualized selection be carried out as near as possible to the point of use (the individual consumer). As Fader points out in *Hooked on Books*, successful selection for another requires more knowledge of that person than even the best teacher or librarian is likely to have. On the other hand, the adult is presumably more informed on the range of materials and their relation to the curriculum. To my mind, adequate individualized selection requires at least some student choice.

In the more formal systems of "individualized education" individualization merely involves locating a child's particular skills and ability levels on prescribed curricula and assigning tasks and materials designed to bring him/her up to a certain mastery level. While this targeted instruction does avoid teaching the child something s/he already knows and attends somewhat to his/her strengths, it bypasses interests almost completely and involves more or less complex assessment meetings and record keeping.

Somewhat simpler forms can be used if children accept responsibility for choosing and recording materials—with or without the consultation of adults. The very process strengthens a child's decision-making abilities and commits him/her to an act of his/her own volition, not that of another.

In this situation the adult needs to supply the parameters of the materials, help define their purposes and ascertain that appropriate materials are available from which children can choose.

Fader's *New Hooked on Books*, among other works, offers a multitude of methods to help adults work with children to choose their own materials. I recommend it strongly to teachers who want to individualize but lack knowledge or courage.

EVALUATING SUCCESS IN INDIVIDUALIZED LEARNING

Since standard evaluation methods are not always easily adapted or appropriate for individualized programs, the For Further Reading and Key Publications section of this chapter include idea sources for alternative evaluation methods appropriate for individualized programs.

KEY ORGANIZATIONS

Association for Individually Guided Education (AIGE)
Tulare County Department of Education
Education Building
Visalia, CA 93277   (209) 733-6334
A national forum for the exchange of information on individually guided education, the AIGE was founded in 1973 by representatives of local schools, state and intermediate education agencies and organizations engaged in Individually Guided Education (IGE).
The objectives include:

- establishing minimum standards of organization and instruction for IGE

- supporting and encouraging the establishment of state and regional networks

- serving as a forum for communicating research and development and successful practices

The AIGE publishes a quarterly journal, the *AIGE Forum*, to report on successful practices and to keep schools abreast of current research.

Edmark Associates
P.O. Box 3903   (202) 746-3900 or
Bellevue, WA 98009   (800) 426-0865
Edmark, which specializes in materials for special education, has an Instructional Based Appraisal System (IBAS), which includes *Objective Cluster Banks* in four volumes: *Mildly Handicapped* and *Severely and Profoundly Retarded* (at $37.50 each), *Career Education* (at $24.50) and *Pre-Vocational Skills* (at $19.50).
Their introductions and assists to the IBAS system include a helpful pamphlet on *Analyzing and Evaluating Instructional Objectives* which includes an explanation of the IBAS system as well as checklists of objectives and suggestions of ways to use IBAS clusters with locally-available materials.

Institute for the Development of Educational Activities (I/D/E/A)
Information and Service Program
P.O. Box 446
Melbourne, FL 32901   (305) 723-0211
I/D/E/A was founded in 1965 as the educational affiliate of the Charles F. Kettering Foundation (founded in 1927). It might be considered a "think tank" in educational research, evaluation, development and innovation, with an emphasis on the total environment (ranging from urban to international).
The I/D/E/A Change Program for Individually Guided Education (IGE) has the dual goals of combining continuous improvement of schools and school staff

with individualizing learning programs for students. I/D/E/A does not work directly with schools, but carries out its programs through cooperating school districts, state educational agencies, and cooperating colleges and universities. IGE implementation efforts in participating clusters and leagues of schools are bolstered by I/D/E/A's own package of films, filmstrips, cassettes and print materials. While most of these are not generally available, three helpful background publications on individualizing, *Learning Styles, Assessment* and *Multiage Grouping* (each available for $2.00), can be obtained from the above address. Schools considering participating in the IGE Leagues should contact I/D/E/A at 5335 Far Hills Ave., Dayton, OH 45929.

Instructional Objectives Exchange (IOX)
10884 Santa Monica Boulevard
Los Angeles, CA 90025   (213) 474-4531
    IOX, formerly a project of the UCLA Center for the Study of Evaluation, has been a separate educational corporation since 1970, specializing in compiling instructional objectives, criterion-referenced test sets, and various planning aids. It is currently developing minimal-competency test sets in reading, writing and mathematics for secondary students.

    These sets of alternative objectives can be quite handy for teachers or administrators who wish to approach individualization by choosing or adapting items congruent with their educational philosophies, student bodies and teaching goals.

    The sets of instructional objectives, which span grades K-12, are frequently revised and are arranged by topic, grade levels, skills and attitudes. Their current catalog includes about 50 sets of objectives in all subject and curriculum areas from *Language Arts* (many sets) to *Early Childhood Education* (364 objectives) to *Woodworking* (56 objectives). There are cognitive, skills and affective objectives such as *Self-Concept* (30 objectives), *Judgment: Deductive Logic and Assumption Recognition* (7 objectives) and *Study and Reference Skills* (117 objectives)—all at $9.95 each.

    Their planning aids, $2.95 each, include one by H. J. Sullivan on *Considerations in Selecting and Using Instructional Objectives.*

Wisconsin Research and Development Center for Cognitive Learning
University of Wisconsin
1025 West Johnson St.
Madison, WI 57306   (608) 263-4200
    The Individually Guided Education (IGE) plan of individual instruction has been developed largely by the Wisconsin R&D Center. It was implemented in Wisconsin in 1966 and nationally, in cooperation with I/D/E/A, from 1969 through 1972. In 1973 they helped establish an Association for Individually Guided Education as part of a network/dissemination effort.

    IGE as a method involves seven major components:

- a multi-unit school organization
- a model of instructional programming for individual students
- appropriate curriculum and instructional materials
- models for measurement and evaluation

- a program for home-school-community relations
- facilitative environments
- research and development

Several of these programs are now available from commercial publishers: *Developing Mathematical Processes* from Rand McNally, *Pre-Reading Skills Programs* from Encyclopaedia Britannica and *Wisconsin Design for Reading Skill Development* from National Computer Systems. In accordance with Wisconsin's philosophy of individualization, these three programs all afford opportunities for continual assessment of the skills of individual children and provide a management system to facilitate appropriate instructional arrangements (individuals, pairs, large or small groups).

Wisconsin itself distributes an *Individually Guided Motivation* series for planning motivational instructional procedures (such as adult-child conferences for goal setting and independence) and ways to guide children toward self-direction for successful tutoring.

Their *Whole IGE Catalog*, available on request, contains prices and descriptions of about 75 print and nonprint materials, films and filmstrips relating in some way to individualization.

The Center has also published a *Directory of IGE Implementators and Coordinators* that lists about 175 implementators and coordinators in about 24 states and includes their areas of expertise. Most can offer some assistance to schools using IGE. And their handout to parents explains the benefits and characteristics of IGE to parents.

KEY PUBLICATIONS

Building Independent Learning Skills, by Beth S. Atwood, with the editors of
Learning magazine. Palo Alto, CA, Learning Handbooks, 1974. 94p. $2.50.
"What we want to do in this book is to identify, organize, analyze and mull over learning skills, and see how they can be used to develop independent learners." Self-directed study—the essence of individualized instruction—does not just happen; this book provides about 100 classroom-tested approaches and ideas with appropriate inexpensive materials that can help students become successful independent learners. Materials are arranged by student skills: communication, investigation and organization, analysis and evaluation and transformation. The book also includes a very useful annotated bibliography of teacher and student resources.

Classroom Learning Centers: A Practical Guide for Teachers, by Marilyn L.
Kourilsky and Elizabeth F. Barry. Glennville, CA, Educational Resource
Associates, Inc., 1977. 81p. $4.00. (Quantity discount).
This book provides detailed descriptions of types of learning centers and explains the underlying principles and rationales for each, with step-by-step instructions for teachers preparing learning centers. It includes a discussion of how and why learning centers can be useful and examples of several types.

Creating a Learning-Centered Classroom: A Practical Guide, by Howard E. Blake.
   New York, Hart, 1977. 338p. $7.95pa.

An interesting, convenient book on how to establish or to expand learning
centers. Covers rationale and assumptions, procedures for organizing and managing classrooms and means of evaluating the program with sample checklists and
ratings. Indicates steps to be taken in designing and stocking centers, with examples
of activities for each level. Also includes an extensive list of additional ideas.

How Do We Know They're Learning? Evaluation in the Informal Classroom, by
   Pat Hopson King. Encino, CA, International Center for Educational Develop-
   ment, 1975. 88p. $4.95pa.; with set of checkup cards, $6.95pa. (From
   International Center for Educational Development, 16161 Ventura Blvd.,
   Encino, CA 91316.)

This informal approach to evaluation was researched at the primary school
program of Pacific Oaks College. It examines and documents a myriad of ways to
gather information on children, including observation (of behavior, interactions,
etc.), spontaneous dialogs and examinations of works. The author includes many
useful outlines, charts, examples, and well-chosen suggestions for further readings.

How to Individualize Learning, by Alan Gartner and Frank Riessman. Bloomington, IN, Phi Delta Kappa Educational Foundation, 1977. 29p. $0.75. (Fast-
   back 100).

A helpful, simple exposition of individualization—though it does not focus
on materials per se—with particular attention paid to the diagnostic and prescriptive approach, learning styles and learning by teaching.

*The Individualized Education Program: Key to an Appropriate Education for the
   Handicapped Child, 1977 Annual Report*, by the National Advisory Committee on the Handicapped. Washington, GPO, 1977. 37p. $2.00.

Examines the implementation required for the individualized education program concept in the Education for All Handicapped Children Act of 1975.

The Individualized Learning Letter. Huntington, NY, 1971- . $40.00/yr. for 9
   issues and 4 special reports. (From TILL, 67 East Shore Road, Huntington,
   NY 11743.)

Written specifically for administrators who want to effect change, this newsletter covers organizational, curricular and instructional arrangements that meet
the needs of individuals. Includes materials on open classrooms, differentiated
staffing, alternative schools and curriculum alternatives, as well as reports of who's
doing what.

Individualizing Science, by Del Alberti. Burlingame, CA, Nueva Learning Center,
   1973. 32p. $2.50pa. (From Nueva Learning Center, P.O. Box 1366,
   Burlingame, CA 94010.)

This occasional paper for teachers wanting to personalize or individualize
science learning offers criteria through which such teachers can determine the
effectiveness or efficiency of individualized offerings. The practical, well-
illustrated approach may be particularly helpful for teachers who are not well
trained in science.

Another Nueva Learning Center publication by Del Alberti, *The Ecological Theme As a Basis for Individualized Science Experiences* (1972. 33p. $2.50pa.), uses a process approach for pursuing individual projects in ecology.

Individually Guided Elementary Education: Concepts and Practices, edited by
    Herbert J. Klausmeier, Richard A. Rossmiller, and Mary Saily. New York,
    Academic Press, 1977. 394p. $14.95.
An extremely thorough and comprehensive overview of the Wisconsin R&D Center's system of individualized schooling, written by 16 scholars involved in developing or implementing the IGE system. It provides good information on what kinds of materials are involved in individually-guided education, ways to use them, and ways to evaluate the process, as well as insights to the importance of community involvement in the education process.

It also covers organization, measurement, computer support, facilitative environments and research and includes detailed discussions of instructional planning, and math and reading programs using IGE.

Insights into Open Education, edited by Clara A. Pederson. Grand Forks, ND,
    Center for Teaching and Learning, University of North Dakota, 1967- .
    8 issues/yr. $3.50/yr. (From Corwin Hall, University of North Dakota, Grand
    Forks, ND 58202.)
Newsletters, each issue usually about 12 to 14 pages, typically organized about one topic, include good annotated bibliographies on such areas as human relations, organizing learning centers, etc.

Instructor's Guide for Individually Guided Elementary Education, by Joan M.
    Rebeck, M. Lynn Karges, Linda M. Blanchard, and Marvin J. Fruth. New
    York, Academic Press, 1977. 96p. (Available on request.)
This backup to *Individually Guided Elementary Education* corresponds chapter-to-chapter to this book. For each chapter, this instructor's guide includes a topical outline, general and detailed objectives, ways to assess student needs and to measure student mastery of these concepts, activities related to objectives, and related materials and resources.

Knots from a Bored of Education: Ways to Individualize Your Basic Education, by
    Eldon Gran. Amherst, MA, Mandala, 1977. 161p. $8.95pa. (From P.O. Box
    796, Amherst, MA 01002.)
Working not from stringent research but from 30 years of "rattling around children" as teacher, principal, superintendent and consultant, Eldon Gran has written an enjoyable, helpful guide on ways to individualize most elementary areas, using, if necessary, whatever standard texts are assigned.

Underneath the determinedly cutesy format, complete with cartoons and comic strips, this book contains intelligent discussions and suggestions on selecting and using instructional materials. It provides simple yet workable ways to determine the difficulty of classroom materials, ways to maintain records on teachers' and students' use of instructional materials, and ways to use workbooks. It also suggests simple ways for teachers and students to select their own materials and recommends that textbook money be allocated instead to school libraries, an approach that is sure to appeal to librarians.

The discussion covers reading, writing, spelling, language, arithmetic, science, social studies, art and music.

Learning Centers in the Open Classroom, by David H. Kahl and Barbara J. Gast.
Encino, CA, International Center for Educational Development, 1974.
148p. $4.95. (From 16161 Ventura Blvd., Encino, CA 91316.)

Detailed and practical descriptions of ways to develop an open, individualized and child-centered classroom through using interest and learning centers. Covers planning for primary and intermediate grades, types of centers, classroom arrangement, construction of materials, evaluation, record keeping, and the use of teacher and student aides.

Miniguides: 16 Ready-made Mini-Courses, by *Scholastic Teacher*. Englewood
Cliffs, NJ, Citation Press, 1975. 208p. $3.95pa.

These guides won an Education Press Association Award when they first appeared in *Scholastic Teacher* magazine. They provide lesson plans, activity suggestions, areas of investigation and resource materials (print and nonprint) for 14 areas: the supernatural, energy, humor, folklore, sexual identity, art of criticism, humor, living with handicaps, death, war and peace, biography and science fiction. Useful for high school teachers in English and/or social studies in planning lessons and locating materials related to these lessons.

The New Hooked on Books, by Daniel Fader, with James Duggins, Tom Finn, and
Elton McNeil. New York, Berkley Publishing Corp., 1976. 294p. $1.75pa.
(Tenth Anniversary Edition).

This updating of *Hooked on Books—English in Every Classroom*, like the first, focuses on paperbacks as a means of achieving literacy—particularly for children who are turned off by reading. It includes a list of 1,000 current paperbacks of sure-fire appeal, sample plans for achieving reading objectives with trade books, and many suggestions for ways of involving students in selecting their own paperbacks, at about $100.00 per classroom per year for initial investment.

According to Fader and his co-authors, "acts of conscious choice-making can bring even the most diffident children to care about books and printed materials . . . . We can make some generalized guesses about types and fields of interests, but the final decision must be with the reader's peculiar interests and circumstances the moment she chooses something to read."

An Open Education Perspective on Evaluation, by George E. Hein. Grand Forks,
ND, Center for Teaching and Learning, University of North Dakota, 1975.
52p. $2.00.

Suggests means of evaluation of individual children that provide information at the time it is needed and that consider, at a minimum, individual rates of development, horizontal growth and individual learning styles. Hein proposes that evaluations of programs should consider and adapt to the goals of the program, and acknowledge their own interaction as part of the process.

Portfolio of Working Materials for Individualized Instruction, by Charles E.
Reasoner. Englewood Cliffs, NJ, Prentice-Hall, 1976. 285p. $15.00.

Includes a discussion of issues, record keeping and evaluation along with sample lesson plans, teaching suggestions and materials for reading, language arts, math, science and social studies.

The Seed Catalog: A Guide to Teaching-Learning Materials, by Jeffrey Schrank. Boston, Beacon, 1974. 374p. $12.95; $5.95pa.

This highly personal compendium, mostly for high school and adult levels, emphasizes the humanities, communications and media. It is arranged by type of media and includes publications, organizations, periodicals, audio, film, video, games, multimedia and such educational devices as timers and metric scales. It includes many worthwhile items not apt to appear in standard educational catalogs; some are carefully evaluated, and others are represented through producers' blurbs.

The Shoe Box Curriculum: 65 Practical Ideas for Active Learning, by Alex Molnar and Will Roy. Encino, CA, International Center for Educational Development, 1974. 125p. $4.95. (From 16161 Ventura Blvd., Encino, CA 91316.)

Describes shoe-box labs which can be made by teachers, aides or students. These include suggestions for contents, procedures, objectives and goals, and easy-to-make materials for learning and discovery centers in reading, math, social studies and other areas.

UNIPACS, originated by Gardner Swenson. Salt Lake City, Teachers UNIPAC Exchange, 1967. Various prices; approximately $0.10 per page plus $5.00 for each mailing; exchange basis; or lifetime fee. (From 1635 Forest Hills Dr., Salt Lake City, UT 84106.)

UNIPACS are formatted learning packages of single-concept, individualized lessons designed for student use. Each UNIPAC includes a pre-test, a statement of primary concept, behavioral objectives, component parts to be learned, instructions for selecting activities, the activities themselves, opportunities for related learning and a post-test. Catalogs in most curriculum areas are available from the foundation, with hundreds or thousands of items available in most areas.

FOR FURTHER READING

This bibliography, a mere fraction of available articles and books, leans heavily upon practical means of individualizing.

*Items marked with an asterisk include criteria or checklists.
+Items marked with a plus include substantial numbers of references.

*+Aiken, W. M. *The Story of the Eight Year Study*. New York, McGraw-Hill, 1942. 5v.

A monumental study, launched in 1932 by the Progressive Education Association to determine the effectiveness of its programs by following its graduates through high school and college, using evaluation methods that included questionnaires, records, and unobtrusive methods as well as standardized tests. In a summary of 1,475 matched pairs, the graduates of experimental schools were found to be more successful and more resourceful.

Anderson, Robert A. "A Humanized and Individualized Secondary School Program," *Theory into Practice*, v. 11, no. 1 (Feb. 1972), pp. 43-48.

+Association for Childhood Education International. *Individualizing Education.* Washington, ACEI, 1964.

Block, James H. "Teachers, Teaching, and Mastery Learning," *Today's Education*, v. 62, no. 7 (Nov./Dec. 1973), pp. 30-36.

*+Bloom, Benjamin S. *Human Characteristics and School Learning.* New York, McGraw-Hill, 1976.

Buglione, Bruce R. "Transforming Education into an Individualized Process," *The Clearing House*, v. 47, no. 7 (March 1973), pp. 409-412.

*+Charles, C. *Individualizing Instruction.* St. Louis, Mosby, 1976.
Suggests strategies for maximizing cognitive, affective and psychomotor growth.

Cline, Ruth K. J., and Bob L. Taylor. "Integrating Literature and 'Free Reading' into the Social Studies Program," *Social Education*, v. 42, no. 1 (Jan. 1978), pp. 27-31.

*+Davies, Ruth Ann. *The School Library: A Force for Educational Excellence.* New York, Bowker, 1969.
Includes checklists, skills charts, policies, evaluation criteria, and a bibliography.

*De Nike, Lee, and Seldon Strather. *Media Prescription and Utilization as Determined by Educational Cognitive Style.* Athens, OH, Line and Color Publishers, 1976.

+Ducote, Richard L. *Learning Resources Center: Best of ERIC.* Syracuse, NY, Syracuse University, 1977.

+Duker, Sam. *Individualized Instruction in Mathematics.* Metuchen, NJ, Scarecrow, 1972.
Extremely thorough survey.

+Duker, Sam. *Individualized Reading.* Springfield, IL, Thomas, 1971.

Dunn, Rita, et al. "Diagnosing Learning Styles," *Phi Delta Kappan*, v. 53, no. 5 (Jan. 1977), pp. 418-20.

Education U.S.A. *Individualization in Schools: The Challenge and the Options.* Washington, National School Public Relations Association, 1971.

Education U.S.A. *Individually Guided Education and the Multiunit School.* Washington, National School Public Relations Association, 1972.

Eller, M. Linda. "Individualized Learning Using TV," *Educational Broadcasting*, v. 8, no. 4 (July/Aug. 1975). pp. 27-32.

Esbensen, Thorwald. *Working with Individualized Instruction: The Duluth Experience.* Palo Alto, CA, Fearon, 1968.

*Frymier, Jack S. *The Annehurst Curriculum Classification System: A Practical Way to Individualize Instruction.* West Lafayette, IN, Kappa Delta Pi, 1977.
A classification system for curriculum materials based on ten human factors:

experience, intelligence, motivation, emotion-personality, creativity, social, verbal expression, auditory perception, visual perception and motor perception. Suggests that learner and materials characteristics should be congruent for best learning situations.

*Gartner, Alan, and Frank Riessman. *How to Individualize Learning.* Bloomington, IN, Phi Delta Kappa Educational Foundation, 1977. (Fastback 100).

*Godfrey, Lorraine Lunt. "Take a Subject, Any Subject and Individualize with Learning Stations," *Teacher,* v. 91, no. 1 (Sept. 1973), pp. 59-108.

*Gow, Doris. *Design and Development of Curricular Materials.* Pittsburgh, PA, Learning Research and Development Center, University of Pittsburgh, 1977. 2v.

*Hecht, Alfred R., and Kristine R. Klasek. "PAS: A Tool for Developing or Selecting Self-Instructional Materials," *Audiovisual Instruction,* v. 20, no. 4 (April 1975), pp. 27-29.

Howard, Eugene R. "Developing Student Responsibility for Learning," *NASSP Bulletin,* v. 50, no. 309 (April 1966), pp. 235-46.

Joyce, Richard, and Patrick Kearney. "Individualized Science Program: A Guide for Developing Your Own," *Science Teacher,* v. 39, no. 7 (Oct. 1972), pp. 45-46.

Kapfer, Philip C., and Glen F. Ovard. *Preparing and Using Individualized Learning Packages for Ungraded, Continuous Progress Education.* Englewood Cliffs, NJ, Educational Technology, 1971.

Kaplan, Sandra, et al. *Change for Children: Ideas and Activities for Individualizing Learning.* Pacific Palisades, CA, Goodyear, 1973.

Kohl, Herbert. *Math, Writing and Games in the Open Classroom.* New York, New York Review Books, 1974.

Langstaff, Nancy. *Teaching in an Open Classroom: Informal Checks, Diagnoses and Learning Strategies.* Boston, National Association of Independent Schools, 1975.

Lickona, Thomas, et al., eds. *Open Education: Increasing Alternatives for Teachers and Children.* Cortland, NY, State University of New York, 1973.

Marshall, Kim. *Opening Your Class with Learning Stations.* Palo Alto, CA, Learning Handbooks, 1975.

Murray, Dennis. "Learning Contracts: Better than Assignments," *Instructor,* v. 85, no. 1 (Aug./Sept. 1975), pp. 74-75.

Musgrave, G. Ray. *Individualized Instruction: Teaching Strategies Focusing on the Learner.* Boston, Allyn & Bacon, 1975.

+National Society for the Study of Education. *Adapting the Schools for Individual Differences.* Edited by Carleton Washburne. Chicago, NSSE, 1925.

Newsom, R. S., et al. "Intrinsic Individual Differences: A Basis for Enhancing Instructional Programs," *The Journal of Educational Research,* v. 65, no. 9 (May/June 1972), pp. 387-92.

Noar, Gertrude. *Individualized Instruction: Every Child a Winner*. New York, Wiley, 1972.

North, Stafford. "Personalization by Mechanization," *Drexel Library Quarterly*, v. 4, no. 2 (April 1968), pp. 77-83.

*Raths, James D. "Teaching without Specific Objectives," *Educational Leadership*, v. 28, no. 7 (April 1971), pp. 714-21.

Rollins, Sidney P. *Developing Nongraded Schools*. Itasca, IL, Peacock, 1968.

Schuster, Sister Marie. *The Library-Centered Approach to Learning*. Palm Springs, CA, ETC Publications, 1977.

Talmage, Harriet, ed. *Systems of Individualized Education*. Berkeley, CA, McCutchan, 1975.

Thelen, Herbert A. "Pupil Self-Direction," *NASSP Bulletin*, v. 50, no. 309 (April 1966), pp. 99-109.

Triezenberg, Henry J. *Individualized Science—Like It Is*. Washington, National Science Teachers Association, 1972. (ED 076 366).

Walberg, H. J., et al. "Evaluating 'Individualized' Materials," *EPIE Educational Product Report*, no. 46 (1972).

Ward, Beatrice A., et al. *Organizing Independent Learning: Primary Level*. New York, Macmillan, 1971. 2 vols. (Far West Laboratory for Educational Research and Development Mini course 8).

SELECTION FOR SPECIAL EDUCATION

"The patient should be educated to liberate and fulfill his own nature, not to resemble ourselves."
                              —Sigmund Freud

"The real message is that even though special children have special needs and problems, essentially they are children. They have the same needs as everyone else for love and affection, for positive experiences, for self development, and for people to accept them."
                              —Betty Fast, "Media and the Handicapped Child,"
                              Wilson Library Bulletin, October 1977

■ ■ ■

While disabled or "special education" children are most certainly individuals, with individual needs, they have often been grouped and categorized for educational convenience. The National Center on Educational Media and Materials for the Handicapped (NCEMMH) selected materials for children with the following difficulties and disabilities:

- visual impairment
- hearing impairment
- speech and language impairment
- mental retardation
- behavior disorders
- learning disabilities
- physical disabilities
- other health impairment
- multihandicapping conditions

The Council for Exceptional Children used similar categories, and added gifted children, as exceptionalities.

What these children (including the gifted) have in common is a need for special or extra attention, since standard teaching methods and materials are not necessarily successful with them.

Children with special needs and disabilities require more personal and rational approaches to teaching and selection. The task of locating and selecting materials can be both a challenge and a reward for educators. Selection demands a thoughtful analysis of each child's needs, strengths, learning modalities and interests, of the curriculum content, and of the teaching process as a whole. The educator must—as educators should in all selection—analyze materials for their cognitive aspects, the appropriate media and mode, and for their relevance to the total educational environment and means of teaching.

If standard materials are adapted or used—as they often can be—they must be rigorously analyzed for their relevance and suitability for particular educational tasks with particular children. Locating and selecting these materials requires not only a broad knowledge of sources, systems and materials, but an in-depth knowledge of each individual child. The former need may be met by computer retrieval, printed indexes or other systems that organize information on particular parameters. The latter demands sensitivity and awareness as well as diagnostic forms.

Though materials for the disabled are now prominent in education, many basic tools and means to reach these special children were designed and developed outside the field of education. Until quite recently, most professional educators tended to shunt aside these children and their needs.

The gaps were filled by parents, friends and advocates, and by voluntary organizations like the charitable American Foundation for the Blind, an advocate which also provides the blind with medical assistance. Similar organizations and commissions, founded by friends, proponents and the disabled themselves, have been the main proving ground for designing, financing and distributing materials and equipment to the disabled. Funding has been a continual challenge.

Sometimes the disabled themselves, as in the case of sign language, have forwarded their own means of education or communication. The Braille alphabet, as an example—still a major means of communication for blind persons—was originally invented and promoted by Louis Braille, a French teenage student who had been blinded as a young child.

Other useful materials were developed by the medical profession, particularly by doctors, technicians and therapists in psychiatry, rehabilitation and military medicine. Maria Montessori, as a doctor of medicine working with retarded children, developed the superb—and much copied—Montessori materials which succeed so well in translating abstract concepts into concrete forms that appeal to children. More recently, disabled students have benefitted from medical equipment developed for injured veterans and those with orthopedic problems. New technology applied with thought and care may do much to extend life experiences.

Since associations are still major sources of information on materials and resources, I have included some of the more substantial agencies as Key Organizations, and have indicated directories that list others.

FEDERAL SUPPORT AND FEDERAL DATA BANKS

One of the few early federal efforts for distributing materials to disabled children was the 1879 "Act to Promote the Education of the Blind" which still provides for the distribution of school books for blind children. This was followed in 1958 by a less extensive distribution of captioned films for the deaf under the auspices of the Office of Education and the authorization of Public Law 85-905. Two 1964 amendments to the National Defense Education Act of 1964 slightly extended the scope of the Act to include some exceptional children by designating reading as a critical subject and by authorizing teachers' institutes of reading for the benefit of exceptional children.

Subsequent enabling acts for Title III, Section 302 of Public Law 88-164 made funds available in theory for research and development projects relating to education of disabled children, while the Elementary and Secondary Education Act of 1965 (Public Law 89-2010) accepted physically, mentally, and emotionally impaired children as part of its target group of educationally disadvantaged children.

In 1972 the National Center on Educational Media and Materials for the Handicapped (NCEMMH) was established under the authorization of Public Law 91-230 "to facilitate the use of new technology for the education of persons with handicaps." From 1972 to 1977 as government contractee the Center located, developed and facilitated the distribution of media materials and educational technology for the disabled. It worked through a computerized information bank, area learning resource centers, three offices specializing in types of impairments, and a backup loan source—at Indiana University—for lending or renting these materials. During these years, the Center compiled and annotated 36,000 materials appropriate for the disabled and produced some excellent finding tools: directories of publishers, lists of films, and other format lists, as well as a thesaurus and criteria for evaluating and appraising instructional materials. (The two *Standard Criteria for the Selection and Evaluation of Instructional Material—Teacher Level* and *National Level*—are reproduced on pages 104 and 206.) During the same period the Center, in cooperation with the Council for Exceptional Children, prepared guidelines for portraying disabled persons in instructional and mass media (see page 167).

Through symposia, meetings, a newsletter, bibliographies and other productions, NCEMMH made information on instructional materials available to parents, teachers, and other professionals. It is continuing this process in a diminished way since it lost its contract in 1977.

The reassignment of this contract to the National Information Center for Education Media (NICEM) in 1977 resulted in the creation of a new entity, the National Information Center for Special Education Materials (NICSEM) and in a discontinuation of some of NCEMMH's services. However, teachers of the disabled may now have a larger information bank to draw on, since NICEM had about 500,000 media items in *its* computerized system, some appropriate for disabled students.

So far as I can tell, neither NICEM nor NCEMMH has really incorporated most of the materials developed and distributed by various voluntary agencies and medical groups, nor are their programs and activities consistently coordinated with these groups. Again, though NCEMMH and NICSEM share part of a data bank (the original data base developed by NCEMMH), they are going their own ways in designing spinoff products. Since these happen to supplement each other, they provide alternative choices for educators.

But, because of such overlaps among agencies, educators have almost too many choices and too many data banks to use in locating materials and information on curriculum. Two other data banks that deal respectively with exceptional children and medical information are those run by the Council for Exceptional Children (CEC) and by MEDLARS (Medical Literature Analysis and Retrieval System).

The Council for Exceptional Children is particularly worth consulting. It has been in existence since 1922, and currently operates an information service and the ERIC Clearinghouse which has a conscious policy of excluding curricula and materials from its files (quite a number of ERIC documents do, in fact, deal with curricula and materials for disabled children, since it is difficult in practice to distinguish rigorously between research, methods and materials).

These data banks and others are treated as Federal Data Banks under Key Organizations.

COMMERCIAL RETRIEVAL SYSTEMS

While government contractees were developing their data banks, other retrieval systems for analyzing materials by learning increments and objectives were independently developed by school districts, states and commercial enterprises. As a group, these can be quite helpful for educators interested in identifying materials for individualizing, as well as for identifying, special education materials. Some of these systems are described rather fully in the chapter entitled "Commercial Retrieval Systems," on pages 328-32.

EDUCATION FOR ALL DISABLED CHILDREN

The thrust of recent legislation for disabled children has changed somewhat from the development and identification of materials to the promotion and expansion of programs. The Mathias Amendment of 1974 authorized $600 million to expand and improve special education programs and established due process procedures and a time table for full delivery. Public Law 94-142, the Education for All Handicapped Children Act (passed November 29, 1975), mandates "a free appropriate public education for all handicapped children" and authorizes grants to assist states in initiating, expanding and improving programs for disabled children. The initial appropriation for this Act was $315 million; the sum may reach $3.2 billion by 1982.

Aside from its fundamental guarantees of due process, programs, and funding, three aspects of Public Law 94-142 have important implications for materials selection; these are 1) individualized programs which are 2) developed with parental input and 3) aligned with mainstreaming policies.

Schools are now required to develop an Individualized Education Plan (IEP) for each disabled child—a program which must be written jointly with the parent, teachers and, where appropriate, the child. And (according to a November 17, 1977 letter to chief state school offices from Edwin W. Martin, deputy commissioner of the Bureau of Education for the Handicapped) the IEP should include all services and materials required by the child, not merely those which happen to be available in the district. These could be, for example, special materials for language or sensorimotor development, or even psychological materials or services not currently available.

In order to prepare intelligent IEPs, teachers will have to develop their skills in assessing and working closely with individual disabled children. They will need to observe and question, for instance, what each child actually knows, how s/he best learns, the ways different children acquire skills and information, which children are primarily visual or auditory learners, which children are likely to benefit by tactual or movement experiences, and the various ways different learners can best demonstrate their acquired skills and information.

Mainstreaming may open up the possibilities of individualization to other children, who are like special children in having individual learning patterns and preferences. Certainly, many of the materials specifically designed for disabled learners are good tools for learning and reinforcement.

AFFECTIVE MATERIALS

One apparent purpose of integrating handicapped children into the mainstream of education is to avoid the loneliness and isolation often experienced by such children. To succeed in this goal, children with disabilities need to feel accepted and wanted by teachers and their peers. Materials from advocacy organizations are often excellent for orienting students and teachers to the needs of the disabled.

Teachers, again, should be sensitive to the representation of disabled persons in educational materials; to the present, they have simply not been included. The *Guidelines for the Representation of Exceptional Persons in Educational Materials*, reprinted on pages 167-69, represent one tentative standard for examining such materials, as do special curricula recently designed to meet the needs of mainstreaming.

One such curriculum is available from Abt Publications (55 Wheeler St., Cambridge, MA 02138): *Handicapped People in Society: A Curriculum Guide*, published by R. E. Ross and U. R. Freelander (Burlington, VT, University of Vermont, 1977. 178p. $10.00 including shipping and handling). This is a complete curriculum guide for all grade levels, which presents information on individual disabilities—for example the visually impaired in the elementary grades, epilepsy in the middle grades, mental retardation and other motor and sensory disabilities at the high school level, etc., as well as suggestions for motivational lessons with specific objectives, materials evaluations and outside speakers.

A Primer on Individualized Education Programs for Handicapped Children, edited by Scottie Torres (Reston, VA, Foundation for Exceptional Children, 1978), includes a sample individualized program form designed, not only to facilitate the implementation of an IEP, but also to begin the process of selecting materials necessary for that implementation.

Most of the bibliographies and sources listed in the chapter entitled "The Feeling Domain" (in *Media and Curriculum*), especially *The Bookfinder* and *Selective Guide to Mental Health Education Materials*, include hundreds of relevant, easily located, thoroughly annotated references. The criteria for mental health materials, of course, are relevant for teachers who want to use the process of mainstreaming as a learning opportunity for all children.

VALUES OF SPECIAL EDUCATION MATERIALS

Many of the materials developed for special children similarly provide learning opportunities for "normal" children. The excellent maps and science materials of the American Printing House for the Blind are good teaching devices for all children, as are textured materials developed for those learners who are both deaf and blind. Games designed for disabled children can be played by all children in a class. Many normal children, say at fourth grade level, would thoroughly enjoy learning braille or manual sign language in a unit on communication.

Overall, materials specifically developed for handicapped children are apt to be strong in qualities that promote cognitive and sensorimotor processes. Many are appealing and interesting, . . . the best have the lessons implicit in the form of the materials.

In locating materials for IEPs and in designing programs for an entire class, teachers need to keep in mind attitudes and skills needed for successful experiences in a mainstreamed class.

PARENTAL ROLES

Since parents are legally included in the team preparing IEPs, teachers can use this opportunity to learn what parents consider to be the needs and strengths of their child and what kinds of materials and experience the child likes or is familiar with.

Parent groups can be helpful to teachers as sources of resources. Many parent groups have been active advocates for their handicapped children; often they are more knowledgeable about resources than are teachers. Some groups have even been long-time distributors of information themselves. Other groups such as International Association of Parents of the Deaf (IAPD) are actively educating themselves on their rights in their children's education.

One training seminar on Public Law 94-142, sponsored by IAPD, Gallaudet College and Johnson County Community College, included sessions on testing materials and assessment, parent and student involvement, the needs of children as seen by children and parent rights and responsibilities. This seminar marks an increased trend toward parent involvement in selecting materials and in mainstreaming that should be supported in IEPs.

In strong support of this trend the California Association for Neurologically Handicapped Children (CANHC) maintains a Literature Distribution Center (645 Odin Drive, Pleasant Hill, CA 94523) with a "complete" selection of learning disability publications. Their order forms are available on request.

MAINSTREAMING

Mainstreaming may also provide an expanded materials budget (for all children) and more emphasis on the roles of materials in education. It has been estimated that materials costs for disabled children are two to four times those for normal children; it may well be that the per-child expenditure for disabled children is approximately what the per-child expenditure should be for all children.

Daphne Philos, in the *School Media Quarterly* estimated that about $15 million might be needed to develop materials for six million newly mainstreamed children. What teachers may need, actually, is training in locating, selecting and adapting materials for various types of impairment. This is seen as a very high priority by specialists.

Most of the materials in NCEMMH's data bank are standard educational materials which are better indexed for use and selection. Many other materials are already available from special publishers (listed in *Publisher Source Directory*), medical organizations (located through MEDLARS and other data banks) or advocacy groups. Some of these groups are listed as Key Organizations; others can be located through the *Directory of National Information Sources on Handicapping Conditions and Related Services.*

Advocacy materials are especially good for children with hearing and sight impairments.

SPECIAL NEEDS

A recent survey, the National Needs Assessment of Educational Media and Materials for the Handicapped (NNA) (reported under Federal Data Banks), indicated that some high priorities for special education teachers are materials to encourage appropriate social behavior, higher self-acceptance and better interpersonal relations and social interactions. Some materials for these may be located through the tools discussed in *Media and Curriculum*. Other high priority areas are in the field of language: reading comprehension, word-attack skills, remedial reading, vocabulary and expressive language development and connected and fluent speech. Commercial retrieval systems, NCEMMH tools and other sources listed under language should be helpful in promoting these skills. Other areas include computation, reasoning and decision-making skills, concepts and cognitive skills. Criteria for these are presented in the chapter entitled "Thinking about Thinking" in this volume and in the chapter on mathematics materials in *Subject Areas and Implementation*. Materials can be located through NCEMMH-NIMIS bibliographies, NICSEM product lists, and through commercial retrieval systems.

Other priorities are job preparation and employment skills development—an area where there may be few materials (and few opportunities) for the disabled. Attending, responding and listening skills are priority areas where non-print media are preferable. Materials for dressing, grooming and personal hygiene—another priority area—can be located through special education sources. The NNA findings are discussed more fully under the ETS entry in Federal Data Banks.

Gifted handicapped children, severely handicapped children and multiple handicapped children desperately need instructional materials with the combination of stimuli directed toward their particular needs. For some severely impaired children, there are problems in presentation and problems in using the simplest of standard materials. For example, a child with cerebral palsy may need special devices to sit upright, to hold a pencil or to turn a page. Medical sources may be the best for these. Children who see few opportunities to make use of what they learn, may need strongly motivating materials as well as positive attitudes in the classroom. And those who have difficulty handling concepts may need a wide range of materials that present concepts without exact (and boring) repetition. Disturbed children, particularly, need materials that do not promote more anxiety. Speech-impaired students need materials that promote language development.

To facilitate the process of mainstreaming and the treatment of these special needs, Margaret F. Hawisher and Mary Lynne Calhoun, both of Winthrop College, have evaluated and recommended the establishing of a resource room. In their *The Resource Room: An Educational Asset for Children with Special Needs* (Columbus, OH, Charles E. Merrill Publishing Company, 1978), they provide information and sample forms that will enable the concerned educator to establish a supplementary learning environment for disabled students who are enrolled in a regular educational program and to define the process of referring these students to that room.

SELECTION PRINCIPLES AND CRITERIA

The thoughtful standard criteria developed by the NCEMMH—for teacher levels and national levels—are reprinted, respectively, on pages 104 and 206. These are the most thorough and the best single criteria available.

The needs assessment forms developed by Educational Testing Services for National Needs Assessment of Educational Media and Materials for the Handicapped are excellent analytical instruments which could benefit the process of selection. This project (the NNA) is discussed as a Federal Data Bank on page 305.

Simpler methods can be based on analysis and individualization. Special education children, in general, have definite sensory, physical, emotional or intellectual impairments. (As a consequence, they may also have severely limited experiential backgrounds.)

Teachers need to consider and analyze through which methods a child learns most effectively, and which s/he can use to compensate for her/his deprivations.

In general, materials for special education should:

- be multisensory

- be organized logically and sequentially

- include some built-in motivation and appeal

- have a favorable interest/ability ratio

- have some apparent relations to a child's (or a class's) interests and circumstances

- be related to children's functional levels

- facilitate overview by the teacher

- increase the child's independence and abilities

Cognitive criteria, criteria for models and manipulatives, toys and games, and early childhood education are all relevant here.

Teachers selecting materials (or media) need to ask:

- Why do I believe these materials (or media) will help children learn?

- In what (desirable or undesirable) ways can students interact with these materials (or media)?

- If these materials (or media) are not used, what are the alternatives?

Sandra Boland has suggested the following questions in "Instructional Materialism—or How to Select the Things You Need." These questions are reprinted from *Teaching Exceptional Children*, Summer 1976, by permission of the Council for Exceptional Children. (The Council for Exceptional Children retains literary property rights on all copyrighted articles.)

- Is the material suitable for the ages and interest levels of your class?

- Do the objects realistically represent the real thing in regard to proportion and color?

- Are the materials eye appealing?

- Does the material allow for pupil participation?

- Can the material be used in a variety of ways?

- Are the directions easy to follow?

- Do the materials offer concrete learning experiences?
- How much adult supervision does the material require?
- Is the design simple and easy to use?
- Does it represent more than one media format?
- Is it consumable; that is, are dittos and workbooks a recurring expense?
- Is it convenient to store and to transport?
- Does it require extensive preparation before use?
- In terms of cost, is this the most appropriate material that can be purchased?

MATERIALS MODIFICATION

Libby Goodman, in an excellent article in the Spring 1978 issue of *Teaching Exceptional Children*, "Meeting Children's Needs through Materials Modification," suggests alternative ways to adapt materials through modification or to individualize materials. The variables are the:

- specific materials (such as topic, interest level)
- amount of material/information presented (such as fewer problems, shorter readings)
- difficulty level (such as language or conceptual complexity, vocabulary)
- sequence of presentation
- mode of presentation (such as tape or braille)
- mode of response (such as oral tests, untimed examinations)
- development of supplementary learning aids (such as review mechanisms, study guides)

Teachers who control the setting of learning can also alter: groupings, time (when and how long), place, parent involvement, homework and external motivation.

MEDIA AND LEARNING MODES

The variety of media available today, enhanced by modern technology, offers many choices for special educators. In general, educators should start from a child's strengths by using the media and modes which are accessible to the child and try to develop his/her impaired abilities as much as possible. Use of these modes need not isolate handicapped children in mainstreamed classes.

Good communication modes for the deaf, for example, are tactual, visual and such communication modes as finger spelling, sign language, visible English and mime—all of which could be part of communication units for other children and adults in the school community.

Special educators may wish to draw up their own criteria for materials based on their students' characteristics. For example, here is an overall view of some appropriate criteria for materials for slow learners (as a group). Individual student strengths, interests and preferred learning modes should also be included in particular classes.

MATERIALS FOR "SLOW LEARNERS"

Student Characteristic	Appropriate Materials
short attention span	short units
easily bored	materials relevant to student's interests
not used to success	materials which involve student—easy questions, simple quizzes
may be alienated	attend to affective concerns—diaries or journals
limited oral experiences	opportunities to speak, act, listen—tape recordings
limited life experiences	extend first-hand, real-life experiences—theatre
not oriented to academic world	paperbacks, pamphlets, AV formats, practical interests, job related
not oriented to cognitive world	games—card games, math games, word games—to teach practical skills
uninvolved with materials	short quizzes students can answer, humor
fear of new materials	repetition (of words, etc.), new knowledge based on old, expand horizons

For deaf students sign language films or video broadcasts and teletypewriter service are particularly useful communication modes, although they are not necessarily limited to those with impaired hearing. Cameras and other visual modes can also be used successfully in mainstreaming programs. Since deaf children do not learn either lip reading or hand signs as effortlessly as normal children learn to communicate through talking, learning either of these techniques takes time and effort. It is valuable for deaf children to see pictures of objects with pictorial representation of hand signs while they watch the lips of the person saying the word or phrase. For this reason picture books in sign language, which can be shared by deaf children and their parents or deaf and non-deaf children, are valuable materials.

Sources for such picture books are:

Pre-School English Project of Gallaudet College
7th and Florida Ave., N.E.
Washington, DC 20002

Center on Deafness
600 Waukegan Road
Glenview, IL 60025

Alinda Press
P.O. Box 553
Eureka, CA 95501

Typically, deaf children have difficulty with language (sometimes with thinking) and tend to read years below their age level. The usual "high interest-low vocabulary" sources can be consulted for appropriate materials.

Materials for those with impaired sight draw heavily on all sensory modes except vision. Those materials created especially for blind children tend to emphasize touch, shape, size, weight, texture and sound. Interestingly, many are visually attractive and appealing to other children, and most can be used to advantage in all classes.

Math aids, for example, are generally rather inexpensive, and include many means of reinforcing math concepts through tactual methods and materials: abacuses, number cubes, geometric forms, volume- and area-measuring devices, metric-English yardsticks and rulers, and tactile cubes.

Similarly, those biological models, sound sources, simple machines, and light-sensing devices used to teach science to blind children seem appropriate to any elementary science class.

Since blind children are not the only children who have trouble with spatial concepts, the relief maps, doll furniture and wooden building materials developed for blind children are valuable additions to most classes. Similarly, models for other children than blind children should provide a sense of scale and proportion.

In general—except when their disability is compounded by other impairments—blind children have relatively few language problems. Many, in fact, have excellent listening skills and outstanding memories for music, words, and sounds in general. Therefore, ear-oriented materials for such children should meet high audio standards. These children need equipment that is easy to handle and good dramatizations with authentic, pleasing voices backed by interesting and accurate sound effects. Such materials are available not only from special education sources but from the usual commercial producers.

SELECTING MATERIALS FROM CATALOGS

Despite the heavily-sponsored data banks and commercial retrieval services, many teachers prefer to select materials directly from producers' catalogs. This is not necessarily a bad practice as long as the materials selected are based on appropriate criteria, the needs of students and a good knowledge of suppliers and sources. Many special education catalogs are appealing, interesting and well organized. Some small producers are former teachers; others became interested in special education as parents or friends of disabled persons.

Selectors who use catalogs as their mode of selection should compare among materials from a wide variety of catalogs (using appropriate sources from the *Publisher Source Directory*) and should not accept the first item that appears to fill their criteria. Ideally, catalog collections should be well organized and/or indexed by disability, subject and level. Teachers should confer with each other and keep notes—possibly on cards—on materials that have or have not worked out well.

Straight commercial toy sources are frequently good sources of ideas and materials that can bring special education children more into the mainstream. Some creative educators canvass museums for models and realia, coin dealers for interesting coin collections and theatrical supply houses for discarded or loan costumes. The most orthodox means are not always the best for increasing children's experiences and sensory input.

KEY ORGANIZATIONS

Many organizations not listed below are listed fully in the *Directory of National Information Sources on Handicapping Conditions and Related Services*, which is annotated on page 320. Those included here are either sources of materials or sources of information about materials.

Federal Data Bases
(and Their Spinoffs)

The Council for Exceptional Children (CEC)
1920 Association Drive
Reston, VA 22091   (800) 336-3728
                                       (703) 620-3660 (for Virginia residents)
The CEC, a membership organization founded in 1922, has as its principal purpose the advancement of the education of exceptional children and youth. It covers the entire scope of special education: mental retardation, physical disabilities, learning disabilities, communication disorders, children who are homebound or hospitalized, and gifted children. CEC also deals with members of professional organizations who are interested in particular areas.

Parts of the CEC are focused on information, specifically the CEC Center on Technical Assistance, Training and Information on the Exceptional Person and the ERIC Clearinghouse on Handicapped and Gifted Children. Together they locate and identify English language information on the education of disabled and gifted children and prepare abstracts for *Exceptional Child Education Abstracts* and for the ERIC system. These abstracts (about 29,000 in 1978) are compiled into inexpensive topical bibliographies which sell for around $4.00 each and which can be searched through customized computer searches, at a cost of $25.00 for members and $35.00 for others.

The CEC has an ambitious publishing program, with materials on curriculum, instruction, learning activities, assessment and placement, mainstreaming, professional trends, teacher education, early childhood, working with parents, public policy, delivery of services, career education and cultural diversity. A few of these are available in Spanish. (Some individual publications on games and early childhood are included in the chapter entitled "Toys and Other Manipulatives," in *Media and Curriculum*.)

One of the periodicals, *Teaching Exceptional Children*, is loaded with ideas on programs and materials. *Exceptional Children* emphasizes research; while *Insight* focuses on legislation and governmental activities. Their topical bibliographies ($4.00 each) can also be helpful in selecting materials, particularly *Aurally Handicapped—Instructional Materials* (no. 677).

Perhaps their most valuable bibliography is *Audiovisual Resources for Instructional Development* (1975. 256p. $6.00). This guide to materials for special education includes 1,000 annotations to materials in all kinds of media—audio, films, filmloops, filmstrips, multimedia, slide shows, transparencies, and videotapes—cross-indexed under curriculum areas, exceptionalities, materials, methods, program development, community models and facilities.

Educational Testing Service
1947 Center St.
Berkeley, CA 94704   (415) 849-0950
Attn: Dr. Carol Vale   Extension 355

The Educational Testing Service has undertaken an ambitious national attempt to research and document the materials and media needs of disabled students. Their National Needs Assessment of Educational Media and Materials for the Handicapped (NNA) is a multi-targeted survey of 150,000 special educators which has been funded by the Bureau of Education for the Handicapped.

The instrument used was a 12-page, machine-readable questionnaire in six versions for teachers (each version treating a specific disabling condition) with separate versions for supervisors and specialists in media, curriculum and in-service education. This questionnaire was used to obtain a broad range of data on instructional materials development, media and materials information, materials distribution, training for media materials and instructional technology.

Respondents were asked to indicate their three highest priorities for media and materials by curriculum area, student age, functional level of students and impairment. Other questions deal with preferred formats and perceived inadequacies in current materials. This information, which is currently being collected and analyzed, will provide an unparalleled data bank of needs and priorities in media and materials for disabled students.

Market Linkage Project for Special Education
LINC Services, Inc.
829 Westwind Drive
Westerville, OH 43081   (614) 890-8200

LINC Services, as a result of a Bureau of Education for the Handicapped contract awarded in September 1977, acts as linking agent between the Bureau and commercial publishers, producers and distributors. Overall, it provides market analysis and development services to facilitate the commercial development of materials for the handicapped. It receives, assesses and catalogs these materials, confirms needs and development information, assesses the marketability of these materials, verifies compliance with legal requirements, provides editorial and technical appraisals, and helps commercial distributors obtain user feedback about the effectiveness of their materials.

Medical Literature Analysis and Retrieval System (MEDLARS)
National Library of Medicine (NLM)
8600 Rockville Pike
Bethesda, MD 20014   (301) 496-6095

MEDLARS is a computer-based system that provides rapid access to about 2.5 million medical references dating back to 1964. Though it is primarily for health professionals, it includes a great deal of current reporting and information on learning disabilities, speech, hearing, reading and communication disorders, rehabilitation, and other areas where medicine and biology intersect with learning. It can be used—at rather reasonable cost—through local medical libraries.

**National Center on Educational Media and Materials
for the Handicapped (NCEMMH)**
Faculty for Exceptional Children
Ohio State University
Columbus, OH 43210   (614) 422-7596

From 1972 until the fall of 1977, NCEMMH held the major contract for locating and disseminating information on educational media and materials for disabled persons under the auspices of the Bureau of Education for the Handicapped to fulfill the purposes of Public Law 93-380. When its contract and funding expired in November 1977, NCEMMH decided to continue its work under the auspices of the Faculty for Exceptional Children of Ohio State University, in a self-supporting, self-sustaining, and more thrifty fashion.

The thrust of this organization—in conjunction with Area Learning Resource Centers—has been to review and disseminate instructional materials, in order to help groups at regional, state and local levels to locate and provide media materials and educational technology resources for handicapped learners.

Materials reviewed include standard educational media—films, recordings, slide tapes, video tapes, instructional kits and teaching machine programs, as well as educational games, mixed media items, books and other printed matter, and materials specially developed for disabled children and their parents.

The intended audiences for these materials are disabled children and their parents, educators at all levels, related professionals such as physical therapists and speech therapists, and researchers who are concerned with or interact with disabled children.

Information on 36,000 selected materials was compiled into NIMIS (National Instructional Materials Information System), a data base of items considered relevant to the education of disabled children, and coded for impairment and educational situation. Interestingly enough, about 90 percent of these items—according to Dave Elliott of EPIE—are materials which can be used in other educational situations and/or with other types of learners.

This NIMIS data bank has been handed over to the National Information Center for Special Education Materials (NICSEM) (listed below) which now holds the contract. However, NCEMMH/NIMIS is continuing to use the same data base to compile "mini-bibs," brief, targeted bibliographies of materials for particular educational applications. These are being expanded at Ohio State University according to requests from teachers, parents and other helpers of disabled students. They are useful in locating materials for unique situations and for planning IEPs (individual educational programs). Each of the mini-bibs is well indexed and includes descriptions of materials and abstracts of the content of each item, arranged by specific content areas, exceptionalities and/or age or grade level, with information on titles, publisher, prices, date and sources. (Order forms are available from Publications Sales Division, Ohio State University Press, 2070 Neil Ave., Columbus, OH 43210.)

Other NCEMMH publications include a new quarterly newsletter, *The Directive Teacher* (1978), a combination of two newsletters, *Directive Teaching* and *Apropos* which were issued respectively by the Faculty for Exceptional Teaching at Ohio State and by NCEMMH. This deals largely with teacher-made materials and technologies or their applications in homes and schools.

Their new catalog, available on request, lists NCEMMH products, which are distributed in four different ways: through the National Audiovisual Center (NAC), through ERIC, through commercial vendors, and through Ohio State University Press. NAC products are described in *Media and Curriculum*. Several of these products are listed below as Key Publications.

National Information Center for Special Education Materials (NICSEM)

University of Southern California
University Park   (213) 741-6681 or
Los Angeles, CA 90007   (213) 741-5408

In October 1977, NICEM (the National Information Center for Educational Media) was designated and funded by the Bureau of Education for the Handicapped to assume responsibility for the national bibliographical information retrieval system for disabled persons (formerly carried out by NIMIS/NCEMMH at Ohio State University).

Its major task is to continue the work of its predecessor in operating and developing a system which correlates instructional materials and objectives with specific disabling conditions. As of March 1978 the reorganized NICSEM data base included about 36,000 NIMIS materials and media correlated to specific types of impairment.

The NICSEM/NIMIS data bases, which can be accessed by both computer and print, can be supplemented with other materials from NICEM's total data base of more than 500,000 items discussed in *Media and Curriculum*. Printed access tools to these data bases included the following (as of May 1978):

Index to Deaf, Hard of Hearing, Speech Impaired. $60.00.
Contains approximately 11,000 entries describing media and materials considered particularly suited for 1.3 million individuals with hearing and speech impairments. Entries can be selected by title, source, subject and grade level as well as by specific skills and disabling condition.

Index to Mentally Retarded, Specific Learning Disabled, Emotionally Disturbed. $55.00.
Lists and describes over 10,000 media and material items which can be correlated to the mentally retarded, learning disabled and emotionally disturbed.

Index to Staff Special Education Media and Materials Training. $33.00.
An extensive listing of available media and materials especially designed for staff training use, cross-referenced for instant retrieval.

Index to Visually Handicapped, Orthopedically Impaired, Other Health Impaired. $40.00.
More than 10,000 annotations.

Master Catalog of NIMIS/NICSEM Special Education Information. 1978. 2 vols. $121.00.
Contains the total NIMIS I data base with more than 36,000 abstracts, describing in detail media and materials applicable to the education of disabled persons.

NICEM Catalog to Special Education Non-Print Materials. $47.00.
A special master catalog compiled from over 500,000 entries in the
NICEM data base.

NICSEM also distributes without charge two newsletters. *The Program Tree*,
a monthly newsletter specifically for state education agencies, has a great deal of
information on state-level projects, publications, information, activities, networks
and materials. *Frankly Speaking* is intended to meet the information needs of
persons involved in special education at the local level.

High-volume professional users requiring immediate access to information on
professional and child use special education materials can use the on-line computer
search services of NIMIS/NICSEM and of the agencies listed below:

Lockheed Information Systems   Bibliographic Retrieval Service
3251 Hanover Street   Corporation Park, Building 702
Palo Alto, CA 94304   Scotia, NY 12302
(800) 982-5838   (518) 374-5011

Other data banks outside the NIMIS/NICSEM cluster can also be searched for
special education data.

Other Broad-Scope Federal Agencies

U.S. Bureau of Education for the Handicapped (BEH)
U.S. Department of Health, Education and Welfare
U.S. Office of Education
400 Maryland Ave., SW
Washington, DC 20202   (202) 245-2709
The Bureau of Education for the Handicapped is the principal agency within
the Office of Education for developing policy and administering programs and
projects relating to the education of disabled individuals. Its *Division of Media
Services* administers a loan service of captioned films for deaf persons and disseminates media materials, such as films, tapes and videotapes, to disabled persons, to
the parents of disabled children and to people who work with disabled persons.

A Ten-Year Catalog of BEH-Funded Projects (there have been about 2,000),
soon to be published by the Superintendent of Documents, is currently being compiled by Biospherics of Rockville, MD.

The Bureau's Learning Resources Branch—(202) 472-1366—is in charge of
the Regional Resources Center's programs designed to assist state educational agencies through technical assistance and demonstration of exemplary services. Areas of
expertise include appraisal, educational programming, placement, implementation
of educational programs and review of individualized educational program processes.

The staffs at these regional centers should provide assistance and workshops
for at least some of the areas below:

● Selecting and utilizing instructional media and materials based on goals and short-
term objectives for disabled students and media centers

● Modifying and adapting instructional materials for disabled students

- Using behavioral bases to implement goals and short-term objectives and to correlate instructional activities with media and other materials
- Implementing specific learning processes and assessment procedures to provide a specific approach or diagnostic process to improve programs for disabled persons
- Matching the characteristics of specific impairments with the characteristics of media and materials
- Providing inservice/preservice personnel for instructional materials that relate to handicapped programs for disabled persons
- Identifying and providing media/materials appropriate for an individualized, diagnosed student concern
- Providing inservice training on ways to utilize materials to motivate and challenge or adjust behaviors of disabled children
- Facilitating communication between producers, media project development, authors and special educators
- Utilizing instructional materials in program planning with environmental media and teacher-made and student-developed materials

Addresses for these regional centers have been compiled into a directory which is available from the Learning Resources Branch of BEH.

U.S. Office for Handicapped Individuals (OHI)
Clearinghouse on the Handicapped
(U.S. Office of Human Development)
398-D South Portal Building
Washington, DC 20201   (202) 245-1961
The Office for Handicapped Individuals is a staff resource for the Department of Health, Education and Welfare. Established in 1973, its function is to assist in planning, coordinating and evaluation by collecting information on services to disabled persons. The Clearinghouse acts as broker of information services by referring inquirers to appropriate national or state information sources.
One of its first major tasks was the compilation of a substantial directory of national private and government institutions and agencies concerned with the handicapped: *Directory of National Information Sources on Handicapping Conditions* (see Key Publications).

Other National Agencies

American Alliance for Health, Physical Education and Recreation
  Information and Research Utilization Center (AAHPER/IRUC)
1201 6th Street, NW
Washington, DC 20036   (202) 833-5541
Since 1972 AAHPER/IRUC (funded for a time by BEH) has been charged with collecting, reviewing, interpreting, evaluating, cataloging and disseminating information on materials dealing with physical education, recreation and related

activities for disabled persons. Basic areas include sex education, movement education, health and music.

Some specific services include:

Reprints: Xerox copies for hard-to-find, out-of-print, non-copyrighted and other fugitive information and materials—such as curriculum guides, bibliographies, program descriptions, research reports and demonstration projects—at a standard charge of $0.10 per page.

IRUC Briefings ($4.00/yr.), a periodic newsletter with information on programs, activities, methods, audiovisual enrichment, and other areas of interest and importance to personnel in the field. Individuals in AAHPER structures receive *IRUC Briefings* as a part of their membership.

Practical Pointers ($2.00 each) emphasize functional, how-to-do-it assistance.

Information Updates (monthly; $4.00 each) contain information and summaries on books, periodical articles, audiovisual materials and related professional items received and reviewed during the preceding month, with a cumulative index in each issue.

Topical Updates ($2.00 each) and *Topical Information Sheets* ($1.00 and $2.00) provide information and summaries about materials dealing with high-interest topics such as mainstreaming, competitive athletic opportunities, movement exploration, etc.

Closer Look
Parents Campaign for Handicapped Children and Youth
(National Information Center for the Handicapped)
P.O. Box 1492
Washington, DC 20013   (202) 833-4163

This organization is a national information center established to help parents of disabled children locate educational programs and other kinds of special services and resources. It places special emphasis on the rights of disabled individuals and encourages parents of disabled children to press for their children's rights to an equal education.

It publishes an informative but infrequent newsletter, *Report from Closer Look* (whose Fall 1977 issue contained a clear, concise summary of Public Law 94-142). Its information activities are somewhat constrained by lack of funds but lean toward information packets, brochures, pamphlets, fact sheets, bibliographies, abstracts, indexes and critiques of films (all free).

The National Association for Retarded Citizens, Inc. (NARC)
2709 E. East
P.O. Box 6109
Arlington, TX 76011   (871) 261-4961

Inspired originally by parents of retarded children in 1950, NARC's 250,000 members include parents, friends, interested citizens and professional workers in the field of mental retardation, united by a common determination to see that every child and adult has a chance to develop to his fullest potential.

It operates through state and local associations and has a rather substantial publication program that includes books, monographs, pamphlets, periodicals, films, slide shows and the *Mental Retardation News*, the only newspaper in the U.S. devoted to the field of mental retardation.

National Easter Seal Society for Crippled Children and Adults (NESSCCA)
2023 W. Ogden Ave.
Chicago, IL 60612   (312) 243-8400
    This group, founded in 1919, is the oldest and largest voluntary organization
providing rehabilitation services to disabled persons, with a nationwide program of
education, research and treatment. It also provides information on disabling conditions, formal education of disabled individuals, personnel training, recreation,
physical education, equipment, and on other topics such as barrier-free design and
legislation.
    The organization's *Rehabilitation Literature* (available for $12.50/yr.) is a
monthly interdisciplinary journal published since 1940 that abstracts and indexes
materials related to rehabilitation. Highly recommended by special education
people, it includes an index to book reviews in the field.
    A Publication Catalog—available free on request—lists many fine materials on
280 items including careers, occupational therapy, camping and recreation.

National Association of State Directors of Special Education (NASDSE)
1201 Sixteenth St., NW
Washington, DC 20036   (202) 833-4218
    NASDSE is a non-profit educational organization representing personnel from
state education agencies who have legal responsibility for administering special
education programs. From a vantage point in Washington, DC, it monitors legislation, governmental rules and the works of agencies working with and for exceptional individuals. It designs workshops and provides consultation on special education
and has a variety of training products designed to explain Public Law 94-142 and
individualized programs.
    Their *Special Education: State Developed Products* ($3.00) includes 170
products from 20 states: curriculum guides, annual reports, procedures for setting
up programs, and project reports, indexed by content area and by exceptionality,
as well as by state.

National Committee, Arts for the Handicapped
1701 K Street, NW, Suite 801
Washington, DC 20006   (202) 223-8007
    This educational affiliate of the John F. Kennedy Center for the Performing
Arts is a coordinating committee—with representatives of major arts organizations,
organizations representing handicapped citizens, general education organizations
and private foundations—which acts to develop and implement arts programs for
handicapped children and youths.

Agencies Specifically for Blind Persons

American Foundation for the Blind (AFB)
15 West 16th St.
New York, NY 10011   (212) 620-2000
    The American Foundation for the Blind is a private, non-profit agency estab-
lished in 1921 to carry out research, to collect and disseminate information and to

provide advice and counsel on matters that strengthen services to persons with visual impairments.

Its services now include the development of sensory and other aids for blind persons, preparation and distribution of talking books to regional libraries, promotion of legislation and activities for persons with sight disabilities, and provision of regional consultants to schools and other government agencies to improve direct and indirect services to visually impaired persons.

AFB issues three very helpful free catalogs:

Aids & Appliances for the Blind & Visually Impaired, published each summer in print, braille and recorded editions, includes descriptions, prices and ordering information for household and personal items, communication aids, medical devices, tools and other aids for visually impaired persons.

Catalogue of Publications is a very interesting list of materials (some free), many relevant to school situations.

Films about Blindness annotates and lists 15 films that are available for preview, rental or purchase and many of which are suitable for inservice education. For a full catalog and information on service copies, contact Film Librarian, Public Education Division, AFB, 15 West 16th St., New York, NY 10011.

(AFB's Regional Offices are located in Chicago, Atlanta, Denver and San Francisco.)

American Printing House for the Blind (APH)
1839 Frankfort Ave.
(P.O. Box 6085)
Louisville, KY 40206   (502) 895-2405

The American Printing House for the Blind, founded in 1858, is a private, non-profit corporation, the oldest national agency for blind persons in the United States, the largest publishing house for the blind persons in the world, and the only independent organization whose sole purpose is to publish materials and design aids for the visually impaired.

The AHP produces printed materials and tangible aids for distribution through non-profit groups such as the Library of Congress, Division for the Blind and Physically Handicapped, and since 1879 it has been the national official publisher of school materials for blind children, under the authorization of the 1879 "Act to Promote the Education of the Blind." It has grown since that time from an organization with six or eight employees and a budget of about $10,000 to one that has about 500 full-time and 40 part-time employees and a budget in the millions.

APH goes to a great deal of effort to see that basic textbooks are provided for blind children in public, private and parochial schools at the same time that new school adoptions are available for sighted children. Eligible children are registered annually in January to establish a materials quota for the following July. Individual registrations are submitted on prescribed forms distributed by APH to individual schools, which are then given quotas, based on head counts. School orders are funneled through state officers—ex-officio trustees of the APH—who submit their requests to the Printing House. A per-capita allotment is then set up by dividing the numbers of students into the dollars of Congressional funding.

Though these books represent an important third of APH's production, they offer many more materials at all levels which can be purchased with local funds.

Aside from books in braille, talking books, cassettes and large-type books, the APH produces many teaching devices based on sound, touch and memory, which seem useful in many educational applications.

They have outstanding relief and segmented globes, maps and landform models at reasonable prices; many interesting, well-designed math aids, including abacuses, slates, cube and volume forms, metric-English braille rulers and volume-measuring devices; educational games; science devices, such as biological models, simple machines and individualized kits for primary science; a great many sensory and textured aids for early childhood education and reading readiness; interesting devices to extend or vary audio materials and an extensive catalog of music materials.

Overall, their catalogs (free on request) seem appropriate for many educators of children whose strong modes are not visual. Some of the larger catalogs are those for music publications, braille publications, cassette tapes, large-type publications and vacuum-formed (a printing process) publications. Most of these catalogs include regular textbooks arranged by curriculum area, high-interest, low-vocabulary textbooks, fiction, non-fiction, music, and supplementary readings, and sometimes easy books and periodicals.

Their *Central Catalog* is sort of a union list for finding materials from other sources. It is a title-index to volunteer- and commercially-produced materials for blind and visually impaired persons, including braille, large type, recorded textbooks and supplementary materials.

The American Printing House for the Blind provides a backup service in providing thermocopies of books. Individuals or institutions seeking copies can arrange to send a master copy to the APH.

Division for the Blind and Physically Handicapped (DBPH)
U.S. Library of Congress
1291 Taylor St., NW
Washington, DC 20542   (202) 882-5500

One important source of free loan materials for blind and physically impaired persons is the program administered by the Division for the Blind and Physically Handicapped of the Library of Congress. This Division, first established by Congress in 1931 to provide services and materials for blind adults, expanded its services to children in 1952, and was further expanded—by Public Law 89-552 in 1956—to include other individuals whose physical impairments prevent reading standard print—for instance, those with a lack of muscle coordination, paralysis, prolonged weakness or missing limbs.

There are an estimated 7.6 million individuals in the U.S. who might use these services—about two million individuals with visual impairments and about five million more with other physical problems. Of this total, only about 558,000 individuals—children and adults—use the services provided by DBPH. About 500,000 use recorded materials; 38,000 use large-type materials; and about 22,000 use braille. In 1976, the program circulated about 13 million items, as well as playback equipment for records and cassettes.

For this clientele, the Library of Congress—if granted copyright permission by authors and publishers—selects and produces full-length books and magazines in three formats: braille, recorded discs or cassettes, and large type. These materials, distributed through a cooperating network of regional and local libraries, are mailed postage-free from libraries to users and back.

The DBPH itself is funded annually by Congress (about $22 million for fiscal year 1977) while cooperating libraries are funded by local and state sources.

DBPH selects for republication on the basis of appeal to a wide range of interests: best sellers, biographies, and how-to books are in greatest demand. Print/braille and other special format books are popular with very young children and with visually impaired parents of young children. The DBPH produces about 1,650 titles per year for distribution through its network of libraries. About 700 more titles are taped or transcribed into braille by volunteers. About 70 popular magazines are also reproduced, including *National Geographic, Jack and Jill, Weekly Reader, Ranger Rick, Cricket, Children's Digest* and others.

In addition, the DBPH circulates music materials directly from its Washington headquarters from a large selection of braille and large-type music and music scores, recorded music books and texts, and elementary instruction in cassette form for piano, guitar and organ. Music periodicals are available in braille and on records; demonstrations and discussions of music are available on discs and cassettes. These materials are often appropriate for school situations.

In 1977 the DBPH began the first phase of a national automated bibliographic information project which should, eventually, enable libraries to identify and locate all books produced in special format for visually impaired readers.

As an information source on various aspects of blindness and other physical impairments, the DBPH can also answer without charge questions sent directly to the Reference Section or brought to any cooperating library. In addition, the Reference Section issues many free pamphlets on DBPH services, on disabling conditions and materials sources for their users which are revised as needed. Some titles appropriate for school situations are listed below. (Single copies are free on letterhead request.)

- *Talking Books for Physically Disabled Children and Adults*
- *Braille Book Review* (bimonthly listing of current titles and program news)
- *Musical Mainstream*
- *Talking Book Topics* (bimonthly listing of current recorded titles and program news)
- *Commercial Sources of Spoken Word Cassettes*
- *National Organizations Concerned with Visually and Physically Handicapped Persons* (annotated guide to 65 voluntary and federal organizations)
- *Sources of Large Type Books* (includes publishers, sellers and lenders)
- *Subject Guide to Spoken Word Recordings*
- *Books for Children Who Read by Touch or Sound*

DBPH also provides free library service for students who are certified as eligible by public or private schools. The application blank for this service is available from the Washington office.

National Association for Visually Handicapped (NAVH)
305 East 24th St.
New York, NY 10010   (212) 889-3141

     and

3201 Balboa St.
San Francisco, CA 94121   (415) 221-3201
     This voluntary agency, which includes both parents and professionals, addresses itself to the needs of persons with partial sight and serves as a national information clearinghouse on services available from all levels of government and from private organizations.
     They offer comprehensive group programs and educational counseling for low-vision youth, as well as discussion groups and other programs for parents and professionals. They also disseminate information on optical aids from commercial sources, and cooperate in field testing new aids.
     NAVH is the world's largest volunteer source of free print books prepared and distributed without charge. They also act as consultants to commercial publishers, and have worked with them for 20 years in setting standards and representing needs of partially seeing. Their large-print program, now resumed after a hiatus in funding, has produced more than 120,000 volumes in large print.

National Braille Association
654A Godwin Ave.
Midland Park, NJ 07432
     Includes volunteers who transcribe materials for the blind, and persons who work with these materials. It also operates a Braille Book Bank to provide college students with textbooks in braille at approximately the cost of printed texts.

Recording for the Blind
215 East 58th St.
New York, NY 10022
     This group includes volunteers who will record textbooks for blind students without charge on individual requests.

Agencies Specifically for Deaf Persons

Alexander Graham Bell Association for the Deaf, Inc.
3417 Volta Place, NW
Washington, DC 20007   (202) 337-5220
     The Bell Association, founded by its namesake, is a private, non-profit organization (not subsidized by federal or corporate grants) which provides programs and services for the hearing impaired and their parents, educators, physicians and legislators. Essentially, it strives to broaden educational, vocational and personal opportunities for all hearing impaired persons by operating through three sections: one for educators, one for parents, and one for deaf adults.
     Through its non-profit publishing program, the Bell Association publishes and distributes hundreds of books and pamphlets on deafness, hearing and speech, as well as *The Volta Review*, a bimonthly periodical on education, training,

language development, speech and speech reading, and *Newsounds*, a newsletter on current events at state and national levels. A $20.00 membership includes these two periodicals, reduced prices on publications and audiovisual aids, reduced prices at conventions and the privilege of borrowing materials (via mail or in person) from the Volta Bureau Library, one of the world's largest collections on deafness.

The publication program is impressive, with tape-slide shows, videotape cassettes, films and a variety of printed forms. There are many items on deaf children and education (for both parents and teachers) with special school package discount prices for some items. A few particularly relevant items are:

Nix, Gary W., ed. *Mainstream Education for Hearing Impaired Children and Youth*, 1976. 288p. $16.00.
Covers social, psychological, auditory, perceptual and administrative aspects, with a section on exemplary programs and materials.

Northcott, Winifred H., ed. *The Hearing-Impaired Child in a Regular Classroom: Preschool, Elementary, and Secondary Years*, 1973. 301p. $7.95.
A practical handbook with chapters by resource specialists, includes first-hand information on objectives, organizational patterns, etc., with bibliography and glossary.

Silverman-Dresner, Toby, and George R. Guilfoyle. *Vocabulary Norms for Deaf Children*, 1972. 190p. $7.00. (Lexington Series, Book VII).
Lists 7,300 words known to deaf children, ages 8 to 17, by age, parts of speech and topical classification. An invaluable reference for evaluating reading materials or constructing tests.

Convention of American Instructors of the Deaf (CAID)
5034 Wisconsin Ave., NW
Washington, DC 20016   (202) 363-1327
This organization was founded in 1850 by a group of instructors from schools for the deaf in order to improve the education of the deaf. It is one of the oldest professional organizations in the United States and one of the largest organizations of educators of the deaf in the world, with members from all types of schools—residential, day, private and public. Today it is an advocate-and-information organization as well as a professional organization of educators.

It is the co-publisher of the *American Annals of the Deaf*, a bimonthly journal which publishes a *Reference Issue* each April. This issue—available separately for $5.00—provides a comprehensive annual listing of services for the deaf, with information on teacher training programs, research and publications on deafness and a listing of schools, classes and clinics in the U.S. and Canada. The yearly subscription (including the *Reference Issue*) is $13.50.

As an information organization CAID responds to inquiries from members and non-members for information on education or service for the deaf and refers inquiries to other services as needed. Since 1977, CAID has produced educational materials for dissemination.

International Association of Parents of the Deaf, Inc. (IAPD)
814 Thayer Avenue
Silver Spring, MD 20910   (301) 585-5400
    IAPD is in part a pressure group advocating better services and in part an information exchange and liaison agent between deaf persons and those educators, organizations and government agencies that deal in some way with the deaf. Membership at $10.00 a year includes discounts on publications and a bimonthly informative newsletter, *Endeavor*, which provides background information on the concerns of the deaf. Publications include books for deaf children in signed English, sign-language playing cards, workbooks in basic sign language, *Sign Language Flash Cards* (deck of 500 for $6.25), *Games and Activities for Sign Language Classes* ($3.50), and high-interest, simple-language books and magazines for children, including *World Traveler*, a 16-page magazine at third grade reading level, liberally illustrated with *National Geographic* photographs. They have, as well, materials for interpreting the world of the deaf for both adults and children. *The Deaf Child in the Public Schools: A Handbook for Parents* may be as valuable for educators as for parents. A complete catalog of their publications is available on request.

Lexington School for the Deaf
30th Ave. and 75th St.
Jackson Heights, Queens, NY 11370   (212) 899-8800
    The Lexington School has an active education and information program with materials and services in audiology, education, mental health, psychological testing and medicine, with something of a specialization in early detection of deafness, remediation of deafness, and location of materials for and about the deaf, including films, hearing aids, and electronic manikins.
    It is well known for its national conferences which include such topics as adaptation of materials, demonstrations of instruments and evaluation of new techniques. The early *Lexington Education Series* (practical and scholarly), now available from the Alexander Graham Bell Association, stressed materials and methods for reaching deaf children.
    Their *Family Series* has many inexpensive flyers and leaflets, books and cassettes that are appropriate for mainstreamed classes.
    Two helpful *Family Series* titles still in print are:

Hart. *Teaching Reading to Deaf Children*, 1963. Lexington School for the
    Deaf Education Series Book IV. $8.85.
    Steps in teaching reading from preschool through upper grades.

Mignone-Mignone. *Educational Strategies for the Youngest Hearing Impaired
    Children* (0 to 5 Years of Age), 1977. Lexington School for the Deaf
    Education Series Book X. $7.00.
    Over 100 new ideas for developing listening and language expansion
are contained in this new practical, "hands-on" resource book designed
basically for home use by parents and teachers of hearing impaired young
people.

Media Development Project for the Hearing Impaired (MDPHI)

318 Barkley Memorial Center
University of Nebraska at Lincoln
Lincoln, NB 68583   (402) 472-2141

The MDPHI, a successor to the Midwest Regional Media Center, was recently awarded a contract as a three-year project under the auspices of the Captioned Films and Telecommunication Branch of the U.S. Bureau for the Handicapped. Its functions are to identify the educational needs of the hearing impaired and to locate, adapt, develop, evaluate and market materials to meet these needs.

It is actively searching for teacher-made materials to evaluate for possible production and distribution. It is also distributing limited quantities of materials, such as "The Nebraska Transparency Masters," developed by or through former projects for the hearing impaired.

It conducts yearly symposia for administrators and directors on current research and utilization of educational media, technology and materials for teaching deaf learners. Proceedings of former symposia, from 1965 to 1974, conducted under the auspices of the Midwest Regional Media Center, are available without charge. These include topics like *Individualizing Instruction for the Deaf Student* (1969), *Programmed Learning for the Deaf Student* (1971), *Career Education and Educational Media for the Deaf Student* (1973) and other materials that relate to uses of media with the hearing impaired.

National Association of the Deaf (NAD)

814 Thayer Avenue
Silver Spring, MD 20910   (301) 587-1788

The NAD was established in 1880 to facilitate contact between deaf persons in different sections of the United States and to meet the unique needs of deaf individuals as a class—in education, communication, health, research, information, etc. It emphasizes the rights of deaf persons to learn all available forms of communication in order to develop language competence. This includes gestures, speech, formal sign language, fingerspelling, speech-reading, reading, writing and amplification of residual hearing.

The NAD is an information source on the deaf, with a substantial library and a publication program that includes brochures, pamphlets and fact sheets, mostly available at little or no cost.

Some special activities include:

- a National Census of the Deaf which surveys the extent and location of deaf persons in the United States

- a program to develop curricula and guidelines for high-quality communications programs

- a program for screening and evaluating general entertainment motion pictures to determine which motion pictures should be captioned for deaf audiences

- sponsoring research in all aspects of deafness.

The NAD Publishing Division has a free 18-page catalog of printed materials, films and special equipment for the hearing impaired, available on request. Some relevant items are:

Hoemann, Shirley. *Children's Sign Language Playing Cards*, 1973. 52 cards. $2.00.
   Uses games like Old Maid, Concentration, etc. to teach signs.

O'Rourke, Terence J. *A Basic Vocabulary of American Sign Language for Parents and Children*, 1978. $7.95pa.
   Includes 1,200 illustrations based on research in basic word lists.

Royster, Mary Ann. *Games and Activities*, 1973. 49p. $3.50pa.
   Includes 42 games designed to help children become more fluent and expressive in using sign language; the games require very little in materials or preparation.

Boatner, Maxine, and John Gates. *Dictionary of Idioms for the Deaf*, 1975. 392p. $6.95; $4.95pa.
   This reference book, intended for deaf students of ninth through twelfth grades explains the meanings of phrases for which dictionary meanings might be difficult to understand.

Pre-College Programs of Gallaudet College

Kendall Green
Washington, DC 20002   (202) 447-0633
   The Pre-College Programs of Gallaudet College include two federally-funded demonstration schools—the Kendall Demonstration Elementary School and the Model Secondary School for the Deaf (MSSD)—both set up, in part, to develop, test, and disseminate improved teaching techniques and materials for hearing disabled and hearing impaired children.
   News of such developments and materials is carried in a free newsletter, *Pre-College Program Perspectives*, which lists upcoming publications and results of field tests. Essentially, it is a sharing of national news. *Panorama*, produced by MSSD, provides more specific information on instructional materials developed by the school.

KEY PUBLICATIONS

   Other good sources can be found in the chapter on commercial retrieval systems (see pages 326-32) and in both companion volumes to this handbook.

Auditory Learning Materials for Special Education, by Martha C. Smith and Phyllis O 'Connor. Washington, National Audiovisual Center, 1975. 152p. (Out of print but available from ERIC Document Reproduction Service, as ED 102-757). $9.14 hard copy. (From P.O. Box 190, Arlington, VA 22210.)
   This NCEMMH teachers' catalog, accurate as of 1973-1974, provides page-long descriptions of more than 100 auditory learning materials for special-education students from preschool through twelfth grade, with information on chronological and mental age level, student objectives, procedures for using products, required equipment and brief comments on each project.

The Directory of Agencies Serving the Visually Handicapped in the United States,
    20th ed. New York, American Foundation for the Blind, 1978. 448p. $10.00.
    This directory, issued every even year, includes names, addresses and services
of most local, state and national agencies, organizations, schools and government
bodies which serve the visually handicapped. Includes a special section on low
vision services.

Directory of National Information Sources on Handicapping Conditions and Related
    Services. Washington, OHI Clearinghouse on the Handicapped, 1976. 405p.
    looseleaf, $6.50. (Free from the Office of Handicapped Individuals; see
    "Other Broad Scope Federal Agencies," pages 308-309.)
    Includes names, addresses, scope of activities, services, and user eligibility
(and fees) for 270 national organizations that serve the handicapped (with an
appendix listing organizations that preferred not to be included). The guide provides indexes by name, by subject area (employment, recreation, equipment, etc.),
by target population (veterans, children) and by disorder.

A Directory of Selected Resources in Special Education, ed. by Kathy Adams.
    Chelmsford, MA, Merrimack Education Center, 1977. 34p. $1.25. (From
    101 Mill Road, Chelmsford, MA 01824.)
    This directory, the second in a series, includes information on organizations
and publications which constitute "selected resources in special education."
    Like the earlier guide (produced in 1975 and also available for $1.25), this is
a helpful, compact annotated directory to products designed to meet the needs of
children with diverse learning styles. Areas covered are home-school communications, classroom techniques, testing and assessment, as well as media, materials and
resources.

Federal Assistance for Programs Serving the Handicapped. Washington, OHI Clear-
    inghouse on the Handicapped, 1977. 333p. $5.00. (Free from the Office of
    Handicapped Individuals; see "Other Broad Scope Federal Agencies," on
    pages 308-309.)
    A guide to more than 200 federal programs that dispense $22 billion
annually.

Instructional Materials for the Handicapped: Birth through Early Childhood, by
    Arden R. Thorum, et al. Salt Lake City, Olympus Publishing Co., 1976. 194p.
    $6.95pa. (From Olympus Publishing Company, Two Olympus Plaza, 1670
    East 13th, Salt Lake City, UT 84108.)
    This handbook for consumers and developers is a convenient, three-section
guide to instructional materials for young disabled children. The three sections deal,
in slightly different ways, with toys and games, instructional kits, and activity
guides. The book includes guideline definitions of terms, intelligent discussion and
selection criteria for each and a how-to-use-this-book guide.
    The section on toys and games includes addresses of about 550 vendors and
manufacturers and a few vendors of medical equipment, with descriptions of their
products and a back-up bibliography of selected references. The section on instructional kits includes matrices that describe more than 270 instructional kits and an
excellent critique of their uses. The matrices cover vendor, name of kit, cost,

suggested age range, developmental skill area (auditory perception, visual perception, tactile perception, etc.), subject area (such as reading readiness, math readiness and language arts), format (diagnostic/evaluative, individualized instruction, adult involvement, performance objectives, etc.), and components (specialized equipment, books, tape cassettes/records, etc.).

The final section is an annotated bibliography of about 100 activity guides suitable for use in some way with young disabled children—though many were intended for other purposes. These embrace all areas of early childhood curriculum: movement, language and reading, rainy-day books, holiday fun, math and other cognitive activities. All emphasize the use of toys and games—often games made with scrounged materials. Many of the guides are appropriate for parents.

International Guide to Aids and Appliances for the Blind and Visually Impaired Persons. New York, American Foundation for the Blind, 1977. 255p. $3.00.
This comprehensive directory includes descriptions, prices and ordering information for more than 1,500 special aids and devices for visually impaired persons.

National Catalog of Films in Special Education. Compiled by New York State Education Department, Area Learning Resource Center and National Center on Educational Media and Materials for the Handicapped. Columbus, OH, National Center on Educational Media and Materials for the Handicapped, 1977. 70p. $4.00. (From Ohio State University Press, 2070 Neil Avenue, Columbus, OH 43210.)
This comprehensive catalog, compiled by arrangement with NCEMMH, is the most inclusive catalog so far on films for special education and will be updated periodically if funds permit. It includes information on more than 700 films (mostly sound films in 16mm) including title, name, address of producers, distributor or other source, prices for sale or rental, running time, and a short but fairly detailed summary of the contents of each film. Fully indexed.

NAVA Special Report: Education of the Handicapped. Fairfax, VA, National Audio-Visual Association, 1977. 27p. $5.00.
A detailed explanation of the new Handicapped Act (Public Law 94-0142) with special emphasis on the use of funds for audiovisual materials and equipment. Another volume on a related topic is *Federal Assistance for Programs Serving the Handicapped*, by the U.S. Office for Handicapped Individuals (cited on page 320).

Nonverbal Communication and the Congenitally Blind: A Subject Bibliography of Print and Non-Print Materials for the Development of Training Programs, by Marianne May. New York, American Foundation for the Blind, 1977. $2.00 (AFB Practice Report).
This annotated bibliography on kinesics (nonverbal communication) is intended to stimulate the development of training programs by identifying printed materials.

Non-Vocal Communication Resource Book, ed. by Gregg C. Vanderheider. Madison, WI, Trace Research and Development Center, 1977. 4 vols. in 3-ring binder. $12.50 plus subscription to *Updates* ($5.00/yr). (From 314 Waisman Center, 1500 Highland Ave., Madison, WI 53706.)

This resource book is also available from University Park Press in Baltimore, MD. Trace Center also sells separate sections as follows: 1) *Illustrated Digest of Non-Vocal Communication and Writing Aids for Severely Physically Handicapped Individuals*, compiled and edited by Jana Fothergill, et al. 230p. ($8.00); 2) *Master Chart of Communication Aids*, by Gregg C. Vanderheiden, et al. 20p. ($2.00); 3) *Interface Switch Profile* and *Annotated List of Commercial Switches*, by Craig S. Holt, et al. 18p. ($1.50); and 4) *Bibliography on Non-Vocal Communication Techniques and Aids*, by Warren P. Brown, et al. 21p. ($1.50).

As a whole, this book provides descriptions and summaries of communication aids, current information on sources and frameworks for identifying and selecting such aids.

The Trace Research and Development Center for the Severely Communicatively Handicapped, which originated this book, is part of the Waisman Center for Mental Retardation and Human Development at the University of Wisconsin and is concerned with using technology to augment communication systems for individuals whose physical impairments create communication problems. Though it is not a service agency, it does collect and disseminate information on communication aids. Its publications include *A Survey of Critical Factors in Evaluating Communication Aids*, by Deborah Harris, 1975. 22p. (Available in Xerox for $0.01 per page) and other materials that suggest communication techniques for non-vocal children. Send a stamped, self-addressed envelope for a description of the Center and/or a list of its publications.

Patchwork, compiled by Southern Regional Media Center for the Deaf. Columbus, OH, National Center on Educational Media and Materials for the Handicapped, 1973. Filmstrip with audio cassette. Twelve-page booklet with script and operating instructions. $12.50. (From National Audiovisual Center, General Services Administration, Washington, DC 20407.)

This filmstrip-cassette set, designed to introduce public school teachers to the problems of mainstreamed hearing impaired students ("patchwork learners"), presents information to help teachers recognize this disability and to use appropriate media and teaching techniques with such students.

Publisher Source Directory, 3rd ed. Compiled by New York State Education Department, Area Learning Resource Center and National Center on Educational Media and Materials for the Handicapped. 3rd ed. Columbus, OH, National Center on Educational Media and Materials for the Handicapped, 1977. 137p. $5.00. (From Ohio State University Press, 2070 Neil Ave., Columbus, OH 43210.)

Essentially, this tool provides an alphabetical listing of nearly 1,700 sources which sell or rent instructional materials and other educational media, aids and devices. It has a coded summary of the major product lines of each producer or distributor, a glossary of definitions of these products and a rotated index which lists sources of particular kinds of materials such as manipulatives, games or curriculum guides.

The Resource Room: An Educational Asset for Children with Special Needs, by Margaret F. Hawisher and Mary Lynne Calhoun. Columbus, OH, Charles E. Merrill Publishing Company, 1978. 202p. $6.50pa.

A well conceived and presented program for meeting the problem of approaching the special needs of the individual mainstreamed child. Includes useful information on child referral, on the implementation of IEPs and on the organization and selection of materials for the resource room, as well as a plan for evaluating the program itself.

The Special Child in the Library, edited by Barbara Holland Baskin and Karen H.
    Harris. Chicago, American Library Association, 1976. 199p. $9.00.
An extremely well-selected book of readings equally valuable for librarians and teachers working with exceptional children. Current, cogent selections deal with many aspects of materials, programs and learning environments. Includes six articles on physical environments, seven on selection criteria, thirteen on the utilization of materials, ten on instructional programs, seven on using literature for conflict resolution, and eight guides to supplementary resources.
According to the authors, "selection of materials for exceptional children is predicated on a clear understanding of each child's functional level, how the disability interferes with optimal learning, and what kinds of materials are available which would capitalize on the child's assets and bypass, if possible, the disabilities."

Teaching Aids for Visually Handicapped Children, by Barbara Dorward and Natalie
    Barraga. New York, American Foundation for the Blind, 1968. 132p. $3.50.
This workbook includes construction directions for 30 educational aids for mathematics, spelling, matching and other puzzles, with a braille appendix.

Tool Kit 76, by Houston Head Start Workshop. Washington, Office of Child
    Development, 1976. 67p. Free. (From Project Head Start, Office of Child
    Development, D.H.E.W., P.O. Box 1182, Washington, DC 20013.)
This catalog of materials, methods and media for handicapped pre-school children was put together by the Houston Head Start Workshop in 1975. It is loaded with prices, addresses, checklists, ideas and sources of programs and materials arranged in a free-flowing form by editor Dan Prince.

Turn Off the Sound, originated by Northeast Regional Media Center for the Deaf.
    Columbus, OH, National Center on Educational Media and Materials for the
    Handicapped, 1978. 80p. (From Ohio State University Press, 2070 Neil Ave.,
    Columbus, OH 43210.)
This manual provides clear, well-illustrated, step-by-step instructions for adapting sound filmstrip programs to silent programs for hearing impaired students. Includes the steps, materials and equipment needed for ten separate methods of adaptation, as well as guidelines for captioning and appendixes that include resources.

Workshop: Creating Instructional Materials for Handicapped Learners. Columbus,
    OH, National Center on Educational Media and Materials for the Handicapped,
    1975. Three audio cassettes; two color filmstrips; Coordinator's Guide for
    Workshop Leader, 1974. 117p. $20.00. (From National Audiovisual Center,
    General Services Administration, Washington, DC 20409.)
This NCEMMH product (originally issued by the former Northwest Special

Education Instructional Materials Center) is intended for two-session in-service workshops. It has two main purposes: to show teachers how to make instructional materials for handicapped learners and to guide teachers in selecting, adapting and using existing commercial materials for such learners. Session I, on adapting and improvising instructional materials, requires a day; Session II, on evaluation, should follow two weeks later and can be accomplished in one evening. The coordinator's guide includes master copies of activity sheets to be duplicated and distributed to workshop participants, as well as the complete scripts for the other components of the kit. These titles are: *Selecting Instructional Materials* (seven-minute audio-cassette and filmstrip), *Educating Young Handicapped Children, Getting the Most Out of Materials* (15-minute audio-cassette and filmstrip), and *Creativity* (13-minute audio-cassette).

This set, formerly known as TIP No. 5, is part of a series of Total Information Packages produced by NWSEIMC.

FOR FURTHER READING

*Items marked with an asterisk include criteria.
+Items marked with a plus have substantial lists of references.

*+Baum, D. D. "The Attitude of Teachers of the Mentally Retarded toward Teacher Evaluation of Instruction Materials," *Education and Training of the Mentally Retarded*, v. 7, no. 1 (1972), pp. 46-50.

Bleil, Gordon B. "Characteristics of Handicapped Learners," in *Footnote* (Bellevue, WA, Edmark Associates, n.d.). (From Edmark, 13241 Northrup Way, Bellevue, WA 98005.)
A very brief but helpful summary of professional opinions concerning the particular problems met by special educators.

*+Boland, Sandra K. "Instructional Materialism—Or How to Select the Things You Need," *Teaching Exceptional Children*, v. 8, no. 4 (Summer 1976), pp. 156-58.

Buist, Charlotte A., and Jerome L. Schalmon. *Toys and Games for Educationally Handicapped Children.* Springfield, IL, C. C. Thomas, 1973.

Cassell, John T. *Suggested Aids to Educating the Exceptional Child.* Springfield, MA, Milton Bradley Company, 1974.

*Delp, Harold A. "Social Development of the Mentally Retarded," in *Training the Developmentally Young*, edited by Beth Stephens. New York, John Day, 1971.

*Fast, Betty. "Mediacentric: Media and the Handicapped Child," *Wilson Library Bulletin*, v. 52, no. 2 (Oct. 1977), pp. 133-35.

*Fokes, Joann. "Developmental Scale of Motor Abilities and Developmental Scale of Language Acquisition," in *Training the Developmentally Young*, edited by Beth Stephens. New York, John Day, 1971.

Goodman, Leroy V. *Education of the Handicapped Today and a Bill of Rights for the Handicapped.* Washington, National Advisory Committee on the Handicapped, 1976.

*+Junkala, J. "Teacher Evaluation of Instructional Materials," *Teaching Exceptional Children*, v. 2, no. 2 (Winter 1967), pp. 73-76.

Moffatt, Samuel. *Helping the Child Who Cannot Hear.* New York, Public Affairs Pamphlets, 1975.

*Parker, Scott L., et al. *Improving Occupational Programs for the Handicapped.* Washington, GPO, 1976.

"Progress by Partners in Step: Special Issue," *Teaching Exceptional Children*, v. 10, no. 3 (Spring 1978), pp. 57-100.
    Includes 11 articles devoted to the implementation of the individualized education program, many relevant to materials.

*Schmitt, Robert. "The Affective Domain: A Challenge to ITV," *The California News*, v. 88, no. 3 (Nov.-Dec. 1972), pp. 1-3.

*Smith, Lotsee Patterson, and Bill Watson, eds. "Special Education: A Continuum of Services," *School Media Quarterly*, v. 6, no. 4 (Summer 1978), pp. 229-63.
    Includes four articles, covering law, parents and materials.

*"Special Education," *Audiovisual Instruction*, v. 11, no. 9 (Nov. 1966), pp. 708-761.
    This entire issue of *Audiovisual Instruction* explores the use of media for children with various impairments: mental retardation, language disability, hearing impairment, visual impairment, etc. Ten articles in all whose concepts and techniques still are relevant and under-utilized.

*Van Etten, C., and G. W. Adamson. *Analysis of Instructional Materials: A Prescriptive Materials Laboratory.* Pittsburgh, PA, Association for Children with Learning Disabilities, 1969.

+Wright, K. C. *Library and Information Services for Handicapped Individuals.* Littleton, CO, Libraries Unlimited, 1979.
    A first text on planning library services for all major groups of handicapped individuals: those who are blind or visually impaired, deaf or hearing impaired, mentally disabled, aging, or physically disabled.

COMMERCIAL RETRIEVAL SYSTEMS

While systems like NICSEM and NCEMMH were basically developed under federal contracts and auspices, other retrieval systems have been developed by school systems and commercial firms to locate instructional materials to meet the specific needs of individual children.

These commercial systems range widely in price and in method, and they use a wide variety of variables and information gathering techniques to analyze commercial instructional materials and to correlate these materials with student characteristics. Successful approaches include computerized systems, optical scanning cards ("peek-a-boo systems"), punched cards, keysort cards, updated resumes and annual printed indexes—all serving as interfaces between materials and consumers.

These systems are quite helpful when carefully chosen to meet a specific need. They may, however, be expensive or difficult to use or maintain; often they require extensive in-service training. In addition, since new products are continuously being developed, the systems can never include all the products that might be helpful for particular purposes or for particular students.

Though these systems can be valuable in selecting appropriate materials, potential users hoping to simplify selection are faced with the problem of selecting the appropriate retrieval system. Little help is available, except from one study supported by the Massachusetts State Department of Education, *Guide to Finding Appropriate Instructional Materials: Existing Retrieval Systems*, by James H. McCormack, Cathy Doyle and Jody Bleiberg (Medford, MA, Massachusetts Center for Program Development and Evaluation, June 1977). In this study the authors suggest certain questions to consider in selecting commercial retrieval systems for educational situations. The questions below are basically my adaptations of their questions:

- For what skill areas (reading, mathematics, etc.) is information required?
- Is this system intended for one teacher, one school, a school district, an association or _____?
- What does this system (and its updates) cost?
- Are updates included in the quoted price? For how long?
- Can this system absorb teacher-constructed materials?
- Is the format arranged to allow the identification of the best available materials within five minutes?
- Does the system require extensive training?
- Has the system been validated?
- Is this system and its follow-up service reliable?

An additional point is whether or not this system indexes materials that are available. If these materials are not owned and cannot be borrowed, a particularly effective system will provide merely an exercise in frustration.

Decisions on selecting such systems should be made by the persons using them on the basis of hands-on comparisons and try-outs since systems vary as widely as individual preferences. If the user's thinking and approaches to materials are congruent with a particular system, if the system is set up so that it indexes materials the user has or can purchase, and if it is not too expensive in time or money for each item located, the system is worth considering. Some worthwhile systems are briefly listed and described under firm names at the end of this section.

Since retrieval systems are merely guides (somewhat comparable to headings or index terms) the materials identified through such systems may or may not be appropriate for particular teaching approaches or for targeted students. The McCormack study (cited above) suggests that teachers should use the following questions to evaluate the materials they have located for practicality and relevance. These questions, of course, are appropriate for any selection situation.

- Are instructional objectives stated?
- Are there prerequisite skills required of the teacher to use effectively the material stated?
- Is the presentation mode appropriate for the student?
- Does the instruction follow a logical sequence?
- Are the directions complete and accurate?
- Is the teaching strategy clearly and completely indicated?
- Are storage and/or retrieval requirements prohibitive?
- Will preparation time prevent regular use?
- Is the answer key (if provided) useful or can one easily be constructed?
- What student/teacher ratio is necessary to use the material?
- Is the material capable of maintaining student interest?
- Is the procedure for detecting errors and making corrections sufficient?
- Is the material self correcting?
- Is the stated mastery level (criteria for success) indicated?
- Are there alternative approaches to using the material to attain the same objectives?
- Is the material capable of maintaining instructor interest?
- Is the material durable?
- Is the teacher's guide (if one is provided) complete?
- How often will it be necessary and how difficult will it be to replace consumable parts of the material?
- Is validation information provided?
- What are the strengths and weaknesses of the validation information if provided?
- What is the cost/price/value estimate?
- Are the materials' technical aspects, i.e., size of print, quality of pictures, etc., acceptable?

KEY ORGANIZATIONS

Adaptive Systems Corporation
1650 So. Amphlett Blvd., Suite 317
San Mateo, CA 94402   (415) 573-6114

Adaptive Systems' ISAARE (Information System for Adaptive, Assistive and Rehabilitative Equipment) is a method for finding information on educative and rehabilitative equipment for use in schools and special education programs. Many items in ISAARE are also appropriate for physical and occupational therapy and have other medical applications.

This expanding directory now includes about 800 items by 270 manufacturers arranged by developmental categories. These categories include interaction and communication with the surrounding environment, in-situ motion, travel, adaptation to and of the environment, rehabilitation and existence.

The system is currently available in printed format at $57.58 for institutions ($39.58 for individuals). This price includes a set of six indexes with glossaries, a locator with an outline index, an alphabetical index and cross references from equipment to manufacturers. In essence, it is a relatively inexpensive index to catalogs of equipment services in the special-education/rehabilitation spectrum.

Educational Patterns Incorporated (EPI)
63-110 Woodhaven Blvd.
Rego Park, NY 11374   (212) 894-7217

EPI is a manual card sorting system for regular classroom instruction, developmental teaching, special education and remedial instruction, which can be used in school districts, media centers, learning resource centers, special education materials centers and in other learning situations. (A separate component, the S/PH module for severely and profoundly handicapped is also available.)

The basic retrieval system includes information on about 10,000 items from 300 publishers, coded for grade level, modality, interest, format and interaction, as well as skill. Skills themselves include the following which are broken down into language and math skills:

Comprehension	Perceptual Skills
Grammar and Composition	Phonics
Handwriting	Readiness
Language Development	Spelling
Literature	Structural Analysis
Motor Skills	Study Skills
Oral/Silent Reading	Vocabulary Development
Addition	Money/Time/Measurement/Geometry
Division	Multiplication
Fraction/Decimals/Percent	Numeration
Math—General	Subtraction

Costs range from a $360 do-it-yourself system to the most expensive customized system—around $3,000—which includes more than 2,000 cards representing about 10,000 items, 500 cards prepared for the user's own inventory, 400 cards of teacher-created ideas, plus storage boxes and dividers, sorters, materials source lists and 20 guides to the EPI system.

Update services based on the user's new acquisitions cost about $160 for 100 cards, $420 for 300. If the user wishes to correlate instructional materials with his/ her own behavioral objectives, EPI will do it for about $60 to $85 for each item.

Their *Project Mainstream*, a "learning system for students with special education needs," is a two-level system based on 266 Desired Learning Outcomes (DLOs) which are essentially concise behavioral statements of learning behaviors for developmental ages 4 through 10.

Part of *Project Mainstream* is a "Behavior Resource Guide," available for $26.95. This is a series of three types of lists and four types of correlation charts that link diagnostic and prescriptive information with the desired learning outcomes. One of these consists of "Instructional Media," arranged by title and publisher to be used with a chart which correlates 21 desired learning outcomes to specific learning materials.

Educational Progress Corporation
P.O. Box 45663
Tulsa, OK 74145   (918) 622-4522

Educational Progress Corporation, which publishes its own programs, has one math program based on Individualized Criterion Referenced Testing (ICRT) which locates materials in 15 other standard mathematics programs. *ICRT Math Basics +* is an assessment and a classroom instructional management system, which assesses and monitors each student's progress in learning basic math skills from the first to the eighth grade.

It is based on a set of 384 learning objectives (categorized for difficulty, topic and skill) and correlated to specific titles, editions, and page numbers of other reference numbers of 15 recent math books; additional correlations are planned with new materials. Prices are available on request.

FOREWORKS
7111 Teesdale Ave.
North Hollywood, CA 91605   (213) 982-0467

FOREWORKS' *System FORE* (Fundamentals-Operations-Resources-Environment) is a means of correlating lists of instructional materials with particular developmental sequences worked out cooperatively back in 1968 by the Los Angeles Unified School District, the Northwest Regional Resource Center, the West Linn Learning Resource Center and other learning resource centers.

The developmental sequences (the Fundamental "F" of *FORE*) integrate criterion-referenced objectives, specific skills and developmental scales for children from six months to ten years old, with categories related to language, reading and mathematics.

The system offers strategies for organizing learning and provides sequential program development through arranging color-coded printed materials by subject (skill) area, using instructional objectives organized by strand, level, and item. Strands are consecutively-numbered, major divisions of three areas (language has four strands; reading and math have three each). Each instructional area is divided into 18 levels, or developmental stages, covering learning from six months to ten years. The items are specific skills and behaviors which translate into instructional guidelines for teachers and measurable objectives for students.

The Instructional Materials List (1976. $12.00) color codes instructional materials to match the sequence, and organizes materials by strand, level and item, with up to 15 materials listed for each objective. Materials are also coded for the type of classroom learning center where they might be most effective, by the mode of sensory input and by the type of response.

About 8,360 materials are listed. For language there are 682 in phonology, 616 in morphology, 330 in syntax and 126 in semantics. Reading includes 1,012 for visual/motor skills, 836 for decoding, 1,760 for comprehension and 1,232 for study skills. Math has 242 under geometry and measurement, 286 under numbers and 902 under operations/applications. The series has been further extended to include sequences in metrics and motor development, and to include some more advanced developmental levels (levels 19 through 32) for secondary students.

Eric Bagai of FOREWORKS estimates that the system has been used for about two million children, including children in regular classes, gifted children in early childhood education and disabled children up to 14 years old. Since the system is self-contained and inexpensive, it is often used by isolated teachers who lack district support or funding.

Vort Corporation
385 Sherman, Suite 11
(P.O. Box 11132)
Palo Alto, CA 94306   (415) 965-4000

Vort Corporation, operating from a data base in Palo Alto, offers several options to educators selecting instructional materials.

Their most inexpensive retrieval system consists of five annual printed indexes, *Guides to Instructional Materials* ($49.95 total), which index and cross-reference about 14,000 supplemental materials by 300 skill areas. Each of these 8½x11-inch guides includes an index of skills, an appendix of titles cross-referenced by skill, and a directory of publishers/producers. The main section, categorized by skill, provides compact one-line information on each instructional item: title, publisher, type of material, interest level, edition, price and producer's catalog number.

Separate annual guides are available for:

Math (1978. 196p. $12.95). Includes 5,350 references to 100 skills in the areas of numbers, computations, time, money, standard and metric measures, fractions, decimals, maps, graphs, geometry, etc.

Reading (1978. 252p. $17.95). Provides 7,000 references under 120 specific skills related to word analysis, vocabulary, comprehension, reference, high-interest controlled vocabulary, etc.

Language Arts (1978. 114p. $9.95). Provides 2,578 references under 70 specific skills related to listening, speaking, writing, library, role playing, etc.

Vocational Education (1978. 122p. $6.95). Provides 3,192 references under 30 specific topics under areas like career awareness, finding jobs, trades, occupations, career guidance, consumer education, money, banking, etc.

Motor Development (1978. 70p. $6.95). Provides 1,680 references under specific motor skills, such as gross motor, perceptual motor, sensory, etc.

Though these guides are not specific enough to use in prescriptive education without reviewing the materials, they are helpful as a quick method to locate materials for forther consideration.

A somewhat similar series which can help in selecting methods and materials is the *Behavioral Characteristics Progression* (BCP) which correlates 2,200 teacher-developed materials and methods with objectives and behavioral characteristics.

Vort's *Instructional Materials Listings* (IMLs) are part of an ambitious, computer-based, instructional-materials management-and-retrieval system set up to help educators—preferably all those within a school district or a larger unit—to correlate their existing materials with behavioral objectives, individual education programs (IEPs) and new materials as these become available.

The IMLs process begins with a materials checklist for inventory, followed by title labels for labeling and cataloging. The materials noted on the checklist are computer-indexed by skill and objective. Vort also includes a purchasing analysis report suggesting titles from their master files which meet behaviors and objectives not covered in the titles checked on the materials checklist. The master file on which this is based includes 20,000 current instructional materials correlated with 2,000 behaviors.

The IMLs system, in turn, is a subset of Vort's *Pupil-Based Information System* (PBIS)—a multilevel, automated information system set up to provide special education teachers with appropriate assessment techniques, grouping reports, IEPs and parent conference reports, as well as materials. Prices for both systems are available on request.

The corporation's *The Delivery of Educational Services . . . and the Special Child* ($10.95) uses a book-chart format to detail the 150 procedural steps involved in the delivery of educational services to "special education" children. Some of these services are, of course, appropriate materials.

B. L. Winch & Associates
45 Hitching Post Dr., Building 2
Rolling Hills Estates, CA 90274   (213) 547-1240

B. L. Winch, founded in 1971 after a lengthy research project on the state, direction and needs of education, specializes in special education, early childhood education, affective education, career education and vocational education.

Their *Prescriptive Materials Retrieval System* (PMRS), developed essentially for special education, comes in two forms, manual and computerized. The manual system uses computer-punched descriptor cards and a light box for optical matrix readouts. The computerized format has a program deck, tape, and documentation instruction.

The current base is 10,000 materials from 200 publishers; ultimately, they plan to expand to 25,000 materials. The initial selection is based on hands-on teacher evaluation of high-use materials in 17 major curriculum areas. These are indexed by 418 descriptors that cover:

specific skill or content	mental age level
format	stimulus/response
grade level	process
reading level	major areas.

The manual process is somewhat intricate, though it eventually provides detailed information. First the user must find the term, then s/he must locate a descriptor code and then the descriptor card whose punched holes represent published materials. When these cards are stacked on an optical reader, holes that remain lit provide a number key to Descriptive Analysis Sheets (DAS) which, in turn, provide detailed, 1½-page analyses of appropriate materials.

The complete manual set with light box, equipment guides and 33 descriptor lists is $3,250.00 with a year's update included. Other updates are about $500.00 per year. The computer format is available for $1,500.00.

Richard L. Zweig Associates
20800 Beach Blvd.
Huntington Beach, CA 92648   (714) 536-8877

The *Fountain Valley Teacher Support System* for identifying instructional materials is now a self-contained printed system, with separate materials for elementary reading, secondary reading, and mathematics, all revised completely every two years. In-service is not required.

The system for elementary reading (1977. 3 vols. $19.95 each; $49.95 for three) cross-references 330 programs from 92 publishers to 367 reading behavioral objectives for the first through the sixth grades. Each manual is organized first by skill area (phonetic analysis, structural analysis, vocabulary development, etc.) then by behavioral objectives presented sequentially by achievement levels. Within the levels and skill areas, materials are categorized by type of media (including textbooks, audiovisual media, laboratory materials and kits, workbooks, spirit masters, games and activities). Volume 1, for primer and first grade, includes 20,600 prescriptions. Volumes 2-3, for second and third grades, includes 15,400 prescriptions. Volumes 4-6, for fourth to sixth grades, includes 10,600 prescriptions.

The support system in secondary reading (1976. 3 vols. $10.00 each; $24.95 set) comprises three saddle-stitched manuals which deal, respectively, with "Vocabulary Development," "Comprehension," and "Study Skills," cross-referencing 64 programs from 25 publishers to 61 reading objectives, for the seventh through the ninth grades.

Each volume is organized first by domain (word meaning, structural analysis, vocabulary in content areas, etc.) then by specific objectives. These prescriptions are then categorized by medium. The "Vocabulary Guide" includes 1,050 prescriptions; "Comprehension" has 2,100; "Study Skills" has 1,150.

The support system in numbers and operations (1975. $19.95) cross-references 134 programs from 50 publishers to 373 basic math behavioral objectives, grades K-8. The manual is color-coded by achievement level, then by sequential behavioral objectives. Specific prescriptions are categorized by types of materials, as in the other support systems. There are 21,150 prescriptions in this volume.

These resource guides are all part of more extensive systems which have diagnostic and management components.

SELECTION FOR GIFTED EDUCATION

"Education should be seen as the essential period of preparation, training, behaviour and attitude modification, necessary to enable a student to *contribute*. From this it follows that educational and training preparation *cannot* be equal. The gifted must contribute more, work longer and harder during the educational process and if this means that they have to have different methods, different teachers, different teaching aids, books and apparatus, then we must accept this as we accept the fact that you cannot train an accountant with bricklayer's tools or a surgeon with the plumber's."
—Victor Serebriakoff (International Chairman of Mensa)

"To sum up, the methods and materials of creative teaching are group discussion with freedom to dissent; uninterrupted individual study; a wide variety of books and other teaching materials readily available for individual and group use; much purposeful movement and activity; and most of all, an atmosphere that encourages children to look critically at facts and ideas, test ideas, think of alternative methods and ideas, question, doubt, develop tolerance for new and unusual ideas, and to express their own ideas in new and unusual forms."
—J. P. Guilford, *Characteristics of Creativity*

"In addition to the 'rising cream' notion, there is another major reason why youngsters with outsize abilities are often neglected and submerged. It arises from a somewhat astonishing apprehension on the part of many parents and teachers and other school people that these young people will form an elite and come to dominate their classmates and make them feel inferior."
—Harold C. Lyon, Jr., "Talent Down the Drain," *American Education*, October 1972

■　■　■

Interestingly, while there are several national organizations—government and private—concerned with gifted education, none of these organizations, so far as I can tell, has devised standards for materials for gifted education—though some have considered desirable characteristics for programs. Criteria issued are more apt to be criteria for gifted children themselves—sometimes an IQ score, sometimes a list of characteristics. The Office of the Gifted and Talented of the U.S. Office of Education, for example, suggests that "gifted or talented children are those having high potential or performance in one or more areas." According to the Office of Education, these areas include:

- general intellectual ability
- specific academic aptitude
- creativity or productive thinking
- leadership ability
- visual and performing arts
- psychomotor ability

or any combination of these.

By consensus, academically gifted children, as compared to other children, seem apt to demonstrate:

- longer attention spans
- more persistent curiosity
- greater desire to learn
- greater ability to learn rapidly
- better memory
- wider vocabulary and greater verbal fluency
- greater enjoyment of and ability to handle abstractions
- greater appreciation and awareness of people and things
- wider range of interests
- greater ability to solve problems
- tendency to prefer companionship of older children or adults
- greater ability to work independently

Other gifted children might exhibit:

- special abilities and talents in fields like art and music
- social relations leadership
- mechanical ability
- athletic skills
- creativity
- originality

Arthur Koestler, an indubitably creative individual himself, defines creative acts as "the combination of previously unrelated structures in such a way that you get more out of the emergent whole than you have put in" (*Act of Creation*, New York, Macmillan, 1964). He divides creativity or originality into three segments: artistic originality (the "ah!" reaction), scientific discovery (the "aha!" reaction) and comic imagination (the "haha!" reaction).

According to the Office of Education, gifted children constitute three to five percent of our school population—perhaps a total of 1.5 to 2.5 million children— from all races and levels of society, rich and poor, urban and rural, sometimes physically or emotionally impaired.

But such children are often neglected in our school systems, particularly if they are disadvantaged by poverty or disabling conditions, or even if they exhibit too much of that comic imagination that Koestler considers a vital segment of originality and creativity.

Our traditional intelligence tests, which test to measure intelligence components like memory, cognition and convergent thinking, tend to uncover the Lewis Terman set of (teacher-identified) gifted children, those whose particular abilities correlate rather well with success in school. Even for those gifted children who work hard, memorize well and obey rules without questions, traditional instructional materials are inappropriate. All but the most docile gifted children find these repetitive, unchallenging and, above all, excruciatingly boring.

In too many school situations, gifted children, who may be pushed by parents and who may have problems coping with their own intellect, are confronted by unrealistically high expectations from teachers, resentment from other children and a lack of appropriate programs to challenge their abilities and interests. Many educators, unfortunately, are indifferent or hostile to the needs of the gifted. As one study of the self-images on Stanley Coopersmith's Self-Esteem Inventory by Robert Trotter in *Science News* indicated, children of high intelligence, as compared to children of average intelligence, have significantly lower self-concepts except in the roles related to home and family. While average children feel themselves easy to like and fun to be with, gifted children feel less sure of themselves with teachers and peers and believe that their teachers expect too much of them. Despite this, they are more prepared than average children to say what they have to say and to stick to their opinions. Because of their impressive intellectual development, it is sometimes hard for teachers (or parents) to recognize that gifted children function on the same emotional level as other children, they are not miniature adults with adult strengths or aims or interests. To cope with their own intellect, gifted children may need help in bringing their emotional and intellectual capacities into balance.

They do thrive on intellectual stimulation and recognition when their needs as children are met in the process. Gifted children need a scholarly and/or stimulating education within a humane school environment. Too many gifted children in too many schools are lonely, alienated, bored and shunned by other children. If they are limited to standard texts or easy reading materials, they are frequently able to get by without working or thinking. They may become scornful of teachers, school and other students, or may substitute bizarre behavior or pursuit of their own interests for academic achievement.

Cognitive and affective criteria can be helpful in choosing materials for gifted children, who should be exposed to a wide range of intellectual processes. These children are always in danger of becoming premature specialists or walking encyclopedias. Generally, gifted children learn holistically; they are impatient of repetition (especially exact repetition) and enjoy handling abstractions.

While they do need individualization, they should be encouraged to handle problems sufficiently challenging that they cannot get by without effort. Since gifted children work largely from intrinsic motivations, their individual projects should be on a level consistent with their aptitudes and abilities.

Gifted and creative children, in general, learn best from materials that are intellectually challenging, experimental, offbeat, playful and attuned to discussion and problem solving. Most of them, if they are interested, are capable of concentration and hard work, and may be better off working with other students. Even the strong individualists need some successful group experiences.

For gifted children who are adept at abstractions, materials should be included that are high on Dale's Cone of Experience (page 19). Art and print should include humor, divergent thinking, first-hand source materials, a good variety of reference books, divergent points of view, a variety of perspectives and materials that emphasize concepts and values rather than accumulations of information.

Since gifted children are capable of high-level productions, materials with high aesthetic qualities should be selected from all media. Materials for the gifted should illuminate and expand their horizons by being academically provocative and by providing opportunities for interaction and the development of empathy. Materials that integrate several fields provide horizontal enrichment, but should be combined with some materials that can be pursued independently.

Gifted children need materials that enable them to tap into their own possibilities. Print materials should be well-written and should examine emotional areas and/or encourage precise writing and exact shades of meaning. Historical fiction and science fiction are two genres particularly appropriate for gifted students. But those who learn well with words and memory also need some hands-on experiences—original discovery—so they are not constantly regurgitating or rearranging other people's words and ideas. Creative students who learn better through creation rather than authority also need exploratory and manipulative materials. Games are challenging and inviting, particularly if they can be played with peers. Simulations and drama can help students imagine and perceive other points of view.

A Program Checklist of Gifted-Child Education and Talent Development, prepared by the California State Department of Education in 1971, suggests that gifted children needed access to the following materials and equipment:

- books, magazines, scholarly journals and newspapers

- items used in biology, chemistry, physics and other laboratory work

- materials needed to build experimental equipment

- art materials such as paints, plastic clay, portfolios, prints

- realia

- films, filmstrips, charts, maps, blueprints, slides, diagrams

- computing devices like abacuses, calculators, computers

- tape recorders, telescopes, sextants, surveying and mapping equipment

- cameras, microscopes and meteorological equipment

This *Checklist* also suggests access to a variety of environments (social, economic, cultural, ecological and educational), access to ideas, access to experiences, and access to persons. While all of these seem important, access to persons may be the most important. Studies of genius stress the importance of a long and continuous contact with supportive adults or adults who serve in some way as mentors or teachers. Beyond their first-hand experiences, children should be aware of exemplary creators in all fields. Women models may be particularly important for gifted girls.

In response to my query, Virginia Coatney, coordinator of gifted elementary programs in the Richmond (California) Unified School District, defined the proper materials for gifted students as those which "enable the student to perform the creative processes of substituting, rearranging and redesigning in order to create or generate 'new' ideas." She also included the following list of criteria for selection of materials for mentally gifted minors:

- Flexible
- Open-ended
- Multi-disciplinary
- Versatile
- Process Oriented
- Adaptable
- Sequential
- Consumable
- Issue Oriented

- Accessible
- Durable
- Stimulate divergent thinking
- Self-correcting
- Availability
- Promotes in-depth learning
- Self-pacing
- Provides for advanced learning

Gifted children need access to community resources such as beaches, parks, natural history walks, museums, concerts, plays, art galleries, historical sites and special classes where they have a chance to extend their interests and develop a knowledge of history, institutions and culture.

A few criteria for choosing among activities and materials were developed by Operation ASTRA in Hartford, Connecticut. The questions below are based on a report by Joseph Renzulli in *Exceptional Children* (April 1970):

- Are specific intellectual skills and abilities being challenged by these materials or activities?
- If so, which ones?
- Would these materials or activities extend or intensify curricular areas?
- Do the materials emphasize knowledge for its own sake or are they directed toward activities with transfer value?
- Does mastery depend largely on memory?
- Do the learning experiences differ from those in the standard curriculum?
- Do they provide students with opportunities to draw conclusions, to generalize and to suggest other applications?
- Do they allow opportunities for creativity and originality?
- Are the materials intrinsically interesting?

Disadvantaged gifted children, or disabled gifted children, depending upon their educational and home experiences, may have relatively weak academic skills. A surprising number read considerably below their potential abilities—sometimes to the point of remediation. But there are also those children who learned to read before they went to school, who are understandably restless and disruptive when given assignments in preprimers. (I know one child from a non-reading family who taught himself to read at four with stolen comic books.)

Because of their life circumstances, the abilities of gifted and disabled or disadvantaged children may not shine through on standard IQ tests. In kids from deprived backgrounds, experienced educators look for unusual resourcefulness; outstanding skills, achievements or creative products in any area; precocious development or maturation in primary years; or a score in the 98th percentile on non-verbal performance parts of individual intelligence tests. (Parents tend, overall, to be better at identifying such children.)

Educators in Los Angeles, who work with large groups of disadvantaged gifted children, recommend spending blocks of time on teaching thinking skills—such as general comprehension, memory and concentration, vocabulary and verbal fluency, judgment and reasoning, and visual and motor ability—through games, experiences in critical thinking, lessons in problem solving and vocabulary enrichment. For raising self-confidence, they advocate a wide exposure to creative, intellectual and social experiences. For creativity, they work with fine arts and manipulative skills. They use, as well as games, a variety of direct life experiences, from judging distances to observing court systems.

Disabled or disadvantaged gifted children, like other gifted children, may not be equally gifted in all subjects or skills. I have known many verbally-gifted, high-IQ children with average or below average mathematical abilities who have been forced into advanced math groups and humiliated by their failures. A high score on an IQ test, of course, is no guarantee that a child is well organized, the possessor of good work habits or equipped with large stores of knowledge and skills.

Conversely, many children with modest IQ scores may be gifted in particular fields or have such strong interests in these fields that—for practical purposes—they are gifted. Gifted children, like other children, have strengths, weaknesses and individual preferences that should be respected.

The S.O.I. Institute's tests and templates discussed in the chapter on cognitive criteria (see pages 125-43) do provide one means of assessing abilities and skills more precisely, as well as means to balance deficiencies.

KEY ORGANIZATIONS

The Key Organizations listed in the chapter entitled "Thinking about Thinking" are perhaps more important in providing criteria for gifted education than the organizations more specifically directed toward the gifted.

Since giftedness is considered an exceptionality, the chapter on special education covers some organizations which may be helpful, including the Council for Exceptional Children which houses a clearinghouse on the gifted.

The federal agency most aware of legislation and funding may be:

> Office of Gifted and Talented
> U.S. Office of Education
> Donohoe Bldg., Room 3827
> Sixth and D Streets, SW
> Washington, DC 20024
> (202) 245-2483

**National State Leadership Training Institute on the
Gifted and Talented (N/S-LTI-G/T)**
316 West 2nd St., PH-C
Los Angeles, CA 90012　　　　　　　　(213) 489-7470

The N/S-LTI-G/T was founded in 1971 following a U.S. Commissioner's Report to Congress on gifted and talented education. Its purpose is to train state teams to write plans and/or strengthen programs for gifted and talented children. Currently it is funded under Section 404 of Public Law 93-380 and administered by the Ventura County (California) Superintendent of Schools.

It offers contractual services in all phases of gifted education including awareness, identification, programming and evaluations. It has developed workshops, trained consultants and advocates at all levels and established exemplary programs cooperatively with local school districts.

Its publications include a monthly *Bulletin* of about eight pages ($12.50/yr.) with semi-annual topical supplements ($1.10 each). *Groups for Gifted and Talented* is a monthly four-page excerpt from the *Bulletin* priced low for quantity distribution. Other publications are directed to parents, teachers and administrators. A few posters, brochures and flyers are also available. A free publications list is available on request. Some publications that deal—to a degree—with materials are:

> *Providing Programs for the Gifted and Talented*, by Sandra Kaplan. 264p. $5.75.
>> A supplemental resource book for designing and activating programs that covers initiation, program prototypes, designing curriculum and preparation.

> *Developing a Written Plan for the Education of Gifted and Talented Students*, by Irving S. Sato, et al. 62p. $3.00.
>> Provides a framework for writing individualized plans.

> *A Guidebook for Evaluating Programs for the Gifted and Talented*, by Herbert Kanigher. 97p. $3.75.
>> Includes a chapter on evaluation models and concepts, as well as sample forms, instruments, scales and four topical bibliographies.

> *Everyday Enrichment for Gifted Children at Home and School*, by Herbert Kanigher. 97p. $3.75.
>> Provides projects and ideas in art, geography, language, mathematics, music, and science.

> *Promising Practices: Teaching the Disadvantaged Gifted.* 57p. $2.70.

KEY PUBLICATIONS

Other important publications are prepared by the Council for Exceptional Children (discussed under Special Education) and the National/State Leadership Institute on the Gifted and the Talented, listed as a Key Organization. Many school districts and states compile lists of criteria for gifted programs or listed materials they believe to be appropriate for gifted students. I have included here only materials I was able to inspect myself and which include useful materials, programs or approaches for understanding or educating gifted students.

Activities for Motivating and Teaching Bright Children, by Rosalind Minor Ashley. West Nyack, NY, Parker, 1973. 204p. $9.95.

Includes ideas, activities and suggestions for materials for children who are verbally bright and talented in mechanics, math, art and in other fields. Suggests sources for information and/or materials at nominal costs, and for games, math, art, science and social studies.

Brain and Intelligence: The Ecology of Child Development, edited by Frederick Richardson. Hyattsville, MD, National Education Press, 1973. 326p. $16.00.

An authoritative anthology which discusses the complex developmental, genetic, environmental, nutritional and biochemical influences on concept formation, brain functioning and other aspects of intelligence.

Career Education for Gifted and Talented Students, edited by Kenneth B. Hoyt and Jean R. Hebeler. Salt Lake City, Olympus, 1974. 293p. $9.95; $6.95pa.

Explores the future of work, special career development problems of gifted students and the value considerations in career education. Separate chapters summarize exemplary programs and analyze administration and policy considerations in career education for the gifted.

Developing Creativity in Children: An Idea Book for Teachers, by Charles E. Schaefer. Buffalo, NY, D.O.K., 1973. 99p. $4.95.

Includes 63 interesting, provocative activities to stimulate sensory awareness, scientific thinking and/or expression through graphics, construction, drama, poetry and prose. Many possibilities for creative variations.

The Farther Reaches of Human Nature, by Abraham Maslow. New York, Viking Press, 1971. 340p. $12.50. Penguin, $2.95pa.

Posthumous papers by Abraham Maslow deal with creativity, the goal of education, neurosis as a failure of personal growth and with other factors related to education and actualization.

Games Students Play (and What to Do About Them), by Kenneth Ernst. Millbrae, CA, Celestial Arts, 1972. 127p. $7.95; $4.50pa.

Applies Eric Berne's transactional analysis model to some student-teacher classroom interactions often found in gifted classes.

Memory and Intelligence, translated and edited by Arnold J. Pomerans. New York, Basic Books, 1973. 414p. $12.50.

Carefully detailed exploration of memory, with a number of constructive ideas on its development and utilization.

Process Education, by Henry P. Cole. Englewood Cliffs, NJ, Educational Technology Pubs., 1972. 261p. $12.95.

Provides definitions, rationales and goals for process education—a form of education that places major emphasis on mastering the intellectual processes that promote learning and problem solving.

Programs for Gifted/Talented/Creative Children, by Ruth F. Lawless. Buffalo, NY, D.O.K., 1977. 48p. $2.95.

Provides a guide for kindergarten through twelfth grade and curriculum areas for inexpensive program alternatives for gifted youngsters, with bibliographies of sources.

The Range of Human Capacities, by David Wechsler. New York, Hafner, 1969. 190p. $11.95.

A study of human behavioral and physical capabilities based on such socio-scientific disciplines as sociology and anthropology.

FOR FURTHER READING

*Items marked with an asterisk include criteria.
+Items marked with a plus include substantial lists of references.

+American Associated for Gifted Children. *The Gifted Child*, ed. by Paul Witty. Westport, CT, Greenwood, 1972.

Baughman, M. Dale. *Challenging Talented Junior High School Youth*. Danville, IL, Interstate, 1977.

*California State Department of Education. *Gifted-Child Education and Talent Development Programs Checklist*. Sacramento, CA, 1971.

Chicago Board of Education. *Enrichment Materials for Gifted and Advanced Children at All Levels and in All Curriculum Areas*. Chicago, Programs and Services for the Gifted, 1974.

*Cohen, Daniel. *Intelligence: What Is It?* New York, Evans, 1974.

+Cohen, Monroe C., ed. *Literature, Creativity, and Imagination*. Washington, Association for Childhood Education International, 1973.

+Council for Exceptional Children. *Productive Thinking of Gifted Children in Classroom Interaction*. Reston, VA, CEC, 1967.

Davis, Gary A. *Training Creative Thinking*. New York, Holt, Rinehart and Winston, 1971.

DeBono, Edward. *Lateral Thinking. Creativity Step by Step*. New York, Harper & Row, 1970.

*+Gallagher, James J. *Teaching the Gifted Child*. 2nd ed. Boston, Allyn & Bacon, 1975.

*+Cowan, John C., and Ellis Paul Torrance, eds. *Educating the Ablest: A Book of Readings*. Itasca, IL, Peacock, 1971.

Kaplan, Sandra H. *Activities for Gifted Children*. Santa Monica, CA, Goodyear, 1979.

Koestler, Arthur. *Three Domains of Creativity.* New York, Macmillan, 1964.

Labuda, Michael, ed. *Creative Reading for Gifted Learners: A Design for Excellence.* Newark, DE, International Reading Association, 1972. (ED 094 357).

*+Lord, Ann, and Philip Seyer. *Teaching Mentally Gifted Students in Rural Areas* (book and cassettes). Berkeley, CA, University of California Extension Independent Study, 1978.

Lyon, Harold C., Jr. "Talent Down the Drain," *American Education*, v. 8, no. 8 (Oct. 1972), pp. 12-16.

*+Maker, C. June. *Providing Programs for the Gifted Handicapped.* Reston, VA, Council for Exceptional Children, 1977.

+Nazarro, Jean, ed. *Exceptional Timetables: Historical Events Affecting the Handicapped and Gifted.* Reston, VA, Council for Exceptional Children, 1977.

*Raph, Jane B., et al. *Bright Underachievers.* New York, Teachers College Press, 1966.

*Renzulli, Joseph S. "A Curriculum Development Model for Academically Superior Students," *Exceptional Children*, v. 36, no. 8 (April 1970), pp. 611-14.

*Renzulli, Joseph S. *The Enrichment Triad Model: A Guide for Developing Defensible Programs for the Gifted and Talented.* Weathersfield, CT, Creative Learning Press, 1977.

*+Rice, Joseph. *The Gifted: Developing Total Talent.* Springfield, IL, Thomas, 1970.

*+Torrance, Ellis Paul. *Education and the Creative Potential.* Minneapolis, University of Minnesota Press, 1963.

*+Torrance, Ellis Paul. *Guiding Creative Talent.* Englewood Cliffs, NJ, Prentice-Hall, 1962.

*+White, Alan J., ed. *Curriculum Guidelines for the Gifted and Talented: Report of the Connecticut Task Force on Curriculum.* Hartford, CT, Connecticut State Department of Education, 1974. (ED 093 118).

SELECTING MATERIALS FOR YOUNG CHILDREN

Among those selecting materials for young children, there is widespread agreement that developmental criteria are the most important. There are, however, several schools of thought about child development. *A*, or perhaps *the*, key question on EPIE's *Report 42, Early Childhood Education*, was: Where do you stand on development? The choices included behavioral-environmental, maturational and comprehensive-interactional, a less than exhaustive list.

Inevitably, one's view of the process of development affects the selection of programs, materials and experiences. While research shows that young humans (like young monkeys, rats and dogs) are more successful as social animals and problem solvers when raised in an enriched environment, we have not reached absolute agreement on what the optimum enrichment should be. We know these experiences are particularly vital for children whose home environments may be deficient for one reason or another.

For this age group it is particularly difficult to isolate materials since they are part of a total environment and total program, which together should meet the physical, emotional, social and intellectual needs of young children. For this reason I have cited a few references that deal with requirements for programs and learning environments. Since parents are often the major educators, I have also included some materials written for parents that seemed educationally sound.

The Equipment and Supplies Committee of the Association for Childhood Education International (ACEI)—see Key Organizations—suggests that the developmental needs to be considered in educational equipment and materials are:

- Basic environmental needs, such as furniture, permanent equipment, housekeeping and maintenance, audiovisual equipment and materials and expendables

- Physical growth considerations, such as health and safety and motor skills

- Intellectual growth in terms of perception, communication, computation, scientific thinking, etc.

- Socio-emotional balance, which involves community awareness, creative expression, arts and crafts, construction, music, dramatics and puppetry, etc.

Nancy Quisenberry and her colleagues, in their "Criteria for the Selection of Records, Filmstrips and Films for Young Children" (*Audiovisual Instruction*, April 1973), suggest the developmental concepts of aesthetic value, concept development, experience with literature, interpersonal relationships, language development, movement and self-actualization for selecting particular items. They suggest that aesthetic values should:

- foster an appreciation of beauty, art forms and creative effort

- arouse feelings of pleasure for elements of color, texture and line

Concept development should:

- be based on a child's natural curiosity
- refine meanings
- promote awareness, understanding and general principles

Experiences with literature should:

- provide vicarious awakenings
- introduce children to past and distant worlds
- expand horizons
- encourage fantasy
- promote self-actualization in different roles: Who am I? What might I be?

Language development aspects should enhance:

- vocabulary
- expansion of speech patterns
- fluency
- flexibility
- dialectal identity

Some other developmental values advocated by Robert James Havighurst in *Developmental Tasks and Education* (1972) are self-appraisal, overcoming fears, age-mate relationships, family relations, intercultural understandings and social responsibility. Many of these developmental tasks can be enhanced through works of literature selected on a young child's level. Barbara Williams, in *Toys to Go* (1976) merely suggests materials for strengthening large muscles, stretching the mind, pretending and releasing emotions.

In terms of Dale's Cone of Experience (see page 19), then, young children would need direct experiences, concrete materials (manipulatives, toys, realia and physical development equipment—all appropriate to their developmental stages), materials for concept development (books, films, live dramas and stories, art, manipulatives and realia) and materials for arousing sympathy (direct experiences and vicarious experiences through literature as well as art in different media).

Patricia Markun's *Play: Children's Business* (1974) cited in *Media and Curriculum*, suggests some relationships between types of play activities, like sorting and matching, and such school skills as reading skills, science skills, mathematics skills, and writing skills. This book also includes suggestions for toys and activities appropriate for particular developmental ages and stages. This approach goes back a long way. Paul Monroe's *Encyclopedia of Education*, published between 1911 and 1913, has a very interesting chart under Games: "A Summary of Active Plays and Games Most Beneficial at Different Ages." Piaget and Montessori, discussed more fully in the chapter entitled "Thinking about Thinking," deal in different ways with concepts of readiness and development, Piaget with a detailed exposition of stages. Montessori's approach—grouping children from the ages of, say, three to seven together, while arranging carefully-selected materials by difficulty—allows children to select materials for themselves, while using other (sometimes older) children as models. In this situation, older children similarly learn by teaching. In these circumstances, Montessori believed, the children themselves would choose to work with didactic materials appropriate to their particular needs and stages of development. The role of the teacher, in this case, is that of an observor-facilitator who sometimes assists children in their spontaneous efforts to use materials. These approaches are covered in more detail in Key Publications.

Sensory education and perceptual education are generally considered an important aspect of preschool education. In addition to manipulatives, realia, real objects and purchased kits, books, art works and non-print materials can also be useful in sensory training. Ronnie Goodfriend's *Power in Perception for the Young Child* (1972) has a thoughtful section on children's books which is arranged by concept (number and sequencing, self and perspective, spatial concepts, etc.) and fully annotated. For example, Phoebe Erickson's *Who's in the Mirror?* (Knopf, 1965) is suggested for use in development of self-image. A good children's librarian working from an adequate children's library could provide comparable lists from his/her own collection. Topics like color, seasons, weather, shapes and music can even be approached through subjects and cross-references in the card catalog. I have included in my citations criteria as well as kits for using books with young children. Books chosen for young children should, of course, meet standards for literary and visual quality as well as for the handling of concepts. Special educators have also paid a great deal of attention to tactile stimuli and tactile learning. Such sources—often useful for preschool youngsters—are treated in the chapter on special education.

Materials from nature—mud, sand, leaves, corn cobs and the like—are valuable sensory tools which have other values for learning. ACEI's *Selecting Educational Equipment and Materials for School and Home* (see Key Publications) has a very sensitive article by Oralie McAfee which addresses the question, "To Make or to Buy?" and weighs the pros and cons of natural materials, locally-produced materials and purchased materials. Other criteria are available in the chapter entitled "Teachers' Roles in Selection," in this volume, and the chapter on free and inexpensive materials in *Media and Curriculum.*

Pictures, which are very easily obtained, are an inexpensive teaching tool for young children, who can use them for such things as naming objects, observing details, drawing inferences, relating pictures to personal experiences, adding imaginative elements and engaging in activities suggested by pictures. Catherine Williams' *Learning from Pictures* (1968) would be a useful tool for selecting or using pictures with young children.

PEN (*Preschool Education Newsletter*) included a list of criteria in its October 1972 issue, which were largely directed toward evaluating collections of purchased materials and which are quite useful in the selection of materials for young children.

Also useful are the "Criteria for Selection of Single Items of Equipment and Materials" (see page 346), which are reprinted here with permission from page 28 of *Selecting Educational Equipment and Materials for School and Home*, a particularly useful publication. This material is published and copyrighted as of 1976 by the Association for Childhood Education International, and is not to be used without permission of the Association, 3615 Wisconsin Avenue, NW, Washington, DC 20016.

Criteria for Selection of Single Items of Equipment and Materials

Equipment and Supplies Committees (1967-1973)

Functional Requirements

Does the material possess the following features?

Safety*

- non-toxic and easily cleaned
- designed to avoid injury from sharp edges, protruding parts, tipping, splinters, electrical, mechanical and thermal hazards
- flame resistant

Durability

- strong enough to withstand heavy usage
- resistant to weathering
- easy to care for and store

Adaptability

- appropriate in size and form for intended ages
- usable in more than one way
- nonsexist

Accountability

- reasonably priced
- appealing on a long-term basis

Educational Requirements

Does the material contribute to growth in the following areas?

Intellectual

- accomplishes a variety of purposes within given or related areas
- adapts to different ages, needs, interests and abilities

Intellectual (cont'd)

- arouses curiosity, stimulates initiative and invites exploration
- provides for concrete experience as a basis for abstract learning
- involves as many of the senses as appropriate
- promotes thinking and encourages practical problem-solving
- stimulates skill development and broadening of concepts

Physical

- motivates action
- allows freedom of movement
- stimulates muscle development and coordination

Social/Emotional

- encourages a favorable attitude toward self and others
- stimulates imaginative and creative responses
- provides opportunities for a variety of individual, partner and group activities
- gives pleasure

---

*For many useful safety suggestions with reference to children's play and educational materials, write to the U.S. Consumer Product Safety Commission, 5401 Westbard Avenue, Washington, DC 20207.

ACEI's *Selecting Educational Equipment and Materials for School and Home* also includes specific suggestions for the selection of materials to foster intellectual growth and for materials that promote socio-emotional balance as well as sections on "Basic Environmental Needs" and "Physical Growth." These suggestions comprise 1) extensive lists of items particularly helpful in the development of a child's perceptual, communicative, mathematic and rational skills as well as of his/her community awareness and creative expressiveness and 2) recommendations for the age levels at which these items should be employed. The example reprinted below from pages 34-35 of *Selecting Educational Equipment and Materials for School and Home*, like the criteria reproduced on page 346, are not to be reproduced further without permission from the Association for Childhood Education International.

MATERIALS FOR INTELLECTUAL GROWTH

PERCEPTION

Perception is the process by which we make sense out of the environment. Through the process of perceiving—seeing, hearing, feeling, smelling, tasting—we receive, select and organize impressions. Since future learnings depend upon earlier perceptions, it is essential that children's earliest impressions be as accurate as possible.

Materials for Perceptual Development	AGES				Materials for Perceptual Development	AGES			
	0–3	3–6	6–10	10–14		0–3	3–6	6–10	10–14
Balloons to blow up, fly, pop		X	X	X	*Crib mobiles*, such as strings of large plastic colored beads or wooden spools strung across the crib	X			
Blocks, to strike or rub together	X	X							
Cloth of different textures to feel: linen, felt, plush, silk, velvet	X	X			*Design blocks*	X	X	X	X
Color cones	X	X	X		*Flowers* to smell	X	X	X	X
Cooking pans, for manipulation and/or cooking	X	X	X	X	*Food* of different seasonings	X	X	X	X
Jigsaw puzzles of varying difficulty	X	X	X	X	*Records* of soft music, simple tunes	X	X		
Kites, to watch, make, fly	X	X	X	X	*Sand boxes* with digging tools and containers for pouring and sifting	X	X		
Nature materials of different textures: rocks, pebbles, sand, clay; hard and soft wood, bark; leaves, seeds, fruits, vegetables	X	X	X	X	*Sorters* for shapes, colors and forms	X	X		
Nested play materials: blocks, boxes, cans, pans	X	X			*Tops* for spinning and watching	X	X	X	X
Rattles of pleasing tone quality	X	X			*Water-play materials* for pouring, floating, measuring, siphoning	X	X	X	X
					Wind chimes	X	X	X	X

KEY ORGANIZATIONS

Some other relevant organizations are listed as Key Organizations in the chapter on toys in *Media and Curriculum*, and on pages 138-39 and 304-324 of this volume.

Association for Childhood Education International (ACEI)
3615 Wisconsin Avenue, NW
Washington, DC 20016   (202) 363-6963

This international, nonprofit organization, which began as the International Kindergarten Union in 1892, is open to all individuals concerned with the education and well-being of children (from infancy to early adolescence), in school or out. Its members include teachers, parents, administrators, librarians, nursery school and day care personnel, community workers, pediatricians and others in more than 70 countries. It sponsors regional, national, and international conferences as well as summer and winter workshops which call attention to the needs of children and facilitate cooperation among groups and individuals who work with children at all levels.

Major interest areas are child development, early childhood education, reading and day care. About 30 volunteer committees provide policies and guidelines for its programs. Its position papers, typically, are broadly based and well thought out.

In its headquarters office in Washington, DC, ACEI houses a Childhood Education Center, an information center that answers more than 6,000 queries each year and includes materials, displays, and a meeting room in addition to a professional library.

Childhood Education, the Association's periodical, is included in membership (five issues a year from October to April/May). This periodical is often a quasi-monograph devoting perhaps four of its five yearly issues to specific themes.

While ACEI is not primarily a publisher, its publications are exceptionally helpful and well researched. Some that deal with materials include:

Bibliography of Books for Children, 1977. 112p. $3.75pa.
　　Annotated list; titles arranged by age level and subject; major awards noted.

Bits & Pieces—Imaginative Uses for Children's Learning, 1967. 72p. $2.00.
　　Recycling of finds, leftovers, giveaways and throwaways for creative learning in school or home.

The Child and Science—Wondering, Exploring, Growing, 1977. 48p. $2.75.
　　More than 30 suggestions for innovative and practical science activities for two to twelve year olds, with a chapter on evaluation.

Children and Intercultural Education, 1974. 72p. $1.50pa.
　　Kit of three booklets; useful in developing appreciation for cultural diversity and in sensitizing teachers to ethnicity. Reports and interprets research.

Children and International Education, 1972. $1.00pa.
　　Portfolio of ten leaflets on ways of developing international understanding and fellowship in children and those who work with them. Suggests many activities and resources.

Children and TV—Television's Impact on the Child, 1967. 64p. $1.25pa.
　　Looks at program content, what TV teaches, use and abuse of the medium, guidance by parents, TV as curriculum. Thirteen stimulating contributions.

Children Are Centers for Understanding Media, 1973. 94p. $3.95.
Fifteen articles; resource list. Ideas for involving children as photographers, filmmakers, videotapers and sound-seekers. Practical help for teachers.

Child's Right to Humane Treatment, position paper by Helen T. Suchara, 1977. 7p. $0.35pa.
　　Advocates humane experience for and a nurturing of humaneness in children. Lists expectations of adults.

Child's Right to the Expressive Arts, position paper by Arne J. Nixon, 1969. 12p. $0.25pa.
　　Encourages development of environments that allow creativity to flourish; summarizes a child's rights.

Creating with Materials for Work and Play, 1969. $2.00.
Portfolio of 12 leaflets. Varied media and materials and building learning from them. Practical, useful ideas for art, dance, science, drama and more.

Developing Programs for Infants and Toddlers, 1977. 76p. $3.25.
Eleven educators discuss practical concerns and program issues;
glimpses of model child care centers and training sites. Bibliography.

Films for Childhood Educators, 1977. 24p. $1.25.
Collection of film reviews for classes on teaching and parenting. Thematic groupings; distributor list and rental/purchase information.

Good and Inexpensive Books for Children, 1972. 64p. $2.00.
Selections chosen for quality and price. Classified by fiction, biography,
picture books, hobbies, etc. Includes author and title indexes; publisher list.

Growing Free: Ways to Help Children Overcome Sex-Role Stereotypes,
1976. 32p. $1.00.
Examination of questions/concerns with suggestions for meaningful
response, building positive futures. Resource list.

Guide to Children's Magazines, Newspapers, Reference Books, 1977. 12p.
$0.75.
Annotated list designed to acquaint parents and teachers with qualitative literature.

Involvement Bulletin Boards, 1970. 64p. $2.25.
The place of bulletin boards in learning experiences; construction of
and relationship to curriculum. Brightly illustrated.

Kindergarten Portfolio, 1970. $2.00.
Portfolio of 14 leaflets on attitudes, environment, teacher-child-
principal relationships, the program and parental involvement. Includes
extensive bibliography.

Learning Centers—Children on Their Own. 84p. $2.50.
Combines theory and practice. Describes models of individualized teaching. Discusses roles, organization, evaluation, helpful hardware and open space.

Literature with Children, 1972. 64p. $2.50.
Explores how to provide rich and balanced contacts with literature. Use
of critiques, records of reading, poetry, choral reading, story telling, dramatization, multi-media. Teacher resource list.

New Views of School and Community, 1973. 64p. $3.50.
Nine educators offer practical and original ideas for relating school and
community. Vignettes of outstanding projects; extensive classified bibliography. Joint publication of ACEI and NAESP.

Nursery School Portfolio, 1969. $2.25.
The whys and wherefores of nursery school. Sixteen leaflets cover many
aspects of early learning, programs, observation, evaluation, discipline, etc.

Young Deprived Children and Their Educational Needs, by Barbara Biber,
1967. 16p. $0.50.
What are the special needs of and the impact of deprivation on young
children? School role in making up for neglect.

Bank Street College of Education
601 West 11th Street
New York, NY 10025   (201) 663-7200
Bank Street College, established in 1916, is a versatile, humanistic institution
of higher education which conducts research and action programs on the learning
process and the roles of school, home and community as factors in personality
development. It simultaneously conducts its own independent school and creates
children's literature as well as materials for training adults in educational fields.
It also runs a bookstore whose shelves reflect the college's general philosophy; the
bookstore is an excellent source of materials for children, with additional books
carefully chosen for parents, teachers and education students working with children.
Since 1972 Bank Street has issued an annual Bank Street Award for excellence in
children's literature. This particular award is distinctive in that books selected by a
panel of adults are field-tested on a variety of children whose views are given equal
weight in reaching the final selection.
Education before Five, a recent publication written by senior faculty and
associates (1978. $5.00), intelligently explores each of the major theoretical posi-
tions and programs in preschool education. Positions reported include those of
Montessori, Piaget, the progressive movement, the behavioral approach, the develop-
mental-interaction approach and the psychoanalytic approach—all with extensive
print and film bibliographies. Models described include infant programs, programs
for the handicapped, day care, head start, home start and parent/child centers.
Bank Street's *Threshold Learning Library* consists of an on-going series of
manuals ($7.95 each) for teachers of children between three and seven. These deal
with "Perceptual and Organizing Skills," "Math Skills and Scientific Inquiry,"
"Language Skills and Social Concepts," "Music and Movement Improvisation,"
"Art Experiences for Young Children," "Creative Dramatization," "Physical Skills
for Young Children," and "Health and Safety for Young Children."
Some other publications related to materials include: *Invitation to Reading*
($1.00), *The Library: Closet or Classroom* ($1.00), *Bank Street Readers* (a
multicultural, urban-oriented reading series), and *Science Experiences in Early
Childhood* ($1.00).

Day Care and Child Development Council of America (DCCDCA)
622 14th Street, NW
Washington, DC 20005   (202) 638-2316
The major purpose of this nonprofit membership advocacy group is to extend
and upgrade child care programs. Its interests include the social, physical, emotional and intellectual development of children, policy roles for parents and adequate training and pay for child care staff. It is a valuable source of data on all
aspects of child care and a major disseminator of information through a catalog,
Resources for Day Care, listing publications selected and assembled from many
sources. The more recent catalogs include some materials selected specifically for
children which are offered at a slight discount to members. Overall, the publications
listed in *Resources* might be most valuable in selecting or evaluating programs.

Montessori: Nienheus
P.O. Box 16
Selhem, Holland
The Montessori materials stemming from this original Montessori developer and supplier are authentic and beautifully constructed. Though expensive, they are built to last.

The Vital Years
Educational Supply Association, Limited (ESA)
School Materials Division
Pinnacles, P.O. Box 22
Harlow, Essex
England
Their extensive catalog of early-childhood materials draws from a wide variety of sources around the world. Many of the European-made materials are considered to be of higher quality than those made in America; often they are cheaper.

KEY PUBLICATIONS

In addition to the publications listed below, some EPIE *Reports* are worthwhile reading for anyone selecting materials or programs for young children. Toys and manipulatives, a frequent choice for young children, and pictures, another effective medium, are both treated fully in *Media and Curriculum.* The annotation for ACEI in Key Organizations includes many of that Association's most useful publications.

Arranging the Classroom for Young Children, by Keith R. Alward. San Francisco, Far West Laboratory for Educational Research, 1973. 237p. $8.95. (From 1855 Folsom St., San Francisco, CA 94103.)
A twelve-chapter Learner's Guide, complete with learning activities and checklists, which concentrates on classroom areas and activities functionally related to curricular and social objectives. The first part of the book deals with arranging and evaluating classroom areas and covers learning centers, the relationship between classroom arrangement and behavior, variations, physical flexibility and a plan for change. The second section, on facilities and resources, covers storage, working places and seating, the floor, raised and enclosed areas, room and area dividers. Appendices include relevant addresses, bibliographic references, a films list and a helpful checklist-chart of found objects.

Arranging the Informal Classroom, by Brenda S. Engel. Newton, MA, Education Development Center, 1973. 88p. $3.60. (From Publications Office, 55 Chapel St., Newton, MA 02160.)
A guide to classroom environment which discusses such basic considerations as walls, doors and windows and furniture options, as well as the kinds of space and materials which are required for or can be used for art, math, music, science and dramatic play. Includes sample plans with an emphasis on ingenuity rather than on cash outlay.

Baby Learning through Baby Play, by Ira J. Gordon. New York, St. Martin's
   Press, 1970. 121p. $4.95.
   This easy-to-read book describes games with a variety of interesting and
challenging things to do; most are designed to bring pleasure, security, self-
esteem and intellectual growth to the child. Games are designed primarily for, but
certainly not limited to, the child from three months to two years.

The Child's First Books: A Critical Study of Pictures and Texts, by Donnarae
   MacCann and Richard Olga. New York, Wilson, 1973. 135p. $12.00.
   This book, complete with fine color and black-and-white reproductions, provides a basic education in aesthetics. The authors discuss graphic elements in picture books by analyzing the works of 13 contemporary illustrators, to establish
standards for line, color, shape, texture, composition and style. Also discusses
desirable qualities in narrative style, using seven writers for examples, and includes
an evaluation of folklore for children.

Early Childhood Curriculum Materials: An Annotated Bibliography, compiled by
   Gloria Harbin and Lee Cross. New York, Walker Educational Book Co.,
   1976. 125p. $6.95pa.
   This annotated bibliography, published for the Technical Assistance Development System (a division of the Frank Porter Graham Child Development Center
at the University of North Carolina), is designed as a sourcebook for educators
selecting commercial programs for early childhood education with some emphasis
on programs which can be adapted to meet the needs of young handicapped children. It provides thorough, descriptive (non-evaluative) annotations for approximately 75 curriculum programs, conveniently grouped by developmental area
(gross motor, fine motor, perception, reasoning, language, social, infants and core)
using analytic criteria developed by EPIE.
   Though the annotations scrupulously avoid the appearance of evaluation,
there is some unspecified evaluation in the selections. A few books are annotated,
while others of equal value are omitted. For the material covered, however, the format provides ample information on price, source, content and purpose. There is an
author index and a complex, ten-page chart of developmental skill sheets which
serve as an analytic index. The appendix includes a glossary of developmental
terms.
   The major defect of this book, its limited coverage, may be related to its
major virtue, its thorough and painstaking analysis of materials.

Early Childhood Education: How to Select and Evaluate Materials, by EPIE
   Institute. New York, Educational Products Information Exchange, 1972.
   82p. (EPIE Report 42). Out of print.
   Though this useful survey is out of print, it may be reprinted and revised.
It includes: 1) self-analysis checklists on human development and on preferences
in early childhood program designs, 2) guidelines for analyzing early learning
materials, 3) discussions of local resources and roles of instructional materials for
early childhood education programs and 4) producer information on more than
80 early learning kits including learning levels, objectives and teacher competency
levels required for each program.

Its purposes are to enable educational consumers to clarify learning objectives for children they deal with, to define learning programs relevant to those children, to identify community resources to benefit children, to develop points of view about instructional interventions and educational programming, and to understand the interrelationships and potential conflicts among these factors.

Early Learning Kits—25 Evaluations, by EPIE Institute. New York, Educational
    Products Information Exchange, 1975. 88p. $20.00. (EPIE Report 68).
    Discusses elements of the instructional design and setting of early childhood programs and shows how to choose instructional materials to best fit specific curricula and settings. It compares producer descriptions and EPIE analyses for 25 early learning kits.

Films for Early Childhood: A Selected Annotated Bibliography, by Marianne
    Pezella Winnick. New York, Early Childhood Education Council of New
    York City, 1973. $3.50. (From 1775 Broadway, New York, NY 10019.)
    A bibliography of approximately 400 films and film series for early childhood teachers, arranged by subject under such categories as development, current trends, program planning, curriculum, parent education, teacher training, comparative education, children and series.
    Other publications dealing with early childhood materials have been produced by the Early Childhood Education Council: one on evaluating art materials, the other on nonsexist materials.

Free and Inexpensive Materials for Preschool and Early Childhood, by Robert
    Monahan. Belmont, CA, Fearon, 1977. 118p. $3.00pa.
    Recommends about 600 free or inexpensive items—most suitable for primary teachers—on such subjects as animals, art, citizenship, dental health, foods and nutrition, holidays, safety and transportation. Provides purchasing and bibliographic information, usually not publication date—though materials were available when the book was printed. These are mostly proprietary materials.

Instructional Materials for the Handicapped, Birth through Early Childhood, by
    Arden R. Thorum, et al. Salt Lake City, Olympus, 1976. 198p. $6.95pa.
    Annotation for this item is provided on page 320.

Montessori Index, compiled from the books of Maria Montessori and related
    authors, by Virginia B. Fleege. 2nd ed. Chicago, Montessori Publications,
    1974. 78p. + appendix. Price not available.
    This invaluable index to Montessori and related authors covers 43 books in multiple editions. Specific materials are covered on pages 5-10 under Apparatus, in appropriate categories (sensorial exercises, geometric cabinet, word games, touch boards, care of the environment, etc.). The theoretical bases of materials are indexed, analyzed and categorized under Materials on pages 39-40.

Montessori on a Limited Budget: A Manual for the Amateur Craftsman, by
    Elvira C. Farrow and Carol Hill. Rev. ed. Ithaca, NY, Montessori Workshop,
    1975. $8.00pa. (From 501 Salem Dr., Ithaca, NY 14850.)
    This guide, now in its second edition, grew out of an Ithaca community

Montessori Workshop. It provides step-by-step measurements and directions for duplicating Montessori's aesthetically pleasing, self-directing, self-correcting preschool materials from scrounged and inexpensive items.

Nine Model Programs for Young Children, by Benjamin F. Quillian, Jr., and
   Kathryn S. Rogers. St. Louis, MO, CEMREL, Inc., 1972. 2 vols. $14.00 (v. 1,
   $8.00; v. 2, Appendix, $6.00). (From 3120 59th St., St. Louis, MO 63139.)

   This two-volume survey compares the basic philosophies, goals, physical requirements, costs and techniques of nine pre-school programs (that represent five program types) to provide a self-contained information resource for selecting and evaluating programs.

   Volume 1 contains resumes for the following types of programs: 1) open classroom, 2) bilingual, 3) structured classroom, 4) individualized and 5) non-institutional. Volume 2 includes sample lessons and other classroom materials typical of each program reviewed.

Non-Sexist Education for Young Children, by Barbara Sprung. Englewood Cliffs,
   NJ, Scholastic Book Services, 1975. $3.25pa.

   Anecdotal but practical approach for creating non-sexist learning areas in housekeeping, cooking, block and workshop areas—all field tested in four preschool centers by participants in a Non-Sexist Child Development Project. Five units are described in detail: Jobs People Do, Families, The Human Body, Homemaking and Sports. It includes an annotated bibliography of non-sexist picture books.

Pre-School Curriculum Utilizing Selected Public Library Books, developed by the
   Religious Education Committee, First (Unitarian) Church. (Three-year curriculum packet with lesson plan and 4x6-inch card index file. 21 units.) Portland, ME, First Church, 1975. $25.00. (From Dale Bryant, First Parish in Portland, 425 Congress Street, Portland, ME 04111.)

   Almost all of these units—21 in all—are sufficiently secular to be used in public school settings. The topics are interesting to children, and the books are well chosen. Each topic includes story synopses, activities, discussion questions and songs or films. Topics are: homes, other cultures, other children, earth, space, seasons and cycles, family and generations, caring and giving, daily experiences, people in our community, pets, responsibility and death, friendship, feelings, self-concepts, reality versus fantasy, concepts and values, and nature. Teachers can use this model with their own favorite books and/or topics.

Selecting Educational Equipment and Materials for School and Home, Edwina
   Deans, coordinator; Monroe D. Cohen, ed. Washington, DC, Association for
   Childhood Education International, 1976. 108p. $3.50pa.

   The first section of this valuable guide, an update of a 1964 title, deals widely and sensitively with criteria for selecting single and packaged educational materials for the classroom and for the teacher center. Includes a bibliography of selection aids and a discussion of the pros and cons of buying as opposed to making materials. In this section, and throughout the book, the approach is developmental and the focus is largely on young children. The second section presents a developmental survey of the needs of all children and suggests appropriate materials for children in different age groups and various learning areas. This section covers the needs of children from birth to age fourteen. The last section is an annotated directory of about 150 manufacturers and distributors—apparently those found most useful by committee members.

This very thoughtful book should be required reading for anyone selecting materials for primary or preschool children. There is an excellent index, simple yet detailed, that makes it easy to correlate criteria with recommended materials or their sources.

Start Early for an Early Start: You and the Young Child, ed. by Ferne Johnson. Chicago, American Library Association, 1976. 181p. $7.50pa.

This book, intended for librarians involved with preschool programs, is a good introduction to methods, techniques, materials and resources that can be used to introduce literature to preschool children. The section on literature includes a very helpful section on requirements and resources for story telling; Charlotte Leonard's article on poetry for preschools has a large selection of poems and picture books. Good for parents and teachers as well as librarians.

What Books and Records Should I Get My Preschooler?, by Norma Rogers. Newark, DE, International Reading Association, 1972. 20p. $0.50.

Recommends that books and records be selected to suit the maturity level of young children, to appeal to their interests and to meet their needs.

FOR FURTHER READING

Other useful references can be found in the chapters on parent involvement and cognitive criteria, and in *Media and Curriculum.*

*Items marked with as asterisk include criteria.
+Items marked with a plus have substantial lists of references.

*Auerbach, Stevanne, and Linda Freedman. *Choosing Child Care: A Guide for Parents.* San Francisco, Parents and Child Care Resources, 1976.

Bell, T. H., and Arden Thorum. *Your Child's Intellect, a Guide to Home-Based Preschool Education.* Salt Lake City, Olympus, 1972.

Dr. Bell, former Commissioner of Education, offers step-by-step instructions and rationales for successful learning experiences for preschool children.

+Burgess, Evangeline, ed. *Values in Early Childhood Education.* Washington, National Education Association (Department of Elementary-Kindergarten-Nursery Education), 1965.

Well-documented text includes Piaget's work and other clinical studies, plus an 18-page bibliography and a thorough section on cognitive thinking.

*Butler, Annie L. *Headstart for Every Child.* New York, Associated Press, 1972.

Kit of ten articles each discussing some aspects of the young child's world and the kinds of preparation a preschooler needs to expand his/her awareness of the world. Includes articles on reading readiness, selecting toys and games and special help for the fast learner.

*+Butler, Annie L., et al. *Literature Search and Development of an Evaluation System in Early Childhood Education.* Washington, U.S. Office of Health, Education, and Welfare, 1971. 3 vols.
Two volumes of this set are particularly relevant for background and for selecting materials. Volume I deals with researched characteristics of preschool children, volume III with behavioral objectives and evaluation instruments.

Cole, Ann, et al. *I Saw a Purple Cow and 100 Other Recipes for Learning.* Boston, Little, Brown, 1972.
Excellent parent-compiled selection with interesting activities and simple experiments.

*DeFranco, Ellen B. *Learning Activities for Preschool Children: A Home Teaching Handbook for Parents and Teachers.* Salt Lake City, Olympus, 1976.
Includes many games to help children understand difficult concepts.

+Durkin, Dolores, comp. *Reading and the Kindergarten: An Annotated Bibliography.* Newark, DE, International Reading Association, 1969.
Covers theory, research and successful practices—large scale and small scale.

*+Furfey, Paul F., ed. *Education of Children Aged One to Three: A Curriculum Manual.* Washington, Catholic University of America, 1972.
Excellent background in development, with a good how-to section and a list of recommended, inexpensive materials such as books, toys, music and puzzles.

+Gilbert, Arthur. *Prime Time: Children's Early Learning Years.* New York, Citation Press, 1973.
Good chapters on values, music, art and outdoor education.

*+Goodfriend, Ronnie Stephanie. *Power in Perception for the Young Child: A Comprehensive Program for the Development of Pre-Reading Visual Perceptual Skills.* New York, Teachers College Press, 1972.

*Gordon, Ira J. *Child Learning through Child Play.* New York, St. Martin's Press, 1972.
"A low-key approach to games and activities that develop the intellectual and physical capabilities of two- and three-year olds"—a sequel, in the same format, to *Baby Learning through Baby Play.*

*Havighurst, Robert James. *Developmental Tasks and Education.* 5th ed. Chicago, University of Chicago Press, 1972.

Holtz, Michael, and Zoltan Dienes. *Let's Play Math.* New York, Walker, 1973.
Suggests materials and criteria for 80 games and puzzles—to aid children in concept development and logical thinking. Many could be made at home.

+Honig, Alice S. *Infant Development Research: Problems in Intervention.* Washington, Day Care and Child Development Council of America, 1972. (Reprint).
Survey of research with implications for infants in day care centers; includes a nine-page bibliography.

Liepmann, Lise. *Your Child's Sensory World.* New York, Dial Press, 1973.
An extraordinary book that brings out the relationships between the senses, behavior and learning. It suggests methods for determining children's individual sensory patterns and includes exercises for children (from three to twelve) which need neither preparation nor specially-prepared materials.

Montessori, Maria. *Montessori Method.* Translated by Anne F. George. New York, Schocken Books, 1964.
A classic report of teaching methods validated on slum children in Italy; considers "structured freedom," programmed instruction, learning by conditioning and reinforcement by approval.

*National Association for the Education of Young Children. *The Good Life for Infants and Toddlers.* Washington, NAEYC, 1970.
Describes requirements in terms of equipment, supplies, food and services, adult-child ratio and daily programs.

+Polette, Nancy, and Marjorie Hamlin. *Celebrating with Books.* Metuchen, NJ, Scarecrow, 1977.
Selects, lists and describes books useful for each holiday.

*+Quisenberry, Nancy L., Terry Shepherd, and Winona Williams-Burns. "Criteria for the Selection of Records, Filmstrips and Films for Young Children." *Audiovisual Instruction*, v. 18, no. 4 (April 1973), pp. 36-37.

Stanley, Julian C., ed. *Preschool Programs for the Disadvantaged: Five Experimental Approaches to Early Childhood Education.* Baltimore, Johns Hopkins University Press, 1972.
The common theme of these pioneers in preschool education is improving the education of preschoolers whose early environments lack cognitive stimuli that most middle-class children receive early in life.

Woods, Margaret S. *Wonderwork: Creative Experiences for the Young Child.* Buffalo, NY, D.O.K., 1972.

ACRONYM INDEX

All of the items listed in this index also appear in the Author/Title/Subject Index under their full names. But, since acronyms are so prevalent in education, organizations and other educational entities commonly referred to by their initials are indexed here under common acronyms and are arranged alphabetically by these initials. Numbers in boldface type refer to the pages on which these entities are treated most fully; addresses are usually included on these pages.

AUTHOR/TITLE/SUBJECT INDEX

This index includes names of organizations, information sources and other items listed in the Acronym Index. Acronyms appear here only when part of a title or when well known outside the education community. *See* and *See also* references to acronyms refer to entries in the Acronym Index.

(SURVEYS continues on page 380)

DATE DUE

NO 17 '82	NOV 30 '82		
SE 23 '87	SEP 4 '87		
GAYLORD			PRINTED IN U.S.A.